JEWISH CU

READER

4

1 9 7 6 - 1 9 8 6

L O U I S   H A R A P / E D I T O R

ESSAYS, SHORT STORIES, POETRY SELECTED FROM THE MAGAZINE

Published by
JEWISH CURRENTS
Editorial Board
Louis Harap, Elliot L. Jurist, Sam Pevzner,
David Platt *(Emeritus)*, Max Rosenfeld, Neil Salzman,
Morris U. Schappes, *Editor*

First Impression — April, 1987

ISBN No. 0—9618122—0—6

966

THE WORKERS' COOPERATIVE COLONY

We dedicate this book
to the caring mothers and fathers
of the Coops in the Bronx.

Their love and courage
have nurtured the lives
of their children and grandchildren
with understanding and love for others.

We consider ourselves fortunate
to have been part of this heritage.

Phil and Miriam Rosenstein
Perry and Dorothea (deceased) Rosenstein
Donald and Grace Rosenstein

CONTENTS

Preface

In perusing the three past decennial Readers of the monthly JEWISH CURRENTS, beginning with the initial 1946-1956 volume, one striking fact stands out — the change in topics emphasized in each succeeding book. With the passage of time one may observe a shift in interests, emphases and cultural needs. It is equally obvious that some issues persist: how our country meets the challenge of peace and nuclear disarmament, of care for the welfare of all its people, especially of the poor and those living under discrimination, and of the Jews in particular, of cooperation in the struggle for Black liberation. We have from our beginnings tried to advance understanding of Israel, but not uncritically. We have focused attention on the problems of secularism and its expression in Jewish culture. Since the start of our magazine in 1946 we have stressed the lessons of the Holocaust. As could be expected, we have continually treated current topical issues which, because of their transiency, we have not included in our Readers.

The Reader for our first decade (when our name was *Jewish Life*), while the loss of the six million was a fresh wound shows an emphasis on cultural material and translations from the Yiddish in our effort to cling to their heritage. This volume was mostly devoted to stories and poems of Jewish life with social implication including poetry concerning Israel. In the second decennial Reader for 1956-1966, we had virtually completed our casting off of our earlier dogmatism and made the transition to surer ground. There were more essays on such topics as exploration of our cultural heritage, as the Holocaust and Jewish resistance to it, as promotion of Jewish-Black relations, and we introduced an emphasis, new for us, on the protest against forced assimilation of Soviet Jews and the struggle for their national rights. We were also much preoccupied with the problems of Israel as they arose. This volume also included fiction and poetry.

In the third decennial Reader for 1966-1976, called *A Ten Year Harvest,* there were fewer storied and poems but many more essays on emergent issues such as feminism, affirmative action and Israel, besides discussions of the prophetic tradition in Jewish culture, the relation of Jews to the Left, the deprivation of national rights for Soviet Jews and our ongoing comemmoraton of the Holocauset and Jewish resistance. Long before the avalanche of memoirs and scholarly studies of various aspects of the Holocaust, we had from our beginning dwelt on them in our pages and tried to draw out their meaning for us and the future of the Jewish people and of society as a whole.

This present, and Fourth, Reader, continues this orientation to changing times with discussion of issues that have come to the fore in the past decade. The problems of Israel and Soviet Jews have become more acute, as our pages show, as has the urgency of the struggle for peace and nuclear disarmament. One emphasis in the Holocaust section of this book is on the preservation of personal memories of Holocaust survivors. We also tried to do justice to the multiplicity of urgent issues which beset our country and the Jews. At the same time we continued to examine aspects of the Jewish cultural tradition in a secular framework.

These four collections of material from our magazine tend to consist of extended treatments, of substantial discussion and material of continued historical interest, which merit the greater permanency and ease of access afforded by existence between book covers, rather than in magazine files. A new feature of the present collection is inclusion of personal documents, previously unpublished, not only of Holocaust survivors but also of American and Jewish labor struggles, such as those in the garment trades which also fulfil the role of history, namely, to throw light on the present. Another new feature is hitherto unpublished material on historical Jewish personages such as Clara Lemlich, Marc Chagall, Leo Frank and the problems in which they were enmeshed.

As in all our past experience with Readers, final selection under pressure of limited space has necessitated hard decisions for inclusion. Another volume of high quality could easily be assembled from material remaining in the magazine. We have reluctantly refrained from including some important, extended articles such as Morris U. Schappes' careful critique and appreciation of Irving Howe's *World of Our Fathers* (September and October, 1977) and Albert Prago's "Jews in the International Brigade" (February and March, 1979), probably the only source in English for this neglected subject, both of which are available as pamphlet reprints by our magazine.

As for all previous Readers, and indeed for all products of the magazine, suggestions for inclusions were made and final approval given by the entire Editorial Board.

Date of publication in the magazine is appended to each item.

LOUIS HARAP

I: Issues And Occasions

Being a Secular Jew

By *ELSIE LEVITAN*

This following article was submitted for discussion at the 1977 Conference of Secular Jewish Organizations.

L ET us imagine that there is a line going entirely around the room; color it whatever you choose, because choice is what it symbolizes. Let us call that line "The American Jew in a Multi-Ethnic Society." The line then becomes a multiple-choice "test" that we *do* answer for ourselves, whether we know it consciously or not.

Let us label one end of the line "Total Uncommitment." Here belong the Jews who have divorced themselves entirely from the Jewish community, whose Jewish identification is either a source of indifference or shame. So our line immediately begins to have branches or tributaries to allow for the subtlety of differences. In my own family there is an example of someone who has separated himself from his Jewishness: a cousin, several decades ago, changed his last name to single-syllabled Nordic elegance. Today he is living in Europe in a small community where several Holocaust survivors also live, but no one knows that he is Jewish. This is his deliberate choice.

At the other end of our imaginary line we might affix the label, "Total Commitment to Jewishness." Here there are many branches, and at this spot we might place the person whose every moment is absorbed by his relatedness to the Jewish community, be it as writer, like Cynthia Ozick, scholar, like Dr. Howard Sachar, or rabbi. Between these two extremes there are hundreds of choices, and the American Jew, consciously or not, makes an individual choice and hangs his or her identity at some spot along that line. Since our society does not force us to identify ourselves as Jews, we make our own choices. I think I know where I have chosen to be. I search and find a long, strong branch of the line marked "secular Jewishness" and place myself somewhere on it. Where are you on that line? Where would you like to be? Are you comfortable where you are?

A secular Jew, by accepting that designation, has already made certain choices. First, he affirms his Jewishness and his ties to the Jewish people. Second, he also affirms a secular view of reality. Twenty or thirty years ago there was no difficulty in understanding or accepting the meaning of the

1

word "secular." Without consulting the Oxford Dictionary, it simply means that secularism is a doctrine that asserts the primacy of *this* world, in order to differentiate it from other-worldly or religious views of the world. The word and the concept behind it are crucially important today, especially when we talk about the separation of church and state, an area full of problems and tensions. We must also differentiate secularism from Judaism, which is the system of religious practices that Jews follow.

Today we are seeing a hightened increase in mysticism, particularly among our young people. This can be an involvement that takes many forms, ranging from fashionable cultic movements to trying to rewrite liturgy in church and synagogue or trying to go beyond liturgy to the mystic heart of the religion. The proliferation of these movements and their use of words in a new context have tended to push and blur the meanings of ideas and words concerning secularism and supraworldiness. We are in danger of creating our own small tower of Babel where different people mean different things when they use the word "secular."

Very recently a young friend told me of his firm belief in reincarnation, his acceptance of flying saucers as being indeed from outer space, his belief that the pyramids of Egypt and the Yucatan were built by men from another planet, and that books like *The Chariot of the Gods* were true in every detail. This young man is married, a college graduate, and he dismisses religion as relevant only to "them" (the uneducated), as a way of keeping some semblance of social order.

Another young friend tells me of her belief in astrology, although this is contrary to her Reborn Church, which she recently joined by changing her denomination. I don't mean to take these two examples and extrapolate them into a social phenomenon, but we have only to read the newspapers, go to the movies or listen to the music of the young people to know that their hunger for answers to the existential questions is very real and is forcing some of them into some bizarre behavior.

When I saw a paperback book on Kabbalah for sale in the lobby of a popular movie house, I knew mysticism was "in." Now I read that the "laying on of hands" is being taught in some hospitals to nursing staffs and I marvel at how far we have sunk in the quagmire of irrationalism.

After the Atom Bomb and the Holocaust, the Western world "stood naked," and some people needed to reinvent a new pantheon of gods because the old ones seemed to have abdicated. And this new pantheon is growing every day.

Those of us associated with secular Jewish schools have to be very thoughful concerning these matters. Our children or grandchildren are at an age of transparent openness to the influence of their peers. It's fashionable to want to "believe" in some form of mysticism, although it's equally fashionable to belittle traditional ritual. Secular Jews know they must have a continuous dialogue with our young people to strengthen their secularism. Clarity begins at home.

Secular Jews accept the primacy of nature or natural causes to explain the universe. This does not mean that the secular Jew does not ask the great questions: "Why am I here? What does life mean? Is death the final answer?" And in asking, he knows there are no glib, simplistic answers. But it does mean that in our public practices and observances the secularist does not celebrate a supranatural force; he/she searches within world history for a tradition that celebrates what *people* can do together for each other to solve problems — the humanist tradition. Jewish history is a treasure house of that tradition.

I was a fortunate participant in a class that reviewed some of the recent findings in biology; Dr. Donald Prococcini, author of books and articles on genetic theory and developmental physiology, was our teacher. He stated unquivocally that life and the creation of the universe can now be satisfactorily explained in scientific terms. The vitalist goes beyond science for further explanations, but it is now possible, for the first time, to prove the materialist basis of life. Intoxicating stuff, this.

It has been charged that secularists, including secular Jews, are only nay-sayers, that they simply say, "We eschew religion and that is our only doctrine." Not at all. We are yea-sayers to a huge number of ideas. The secular Jews believes fundamentally in the world-view of naturalism; that which appears to be a mystery is not unknown at this time. The secular Jew also believes that people, contrary to biblical injunction, were not evolved in order to dominate nature, but to live *within* nature, respecting the circle of life. People live *in* history; every artifact and phenomenon has a history; every idea, every art form has a history. We do not live suspended between Hell or Heaven or Nirvana, waiting for eternal solutions or for the eternal verities to be disclosed to us. The truth is real people, responding to real problems.

The secular Jew says that problems are in their ultimate created by people and nature and must therefore be solved by people and nature. Hunger and disease and poverty do not represent the will of any god, but they do represent the complicated-as-hell will of some people, and when that is better understood, more people will ameliorate these horrors. Cultures do change, perceptions change, behavior changes. Who knows that better than the secular Jew who studies the history of his people? Israel started as a hope in the minds of only a few individuals; much history, laced with blood, ensued to make it a reality.

Jewish history and tradition are splendidly rich in humanist doctrine. Early on, the Talmud spelled out its priorities: "The Sabbath is holy, but life is holier." Secular Jews take the totality of Jewish experience as their province, they look at that experience through their particular world view

3

and then choose those periods, holidays, heroes, heroines and interpretations that strengthen that view.

Surely, this is a process that people have engaged in since the beginning of communication. If we read Jewish history with a view to the desirability of Jewish continuity, certain conclusions loom large. In Israel, one can have sincere political differences as each sees the political extensions of survival. But in the U.S., for the five-million-plus of us, a tiny fraction of the total population, there may not be as much latitude if we are to respond to events in a truly secular Jewish way.

In order to be secure, Jews in the U.S. must forever be part of a collation that seeks to solve social problems in a wideningly democratic way; in that lies safety, a future and the fulfillment of our prophetic tradition. It is not enough only to thunder out for the needs of the widow and the orphan, the hungry and the deprived. *Compassion has a political dimension.* In our awareness of the political process and our ability to act to influence social dynamics toward greater democracy and fuller justice lie the safety of the Jews and all ethnic groups in the U.S. and Canada and everywhere, as we have learned again and again. So the secular Jew believes in joining with others for political answers to human needs.

We should also turn our attention to ethics, not supplant the Ten Commandments but to see if we can supplement them in view of some of our more recent sensibilities. Even a hurried glance at the Ten Commandments reveals that they are overwhelmingly secular. They attempt to regulate the way people should behave toward each other; they are, incidentally, with a single exception, almost entirely negative in the way they are stated.

The exception is the one that urges us to honor our mothers and fathers, and if ever we want to think about the dimension of compassion in politics, we should remember the way older people are treated in this country.

The first commandment, which thunders, "You shall have no other gods before me," not only reveals a self-proclaimed jealous god, but a very insecure one as well. So insecure, in fact, that graven images of any kind are prohibited; and like any insecure parent he threatens punishment for disobedience, on the one hand, but promises life everlasting for obedience.

These first two commandments are usually placed in a religious category, but I should like to propose that they are political, concerned as they are with power and dominance and the hoped-for elimination of pagan rivals.

Another commandment often deemed religious is the one outlining the way to observe a day of rest — the Sabbath. How lovely that the first labor contract had to do not with wages or working conditions, but with time to oneself to abstain form working. What a pity that the fourth commandment did not go further and talk about wages and profits! But

4

here may be a place where some supplemental "commandments" might be indicated.

Was a day of rest already a practice among some tribes in the ancient world? The root of the word "Sabbath" goes back to the Greek and Hebrew, meaning simply "to rest." To sanctify the idea of resting one day out of seven by calling it holy must have been a popular measure indeed; it was one idea in the platform of monotheism that proved irresistible; everybody adopted it, and wherever possible everybody practiced it.

But the other commandments abjuring us not to murder, lie, steal, covet or commit adultery are observed, alas, more in the breach than in the doing; yet they do not lose their moral force, except where modern psychology assures us that we all break some of these for the sake of social grace or the rampant ego.

Perhaps one of the future workshops of this Conference can give us "The Secular Jew's Handbook on Ethics." But here are a few suggestions: Anything that leads to understanding oneself and one's fellow human beings is good. Conversely, anything that tends to distort or becloud or deflect understanding is bad.

Anything that on balance supports our feelings of loving rather than punishing, being positive rather than destructive is good. the converse is evident.

That which keeps our indignation keen concerning the wrongs people inflict on each other is good. Anything that encourages apathy about the pain of other people is harmful.

To repeat the phrase in the hagada, "Remember that you were slaves in Egypt," without thinking through some of its implications is not sufficient. We must go past empathy to action; actively to oppose institutional bigotry, to help promote people's liberation, otherwise our pious declaration could be in Sanskrit.

When we talk about the holiness of life, we must include those forms of life that greed threatens to extinguish; the hoop of life is all of one piece; we cannot diminish it without diminishing ourselves. It is wrong to be exploitive:
of the worker for hire,
of a sexual partner,
of a husband or wife to each other,
of any person, child or adult for personal gratification.

It is wrong to incite to anti-Semitism, whether blatantly or by innuendo. To denigrate any group based on its ethnicity is wrong and feeds the fires that could destroy us all.

The reverse of these coins might read something like this:
value yourself,
value and nurture those you love,

5

value and support your neighbors as they seek to find a more human dimension for themselves.

Your neighbor has become the world. Nuclear weapons and the speed of the machines of technology have placed us into one spaceship, one global village. When we befoul one ocean, we befoul them all; when we develop new missiles systems, we threaten everyone.

These suggestions are incomplete, but they point the way we may want to go.

The secular Jew is curious about everything in the Jewish past: its origins, its borrowings, its similarities to and differences from the rites and concepts of other peoples, the uses and abuses of religion; the history of secularism, and lots more. Secular Jews hope to pass on to their children not only stories and snippets of information, not only some customs and Jewish *Kheyndlekh,* but a proud and unified view of the universe which can provide them scope to grow to the limits of their gifts.

Just as the children read and study, so we, too, should continue to read and study about the Jewish community now and in the past, and what we can do to assure its future; about the limits and responsibilities of ethnicity; about the contribution secular Jews can make to the larger Jewish community.

Of course, we have Jewish music in our homes, go to see films with Jewish content, or a play with a Jewish theme, but we are careful not to become parochial in our vision or the experiences we seek. Marc Chagall is not the only painter; Jewish folk song is not the only folk music; Jewish ceremonial objects are rarely unique in design; American-Jewish literature and Yiddish literature are infinitely rewarding, yet other groups express themselves richly through poetry, novels and plays, and we will be made more deeply human for reading them. If we, as secular Jews, are to understand ourselves *in* the world, we must understand something *of* the world.

Secular Jews experience joy in their explorations of Jewish culture and history; in their endless discoveries that the Jewish heritage is basically secular, that religion is another social institution to be understood within framework along with other historical activities.

Well, that's my profile of the secular Jew. What's yours?

February and March, 1978

6

A Jewish Folk Music Revival

By BOB NORMAN

ANDY Statman's a small, dark fellow whose diffident onstage manner belies the creativity that has won him a reputation as one of the best young bluegrass mandolinists in the country. On June 24, 1980 when he took to the stage of this country's finest new folk festival, the Hudson River Revival, he wasn't doing anything he hadn't done hundreds of times before. But this time his mandolin lay snug in its case. As his partner Zev Feldman began carefully striking out sonorous, hypnotic chords on the interwoven strings of an ancient instrument called *tsimbl,* Statman raised a clarinet to his lips and the steamy summer air shimmered in the first sinuous notes of a *sher* — a *sher* as it might have been played by *klezmorim* at a *shtetl* wedding in the Ukraine a hundred years ago.

Ethel Raim's fine features, her impassioned singing, are of timeless character and beauty. Her contribution to the American folk music movement has been enormous but largely unacknowledged. For over 10 years, as music editor of *Sing Out!,* the nation's leading folk song magazine, she personally compiled, transcribed and published nearly half its 2,000 song treasury, an indispensable resource for American folksingers. Through her work with the Pennywhistlers singing group, the Newport Folk Festival, the Smithsonian Folklife Festival and New York's Balkan Arts Center, she also helped find a place in the American folk musical movement for "ethnic" Americans of European background. But for her own concert at this year's Hudson River Revival she set aside a vast repertoire of Russian, East European, Balkan and American songs to sing something closer to home-songs in Yiddish, like those she heard as a child growing up in the Bronx.

Henry Sapoznik's an intense, bearded young man, capable of intellectual vigor and a crazy Brooklyn humor. As a member of a band called the Delaware Water Gap, he's been known for years in the folk music community as a fiddler and banjo player in the tradition of the Southern Appalachians. But he's chosen to spend the last few years buried in the musty files of the YIVO Institute for Jewish Research, rescuing sounds forgotten by much of the Jewish community and never heard at all by most of the current generation. Not content to garner only the past, he's put together the klezmer and band Kapelye.

Does Jewish music need to be revived? Let me cite my own experience:

I grew up in New London, Conn., a small town with a fairly large Jewish community. I attended Hebrew school at the Conservative synagogue for many years, learning some Hebrew, but only enough to be able to recite the prayers at services. The music I learned was almost entirely liturgical. The only Yiddish song I remember learning was *"Oifn Pripitchok."* It's a beautiful song, but as Henry Sapoznik says, it has come to represent the epitome of longing for a world destroyed. It was at best a token — our sole remembrance of the largest long-standing Jewish community of modern times.

There was more Jewish music in my life when I joined Young Judaea, a Zionist youth group, and spent several summers at their camp in the Poconos. Here there was singing at every meal, but again, almost all the songs were in Hebrew and were about the lives of Israeli halutzim. In Young Judaea thousands of years of history were taught as if they were merely a prelude to the reestablishment of a Jewish national state; virtually nothing was taught about the experience of Jews in America. Once I had made a definitive decision against *aliyah,* I was left with nothing to give meaning to life as a Jew in this country.

In all those years of Jewish music, I'd hardly learned a tune or song that would give me a clear cultural tie to the experience of my parents or grandparents and the great waves of Jewish immigration, mostly working class and more than two million strong, that had come to this country from Europe starting in the 1880s. I was heir, without knowing it, to what Ethel Raim calls the "profound fracture" in Jewish identity that took place in the midpart of our century.

While there had been musical stirrings and important research throughout the '70's, the revival "burst on the scene" with the advent of a Berkeley-based group called Klezmorim. "The Klez," as Henry Sapoznik affectionately calls them, were loud, brash and entertaining. If their Yiddish was sometimes a little garbled and their presentation a bit hokey, they nevertheless made vivid and contemporary the styles of music that had been consigned to archives and history books.

The Klezmorim took their name and repertoire from the Jewish bands that had been popular for centuries in the *shtetlach of* Poland, Byelorussia, the Ukraine and Romania. "The traditional instrumentalist among the Jews of Eastern Europe," writes Zev Feldman in liner notes to a Statman-Feldman record, *Jewish Klezmer Music* on Shanachie label, "was called in Yiddish a *klezmer,* from the Hebrew words for 'musical instrument.' He ... had to be competent in many musical forms — from dance music, wedding melodies and variations of folk songs to music of Hasidic and synagogue derivation. In addition, peasant and Gypsy dance tunes and even light classical suites often found their way into his repertoire, depending on the clientele.

8

"The mass immigration of Jews between 1880 and 1922," he continues, "brought hundreds, perhaps thousands, of klezmorim to the United States and should have ensured the perpetuation of the klezmer tradition in this country. Only the first two decades of this century witnessed a significant flourishing of klezmer misic in America. Even in this period, the repertoire began to be confined to dance music, and soon afterwards the klezmer families themselves turned to more mainstream American music."

"The Klez," then, were attempting to pick up where the old bands had left off 40 years earlier. They experimented with many of the instruments that had been popular — fiddle, clarinet, accordion, flute, trumpet, tuba and bowed bass.

Zev Feldman and Andy Statman have approached the klezmer tradition differently. Eschewing the "big band" sound, they limit themselves to *tsimbl* and clarinet or mandolin, creating intimate, mysterious and very compelling music. Their repertoire is strictly instrumental, presented with seriousness and spirit, subtlety and beauty. Zev's *tsimbl,* the European equivalent of the American hammered dulcimer, can create strong rhythm and full sonority while a lively lmelody is hammered out on its strings. Statman's clarinet and mandolin playing are remarkably expressive, best felt, perhaps, in the free-meter *doinas,* a genre borrowed from Romanian Gypsy tradition that gave the klezmers an opportunity for improvisation. He has studied with Dave Tarras, one of the greatest Jewish clarinetists of the 20th century, and with the talented mandolinist Martin Kalisky. Tarras' early recordings and work in the Yiddish theater with popular performers like Aaron Lebedeff, Molly Picon and Moishe Oysher are legendary. The Balkan Arts Center has now presented him in several concerts, to wide acclaim. They've also released a new album of Tarras playing music from the traditional Jewish wedding. This "rediscovery" of such musicans has been one of the finest aspects of the Jewish folk revival. Statman and Feldman, in conjunction with Balkan Arts, have a grant from National Endowment for the Arts to deepen their research into Jewish instrumental music in America.

Meanwhile, Henry Sapoznik, a cantor's son turned fiddler, banjo player and folklorist, has developed a research project of his own under the auspices of the American Jewish Congress, with funding from the federal CETA program. Part of it involved exhaustive examination of old records and sheet music and taping interviews with musicians. This led to the establishment of an open-access archive of Jewish music at the AJCongress' Martin Steinberg Center.

Henry's research focused on klezmer music, the Yiddish theater and cantorial music. Robin Greenstein examined the Ladino tradition. Michael Alpert and Carol Freeman were recruited to visit senior citizen centers in the New York area, both to collect songs from elderly Jewish people and to sing for them.

Henry's research at YIVO has resulted in the pioneering album, *Klezmer Music 1910-1942,* on the Folkways label. The album includes classic recordings of American Jewish orchestras like those of the violinist Abe Schwartz and the clarinetist Neftule Brandwine. Henry's extensive album notes are invaluable to an understanding of the development and near-disappearance of this music in America.

Henry and Michael Alpert, both fiddlers, are members of Kapelye (which means "band"), along with Lauren Brody, vocals, accordion and piano; Josh Waletsky, vocals and piano; Eric Berman, tuba; and Ken Maltz, clarinet. They recreate pieces from the traditional klezmer repertoire, but also sing a variety of songs from the Yiddish secular tradition, many chosen for their progressive political content. In a genre that has generally been dominated by male instrumentalists, Lauren, like Ethel Raim, carries on an important body of Jewish women's songs.

Much more is happening in the world of Jewish music. In Philadelphia, International House has included a yearly Jewish festival in its exploration of that city's ethnic traditions. In Boston, a 12-piece Jewish orchestra has formed. It's hard to keep up with such a rapidly-developing, national phenomenon and harder yet to give credit where credit is due. No revival springs full-blown from nowhere; there have always been important singers, foklorists, chorus leaders, cantors, communities and institutions who have kept the sound of Jewish music alive.

In a broader sense, too, this revival activity can't simply be seen in isolation. In the remainder of this article I should like very briefly to raise some questions and put forward some ideas about why this revival at this time. I hope they will contribute to the creative ferment always present at the beginning of a new movement and that often helps determine its direction.

The United States has a particularly varied folk music heritage, since it was created by people from all over the world. The result was a multitude of distinct cultures, a wonderful mixing of styles and a number of distinctly American hybrids. These musics, however, developed contending with very concrete historical conditions.

For centuries, mainstream "high culture" was dominated by the European classical tradition; Americana was considered of little importance. Folk and popular music, on the other hand, was left to the mercies of a developing entertainment industry that in the last half-century has become enormously profitable and influential.

This industry has subordinated our rich musical tradition to the profit motive, no respecter of tradition, aesthetics or human needs. Music is marketed like any other commodity — with built-in obsolescence ("fads," "hits") and with packaging ("stars," "lifestyles") taking precedence over quality or human need. While the music industry has created an

10

accessibility to recorded and performed music unheard of in previous generations, it has also consistently trivialized it, obscured its origins and routinely cast musicians aside once they've been sufficiently exploited.

In response to this pressure a folk music movement grew up dedicated to maintaining this country's finest musical traditions, and to rescuing with them the respect due to the generations of workers who created them. Understandably, this movement focused initially on styles of music particularly indigenous to the U.S. — Southern mountain music, Western songs, blues and gospel. But the last 10 years has seen a broadening of that scope to include many kinds of "ethnic" music — Chicano border ballads, Cajun two-steps, French-Canadian fiddle tunes, Irish piping, Serbian *tamburitza* music and, now, klezmer tunes and Yiddish songs.

There has been a new interest in "ethnicity" throughout the '70's; to understand why this has been necessary, we must go back a hundered years, when the great waves of eastern and Southern Europeans, as well as Irish, began emigrating to the U.S. Industrialists were eager to exploit these immigrants' labor, but they were also determined to discourage any form of national pride or class consciousness that might motivate them to challenge the status quo. Henry Ford, for example, the most creative of these manufacturers, sponsored "Americanization" classes for his workers and sent "social workers" into their homes to make sure the new "American values" were being put into practice. At the same time his magazine, the *Dearborn Independent,* extolled the virtues of "Nordic" peoples and attacked urban, immigrant and non-white culture. Ford reserved his greatest venom for Jews, publishing the notorious forgery *The Protocols of the Elders of Zion.* He even sponsored his own "folk revival," a country-dance movement aimed at combatting "Jewish jazz."

The anti-immigrant, anti-radical Palmer Raids of the early '20's, followed by a racist immigration quota policy, left many immigrants cut off from their families in the old countries and convinced that the only way to get ahead here was to reject all outward signs of their cultural traditions. Not suprisingly, this idea was advocated vigorously by the minority of immigrants who had managed to get a toehold in the capitalist socio-economic structure.

In the Jewish community, this insecurity was immensely worsened by the trauma of the Holocaust. As Ethel Raim points out, the Nazi massacres not only destroyed the source of cultural continuity for American Jews, but in the years that followed they were running scared. The anti-Semitism of the McCarthy era made things worse. Stalin's execution of Yiddish artists and intellectuals was yet another blow.

Hernry Sapoznik advances another idea: "Zionism," he says unequivocally, "was the final strike against Jewish culture" It's a controversial idea, but in many ways it corresponds to my own experience

11

as I've described it. In the Zionist movement Yiddish was considered "the ghetto language." A new Jewish people was to be born in the State of Israel and what came before and what happened elsewhere was not important. In the U.S. this negation of the past meant abandoning the Yiddish language, and with it great socialist traditions of internationalism and an immigrant culture that to some in the community was too embarrassingly working class.

It was the upheavals of the '60's that for us finally began to break the hold of "Americanization." "For Blacks, Chicanos, Puerto Ricans, and American Indians," writer Carolyn Golab in Balkan Arts's *Tradition* magazine, "the ethnocentrism of Anglo-America had become unbearable... These groups forced America to re-examine her principles.. Ethnics of immigrant heritage who had been taught to be ashamed could now admit openly their heritage and differences..."

To the extent that we young Jewish musicians explore and understand this history, the new revival of klezmer traditions and Yiddish culture can both be a living link to the past and place us at the heart of the process of social change. These time honored, evocative melodies can provide us with musical expressions of the finest Jewish traditions of class consciousness and internationalism, with both Jewish pride and the strength to resist the narrow chauvinism that would make of us a "chosen people" rather than one of the many working to create a better world.

October, 1980

American Jews Profiled

SOCIOLOGY by and large, is an attempt to analyze and explain modernism. Marx, Weber, Durkheim, and numerous colleagues and followers labor to understand the liberation of the individual made possible by capitalism, industrialism, urbanism and secularism. They have dwelt mightily upon the loss of community, of connectedness, of ritual richness and meaning that somehow seem inevitably to accompany that modern freeing of the self. The convulsions we identify so easily in Iran, the Arab world, and much of Latin America, Africa and Asia are all responses to modernization, a force that seems both to emancipate in the name of development of human potential and also inadvertently, to kill. People, contexts, symbol systems, integrity, die like burned skin cells after the social organism has been exposed to the sun-brilliance of modernization.

And so, modernization and the (American) Jewish question is the topic of demographer Steven M. Cohen's new book *American Modernity and Jewish Identity.** Although, like their mostly European forebears, American Jews do not all choose to modernize, most do. But they are not fully certain how welcome they are, or how comfortable, in American culture and society. Complete acceptance seems impossible without complete assimilation, but we know that in Germany, even total abandonment of all aspects of Jewish identity did not mean an end to anti-Semitism. In the theoretical part of his book, Cohen reasons that many Jews hesitate to attempt full assimilation because their doubts about its possibility combine with lingering respect and affection for some of the pre-modern group characteristics of Jews in community, to yield a most complex, ambiguous present American Jewish identity.

We are as a group, Cohen convinces the reader in a statement that summarizes the book, pointed "neither in the direction of rapid assimilation, more toward sustained and assured group continuity" (p. 175). Thus those foreseeing an end to Jewish identity in the United States and those celebrating returns to origins in the third and fourth generations are both asked to step back and hear a sober, scientific discussion, at the end of which one can most appropriately muse, Hmm, I wonder what is coming next, for and by Jews in American society.

Cohen asks some leading questions about Jews and modernization, but he avoids serious political analysis of his findings and their context, he

---

* Tavistock, N.Y., 226 pages, $18.95 cloth, $8.95 paper.

minimizes and trivializes progressive and experimental traditions among American Jews today, and he assumes an unnecessarily narrow focus on his topic throughout the book.

Cohen introduces generation as a crucial variable in understanding his topic. Not community, not challenge to religious beliefs, and not even major historical events are his focus so much as the response of each Jewish generation in America to those issues and to the realities of its own experience in the United States.

Cohen paints a mixed and often surprising picture: Completely secular Jews are about as conservative politically as orthodox Jews. For what appears to be a majority of secular Jews, despite the reality of progressives among them, full secularity means such total assimilation to the American social class system as to participate in its general political conservatism. Indeed, the most liberal Jews (Cohen rarely distinguished liberals from radicals, past or present) identify as Jews and usually acknowledge one or more Jewish holidays, in one way or another.

The age structures of Jews identifying ritually as Conservative indicates that younger Jews, even the children of those in the Conservative movement, are moving to Orthodoxy, Reform, or nothing, but are not remaining Conservative. What needs Conservatism has fulfilled for Jews in America seem generation-bound, and that generation is aging.

The fewer observances like kashruth, lighting shabbos candles and attending shabbos services Jews honor, the more likely they are to become active in Jewish organizations and fund Jewish philanthropies that are not exclusively or primarily religious in their orientation. The focus of attention moves from home and synagogue to community infrastructure and Israel.

Despite their serious limitations, which I will explore shortly, Cohen's findings are far too rich and complex to summarize adequately in a review. but a few are especially worth noting. He suggests that professions often provide surrogate communities, complete with value systems, for Jews falling away from the ethnic-religious fold. He finds that lawyers participate in Jewish communal life far more than do doctors and professors.

He demonstrates not surprisingly, that singlehood, childlessness, divorce, gay sexual identity, and any other life style alternatives to the traditional nuclear family are considerd threats to Jewish existence, to be coped with aggressively by the mainstream Jewish community rather than welcomed and addressed sympathetically on their own terms. He names programs organized by synagogues, community centers, family agencies and federations for younger Jews outside the nuclear family category, "policies of containment... aimed at containing the rise in alternative households" (p. 131).

14

Social mobility of course disrupts Jewish participation in community activities and hastens assimilation into the mainstream culture, but often a mobile family re-establishes Jewish ties after a few years in a new location. Again we see ambiguity and mixed consequences of serious change.

Basing his larger analysis on the tension between *"the embrace of modernity and lingering insecurity"* (Cohen's emphasis, p. 23), Cohen sees liberalism as "the politics of group integration" and pro-Israelism as "the politics of ethnic survival." He calls American Jewish support for Israel pro-Israelism, to distinguish it from the Zionism of many of our European ancestors and cousins. He sees that support as playing a crucial part in identifying as American Jews, rather than signifiying an ideological commitment to Jewish renaissance in a Jewish-majority society. Nice point, and important.

Unlike people who assume that Jewish support for Israel must be uncritical, Cohen helpfully distinguishes between that position and one of constructive friendly criticism joined with support for Israel. As liberalism increases among younger Jews, Cohen finds, pro-Israelism decreases. Yet Cohen finds the decrease is in hawkishness, not in concern or support for Israel. Cohen speculates that liberalism tends to define the Mideast conflict in ways that tend toward political solutions and conciliation between the contending parties rather than military confrontations and polarization, strategies favored by more hawkish and often traditionally religious supporters of Israel.

Cohen says that Jewish liberalism seemed understandable among immigrants, poor and active in labor unions, but with substantial upward mobility, why, he questions, has it persisted (even if in somewhat diminished degree)? Conviction that a tolerant pluralism is benefical for Jews, comfort and familiarity with Democratic Party politics, and a certain trendiness to leftist politics among the culturally "high-brow" help explain Jewish liberal politics, according to Cohen. By contrast, religiously observant Jews often shun liberalism because of its identification, in their eyes, with assimilation, with relative indifference to Jewish particularism and with a traditional sub-culture that does not embrace liberal social issues. Generationlly, younger Jews tend to be liberal more often than older Jews.

Cohen's data are from a number of sources, prime among them the 1965 and 1975 surveys of metropolitan Boston, gathered under the auspices of the Combined Jewish Philanthropies of Greater Boston. Although Cohen also draws on information from the 1981-82 National Survey of American Jews, supported by the American Jewish Committee, the Boston data are paramount in his book. They may well not be adequately representative of American Jewry as a whole; indeed, they are drawn upon so heavily simply because they are more thorough, informative and useful for the demographer than other data. Perhaps surprisingly, there is not a plethora of good, useful data about American Jews along the dimensions of Cohen's study under review. Given the serious possible limitation of a major part of his data, then, Cohen nonetheless offers us rigor, careful analysis and imaginative interpretation.

Cohen is entrapped, though, in a framework that I believe leaves much to be desired. Sociologists of American Jewry appear to set as their prime issue the maintenance of self-conscious Jewish identity among Jews. Much of the work of these investigators is in counting: how many Jews have fallen by the wayside (no longer identifying as Jews), they want to know, and how many have not. Their method, following classic Jewish attention to ritual behavior, center upon counting observances. Keeping kosher, honoring Jewish holidays, lighting shabbos candles, etc. form the basis for their numbering Jews identified as Jews. More recently, support for Jewish philanthropies, membership in Jewish organizations and pro-Israelism also certify as Jewish identity characteristics.

The advantage of the method is precision (assuming honesty in reporting behaviors defined by investigators as indicating Jewish identity). The limit of the method is in fragmenting Jewish experience and Jews into behavior and little more. Degrees of Jewish identification are established according to number of observances and frequency of performing them. There are no whole people, no living Jews identifiable in such studies and neither individuals nor groups in active processes of transformation. We have no glimpses of the excitement of a Jew returning in adulthood to the study of Jewish texts, of finding new and personal meaning in designing a Seder and carrying it out, or in discovering an innovative celebration and connecting it to millenia of Jewish practice.

Who is "more Jewish," a couple married according to traditional Jewish wedding formula, or a couple steeping itself in a variety of Jewish and secular texts to create their own unique ceremony? Given that both have Jewish ceremonies, is there no useful distinction for the sociologist between the two? Who foretells the future of self-identified Jews more clearly, a Bar or Bat Mitzva reading a *haftorah* and celebrated in an *arriviste* banquet-dance, or a Bar Mitzva doing the whole ceremony himself in orthodox fashion, or a Bar or Bat Mitzva in a *chavurah* creating a new adaptation of an old ceremony according to post-counter-culture liberated communal Jewish lights? Of course all new efforts may turn out to be but chaff in the wind, but ought not they to be explored a bit more fully in a book on American Jewish responses to modernism?

There is little place in Cohen's book for innovation and no indication that out of experiments and discoveries mighty new trends *may* grow. Reconstructionism warrants not even a passing mention (perhaps because of its absence in the Boston area, upon whose Jews so much of the data depends). Jews who observe in order to please parents and grandparents, or from fear of them or at least ambivalence, are not distinguished from those who freely choose their Jewishness, although there are here and there indications that in the third and fourth generations return to Jewish practices may indeed sometimes be voluntary. But if so, the significance of the growing number of such people making such choices is absent.

It is perhaps in his discussion of Jewish liberalism that Cohen's method yields its most problematic fruits. Jews did not only bring over working class consciousness from Eastern Europe, a fact that Cohen correctly ties to leftist tendencies among American Jewish immigrants earlier in this century. They also brought Bundist backgrounds and mutual aid associations. they brought traditions of arguing about socialism and communism, secularism vs. religiosity, and disputations about Zionism as the answer of the Jewish problem, and socialism as the answer and socialist-Zionism as the answer, and more. None of this appears in Cohen's book, not even in the footnotes. He makes barely any effort at all to distinguish liberalism from radicalism, as if the distinction were unimportant in America, or among Jews; and he sees political commitments too sociologically, as reflecting class and mobility interests, as if the content of political ideas had nothing to recommend it at all as an object of serious investigation and influence.

Cohen barely notices that pro-Israelism may have come to be defined by Israeli leaders and by American Jewish establishment leaders as inconsistent with left politics. He suggests only that the American left communnity may have made that claim. That American Jewish consciousness might have been manipulated since 1948 (whether deliberately or not is beside the point), with some effects on political commitments goes unremarked. That assimilation to American social class norms (with their all-important obsessive consumerism at the higher levels) could account for toning down of left politics goes unremarked also.

There is no room in this kind of sociology for how Jews think about themselves and how they explain their behavior. Thus, the likelihood that some Jews active in civil rights, feminism, gay and lesbian rights, the movement against the war in Vietnam, the movement to reduce the threat of nuclear war, environmentalism, etc. might self-consciously act according to their notion of what it is to be Jewish, is nowhere apparent in *American Modernity and Jewish Identity*.

Speaking of generations, social change in America in the past 20 years has seen Jews vastly overrepresented, in terms of our number in the larger population. Activists are often younger Jews who whether deliberately or not find *tikun olam* (repairing the world) a mark of their Jewish identification more than membership in mainstream Jewish organizations,

17

philanthropy through traditional channels, uncritcal support of Israeli governments, or observing kashruth and the High Holidays. That there is a thriving Jewish counterculture, represented by the small but no means insignificant *chavurah* movement, by Jewish feminism and its books and journals, by the several editions of the *Jewish Catalog,* by gay and lesbian synagogues and rituals, warrants little more than notice as "alternative" means of expressing Jewishness, means that the established community wants to "contain" as quickly and effectively as possible. Cohen does not seriously consider that a redirection of American Jewishness could ensue from these movements.

The limits of Cohen's study are the limits of the method and the imagination used in applying it. Most sociologists of the American Jewish community focus on how many people do and do not intermarry, and how many carry on traditional practices in maintaining self-conscious identification as Jews. Exactly as among many of their forebears in Europe before and after emancipation, Jews who study Jews in America attend primarily to maintaining the community; they are terrified of assimilation. They seem, oddly, never to ask if assimilation indicates not simply a greater American magnet drawing the little Jewish filing, male or female, away from the ethnic piece of iron, but whether assimilation could, for some, also represent failure of the Jewish community to present Judaism and Jewishness as vital enough to be worth sustaining.

It happens that in America, people can choose to be free from guilt-laden obeisance, free from automatically wearing a hat because one's ancestors have always worn a hat. From the traditional Jew, like the traditional Muslim or Christian, the curse of modernization is reflection, questioning, wondering if one's group's traditional ways may after all not be neccessary or even all that wise or fulfilling any more. Nervous about that questioning, and perhaps fearful that if one were to engage in it oneself one's loyalities might be found wanting, the Jew, sociologist or otherwise, who takes this approach wants to calm and be calmed, wants assurance that traditional society is not dead, will not die, will hang on no matter what.

The challenge of modernization is thus sidestepped; implicitly the challenge is seen as too great to be taken hold of, too threatening to be met on its own terms. It is fear of modernization, not modernization itself, that most sociologists of American Jewry reflect in their work.

Maybe Jewish identity is heading in new directions, maybe the Jewish insistence on social justice takes new forms in the modern era, maybe American Jews today work out *their* version of the tensions between prophet and priest, and prophet and king. It is the rabbi and the community official (backed by some sociologists) who so far determine who is a proper Jew, who is a good Jew, indeed who is a Jew at all. Where are the activists, the political thinkers and fighters, in all this? Might not the struggle many

18

Jews in America feel reflect that tension between prophecy and ritual observance? American Jewish life is religion, culture and politics. Cohen acknowleges all three elements but looks for consensus, stability, continuity, more vitality, renewal and change. So long as our sociology counts observances and labels Jews accordingly, we will know little of the possibility of genuinely new directions in American Jewish consiousness and practice.

A sociology-of-knowledge approach to American Jewish sociology would show us that the sociologist of the American Jewish community unwittingly takes his/her place in defining Jewishness narrowly, according to the wishes and preferences of established community leaders (who often, as it happens, see to the funding of research on American Jewry: he who pays the piper, etc.). I do not want to fall into the trap of insisting that Cohen should have written another book rather than this one, but I cannot avoid pointing out that the richness of American Jews' responses to midernity is lost in a sea of data on behavior defined according to traditional criteria, and slight modern variations upon them, and defined in ways that sidestep failures in Jewish education and uncertainties on the part of any Jewish elders as to whether there is any point in maintaining Jewishness except as an end unto itself.

Perhaps the survey method can carry us no further. In that case, I would hope for a study according to the case method, of real Jews struggling to define themselves anew in this era, of Jews in social change movements, of *chavurot* and progressive Jewish publications finding new ways to say they are Jewish, to recreate their Jewishness, and to take part as Jews in identifying human survival issues and addressing them successfully.

Sociologists of the American Jewish community do in-house surveys for federations and the American Jewish Committee. Nothing wrong with this, to be sure, but is there nothing more to being a sociologist? Where is the sociologist as skeptic? Where is the critical edge? Marx and Mannheim tell us that intellectuals can serve the interests of established authorities, rationalizing their rule and justifying their claims, or they can point to the discrepancy between what their society is and what it could be. Sociology has a rich tradition of prophecy, but like all of social science, it has a larger tradition of serving the status quo authorities. Thus in Israel and thus in the United States.

Is it too much to hope that a sociologist of Cohen's fine mind and gifts might turn his attention away from contract sociology that is meant to alert establishment leaders to not much more than where, in their terms, Jewish life is today? Might we not ask of Cohen and sociologists of the Jewish community a more imaginative, critical, enlightening sociology that tells us something of human struggles of our era, the possibilities of affecting them positively, and the evolving Jewish role in all this?

January, 1986

If I Am Only for Myself...

By GERALD STILLMAN

S TOP an "average Jew in the street" and ask him what is anti-Semitism in the U.S. today. He will hem and haw and probably tell you that it is painting swastikas on synagogues, desecrating cemeteries, snide remarks or jokes at work, exclusion from certain clubs, discomfort when living in a neighborhood with few Jews, celebration of Christmas in his kid's school...

If he is more sophisticated, he may say that he is worried about rising membership in the Ku Klux Klan and increasing numbers of right-wing preachers calling for a Christian America. He may be worried about Reagan's attempts to introduce prayer into the public schools and to provide goverment funding for religious schools. He may express fear that CIA and State Department officials similar to those who helped Nazis like Barbie and Rauff escape justice are still active in government.

Not that such fears and worries are uppermost in his mind. Jews in the U.S. today by and large recognize that the "Jewish experience" here, especially during the last quarter century, has been one of the best in Jewish history from the standpoint of equality of opportunity — civil, social and economic. Still, when asked what anti-Semitism is in the U.S., the concern will be with anti-Semitic acts, prejudices, discrimination against individuals and institutions here because they are Jewish.

That is not the case of Nathan and Ruth Ann Perlmutter, who have written a book called *The Real Anti-Semitism in America* (Arbor House, N.Y., 1982, 303 pages indexed, $15,50). The very title implies that the rest of us have been overlooking the *important* aspects of anti-Semitism. Nathan Perlmutter is national director of the Anti-Defamation League (ADL) of B'nai Brith. His wife, Ruth Ann, is a director of the women's division of Bonds for Israel in Florida. As if to show that the real aspects of anti-Semitism are not trivial, the dust-jacket design of the title is in the shape of a fat flame, one that cannot help but evoke memories of crematoria and Holocaust — and therefore worries about survival — in the mind of the potential reader.

What, then, constitutes the Perlmutters' perception of the real anti-Semitism in America? It is very different from those of the "average Jew": "For all that we have never, in the millenia of our wanderings, enjoyed a safer harbor than here in the U.S., Jews are nevertheless uneasy. Not because of a sensed personal danger... it isn't even due to anti-Semitism.

Rather is it a fear of Jewish endangerment coiled in state policies, themselves free of anti-Semitism, which in plausible scenarios spring free jeopardizing Jewish security... It is nothing personal — as yet."

Three major state policy areas, "themselves free of anti-Semitism" as the Perlmutters put it, outline the real anti-Semitism here for them: 1) the recognition that oil is the name of the game in Middle East politics and that it "has compromised Israel's international standing and contributed to the sure-footedness of Israel's implacable enemies"; 2) *detente* with the Soviet Union, especially the trade aspects, because those help to stabilize the Soviet system, thereby lending a "helping hand to the one major power in the world today that has institutionalized anti-Semitism"; 3) an imposed Middle East peace which, "though it results in the absence of war and renders oil safe, makes being Jewish in Israel hazardous."

The real anti-Semitism in America thus resides in those aspects of U.S foreign policy dealing with Israel, the Middle East and the Soviet Union. Perlmutter worries: "What if a Middle East war were to deprive the world of oil? Would a darkened world... scapegoat Israel? (and) scapegoat Jews, *Israel's advocates?"*

That's how, according to them, individual Jews in the U.S can be attacked — because of an oil crisis in the Middle East which involves Israel and consequently American Jews. Since the Perlmutters see Israel's security so intimately intertwined with anti-Semitism here, one would think that they would explore policy alternatives that would increase Israel's security. Not a bit of it! Here we have a book, published in 1982, prior to Begin's invasion of Lebanon, which never once mentions issues like the future of the West Bank, Palestinian autonomy, the spirit of Camp David, Jewish settlements on the West Bank. They are not even listed in the index.

Perlmutter has a different approach to improving Jewish security. In a roundtable discussion with editors of the *Long Island Jewish World* in April 1983, he stated his approach succinctly: "The core purpose of the ADL is to fight anti-Semitism... We have learned that the well-being of the democratic process determined the well-being of Jews... That is why the ADL four years ago was the first Jewish organization to publicly call for an increase in the American defense budget.

"We noted that democracy is good for Jews and that communism is bad. A strong democracy is an investment in Jewish security. There is something disingenuous about politicians calling for increased aid to Israel and then voting against military appropriations that would make it possible. An American military budget that can't spare weapons for Israel is no less a danger to Jewish interests than the swastika dauber."

Is it necessary to have a nuclear and missile buildup in the U.S. to the tune of $300 billion per year for the next five years in order to be able to sell weapons to Israel? Or is the Soviet Union the same "evil empire" to Perlmutter as it is to Reagan and worth risking a nuclear war to destroy it? How will Israel fare in a nuclear war — especialy an Israel whose government has volunteered it to be a long-term strategic military supply base for U.S. forces in the Middle East? This topic in not relevant for authors committed to an arms race.

The real anti-Semites the Perlmutters see in the U.S. are those who question American foreign policy which is intertwined with American military posture around the world. Relationships between Jews and their traditional allies of the past are evaluated on the basis of the same criterion: how have they rallied to the support of Israel? Implicit in this criterion is the assumption that all Israeli policies will unquestionably serve to increase Israel's security and guarantee its survival. Therefore, anyone who questions Israeli policy *ipso facto* questions the need for Israel security and becomes part of the real anti-Semitism in America. This can include liberals or leftists, both Jewish and non-Jewish, here in the U.S. and also in Israel. A crazy equation summarizes this approach:

Question Israeli policy equals anti-Israel attitude equals real anti-Semite.

How crazy this can be is seen from the following quotation: "Why then don't we feel more comfortable today with Reverend Bailey Smith, leader of the Southern Baptist Convention, who has seriously declared, 'With all due respect to those dear people, my friends, God almighty does not hear the prayer of a Jew,' than we do with the more socially conscious National Council of Churches?"

Why indeed would they feel more comfortable with fundamentalist right-wing Christians? Because fundamentalists believe in the literal words of the Bible that Jews are God's chosen people and that Israel is their promised land: "... the fundamentalist's relative religious intolerance can and does coexist with religious and political attitudes supportive of Israel's well-being. In short, liberal Protestantism's tolerance is not so helpful to us as its political hostility to Israel is damaging to us. Fundamentalist intolerance is currently not so baneful as its friendship for Israel is helpful... Our friends of yore now insensitive; the fundamentalists... now our limited partners."

The book pleads with American Jews to examine the validity of relationships with allies of the past in light of the new realities as the authors perceive them. Recognizing the strong liberal, yes, even of socialist, heritage of politically conscious Jews of past decades, the Perlmutters urge them to discard this heritage, to open their eyes and see which side their bread is buttered on today.

In doing so, the authors' posture as former liberals, who, themselves, have been disappointed by the turn events have taken: "A decade ago, who

22

would have imagined that the Berrigan brothers, apostles of peace, would today be rationalizers of the terrorist PLO and that a brigade of Christian fundamentalists would be resolutely siding with Israel? Or that the United Nations, once the One World ideal, would turn lexicographers, brew antonyms — Zionism and racism — and in a reeking alchemy reconstitute them as synonyms? Or that Jewish defense agencies would still be filing friend-of-court briefs challenging racial discrimination, but that their legal adversaries would be led by the NAACP?"

Calling the Berrigans "apostles of peace" can only be a deliberate distortion on the part of the authors. The Berrigans opposed the U.S. involvement in Vietnam and the concommitant brutalities which were committted there and to a much lesser degree at home here. Opposition to a particular war is certainly not synonymous with being an "apostle of peace," whatever the author intended that expression to mean. I wonder what they would call the Israeli army officers who refused to fight in Lebanon.

Another deliberate distortion is the implication that the NAACP supports racial discrimination in the courts. The authors are referring to affirmative action. During the last decade, the Equal Employment Opportunities Commission, in an effort to overcome some of the inequities resulting from centuries of discrimination, began to implement plans that would give some form of employment preference to women and ethnic minorities. The ADL and some other Jewish organizations have opposed such preferential treatment as "reverse discrimination" and setting up "quota systems"; they have taken the position that ability should be the sole criterion for employment.

By taking such a position, ADL supports the unbalance resulting from discrimination in the U.S. It tosses aside a heritage of cooperation between Jewish and minority organizations — an alliance which, in the two decades following World War II, was successful in getting Equal Employment Opportunity legislation passed. It also places ADL squarely behind the Reagan administration efforts to dilute, if not eliminate, affirmative action, and consequently places ADL on the side of the oppressors and in conflict with the oppressed.

It is to such a conservative, neo-Right, position that the Perlmutters would like to direct the American Jewish community. Posing as ex-liberals, they offer an explanation of how it came about that Jews were close to the left in the past: "Our allies were 'liberals'; our adversaries 'conservatives'. Among us outsiders... some (Communists, socialists) sought to change the system, while others (liberals, reformers) sought to cause the system to function according to the democratic ideals it espoused... But whatever the reasons for our high profile in the Left, certainly anti-Semitism figured prominently. Long after we lost our

Yiddish accents, long after we vacated the tenements of the lower East Side, established ourselves in the aeries of the upper East Side, even as we began to rue the distance we had put between our acculturating selves and our cultural heritage... *they* still would not fully accept us. So, as marginal Americans we embraced and were embraced by the Left and by minorities, themselves outsiders."

The Perlmutters' view is that "we" embraced the left and that "they" embraced "us" because we were marginal Americans involved in upward mobility — out of the lower East Side tenements and into upper East Side aeries. This is a description that may appeal to upper middle class Jews and Jews who have little knowledge of Jewish history and demography in the U.S., i.e., those who have "made it" or think they have made it. What the Perlmutters chose to omit is the working class character of the large majority of Jews who immigrated here, the sweat shops, the Triangle fires, the formation of socialist oriented trade unions, the socialistic character of some of the Zionist parties in the U.S.

It was not all "Hester Street" — that infernal vision of Abe Cahan's where, among Jewish immigrants in the lower East Side, he saw dog-eat-dog and a lack of concern for one's brethren. Certainly, anti-Semitism stimulated to some degree Jewish prominence in the left, but the basic reasons lay in the reality of capitalist America at that time, in the brutal exploitation of people and the often inhuman conditions under which they had to live, Jewish or not. This misery was also the reason that broad alliances developed between Jews, other national minority immigrant groups, Blacks, Puerto Ricans, and, yes, with some white American workers and their unions. The left didn't embrace "us"; Jews were among the forces that created the left in America in response to the conditions here at that time.

The Perlmutters are convinced that "the liberal agenda and ours are no longer coincident and at times not even parallel" and that "the Jewish agenda must look to Jewish interest." Here are items that will appear on an agenda to serve Jewish interests, as the Perlmutters see them:

1) The development of nuclear power is a *de facto* Jewish issue. 2) Israel's security is related to an "adequate American military budget." 3) Tax deductions for private and parochial school students "are likely to encourage public schools to be more competitive." 4) "In terms of our academic strategies... for whom are we saving public schools?" 5) "We favor ERA... but Jews can live without ERA." 6) "We favor legislation (making) abortions available... (but) Jews can live with restricted abortions. Indeed, societies have for centuries." 7) "Prayer in the public schools... would not... seriously impact Jewish life."

Are the Perlmutters being responsible as far as Israel is concerned? Or as far as American Jewry is concerned? Do they realize that we live in a nuclear age and what that can mean for the human race — including Israel? An approach such as theirs can lead only to greater militarization of Israel and the Middle East, and with greater militarization comes greater insecurity, because war can break out more easily, as it has repeatedly. Greater militarization of Israel also means continued discrimination against Arab minorites within Israel and of occupied Arab populations around Israel — all of which leads to more and more Jewish young men becoming cannon fodder.

The Americn people continue to be supportive of Israel. Poll after poll has shown that up to 50% of Americans would support Israel in a war against the Arabs with less than 5% saying they would side with the Arabs. The remainder aren't sure. The Perlmutters note this: "This continued level of popular sympathy for Israel, whether the offshoot of favorable attitudes toward Jews as compared to Arabs, whether the consequence of American anti-Communism or fundamentalist literalism, is in *realpolitik* terms tons weightier an assurance to Jews than their countrymen's increasing acceptance of them as neighbors, merchants, sons-and daughters-in-law."

The pride expressed in the first part of the quotation is one we can all share. But the reasoning, or, better yet, the lack of reasoning, is a matter of concern. Suppose it's only because of anti-Communism that there is American sympathy for Israel; what would happen if a leftist government were elected in Israel? And suppose further that the fundamentalists conclude that a leftist secular Jewish state in Israel is not the one predicted for the Jews by the Bible; what would happen then? I think that Americans sympathize with Israel because they see it as a democratic state, built by people with a pioneering spirit similar to the one that played a role in building the U.S, and serving as a refuge for the oppressed and tormented as the U.S. did during large parts of its history. This sympathy should not be jeopardized by an increasingly militarized and potentially oppressive government in Israel.

The fact that the Perlmutters believe that American "popular sympathy for Israel," — regardless of the basis, "is in *realpolitik* terms tons weightier an assurance to Jews tnan their countrymen's increasing acceptance of them as neighbors," etc., is troubling, It would appear to predict a basic change in ADL policy. At the bottom of ADL stationery, there is a slogan: "Founded in 1913 'to stop the defamation of the Jewish people... to secure justice and fair treatment to all citizens alike.'" If the Perlmutters really believe that increasing acceptance of American Jews by their countrymen is far less important than sympathy for Israel, then ADL will be much less concerned with anti-Semitism in the U.S. and far more concerned with being a foreign-policy lobby for Israel. This is disturbing thinking, coming, as it does, from the national director of ADL.

The last chapter of the Perlmutters' book is entitled "If I Am Not For

Myself..." It is, of course, the first part of Rabbi Hillel's well-known aphorism: "If I am not for myself, who will be for me? But if I am only for myself, what am I? And if not now. when?"

They have chosen to omit the rest of Hillel's aphorism. The "agenda" items above, also summarized from their last chapter, show that they believe that Jews have long enough been for others, and that now is the time for them to be for themselves, i.e., to be for Israel. Indeed, they say so in so many words: "Jews have been voting for candidates whose political platforms they deem compassionate of the needy, caring of the underdogs, and which are critical of such socially baneful conditions as racism, discrimination and ultranationsalism.

"This voting pattern has seen Jews vote against Jewish candidates and in favor of non-Jewish candidates when the former were viewed as less liberal than the latter... Jews must reexamine their voting impulses. Does the candidate with soothing words for Israel have an understanding of the implication for Israel's security in an inadequate American defense budget?"

In other words, it is time, as the Perlmutters see it, for the Jewish community to separate itself from its century-old political and ethical heritage in the U.S. to look after its "own" interests only, and to turn to the right. Abandoning heritages always raises questions of identity, and Hillel's second question becomes most pertinent in regard to the abandonment proposed by the Perlmutters; if we take care only of ourselves, what are we?

It was a real disappointment to read a book by the national director of the ADL which sees the real anti-Semitism in America almost exclusively in terms of unquestioning support for Israeli policies and for a large American military budget. He has thereby short-changed the Jewish community in the U.S. Unfortunately, since he is in a policy-making position in ADL, the American Jewish community may be further short-changed by ADL abandoning its objectives not only "to stop the defamation of the Jewish people... (but also) to secure justice and fair treatment for all citizens alike."

September, 1985

For its 60th Anniversary

Griffith's "Intolerance"

By DAVID PLATT

INTOLERANCE (1916) was D. W. Griffith's answer to the protests and picketlines organized by the young National Association for the Advancement of Colored People over the pernicious racism in his previous film, *The Birth of a Nation* (1915). That film's salute to the white-hooded Klansmen riding to lynch freed Negroes asserting their rights was rightfully condemned by notables like Lillian D. Wald, Jane Addams, Harvard's Charles E. Eliot and others — white and black. The film, said Oswald Garrison Villard, editor of *The Nation,* was "a deliberate attempt to humiliate 10 million American citizens and to portray them as nothing but beasts," a charge disputed today only by hardened racists and unreconstructed art-for-art-sake film aesthetes.

Griffith (1875-1948), son of "Roaring Jack" Griffith, a Confederate colonel, responded to these attacks with a rambling and unconvincing pamphlet *"The Rise and Fall of Free Speech in America"* castigating his critics for endangering freedom of the screen. No one takes this curiosty of literature seriously any more, but the movie *Intolerance,* which was the major part of his offensive against his detractors, is something else.

True, it is in many respects a continuation of Griffith's banal history and sociology. Floyd Dell, in his review in *The Masses* (Nov., 1916), was the first to note the irony in the idea of Griffith, the maker of the "hate-breeding" *The Birth of a Nation,* "telling us to be tolerant." But beyond that, *Intolerance* towers as a work of pictorial and poetic beauty on the liberating theme of social justice and universal brotherhood — that is, for all but Blacks and Jews. One notes that there are no Blacks to be seen in the American episode of *Intolerance.* Apparently the director had said all that he wanted to say about Negroes in his previous epic. As for Jews — the victims of 20 centuries of the most barbaric form of racial hatred and intolerance — Griffith in his Judean segment chose to portray the alleged intolerance of Jews toward Jesus — but more about this later.

Griffith scoured world history — from ancient Babylonia to modern America — for material for his main theme. He built enormous sets with towers and walls big enough for an army to march around. He hired actors, horses and elephants by the thousands and built a private railroad to transport food and materials and provided special housing for them all. He shot miles and miles of film over a two-year period, then retired to the cutting-room to shape the mass into four parallel stories of intolerance through the centuries that shook the film world to its roots and opened up unimaginable new vistas of film art. In the finale, as Iris Barry pointed out, "history itself seems to pour like a cataract across the screen," as the director cuts back and forth with shattering effect from one story to the other, from the Persian armies of Cyrus advancing in great hordes on Belshazzar's Babylon to the signing of the death warrant of the Huguenots at the Catholic court and the bloody street fighting that followed on St. Bartholomew's Day; from Christ struggling toward Calvary to the breakneck auto race to save a frameup victim from the gallows.

To hold the four stories together the director used the recurring image of a mother rocking a cradle, a not too effective symbol suggested by Whitman's lines, "Out of the cradle endlessly rocking, uniter of here and thereafter." The screen title said: "Today as yesterday, endlessly rocking, ever bringing the same human passions, the same joys and sorrows." But Griffith's undeniably vivid defense of human decency against the corruptive forces of society was in the end vitiated by his idea of intolerance as an unchanging evil that is the same for all times and places, and of course by his failure to deal with the two supreme examples of intolerance in history.

Of the four stories that make up the film, the Babylonian episode was by far the most spectacular and the one on which the director lavished without stint his phenomenal artistry, but intellectually the film is hollow. Its "fatal error," said one observant critic, was that in the great battle scenes "you didn't care which side won. It was just a great show." Similarly, the medieval story of the slaughter of the Protestants by mobs unleashed by the Catholic royalists, described the violence and the horror in minute detail and with matchless art, but the meaning of St. Bartholomew's Day as a major chapter in the long struggle for religious freedom in France is hardly explored. Nevertheless, the continued effectivness of the film is such that one would not want to risk showing it today in Northern Ireland.

The Judean story, widely acknowledged as the weakest of the lot, falsely portrays the Pharisees as the main antagonist of the gentle Jesus. Eric von Stroheim, soon to be cast in World War atrocity films as the "Hun you love to hate," portrayed one of these sinister Jewish characters in Griffith's film. Actually, the Pharisees represented the vast majority of the lower and middle classes of Jews in the time of Jesus and, after the destruction of Jerusalem, became the dominant force in the growth of Judaism. By picturing the Pharisees in conventional Christian fashion as "meddlers" intent on depriving the common people of their simple pleasures, and as "hypocrites" invariably on their knees giving thanks to the Lord "that I am better than other men," the film tended to reinforce the bigotry of the anti-Semites. This was understood by the unnamed critic of the *N.Y. Evening Post* who wrote Sept. 6, 1916: "The story of Christ portrays the intolerance of the Jews for the teachings of the Master." Competent scholars agree that the stinging rebuke attributed to Jesus in *Luke* 11:44, "Scribes, Pharisees, hypocrites!," which the film repeats is unjust and could not possibly have happened, as many of the views of the Pharisees were shared by Jesus, and much of Christianity has roots in pharisaic thinking. St. Paul himself was a Pharisee.

It is of extraordinary interest that in his Judean story Griffith was prevented by the fast action of a nationally known Jewish organization from committing a far more serious offense against the Jewish people. Several months before the film was due to be released, the Los Angeles chapter of the Anti-Defamation League of B'nai B'rith learned that Griffith intended to pin the blame for the crucifixion on the Jews and that for this dangerously provocative act he had gone to the ghetto in L.A. and "signed up all the Jews with long whiskers he could find." Remember, this was the era of the Mendel Beilis "blood libel" frame-up in Tsarist Russia, and still green in every Jew's memory was the tragic figure of Leo Frank, wrongfully sentenced in Atlanta for a crime he did not commit and lynched by anti-Semitic vigilantes in 1915. Understandably alarmed, a committee of ADL leaders met with Griffith to try to persuade him to remove these inflammatory and insulting scenes form his film. He refused.

On April 7, 1916 the amusement weekly *Variety* picked up the story that the group then brought the matter to the attention of notables like Jacob Schiff, Louis Brandeis, Louis Marshall and others, and in a short time the ADL leaders again called on Griffith, this time armed with "indisputable" proof that the crucifixion was the work of the Romans, not Jews. "They supplemented their proof," said *Variety,* with a "48 hour ultimatum to destroy that portion of the 'masterpiece' negative on penalty of a concerted national campaign of blacklisting and other pressure which powerful financial and industrial interests might bring to bear, which included the assertion that censors, governors of states and even the President would do all in their power to prevent the showing of the picture with the objectionable scenes." The story added: "Confronted with such formidable antagonists, Griffith burned the negative with the scene in the presence of the committee and has retaken it, showing Roman soldiers nailing Christ to the cross."

Bnai B'rith News (May, 1916) confirmed that this was essentially what happened, but denied that Griffith was given a "48 hour ultimatum" or that threats of any kind were made or implied. An adjoining editorial spoke of the need for continued alertness against attempts to use the screen to inflame "the passions of the populace against the Jew for a crime supposedly committed by our ancestors." There is no record of any further Jewish protest against the film either before or after its release.

It is of course the modern story of *Intolerance*, with its remarkable scenes of hunger and social deprivation in the midst of inordinate wealth in industrial America in the years before World War I — and especially the militant strike scenes and their suppression by the militia — that commands attention today. The film showed unarmed factory workers striking against a 10% wage cut being shot down by company thugs as their families look on in horror. These scenes are intercut with shots of the factory owner sitting in splendor alone in his sumptuous quarters and telephoning the order to fire on the workers. There's something here close to the massacre in Ludlow, Colorado in 1914, when Rockefeller mine guards, aided by the state militia, burned a tent colony of striking miners and their families, killing 11 children and two women, one of whom gave birth to a posthumous child. John Reed wrote a classic piece of reportage on this tragedy that held Rockefeller and the coal barons reponsible for the crime. Griffith based his film partly on the revelations of conditions in a chemical factory combine, whose owner, a prominent philanthropist, poured his firm's profits into charities while keeping his employees on starvation wages, and partly on newspaper reports of the sensational Steilow murder frameup that included the grim detail that the reprieve for the innocent man arived just as the prison guards had slit his trouser leg for the electrode.

It was undoubtedly the modern story that made such a profound impression on Lenin and the young Soviet filmmakers, Eisenstein, Pudovkin, Vertov and the rest when by an extraordinary stroke of luck a print of *Intolerance* eluded the blockade and found its way to Moscow in 1919. For Lenin, Griffith's film, with its sweeping history, mass scenes of social struggle and eloquent pleading for justice and peace, not unlike what revolutionary Russia was then going through, must have stimulated the idea that films could be a powerful force for socialist progress. And from that moment on, wrote film historian Jay Leyda, "no Soviet film of importance made within the following 10 years was to be completely outside *Intolerance's* sphere of influence." Eisenstein, the maker of *Potemkin* and *October,* whose film career began where Griffith left off, was to say later that "all that is best in the Soviet film has its origins in *Intolerance.*"

In the USA, Griffith's film had nowhere near the fantastic reception it got in the USSR. At the time of its release its pacifism conflicted with the growing spirit of war and it was widely banned. It also encountered sharp criticism for its excessively harsh treatment of the women "uplifters," "reformers," social workers, etc., almost all of whom were depicted contemptuously in the modern story as preying on the misfortunes of the poor. One particularly offensive title read: "When women cease to attract men they often turn to reform as a second choice." Reform women then were playing significant roles in the passage of child labor laws, workmen's compensation and state woman suffrage laws. Heywood Broun, in his review of *Intolerance* in the N.Y. *Tribune* Sept. 7, 1916, expressed his shock that anyone with Griffith's power should want to "go out of his way to attack such a useful institution, for instance, as the juvenile court, and whatever defects of organized charity it no way merits the abuse heaped upon it by *Intolerance*." The *Philadelphia North American* Dec. 30, 1916 called for a boycott of the film for similar reasons. The explosive social struggle theme of the first part of the modern story was defused, and diverted into safe channels by these scenes with the "uplifters," etc.

The adverse criticism of *Intolerance* and of *The Birth of a Nation* angered and unsettled Griffith and led to a steady decline in his artistic power. His films after 1916 continued to deal with major social and political questions: World War, postwar Germany, the French and American Revolutions, but the times were changing and he lacked the intellectual equipment to infuse these events with anything but outworn ideas. In 1917 he was persuaded to use his talent in the service of the warmakers. He made *Hearts of the World,* an elaborate piece of jingo war propaganda that shattered the pacifism that marked the closing scenes of *Intolerance*. In those scenes, after the title, "And perfect love shall bring peace forevermore," soldiers are shown laying down their weapons, flowers spring up where before there was a prison, happy children play in the sunshine.

Although many of his later films, such as *Broken Blossoms* (1919) and *Isn't Life Wonderful* (1924), were marked by flashes of social insight and art, never again was Griffith to attain the heights of *Intolerance*. "He had glimpsed the future," wrote John Howard Lawson, "but he could not go forward to the new territory that lay before him." The last two decades of his life in Hollywood were wasted, bitter, agonizing years for the great pioneer of film art. Griffith died July 23, 1948, a victim of, as well as a contributor to, the destructive social forces that, spearheaded by the House Un-American Activities Committee, were moving to drive from the industry hundreds of talented film-makers who had dared to stand up for freedom of the screen. But his work, as Lawson points out, "continues to instruct all those who seek to carry forward the unfinished tasks which he had begun."

December, 1976

Christians, Jews and Luther's Anti-Semitism

By W. CHRISTOPH SCHMAUCH

AFTER the front-page article in the *New York Times* (May 8, 1983), "Luther being lionized in East Germany," everyone knows that this is the 500th anniversary of the birth of Martin Luther. He's considered the father of the Protestant Reformation, since the events following his nailing of the 95 Theses on the castle church in Wittenburg on Oct. 31, 1514 had a tremendous impact not only on European history but on large parts of the whole world. There are approximately 70 million Lutherans who are members of the Lutheran World Federation, but beyond that all of Protestantism has been influenced by these events, and today even Roman Catholic theology accepts many of Martin Luther's criticisms of the medieval Church and is rehabilitating him on the occasion of the birthday celebration.

An interesting aspect surrounding the 500th anniversary celebration is the fact that most of the places connected with Luther's activities are located in what is today the German Democratic Republic (East Germany), which for its own reasons is making the most of it, even though this means the reversal of government policy. Thirty years ago the GDR government emphasized Martin Luther's reactionary attitudes in the Peasant Wars, over and against the radical Thomas Muenzer, who identified with the peasants and lost his life doing so. There are certainly many reasons for this reversal, not least the fact that the German Democratic Republic is the only socialist country with a Protestant majority of strongly Lutheran backgrund, which raises somewhat different questions for church-state relations and Christian-Marxist encounter than, for instance, in Roman Catholic Poland or among many people in the Soviet Union, Bulgaria or Rumania, who are predominantly of Orthodox Church background. Suffice it to say that today a modus vivendi exists between church and state in the GDR, of which the separate and joint celebrations on the occasion of Luther's 500th birthday are only one obvious expression.

The same *New York Times* article briefly notes "both state and church historians deplore the anti-Semitism that crept into Luther's pronouncements in his later years." This raises the question of Luther's attitudes toward the Jews — a question that must be raised even though it might spoil the celebration of Christians and Marxists, who, each in their own way, can call on the "authorities" to justify their current enthusiasm about Luther's contribution to German history and culture.

Quoting the authorities, Marxists like to use a passage from Frederick Engels in his introduction to *Dialectic of Nature:* "It [the Protestant Reformation] was the greatest progressive change which humanity had experienced up to that point, a time which needed giants and produced giants, giants in the power of the intellect, passion and character, many-sidedness and knowledge. Luther did not only sweep the barn of the church, but also cleansed the German language, created the modern German prose, and wrote the text and music of that hymn, expressing certainty of victory, which became the *Marseillaise* of the 16th Century" (my translation).

Given the joint admiration of Christians and Marxists, to raise the question of Luther's anti-Semitism is awesome and necessary: awesome, because it involves 500 years of Christian-Jewish relations, mainly bad, and culminating in the Holocaust; necessary, since without it the past will not be adequately dealt with (*die unbewaeltigte Vergangenheit*) and a new beginning cannot be made.

Judging by my own experience, Luther's tract "Of the Jews and Their Lies," written in 1543, was not part of catechism or confirmation class, which is the required period of religious instruction of 12-14 year-olds in Protestant churches of Lutheran background. With few exceptions, an uncritical attitude prevailed toward this aspect of Luther's theology through the centuries. It was either ignored or explained away, so that the German fascists found a ready-made support system for their anti-Semitism in Luther's sermons and writings, which were widely disseminated in Europe.

It was only in 1946, after the liberation from fascism, that members of the so-called "left-wing of the Confessing Church" — that small group of Protestant Christians who had actively opposed the Hitler regime — held a major conference on "Self Critique of German Lutheranism." Theologians who had been in the resistance, such as Martin Niemoeller, Ernst Wolf and Hans Joachim Iwand, participated in this conference. H.J. Iwand declared on this occasion: "If we are not determined — in light of what has happened — to deal critically with our Lutheran heritage, in order to use and understand properly what we have received from Luther, then we will do a disservice to Lutheranism" *(Weissenseer Blaetter* 2, 1982, quoted by Rosemarie Mueller-Streisand in her article, *"Zum Lutherjubilaeum").*

Karl Barth, the Swiss theologian, had raised the question whether there was not some truth in the contention first expressed by "clerical fascists, that there was indeed a thread of continuity which led from Luther to Frederick the Great, to Bismarck, to Hindenburg, and finally to Hitler, for

33

instance on issues such as 'the separation of politics and the sphere of privacy' or 'the political ineptness and immaturity of the German *"Untertanen"* [underlings].'" It took another 35 years of dialogue between Lutherans and Jews before the LutheranWorld Federation last year — looking ahead to the 500th aniversary of Luther's birth — urged that "Lutherans must rid their theology of any remaining vestige on Martin Luther's vitriolic denunciations of Jews" and "called on Lutheran bodies throughout the world to include programs that will examine Luther's anti-Semitism, with a view to promoting better relations between contemporary Lutherans and the Jewish people" (reported in Boston *Jewish Advocate,* Nov. 11, 1982).

How significant these statements are one can only appreciate in light of the persistent efforts of Luther scholars and admirers to minimize and explain away the horrendous anti-Jewish tirades of that infamous tract, "Of the Jews and Their Lies." How difficult it is to be objective about Luther on this point for a Lutheran becomes clear once again in the fascinating dialogue on this subject between the eminent Luther scholar, Roland Bainton, author of the American standard work on Luther, *Here I Stand,* and Menachem Begin, published in *Christianity and Crisis* (Oct. 5, 1981 and March 15, 1982).

In his article, "Luther, Begin and the Jews," Roland H. Bainton refers to an Associated Press report in which Menachem Begin, speaking to a large gathering of survivors of the Holocaust, traced German anti-Semitism to Martin Luther. After re-reading the sources, Roland Bainton states, he finds Begin's accusations "not wholly false," and proceeds with a scholarly analysis of the sources and complex history of Luther's attitudes toward the Jews and their lot in the Europe of the 15th and 16th centuries. Prof. Bainton points out repeatedly that "Luther was not anti-Semitic, but rather anti-Judaic." Mr. Begin responds that this distinction is hardly adequate. He quotes the *Encyclopaedia Judaica:*

"Although Luther poured out such violent language on the heads of all his enemies — princes, lawyers, bishops and especially the Pope — in the case of the Jews he also made practical suggestions ranging from forced labor to outright banishment. As many of the Protestant rulers of the times relied on Luther's political advice, his attitude resulted in the expulsion of the Jews from Saxony in 1543 and the hostile *'Judenordnung'* of *Landgraf* Philip of Hesse in the same year. The tenor of his suggestions was equally virulent in his 'Admonition Against the Jews,' a sermon preached in 1546, shortly before his death."

It pains me that for honesty's sake on this point I have to disagree with my friend, Roland Bainton, and agree with Menachem Begin.

In all fairness to historical accuracy one has to state that Luther wrote very differently about this subject in 1523 than in 1543, so that on the surface one could speak of a total reversal within the 20 year period. In his

34

lectures in 1523 Luther wrote: "Our fools, the popes, bishops and monks have treated the Jews so badly, that every good Christian would want to become a Jew. And if I had been a Jew, I would have rather become a pig than a Christian. For they have treated the Jews like dogs and not as human beings... We treat them only with violence and spread false lies about them, such as blaming them that they must have the blood of Christians, so that they do not smell, and all kinds of other foolishness and think of them as dogs... Also, that they are not permitted to work among us, and be part of the human community and are driven to usury; how should this make them better? If one wants to help them, one has to apply not the law of the Pope, but of Christian love, accept them with friendliness, and let them work so that they have reason and the opportunity to be with us, to see our Christian life and teaching. What does it matter that some are stubborn? Not all of us are good Christians either" ("That Jesus Christ was born a Jew," 1523 — my translation). Ronald Bainton must have had this passage in mind when he said elsewhere that one might wish that Luther had died before writing a little book, "Of the Jews and Their Lies."

A legitimate question that might be asked, even though it does not change the bottom line of Luther's anti-Semitism, is this: What happened to Luther between 1523 and 1543? It is true that he was under a death sentence and tremendous pressures from many sides. The emperor would have killed him if he could have gotten hold of him. Luther felt threatened and became vicious. He was deeply disappointed that not everyone accepted the truth of Scripture as he saw it, including the Jews. He had hoped that they would be converted. But most remained Jews.

The final answer must be sought in the Bible itself, especially what Christians call the New Testament. I believe it is true that "Luther, absorbed as he was in all the words of Scripture, rather naturally imbibed the deep hostility of the New Testament against those who had rejected the Messiah. And so it is difficult indeed to argue convincingly that he ever really changed his estimate of the Jews at all. The most that can be said is that he went from thinking of the Jews as reformable felons to perceiving them as criminals who must be damned and that right quickly and forever. It takes a real wrenching of the evidence to say that his hatred of the Jews is "an eccentricity, an aberration, a fault of the hardening of his arteries in old age" (Richard Marius, *Luther,* J.B. Lippincott, 1974, Phila., p. 236).

Rosemarie Radford Ruether of Garrett Evangelical Theological Seminary has most thoroughly traced Luther's anti-Semitism to Christian Scripture and tradition. On Nov. 19 and 20, 1980, a symposium was held on "Religion in a Post-Holocaust World" at the Hebrew Union College-Jewish Institute of Religion in Cincinnati. At that occasion Prof. Ruether presented a paper on "Christology and Jewish-Christian relations." She begins her paper with the following summary:

"The anti-Semitic heritage of Christian civilization is neither an accidental nor a peripheral element. It cannot be dismissed as a legacy from 'paganism,' or as a product of purely sociological conflicts between the church and the synagogue. Anti-Semitism in Western civilization springs, at its root, from Christian theological anti-Judaism. It was Christian theology that developed the thesis of the reprobate status of the Jew in history and laid the foundations for the demonic view of the Jew that fanned the flames of popular hatred. This hatred was not only inculcated by Christian preaching and exegesis. it became incorporated into the structure of canon law and also the civil law formed under the Christian Roman emperors, such as the Codes of Theodosius (A.D. 428) and of Justinian (sixth century). These anti-Judaic laws of the church and the Christian empire laid the basis for the debasement of the civic and personal status of the Jew in Christian society that lasted until the emancipation in the 19th century. These laws were, in part, revived in the Nazi Nuremberg Laws of 1933.

"The understanding of Christology is, I believe, at the heart of the problem. Theologically, anti-Judaism developed as the left hand of Christology. Anti-Judaism was the negative side of the Christian affirmation that Jesus was the Christ. Christianity claimed that the Jewish tradition of Messianic hope was fulfilled in Jesus. But since the Jewish religious teachers rejected this claim, the church developed a polemic against the Jews and Judaism to explain how the church could claim to be the fulfillment of a Jewish religious tradition when the Jewish religious teachers themselved denied this." (Published in *Jews and Christians After the Holocaust,* Abraham J. Peck, ed., foreword by Elie Wiesel, Fortress Press, Phila., 1982, p. 25).

It is obvious that the dialogue between Christians and Jews on this level and depth has only begun. The Luther Anniversary provides an opportunity to deal squarely with a legacy that has led to unspeakable horrors. Yet official government publications in the GDR make little or no reference to Luther's anti-Semitism in connection with the anniversary observance. This is equally true for the official church publications that I have seen. However, the issue is dealt with in great detail in a publication for which a number of theology professors at Humboldt University in East Berlin are responsible. They understand themselves in the tradition of the Confessing Church (*Weissenseer Blaetter* 2 and 3, 1982) Unfortunately, the circulation of this magazine is relatively small.

Much credit for raising the issues goes to Stefan Heym, who in his novel *Ahasver* (Bertelsmann Verlag, Muenchen, 1981) cannot resist the role of spoiler of the Christian-Marxist euphoria displayd at the birthday celebrations in the Luther Year. Heym, who lives in East Berlin, quotes extensively from the tract "Of the Jews and Their Lies" (1543), where, in addition to the recommendation that all synagogues and schools be burned, Luther wrote: "I advise that their houses be razed and destroyed.

36

For they pursue in them the same aims as in their synagogues... I advise that all their prayer books and Talmudic writings, in which such idolatry, lies, cursing, and blasphemy are taught, be taken from them... I advise that their rabbis be henceforth forbidden to teach on pain of loss of life and limb."

In his novel, Stefan Heym uses the imaginary correspondence between a professor from the Institute of Scientific Atheism in Berlin, capitol of the GDR, and a professor from the Hebrew University in Jerusalem, to point out that the responsible ministry in East Berlin considers the dredging up of these statements on the Jews by Luther a bad contribution to the Luther Year. But one expects Stefan Heym to raise sensitive issues.

The statement by the Lutheran World Federation that "Lutherans must rid their theology of any remaining vestige of Martin Luther's vitriolic denunciation of Jews" is a hopeful sign — but not more.

Unless the relationship between Christian traditions and anti-Semitism are intentionally taught in every theological seminary, and every confirmation class, things will change little. Only with this intention can there be any justification for celebrating the positive contributions which Luther has made to church and secular history.

One last observation, which brings the matter close to home and up-to-date: In an editorial, Sunday, May 22, 1983, "Spy Stories and Vile Racism", the *New York Times* refers to the operators of a country music station in Dodge City, Kansas and their "Vicious messages and violent hints" that denounce "Jews as 'children of Satan' and speak loosely about cleansing the land by roadblock and ambush." The editorial continues: "Still, that's what free speech is all about. The Babbses may be unfit station operators by F.C.C. standards because of their refusal to pay taxes, but not because of what they say. So long as they do not incite imminent violence, society can tolerate hearing even their vile racism."

One might want to ask, has history not shown sufficiently that anti-Semitism and violence go hand-in-hand? There is a limit to what can be tolerated. What else has to happen to make this point? It is this conclusion which has made the propagation of fascism, with all its aspects, including anti-Semitism, a punishable offense in the German Democratic Republic, and one wonders whether "tolerating the intolerable" is not stretching the free speech argument. One cannot but concur with Richard Marius *(Ibid, p. 242)*:

"It is not so much that Luther was an ancestor of Hitler's that may strike us with foreboding when we read this tractate ["Of the Jews and Their Lies"]; it is that Luther is yet another example of that nearly ritual bloodiness that in our history is so frequently associated with men whose lives are tied to desks and theories, isolated from the red ground where the blood is shed. Hitler is gone, but the almost ritual propensity for abstract violence among the theory class is still frighteningly with us."

November, 1983

WABC, Blacks and Jews

By LAWRENCE BUSH

WHEN Gil Noble devoted his Oct. 10, 1982 edition of "Like It Is" (WABC-TV, Sundays at 1:00 P.M.) to the Israeli invasion of Lebanon and the massacre in Beirut, the ABC switchboard was flooded with over 200 phone calls pointing out that the show was inaccurate and unfair to Israel. This protest, augmented by many letters to the network, was spontaneous, according to Ilana Stern Kabak, deputy director of the NY. Jewish Community Relations Council (JCRC). "We do organize phone chains around issues like this, " Kabak told JEWISH CURRENTS, "but this time that wasn't necessary."

The protest apparently caused shock waves at ABC, offering an opportunity for vice-president and general manager William Fyffe to threaten that Noble's show be restricted to "dealing with local issues that concern the Black community." No such demands, however, were made by the JCRC or Anti-Defamation League representatives who met with Noble, his staff and ABC management to design a "rebuttal" to the Oct. 10 broadcast.

That rebuttal was finally aired Dec. 5, evoking another storm of protest — this time from a sector of the Black community which insisted that Noble was being coerced by "special interest" groups and that "Like It Is," unique in its representation of Black interests on television, was facing a threat to its editorial autonomy. Some of the Black outcry was marred by both overt and subtle anti-Semitism, as I shall report below. Fortunately, no Jewish organization jumped deeper into the fray, which *was* essentially a conflict between the ABC network and the Black community.

On Dec. 21 Noble reported to a community meeting at the Abyssinian Baptist Church on W. 138 St. in Harlem that ABC had been responsive to the Black protest and that the threat to the independence of "Like It Is" was eliminated. The controversy is therefore cooling down, since the protests of both the Jewish and Black communities have proved effective. Still, in the Black community there seem to be traces of feeling that the Gil Noble controversy resulted from a feud, still ongoing, between Blacks and Jews over "Jewish power" and paternalism. Perhaps a more detailed look at the events, the participants and the issue involved can challenge that perception and help enable, rather than disable, self-criticism and communication between the communities.

"Like It Is" has been an award-winning news program with a uniquely progressive, investigative editorial slant that has won for Noble a broad and lo ᵃl viewing audience, particularly in the Black community. Noble has tackᵢₑd such subjects as FBI persecution of Paul Robeson and infiltration of Black radical groups, destabilization in the Caribbean, Namibia's struggle for independence from South Africa, drug abuse in the ghetto, and many other topics of Black concern that network news departments generally ignore or report from a government press release perspective. Unlike other news programs (such as Ted Koppel's "Nightline" on ABC and "The MacNeil-Lehrer Report" on PBS), "Like It Is" does not use a debate format to present opposing sides of an issue, but is an "advocacy" program seeking to fortify with facts and expert testimony a progressive Black perspective.

This approach, however, led to an Oct. 10 presentation about the Lebanon crisis that was significantly biased against Israel. Criticism of the invasion itself was fair, no harsher than many of the anti-invasion articles in *New Outlook* and other Israeli and Jewish publications. Discredited casualty statistics were presented as fact, but Israeli Defense Force efforts to protect civilian lives were acknowledged more than once. More significantly, though, the presentation of historical material about the Israeli-Palestinian conflict, material that can color attitudes towards Israel's very right to exist, was altogether inaccurate and one-sided.

Regarding the 1948 war, for instance, "international human rights attorney" Gay McDougal underwent no cross-examination from Noble when she asserted that "As soon as the British withdrew, the Israelis at that time, having grown in their military power, immediately overstepped the boundaries set by the partition plan. The 1948 war was a consequence."

McDougal continued: "... from the 1947-48 period on, we get a consistent pattern of military conquests of territory and annexation. And that's what we have in '67, when, in essence, Israel annexed... the West Bank, the Gaza Strip, the Golan Heights, and... Sinai."

McDougal deliberately failed to mention the invasion of Israel by Jordan, Egypt, Syria, Iraq and Lebanon in 1948 after those countries refused to accept the UN partition plan for Palestine. She failed to mention a single instance of the Arab military aggression and non-recognition of Israel that has continued through the years. She did not mention abuse and exploitation of the Palestinians by Syria, Jordan and others; she regarded PLO terrorism exclusively as an exercise of the "right to wage that struggle [for self-determination] by any and all means necessary." McDougal omitted from the historical record every Arab breach of morality, peace and justice that, with Israeli expansionism and intransigence towards the Palestinians have led to the current bloody impasse.

Former South Dakota Sen. James Abourezk followed McDougal with comments about the American Israel Political Action Committee. As a lobby, he said, AIPAC is "smart, clever and is sometimes very ruthless." It "uses supporters of Israel throughout the U.S., who... support Israel unquestioningly, or have, up till now, and blindly, and will let themselves be used to pressure any politician who might step out of line... It's simply because of the fear of the Jewish voters and other people who support Israel... It's political intimidation, political terrorism, if you want to call it that." Abourezk was describing legitimate, highly effective AIPAC lobbying efforts, as well as genuine Jewish electoral influence based on the extraordinarily high percentage of Jews who vote — but his language contained codewords that conjure up classic images of a Jewish cabal, of undue Jewish "power," and of Jewish disloyalty to the U.S. Gil Noble was not sensitive to such language, however, and challenged none of it with statistics or facts (about other lobby groups, for instance, to provide a context for AIPAC's activities).

These and other significant problems in the Oct. 10 broadcast led to the protest — indicating that a sizable sector of the Jewish community in New York is concerned enough with Black affairs and intelligent political analysis to watch "Like It Is." As word got out that Gil Noble was seeking Black voices for a "rebuttal" show, the Black community connected to the Abyssinian Baptist Church began to fume about the "pressure" being exerted on "Like It Is" — a bogus charge, as Noble himself had expressed active interest in producing another show on the Middle East when apprised by JCRC of Jewish impressions of the Oct. 10 show. Two factors were at work in the Black community: a volatile resentment of Jews and of the effectiveness of Jewish protest, and the perception that ABC was trying to exploit the furor to settle old scores and curb the anti-imperialist perspective of "Like It Is." Both these factors, as I shall indicate, were visible in the Black response to the Dec. 5 "rebuttal."

The show itself was fairly ineffective. "Like It Is" presented Hazel Dukes, president of the New York National Association for the Advancement of Colored People, and William Tatum, chairman of the board of the *Amsterdam News,* both of whom had just returned from a seven-day tour of Israel and Lebanon sponsored by JCRC. (The tour had been arranged well before the Noble controversy.) Neither speaker, unfortunately, was well-versed enough in the factual and ideological history of the Middle East conflict to rebut the specific distortions of Oct. 10 about the 1948 war, etc.

Still, Dukes and Tatum did convey a more positive feeling about Israel. "Within the loyal persons of Israel," Tatum pointed out, "you have two substantial... differing factions... That's democracy... some 400,000 people... demonstrated in Israel because of Lebanon... there was room in

Israel for this kind of dissent, this kind of opposition to the government."

Tatum concluded that "The state of Israel must survive, and America must support the state of Israel, but it cannot support Israel right or wrong.... I believe that there is enough thinking in Israel politically and intellectually that there will come a day... when they will sit down with the Arab community, perhaps including the PLO, and come to some accommodation in terms of living together."

Gil Noble then wondered aloud why "a good portion of the Black community, the Third World community, seems to be critical of Israel's role." Hazel Dukes's reply was revelatory: "Because of what happened here in America. Take, for instance, New York City, which is now by the census count, by just plain knowledge of feeling, half... Black... Most of our elected officials in high places... the mayor, the comptroller, several other key positions, relate to the Jewish community... the [Black] response is, 'Why in the hell should we worry about Israel?... Here in our own city they want to take, they want to dominate... and not give us a portion of the pie.' And they feel," Dukes continued, "that the same kind of attitude that exists here from those who are in power exists in the country of Israel, that they want everything, that they have no sense of compassion, no sense of reason, no sense of compromise, no sense of sharing."

Dukes was describing in no uncertain terms the dynamics of Black anti-Semitism: a classic case of the powerless hating the seemingly powerful to the benefit of the truly powerful. Such anti-Jewish expression was uninhibited at a community meeting Dec. 7 at the Abyssinian Baptist Church, led by the Rev. Calvin Butts, whose new "Organization of African American Clergy" organized picketing at the offices of ABC and the *Amsterdam News.*

Butts characterized the Gil Noble affair as "a pound of flesh... extracted from our community." Other speakers, all meeting with applause, suggested that Blacks "get the Jews out of our schools... stop buying at Jewish establishments... The Jews are not the friends of Black people, they have always demonstrated that. They've always used us, abused us, and so forth. Not only TV today, but with movies in 1941, when Black people were getting killed fighting Nazis to save Jews. They were taking us as fools... They hate their mothers and fathers, you know..."

The Rev. Butts considered such statements "cogent and very important." An undated press release from his organization added fuel to the fire: "There are some atrocities that we cannot abide; the premeditated murder of 'Like It Is' at the hands of an alien power is one of them."

Who in the Black community will challenge such poisonous leadership? When Gil Noble Dec. 21 announced to over 500 people at the church that their protest — including "the first demonstration ever" at ABC headquarters and a 3½ hour meeting of the Rev. Butts and his allies, ABC management and Noble himself — had protected "Like It Is" from editorial interference, he said nothing about the anti-Semitic undercurrents of that protest. In fact, Noble repeated the infamous "pound of flesh" line from *The Merchant of Venice,* adding that the Blacks, in response, had "exacted eight pounds of flesh!"

Butts followed Noble by wondering aloud "just who are the 33 groups that make up theJewish Community Relations Council? We tried to find out — ABC couldn't tell us." JCRC, by implication, is a mysterious power group. I asked the Rev. Butts after the meeting whether any effort had been made to call the JCRC directly, and informed him that its constitutent groups are listed on the organization's stationery. He said no such effort had been made.

Innuendo and sloppiness like this can make the Harlem community susceptible to political distortion. I noted at the Dec. 21 meeting that material from Lyndon LaRouche's National Democratic Policy Committee, formerly the U.S. Labor Party, a purveyor of anti-Semitism and bizarre conspiracy theories that support its ultra-right views, was being widely circulated by a woman who presented the material as coming from the "Democratic Party," with which the Committee has no connection. One conspiracy theory, it seems, begets another.

On the other hands, positive developments did arise from the Dec. 21 community meeting at the Abyssinian Baptist Church and the hubbub that preceded it. ABC agreed, for example, that during the 17-week football broadcast season, when "Like It Is" is bumped to a Saturday slot, 2-3 P.M. the show will be rebroadcast on Sundays at 8 A.M., to test whether there is a market for such rebroadcasts on a regular basis. ABC also agreed to explore the idea of turning "Like It Is" into a national network program (it is presently a part of the local New York affiliate and only local).

More significantly, there seems to be energy in the Harlem community for the formation of a Black media watchdog committee that will press Black demands for greater representation on the networks. As the *Amsterdam News* editorialized Dec. 11: "There is clearly a need for more quality Black programming on Channel 7 as there is on all of the television stations. That is, at bottom, the real crime in this situation."

Obviously Black low visibility on television has not been substantially reversed and — judging from the turnout at a symposium for TV writers that I attended in November, at which only five of more than 200 professional N.Y. writers were Black — the industry is doing little in the way of affirmative action. Even the fabulous success of *Roots* produced, in a business that mimics its own successes, more "docudramas" about European history and Jewish history (including *Holocaust, Playing for Time,* and *Masada*) than about Black history. (PBS is a limited but notable exception to this rule.) Popular Black programs like "The Jeffersons" have likewise spawned few offspring, and none without its "Amos n' Andy" quality of stereotyping and humor. In a word, Noble's show is indeed a "rebuttal" to mainstream programming.

But racism is not solved by anti-Semitism. Black disunity will not be overcome by condemning Jewish unity. Black powerlessness will not be solved by fighting the Jews. The need for education about the slave trade and the brutal Atlantic Crossing does not dictate a lessening of education about the Holocaust. Anti-Semitism remains the "socialism of fools" for Blacks who exalt their envy of the Jewish community's relative affluence and relative unity into "revolutionary" or nationalistic rhetoric. As Hazel Dukes of the NAACP concluded Dec. 5 on "Like It Is": "... those who are unemployed, those who are left at the bottom... of the ladder and see no light at the top, they cannot use that as a base for being anti-Semitic..."

Dukes, however, tried to articulate lessons for the Jewish community as well: "Jewish communities cannot get sensitive when questions are asked how come, why and what for, to them about what's happening in the Middle East and what's happening here in New York."

William Tatum added: "I reserve the right to criticize Israel, American Jews, Blacks and everybody fundamentally if indeed I intend to support them."

I understand them to mean that parochialism and defensiveness, both growing attitudes in the Jewish community, do not make for successful Black-Jewish relations. Only an active, progressive involvement in the issues of our day will protect Jews, as ever in the middle in our contentious society, from being trapped in a pincer of anti-Semitism from above and below. Just as the ADL saw fit to engage Southern Baptist Conference leader Rev. Bailey Smith ("God does not hear the prayer of a Jew") in dialogue, so must Jewish groups, in particular Jewish progressives, be willing to encounter and overcome, not disdain to discuss, the very basic shibboleths of anti-Semitism in future Black-Jewish dialogues.

Such dialogues could help Blacks isolate the anti-Semitic opportunists in their midst and enable Jews to confront Jewish reactionaries, who too easily exploit Jewish fear of anti-Semitism to mute criticism and opposition. Perhaps "Like It Is" could aid such coalition-building by airing a show of progressive Black-Jewish dialogue in which Black anti-Semitism and questions of "Jewish power" and Jewish responsibility could be confronted head-on. That, as well as Jewish support for a campaign to increase Black representation in the media, would be a constructive outcome of this feud.

February, 1983

Nairobi

FOR many of the women, especially the Jewish ones, arriving at Nairobi, Kenya this past July 1985 for the third and final conference marking the UN's Decade for Women, the African capital was haunted by ghosts. Ten years before, in Mexico City, the Decade had been kicked off with a conference that passed a resolution equating Zionism with racism (several months in advance of the General Assembly's declaration on that issue) and featured a third-world walkout when Leah Rabin, then wife of Israel's Prime Minister, rose to speak. A number of feminists promptly declared these women had been "used" by their male governments in doing so.

I can still remember how angry this assertion made me in the way it deliberately stepped around the idea that the women themselves might have had feelings on the matter. True, the delegations at Mexico City were official ones, bound by orders from their governments, which were indeed run by men and which had decided to use the conference to make their play on Israel. I accept this. What I reject is the implication that women somehow can't be political beings too, as dedicated to their national causes, as committed to a parochial and tendentious view of right and wrong, as men can be. Let's say all those women were simply obeying orders. The important question for me is, how did they feel while they were doing it? Resentful and rebellious? Just doing a day's work? Or, perhaps, quietly aware that they were doing the minumum required by common decency against a great evil?

But then it was not the Mexico City Conference that chiefly haunted the Jewish women planning to go to Nairobi, but Copenhagen, scene of the 1980 Conference. At Copenhagen, microphones were pulled out of hands or disconnected; arms were twisted (sometimes literally). Discussions disintegrated into shouting matches marked by furious insults and, according to some reports, physical violence. Nothing can convince me this kind of thing happens only on government orders and not because of a real, gut feeling on the part of the people involved. For many Jewish women present, Copenhagen was an experience they never wanted to repeat.

So the approach to Nairobi was marked by trepidation. Jewish organizations held numerous training sessions on issues and parliamentary tactics. Dame Nita Barrow of Barbados, President of the World Council of Churches and a prime organizer at Nairobi, announced that a small committee of Arab and Jewish women were meeting beforehand to try to obviate the possibility of open strife. She also said that "experts in conflict resolution" would be on hand anyway.

Actually two gatherings were held in Nairobi: the official UN Conference (July 15-26), attended by government delegations, and the unofficial Forum (July 10-19), for non-governmental organizations (NGO's) and individuals from around the world. The first was charged with voting on a document embodying the Conference's, and the Decade's programs and aspirations. The second was a deliberately unstructured series of workshops.

About 300 Jewish women attended the Forum, which had some 11,000 participants. Among the many Jewish NGO's sending representatives were the American Jewish Congress, whose deputation included Bella Abzug and Betty Freidan. From South Africa came Esther Levitan, who circulated a petition urging opposition to apartheid. And New Jewish Agenda sent Reena Bernards and Christie Balka, who were optimistic on the basis of pre-Forum networking with Arab and American Black delegates.

So, what happened at Nairobi? Was there good news or bad news?

Both, of course, as always. "Regardless of the scheduled subject of any meeting... anti-Zionist slogans, speeches and accusations took over the discussion," a B'nai B'rith woman stated in remarks reported in the July 28 *Morning Freiheit.* Numerous reports of this type suggested that the ghosts of Copenhagen still walked. Etti Hollander, an Israeli emigre from Ethiopia, was accused of being a traitor to her race and continent by some African delegates. And when Sarah Doron, a Labor Party Knesset member and head of the Israeli delegation to the UN Conference, stood up to make her speech, 200 Arab, African and Eastern bloc women walked out, shouting "Palestine! Palestine!" through the halls.

But one stayed. (Here begins the good news.) One Jordanian woman kept her seat when her entire delegation walked out. "Why should I leave? You want peace. I want peace. So we have something in common," she announced to the hall. Then she went up to Sarah Doron and kissed her.

Incredibly, this courageous act was reported nowhere in the American news reports that I read. Only the London (Zionist) *Jewish Chronicle* — which had been noting the Forum's pro-Palestinian activities with chagrin — ran it.

New Jewish Agenda sponsored a workshop in which Lisa Blum, of Shulamit Aloni's Citizens' Rights Movement, met Mary Khass, director of a preschool program in the Gaza Strip. "I know that the Jewish people have suffered a great deal and that they felt a need for a homeland as a safe refuge," said Khass. "We must agree that there must be mutual recognition between both peoples," said Blum. That Blum would take this view was not surprising. Her position (along with that of the other Israeli Forum

45

participants) toward the leftward end of the Israeli political spectrum was noted, sometimes with acerbity, by the mainstream Jewish press. But Blu Greenberg, wife of an Orthodox rabbi and a noted writer on Jewish and feminist subjects whose commitment to Jewish nationalism has never been doubted, came home saying she had learned a great deal about the Palestinian point of view.

There was more. Charlotte Jacobson, president of Hadassah, reported that at one forum a woman doctor from Hadassah was giving a speech on community health when a Palestinian participant tried to interrupt her. African and Asian delegates at the meeting began to bang on their desks in protest at being prevented from getting information they wanted. At another panel an Arab woman in the audience rose after listening to an extended attack on Israel and said that she had come to learn how women could help each other, not to hear arguments about religion and groups. "Tell us how Arab and Jewish and Christian women can work together," she pleaded.

So what's the final word? Some women came back saying they had reached out across barriers they never thought could be breached. On the other hand, Maureen Reagan, head of the U.S. Conference delegation, while exultant at having brought back a declaration that did not mention Zionism, nevertheless called the conference "an orgy of hypocrisy." And *Al Fajr,* the Jerusalem Palestinian weekly, perhaps closed the circle opened in Mexico City by asserting that the elimination of the Zionism-racism formula was the result of — women acting on the orders of their governments. Two steps forward and one step back, life goes on.

S O *nu,* what was the real thing, the proper business with which an epochal convocation on women's international concerns, such as took place in Nairobi, Kenya, last August, should have occupied itself? Last month's column was devoted to the hovering fears of the unreal, the improper: the possible hijacking of the conference by forces determined to use it to expel Zionism, and Israel with it, from the moral universe.

"Politicization," the term used for this posture, came to assume the status of a code word on both sides of the controversy. The Reagan administration inveighed against the "politicization" of the conference, thus getting two birds with one stone, since it was also argued that attacks on apartheid likewise came under the "political" rubric in this context. And nobody in the administration was going to claim to be in favor of apartheid — although the U.S. did cast the *only* vote against condemning South Africa's racial policies, in the conference's final document, "Forward Looking Strategies" (FLS).

Even so, in the final analysis apartheid took a back seat. It wasn't demonstrations over apartheid that broke up the mid-decade women's conference in Copenhagen in 1980, and nobody ever said it was. It was the other thing. "Sorry, no politics here," ran the caption on the front page of

46

Al Fajr, the Jerusalem Palestinain Weekly, a few weeks before the 1985 conference. The cartoon showed two female figures labeled U.S. and ISRAEL, gotten up as a cross between the Jewish American Princess and the Decline of the West in teased hair, eye makeup, toreador pants and dangling cigarettes. They were addressing a piteous creature who crawled toward them dragging balls and chains labeled "Town Curfews," "House Arrests," "Land Seizures" and so on. Clearly, she was Palestine; clearly the question was Israel.

This was the unreal thing, the tendentious use of the conference for a purpose other than its own. This month my question is: what then is the real thing, the legitimate needs and demands of women as a global constituency?

A good place to start looking is Kenya itself. It has the highest birthrate in the world, with an annual population increase of 4.1% and an average of 7 or 8 children per family, and is desperately strapped for food. Although the government introduced a reduced-fertility policy 20 years ago, contraceptive clinics are still few and far between, and only fitfully staffed or equipped. Even were the services adequate, however, the problem of hyperfertility would probably still exist, since the great majority of young Kenyan women *want* to have six or more children. (There is some evidence that this attitude changes in later life.)

Child-bearing is their immemorial role, the one status-conferring activity open to them. Natural barrenness is a curse, intentional infertility an insult to a husband's virility. Compulsory fertility, whether the compulsion comes from within or without, is a woman's problem. Scorecard: an amendment to the FLS attempted to protect the rights of women to "control their own lives and bodies" (*N.Y. Times* July 25), but was killed by Islamic findamentalist delegates on the grounds of religious traditions.

Agricultural development is a woman's problem, on a continent where 75% of the farming is done by women. Women are traditionally responsible for water and fuel, which often means walking as much as six miles a day for water and firewood. It is women who grow the vegetables that feed her family — all of this under an equatorial sun, with the latest addition to her family strapped to her back and the next to come in her belly.

The men are not necessarily idle, but they will more likely work for wages on the cash crops for which the country's development funds are usually earmarked. Subsistence farming, the women's work that results in the food four fifths of the people eat to stay alive, is "economically invisible." Scorecard: the FLS appealed for economic remuneration for this work and called on governments to construct wells, bore holes and dams to facilitate the collection of water (*N.Y Times,* July 29).

Female circumcision is a woman's problem — my god. This mutilation, widely practiced across Africa, including countries like Kenya and the Sudan, which have officially outlawed it, is not to be thought of in the same class as male circumcision. Female circumcision takes a variety of forms. Sometimes the tip of the clitoris (the seat of female sexual sensation) is cauterized with a hot iron and sometimes snipped off. Sometimes the entire clitoris is split or removed. Sometimes the 3 - or 4 - or 5-year-old girl is held down while a woman rips both her clitoris and her inner labia from her groin with a jagged piece of glass. In a variation called infibulation, a piece of bark is inserted in place of the excised tissues with a hole for menstruation. The operation is said to prevent immorality and marital infidelity. Scorecard: *no* news article in my voluminous file mentioned the FLS taking any position on this issue. This isn't conclusive, but it is suggestive.

Enough of this. We'll move out of Africa into a universal arena. Illegitimate pregnancy and birth are a woman's problem. The fact that mutual sexual passion, lust and rape can all result in babies, and that the concomitant stigma devolves almost exclusively upon those babies and their mothers, is a grief that has been knotted into the human condition since history began. Scorecard: the FLS contained a paragraph calling for the legal elimination of "discrimination against unmarried mothers and their children born out of wedlock." This language proved unacceptable to four countries represented. One was a Catholic entity, the Vatican; two were Moslem countries, Jordan and Syria; and one was a socialist country, Cuba. (Interestingly, Cuba was the only non-Arab country among the sponsors of the "Zionism-is-racism" resolution.) The paragraph passed when the phrase was changed to "single mothers and their children" and the condition "without prejudice to the religious and cultural traditions of countries" was added.

The impetus here came partly from the recent massive surge of Islamic fundamentalism, but fundamentalism has become an endemic weed of late, so that several American groups attended the Non-Governmental Forum at Nairobi University to lobby against abortion and contraception. One of these, the American Life League, declared International Planned Parenthood "bigoted" and "genocidal." And they're not alone in that perspective; closing the circle, many Black Africans, men and women alike, regard Western-sponsored campaigns to reduce Third World population as an attempt of white people to reduce the number of black people. Many black African women shy away from birth control angrily for that reason, and continue to bring forth 6, 7, or 8 children into their parched and overburdened land, to build up their people. It's not easy to sort out right and wrong, rationality and humanity in this mix. It's not easy, but it's the real thing.

November and December, 1985

48

Jewish Activism in the Lesbian-Feminist Movement

By *MELANIE KAYE/KANTROWITZ*
and *IRENA KLEPFISZ*

JEWISH consciousness and activism are coming alive in the lesbian-feminist movement. We are two Jewish lesbians who have recently become subscribers to *Jewish Currents* and begun to acquaint ourselves with various Jewish communities. This extension back towards our roots is not unique; as Jewish lesbians and feminists develop our Jewish identities and encounter increasing anti-Semitism in our movement as in the world, many of us recognize the need to build coalitions among Jewish communities and progressive movements.

Though in the past many Jewish lesbian-feminists have met in scattered friendship, consciousness-raising and study groups, and among the more observant in gay synagogues, and though some writing has appeared in the feminist media, these remained separate from one another, discrete events. What has been occurring, however, in the past year or two, is a leaderless, grass roots political movement of Jewish lesbian/feminists becoming visible to itself. We personally know of groups meeting in New York, Chicago, Madison, Boston, Philadelphia, Washington, Los Angeles, San Francisco, Portland and Belfast (Maine), and Santa Fe; outside of the U.S. we know of groups in Toronto and London. There are undoubtedly others we are not aware of. These groups have been dealing with a variety of subjects, including problems of identity, assimilation, self-hate, class and race and their relationship to anti-Semitism, Israel, Zionism, diverse Jewish cultures, Jewish solidarity, and how to counter anti-Semitism.

The magnitude of this, the hunger — as many have described it — for reconnecting with Jewishness is reflected in a few facts. In April, 1982, *Nice Jewish Girls: A Lesbian Anthology,* edited by Evelyn T. Beck, was published by Persephone Press, a lesbian/feminist publishing house. Consisting of writings of 23 women of Ashkenazi, Arabic, Sephardic, and interracial backgrounds, the anthology's first printing of 10,000 copies sold out in 10 months. A reading by some contributors in Boston, to celebrate the book's publication, drew over 5000 women and concluded with a 20-minute ovation; another reading in Albany drew 200 women. Jewish lesbians also organized readings from the anthology in Washington, San Francisco, Chicago and other areas.

49

Acitivities of Jewish lesbians are not limited to small groups or readings. For example, women in San Francisco organized a Jewish Feminist Conference in May 1982, a conference that included cultural events, caucuses, and workshops on combatting anti-Semitism, Jewish artists, working-class Jews, Zionism and discussions of the Middle East, daughters of survivors, Jews and gentiles in love, etc. (see Marylou Hadditt, "A Thousand Jewish Feminists: Coming Out Jewish in San Francisco" in *Jewish Currents,* Oct., 1982, which unfortunately does not make clear the extent of lesbian participation.) More than 700 women came to the conference, mostly lesbians (and mostly Jews; one of the three conference days was open to Gentile women.) The San Francisco conference also represented an encouraging attempt of lesbian and heterosexual women to work together.

Jewish lesbians have been active recently in countering anti-Semitism. The San Francisco Mime Troupe, for example, presenting in one of its plays a "Jewish American Princess" stereotype (the play's only Jew), has been confronted by Jews in several cities; some Jewish lesbians distributed leaflets critiquing the character. In Albany, Jewish and gentile feminists and lesbian/feminists challenged the Wallflower Dance Order, a woman's troupe with progressive politics, over its monolithic support of the PLO and a flyer which characterized Israel as the new Nazi state that had committed "the worst crimes of any country since 1945."

In Rochester, the scheduling of a feminist concert on Rosh Hashonah met Jewish protest; some Jews involved in the scheduling were prodded to rethink their erasure of an important Jewish holiday. The night of the performance one of them read a moving statement to the audience, affirming her Jewish identity and her solidarity with more observant Jews; and then she lit the New Year's candle and said the traditional Hebrew prayer.

Along with these activities, Jewish lesbians are insisting on more visibility in the various progressive struggles in which, until now, they have worked, visible as lesbians but invisible as Jews. At rallies on nuclear disarmament, gay pride marches, prochoice meetings, Jewish lesbians are carrying signs and symbols of Jewish identification. Jews are demanding that the issue of anti-Semitism be included in discussions of oppression.

And the lesbian-feminist media is responding. There have been special issues on Jewish lesbians and Jewish women. Papers like *Womanews* (New York City), *Big Mama Rag* (Denver), *Plexus* (San Francisco), *Off Our Backs* (Washington, DC), *Gay Community News* (Boston), and magazines like *Sinister Wisdom* and *New Directions for Women* have been carrying articles which document instance of anti-Semitism and resistance to it, and explore the experience of Jews in the lesbian community and lesbians in the Jewish community.

During the Israeli invasion of Lebanon, the lesbian-feminist media carried endless articles from Zionists, anti-Zionists, reflecting the spectrum of opinion observable everywhere else. Arguments were as sharp as those found in the mainstream and left presses.

The voicing of Jewish lesbian concerns has met some response from gentiles. In one issue, *Sojourner* carried a letter by a gentile lesbian who was disturbed by the Jewish sterotype in the performance by the San Francisco Mime Troop and an article written with great sensitivity by a Black lesbian on her perception of relations between Black and Jewish women. *Lesbian Insider* published a strong tribute by a French-Canadian lesbian about the impact of the San Francisco conference; the piece concludes with her commitment to fight anti-Semitism.

None of this, of course, has developed without friction. The lesbian-feminist movement reflects very much the same problems as other progressive movements, not to mention the world. Most disturbing, as always, is the trivializing of anti-Semitism and the denial of support to Jews (often by Jews) in the name of "progressive politics." Self-hate and internalized anti-Semitism are very much in evidence among activists who are Jewish but minimize Jewish issues.

What we describe here is not meant to be exhaustive or comprehensive, but rather a broad sketch of recent Jewish activism in our movement; we want to inform other progressive Jews who, despite their professed support of lesbian and gay rights, are usually ignorant and unaware of what goes on in the lesbian-feminist movement. The biggest fear of Jewish lesbians is to be rejected by the lesbian, Jewish and progressive communities. It is upsetting, to say the least, that Orthodox Jews have been so vocal in opposition to lesbian and gay rights, or that Amnesty International — a progressive group which many Jews support — refused *again* to consider imprisoned homosexuals as prisoners of conscience. The issue is both support for gay and lesbian rights, *per se,* and recognition that gays and lesbians cannot work in, for, or with organizations which treat us contemptuously.

Nevertheless, Jewish lesbians continue to struggle, not only for ourselves, but for our children, parents, friends, and neighbors in the "old neighborhoods" in which we grew up. We ask that the progressive Jewish community actively seek us out, fortify us not only in work on Jewish issues, but on gay issues as well, support us beyond simply adopting a political position which says we deserve to exist. It is critical that lesbian-feminist concerns, issues and activism be reported regularly in progressive journals and newspapers; it is important that our writing be reviewed. It is critical that Jewish lesbians be invited to participate in progressive Jewish events, that lesbian and gay needs and perspectives be considered and consulted as positions are formulated and acted on. In a period of severe backlash like the present, the progresive community must independently as well as in coalitions be unequivocal in its commitment to lesbian and gay rights. No one, lesbians and gays included, is expendable.

We are encouraged by some moves from the progressive Jewish community. New Jewish Agenda has active lesbians and gays in its organization The Medem Jewish Socialist Group has included lesbians in cultural and politcal events. Other groups should be extending themselves too. The lesbian-feminist comminity and movement have many Jewish members, women with years of political expertise, at least three reasons to commit ourselves heavily to progressive politics, and at least three mass movements (feminist, gay, and the overlapping lesbian-feminist) to work within, and to join with the Jewish community against common dangers. We ask Jewish progressives to actively welcome us.

March, 1984

South African Jews on the Spot

Interview with RABBI BRIAN WALT
By Max Rosenfeld

MR: Rabbi Walt, you were born in South Africa?
WALT: Yes, in Capetown, in 1952. I grew up there, went to a Jewish day school. When I was 17, I went to live in Israel. I had become a Socialist-Zionist and I didn't feel there was any chance for the long-term survival of the South African Jewish community. Actually, I doubted the long-term survival of the Jews anywhere outside of Israel, although I didn't know much then about world Jewry.

MR: How long had your family been in South Africa?
WALT: My grandfather had migrated there from Lithuania early in the century, when most of the Jews came to South Africa.

MR: How long did you stay in Israel?
WALT: Two and a half years. I returned to South Africa because my father was mortally ill. I stayed there for about three more years and then came to America. So I've been here eleven years.

MR: Why did you come to the U.S.?
WALT: I came to pursue graduate studies in Jewish Education. I was attracted to the *havurah* movement in America and wanted to connect with groups of Jews who were connecting their Jewish religious life with the pursuit of social justice. I was particularly inspired by the activities of a small group in Washington that called itself Jews for Urban Justice.

MR: I understand you've been in South Africa recently?
WALT: Yes, this past December (1984). My wife's family still lives there.

MR: What was the mood among Jews when you were there in December?
WALT: The general feeling was that apartheid couldn't perpetuate itself forever, that this was the beginning of the end. I think there will be another wave of emigration of Jews from South Africa generated by the present "unrest" — that's the government term for Black resistance. But I think it's important for American Jews to understand that this is primarily an economic migration — the economic position of most Jews there is being threatened. Of course, many of these Jews may have moral qualms about apartheid too. Even some of those who have been active against apartheid may be leaving.

MR: Are there many Jews there who have been opposing apartheid?
WALT: Yes, but as a group they need to be distinguished from the

established Jewish community. For the most part they are not very connected to their Jewishness. Then there is a big segment of Jews who are liberals — they are good people, concerned about human rights. Helen Suzman, for example, who represents the Progressive Federal Party. People on the left usually join the African National Congress or the United Democratic Front. There is no organized group among South African Jewry that defines itself as Jewish *and* Progressive. Although many South African Jews are liberals, South African Jewry has not, until June of this year [1984] taken an official stand against apartheid.

MR: What do you think was the motivation for the anti-apartheid resolution that the Jewish Board of Deputies recently passed?

WALT: South Africa's Jews are in a very precarious situation at this point in history. They have been living with a dilemma for many years but now they can no longer ignore it. South Africa is undergoing a major transformation that is a result of Black resistance and that will inevitably end the apartheid system. If apartheid could be perpetuated for a longer period of time, the Jews would be safe in South Africa. They could maintain their freedoms and their economic security and that would be "wonderful." But it's not wonderful, because there's a moral issue here. Their privileged status as whites is at the expense of the Black majority. I don't want to minimize the difficult choice they have to make. If a truly democratic government comes to power, it will be a Black-majority government, and the whites will have to give up some privileges, economic privileges. So I think the Jewish Board of Deputies wisely recognized that in any real transformation of South Africa, Black leaders will have political power and that it makes sense to have some connection with them. Apartheid is doomed — even Botha realizes that now. He is beginning to dismantle the system. That's why he had a right-wing opposition. But what Botha is offering is much too little and much too slow. So the resolutions in my opinion are an indication that South African Jews realize that apartheid is doomed and they must be on the right side.

MR: You started to speak about the difficult choice facing Jews in South Africa?

WALT: Yes. I see three basic choices facing them. They can support the ruling party and go along with "apartheid with a human face." In the long run, I think that will be self-destructive. The second option is emigration. I think the reality is that most Jews will choose that. The third choice is to become a voice for progressive change — to educate the Jews there to adjust to life in a totally different kind of society. There is a wide variety of government that may emerge from the transformation of society in South Africa. The Jews could play a role in facilitating this change to a more democratic system. But to follow this course, the Jews would have to put themselves on the line. You are dealing with a ruling class that was sympathetic to the Nazis during World War II. The Nationalist Party that

54

runs South Africa dropped the anti-Semitism from its program in the 1950s, but there is still a reservoir of animosity that could be vented on the Jews, who have always feared that if they take the moral course and oppose apartheid they could become the targeted group.

MR: With regard to that, you said that the Jews in South Africa could play a role in facilitating democratic change. How effective could they really be, when they are only 2.6% of the white population and 0.4% of the overall population?

WALT: As members of the ruling white group, Jews have the opportunity to make it more amenable to change. Jews can't change apartheid by themselves but a moral decision by South African Jewry to place itself squarely on the side of change would help to create an environment in which change could take place. Moreover, Jewish support for change would be just one more pressure on the apartheid system.

MR: Representatives of several Christian denominations met with Botha recently to protest apartheid. What is the relationship of the Jewish community to those groups?

WALT: Generally, the Jewish community does not officially support the protest actions of church groups in South Africa.

MR: What about relations between Jews and Afrikaners now?

WALT: On the day-to-day basis, Jews deal with Afrikaners in business and professionally, but there is no general close social relationship. When I was growing up, there were very few Jews who supported the Nationalist Party. In fact, the Nationalists officially barred Jews from membership in their party until 1953. That changed in 1967, and you now have one or two Nationalist members of Parliament who are Jews.

MR: Is there some special significance to the year 1967?

WALT: 1967 marks the beginning of friendly relationship between Israel and South Africa and the Jews had a lot to do with that. The '67 war produced the talk about Israel and South Africa being in parallel situations. The Jewish community here in the U.S.A feels attacked when Israel's ties with South Africa are mentioned. The usual defense is that Israel's trade with South Africa is less than 1%, while the U.S. does 7%, and even African countries and Arab countries trade with South Africa.

Well, all that is true, and very often, bringing that issue up *is* anti-Semitic. I often speak at anti-South-African rallies and somehow the onus is on me, as a rabbi and a Jew, to explain Israel's policy. I contend that approach is anti-Semitic. I'm not a citizen of Israel, I'm not responsible for their policy, I actually oppose any and all connections with South Africa and I include Israel in that. It saddens me to think that the government of Israel has close connections with the present government of South Africa, but I can't do anything about it except to support those people in Israel who

55

have the same opinion as I do and to publicly protest Israeli along with all other foreign government ties with South Africa.

The Jewish community, however, should be honest with itself and realize that Israel's trade with South Africa is more than one percent. How much more, I don't know. But the one percent covers only official trade, not military trade nor diamonds.

[When arms are added to Israeli exports, the total in 1983 leaped from $15 million to $419 million; when diamonds are added to imports from South Africa, the 1983 total leaped from $142 million to $893 million (L.H. in our Oct., 1985 issue, p. 11, citing *Nation,* Aug., 17, 1985) — *Ed.*]

MR: Has this become a public issue in Israel?

WALT: Only to a limited extent. Whenever it's raised in Israel it's part of a wider issue, in conjunction with policy toward Central America. Israel as an arms exporter to right-wing, fascist governments is a limited issue there, given the totality of what Israel faces.

MR: In this complex situation, what do you think is the best course for American Jews to follow?

WALT: In my opinion, American Jews should support moves for divestment and sanctions against South Africa. The Blacks in South Africa will liberate *themselves,* but what America does will have a significant effect in aiding the Blacks achieve their liberation. Were our large-scale trade and economic ties with South Africa to be cut, this would put a great deal of pressure on the South Africa government to change.

MR: Do you really think the present South Africa government is capable of changing for the better?

WALT: Yes. I have to believe that. It may take a lot of pressure to make them change, but even now they are beginning to make changes, small as they are. When I was there in Dec. 1984 I was startled by all the talk about secret meetings between government people and the African National Congress. When I was growing up, the ANC was a dirty word. Of course, it's also possible that when they are pushed to the wall, the government will become even more defensive and more hard-line. But in the long run, they can't maintain that line.

MR: And you think the "hard-line" will make it worse for the Jews there?

WALT: Sure. The most deadly threat to the physical safety of the Jews in South Africa is apartheid. It's a deadly threat to the safety of all the whites there. It's deadly to the safety of Blacks. Because it's a system that cannot endure. My fundamental religious conviction is that, in the long run, justice will win out. In the end apartheid will lead to rebellion, because the world is so structured that people seek and create justice. That's the essence of Judaism — we remember how we rose up against Pharaoh. As Jews we must support those who are working to bring down the South Africa Pharaoh.

January, 1986

56

Jewish Witness in Nicaragua

Interview by MAX ROSENFELD

Annette Jaffe, Marc Breslow and Phyllis Taylor were part of a Jewish Witness for Peace delegation that spent Dec. 12 to 23, 1984 in Nicaragua. Jaffe, 30, and Breslow, 29, are members of New Jewish Agenda in Philadelphia. Taylor, 33, also of Philadelphia, is on the National Steering Committee of Witness of Peace. The following is excerpted from an interview I conducted with them a few days after they returned. M.R.

MR: First, give us a general idea of what you folks did there.

BRESLOW: We spent the first three days in Managua, the capital, then we rode up (in a truck) to Somotillo, a town near the Honduran border. We spent one night there, then one night in Achuapa, also near the border, then three nights again in Somotillo. From there we went to Corinto, on the Pacific, then back to Managua. Wherever we went, we talked to people. In Managua we spoke with the few Jews there. We also talked to several religious groups which are supporting the Sandinista government, such as the Protestant "Evangelicals" and a Baptist group.

MR: Who is "we"?

JAFFE: Our whole group of volunteers — 18 Jews from the U.S. We were from many different cities and of diverse ages and beliefs, from atheists to *Shomer Shabbos* (Sabbath observers). We traveled together the whole time we were in Nicaragua.

BRESLOW: Transportation is extremely difficult there, and outside of Managua it's not safe to travel alone. Besides, most of us didn't know Spanish.

JAFFE: Very few Nicaraguans know English, so Felicia Hirsch of New York, who speaks Spanish fluently, acted as our interpreter. Her family emigrated from Europe to Cuba after World War II.

MR: Please tell us something about Witness for Peace.

TAYLOR: The idea of Witness for Peace grew out of a trip to Nicaragua in April, 1983, when 30 religious folks from the Carolinas went there on a study tour. They arrived at one town up at the Honduran frontier right after it had been attacked by the Contras. Some of the homes were still burning. People had been killed. The survivors were in a state of shock. One of the comments made to the group that year was: "We can relax when you are here because when there are U.S. citizens here the Contras won't attack."

In July, 1983 a group of 150 people went to Nicaragua to see for themselves what was happening there. In Aug., 1983 I was in Washington for the anniversary of the Martin Luther King, Jr. march. Some of the people who had been in Nicaragua were there and got together to talk about what might be done, in view of what they had seen and heard. And that's how we organized Witness for Peace.

MR: For what purpose?

TAYLOR: Three things: We wanted to affirm that we were coming out of a religious base, out of a commitment to non-violence, and out of a commitment to change U.S. foreign policy where Nicaragua was concerned. We felt it was very important that we remain politically independent. We were invited to Nicaragua by the churches there, not by the government. We are not there to "protect" the Nicaraguan government. We are there to help U.S. citizens find a way to challenge our own government's policies. As for myself, I coordinated the first short-term group that went down in Dec., 1983, so the 1984 trip was a repeat for me.

Witness for Peace has been working there for a little over a year. We have to get permission from the Nicaraguan government to travel into the war zone, so we have the same status as a foreign correspondent. We now have long-term volunteers who give six months or more, at very minimal wages — they have to raise much of their own money. Their job is difficult and dangerous. They do three things: they help to host the short-term delegations, they investigate Contra incursion (they all speak Spanish), and they help the Nicaraguan people in any way they can. (One of them is a physician, for example.)

JAFFE: One of the first things we did in Somotillo was to hear a Mass for 20 telephone-telegraph workers who were killed by the Contras. They had come out to the countryside to help people with the harvest.

MR: Contras — is that a word that the Nicaraguans use?

JAFFE: They refer to anybody who is against them as "Contras." The word means "counter-revolutionaries" — armed insurrectionists.

MR: How many are there?

BRESLOW: The U.S. embassy says 15,000. About 4,000 are from Somoza's National Guard. They seem to be the driving force behind it.

JAFFE: The U.S. Congress voted down the appropriation for military aid to the Contras, so now they are being funded by private donations, but they are getting more money privately than they would have through Congress. And since people are giving money, not arms, it's legal.

MR: How much of this were you familiar with *before* you went down there?

JAFFE: We knew things in a general way. But the impact on the people, what it's like to live in a border area in fear of attack every time you go out on the road, that's something you experience only when you live with it.

58

They carry weapons all the time to defend themselves. A couple of people in our group who have spent time in Israel say it's comparable to Israel that way. In other ways, too. The farm co-ops, the spirit of a people struggling to build its own country in a hurry. And the people are young — it seems like all the women are pregnant!

MR: What moved you to go to Nicaragua? It's not exactly a vacation.

BRESLOW: I've been wanting to go there for the last couple of years; I wanted to see what it's like to live in a revolutionary situation. I've been active in New Jewish Agenda's Middle East work and when I heard there was going to be a Jewish Witness for Peace trip, I volunteered. As Phyllis (Taylor) said, they have the feeling there that if U.S. citizens are in an area, the Contras are not likely to attack. I must admit, though, *that* argument didn't make me feel any safer!

MR: What does Witness for Peace do to prepare the volunteers for their "tour of duty" down there?

TAYLOR: We have a training period in the U.S., before they go, because we want to make sure they understand it's *not* a vacation, that they are freely choosing to go into a dangerous area, and that we are coming out of a religious base and a commitment to non-violence. We go over the history of Nicaragua-U.S. involvement. For this particular group there was additional training on the Jewish aspect. And we've got to be careful we stay healthy — outside of Managua the food and water is different from what we are accustomed to. We talk about the customs of the Nicaraguans, so that we don't inadvertently do something offensive to them. We learn how we're going to function as a group. And going to Nicaragua is only part of the commitment; people must also make a commitment to work to change our foreign policy when they come back home. The training period is two and a half days.

MR: What did you do there that characterized you as a "Jewish presence"?

BRESLOW: We were staying in a compound that belongs to the BLOQUE, a Protestant group that supports the Sandinista government. We organized a Hanuka observance in the courtyard, led by Paula Marcus, a Hebrew School teacher and cantor. For one of the Hebrew songs we wrote English and Spanish versions! It goes like this: *Hanuka, Hanuka, b'herut/Hanuka, Hanuka, b'neyrot/Hag la nisim v'neyrot/b'kol bayit l'vivot.* Hanuka is freedom/Hanuka is the reason/To remember we must be/Always fighting to be free. *Hanuka, Hanuka, es libertad/Hanuka, Hanuka, es la verdad/ Siempre tenemos que luchar/Frente por la libertad.*

MR: Who was at the service?

BRESLOW: The people in our group, plus some American Jews who happened to be in Managua, plus some North American Christians who are living down there and helping the people, and a few Nicaraguans connected with the Center.

(Ruth Perk, a member of the delegation who knows Spanish, told me in a

59

telephone conversation: "We celebrated one of the nights of Hanuka with a Baptist congregation in Corinto. The pastor, Elmer Barahorra, said he was very moved when he realized that the Hebrew words we sang were in the same language that Jesus spoke. He impressed his congregation with the mystical nature of the occasion."

*(In the same vein, Robert Rosenberg, another member of the delegation, reported (*Morning Freiheit, *Jan. 13) that at the Jewish section of the Nicaraguan cemetery in Managua, "We said kaddish for the Jews buried there, as well as for the Nicaraguans who have died a senseless death in the war against their country. I was impressed by the profound sense of faith on the part of the Nicaraguans and that the revolution has been a spiritual awakening for them, as well as a political struggle for freedom." — M.R.)*

BRESLOW: Also, the U.S. residents in Managua gather every Thursday morning before the U.S. embassy to protest our government's policy. Our first full day in the capital was a Thursday, so we wrote a statement of our own and it was read by Phyllis Taylor at the meeting. Later, it was translated into Spanish and when we were in Achuapa we read it to a gathering of the local people in the town square.

MR: Did you find any evidence of anti-Semitism in Nicaragua today?

JAFFE: Judging form what we saw and heared, that's a non-issue. However, since Israel sold arms to Somoza, their propaganda does reflect that.

BRESLOW: We were told that they are now reconsidering their relations with Israel. There are practically no Jews left in Nicaragua now and people generally agree that there is no insitutional anti-Semitism. Even Robert Fretz, the U.S. Consul, told us that the Nicaraguans are not anti-Semitic and that the Reagan administration had been wrong on that. But our group felt it was important to check on the allegation of anti-Semitism.

TAYLOR: The Jewish community in Nicaragua was tiny from its inception. Most of the initial settlers came in the late 1920s. The boats from Europe stopped in Panama. Nicaragua and Honduras were two possible countries that the Jews on those boats looked at, but they were such totally undeveloped countries that they didn't seem to be a good prospect for earning a living. By the 1950s and 60s, the small number that did remain were primarily wealthy business people. After the earthquake in 1972, some of them migrated to the U.S. Those that remained were associated with Somoza. So they did have a reason to be fearful, not because they were Jewish but because they were "bedfellows" of Somoza, as the embassy man said. Their businesses were expropriated for that reason.

No doubt there's anti-Israel feeling there because Israel supplied arms to Somoza after the U.S. stopped doing so. This feeling exists mainly among the intelligentsia. The people out in the countryside don't really know anything about it. People there asked us if we came to Nicaragua out of our

Christian values! They had no concept of who the Jews are.

We talked with Hertes Lewites, the Minister of Tourism. He told us that he is now meeting with some Panamanian Jews about investing in Nicaragua. He himself was born of Jewish parents and identifies himself as a Jew, but says that in his youth he became alienated from the synagogue. He denied that there is anti-Semitism there. We also talked to Michele Najalis, a poet and a writer for *Nuevo Diaro,* a progovernment newspaper. She was wearing a Star of David. We asked her about the star and she said that she had been very close to her grandmother. Her grandparents were French Jews. Her grandfather was a highly decorated military man after World War I. When he died, he left all his medals to his wife. When the Nazis came to France and ordered the wearing of the yellow star, she went to the Vichy government and said; "I will take this yellow star and give you back these medals."

On her mother's side, Michele stems from Roman Catholics. She herself went to a Catholic school, so she knew very little about Jewish culture and tradition. She told us, however, that she discovered in herself an affinity to Jewish culture and to what Jews have contributed to humanity. Then she said something that was so moving that I wrote it down so I would remember it exactly. "From the chimneys come the smoke and souls of the Jewish people." I believe she meant what she said when she told us: "I feel my identity as a Jew and I am proud to inherit the history of the Jewish people." She also insisted that there was no anti-Semitism in Nicaragua, but that there is little sense of Jewish culture because there was such a tiny number of Jews there.

We also met with Oracio Ruiz Hijo, an editor of *La Prensa,* the opposition newspaper, and even he agreed that the stories about anti-Semitism had been exaggerated.

MR: What does this opposition in his paper reflect?

TAYLOR: It's owned by the Chamorro family, a newspaper family. It was the assassination of one member of that family that finally turned the middle class and the newspapers against Somoza. They feel that there has been an erosion of human rights in Nicaragua. They are very angry about press censorship, and it's true, there is some of that. As a civil libertarian, I don't approve of it. But you can go to the front of the *La Prensa* building, where there is a big bulletin board every day with the articles that have been censored. Some of the items censored have to do with military security, but some are stupid, like pot-holes in the streets. The justification of the government is that they will relax the censorship when the war is over.

We also met with Marta Baltodano, of the Permanent Commission on Human Rights, which played a key role in the fight against Somoza. She spoke of human rights abuse in Nicaragua today. However, being with

Amnesty Internationl and familiar with their research on this, I question some of the charges she made. I know that there have been violations of human rights in Nicaragua, but I also know that military persons there responsible for those violations have been courtmartialed and imprisoned.

MR: What is the Catholic Church's attitude toward the government?

BRESLOW: It's pretty clear that the upper levels of the Church hierarchy oppose the government. The lower level priests support it. Some of the priests and the lay people talked to us about their Liberation Theology.

JAFFE: It's powerful stuff! These priests really do community service — and they take great risks. They are prime targets for the Contras. They asked us not to use their names, for that reason. The popular slogan in Nicaragua is: "Between Christianity and the Revolution there is no contradiction."

MR: Did you get a chance to talk with some Nicaraguans privately?

JAFFE: One night our group slept in ten different homes, in pairs. The women's organization, ANNLAE, had arranged for us to stay with different families. ANNLAE tries to bring the ideas of the revolution into women's lives. They still have a lot of work to do about male chauvinism. Machismo is prevalent even in revolutionary Nicaragua.

BRESLOW: The women talked to us about that. They have a tremendous feeling about the feminist part of the revolution. They did all these chants and songs — it was great! We asked them many questions and they were quite open about the problem — they are trying to bring the men along, but it's hard work.

MR: I'm getting the feeling that there is a general fervor there about what they are doing.

JAFFE: Very much so! In Achuapa we went to one of the farm co-ops. It's like a big ranch. People ride horses — there are no cars except for the military. Before the revolution, all that land had been owned by one man, a colonel in Somoza's army. Now it's being worked by 20 families. It belongs to them.

MR: They get to keep what they grow?

JAFFE: Yes. They can sell their products. They are trying to build a new life for themselves — which means, for example, having a school teacher for their children.

MR: How would you characterize their revolution?

BRESLOW: I think they consider it a democratic nationalist revolution. The main impetus was to throw out the dictator along with U.S. dominance of their country. The economy is mixed.

JAFFE: In their first elections, the Sandinista Party got 63% of the vote; the rest went to a variety of parties.

MR: Why is little Nicaragua so vital to U.S. interests?

JAFFE: Well, the clear line of the U.S. government is that "there will be no more Cubas in Central America" or anywhere near our borders. I think that's the bottom line for the Reagan administration — Not more governments that we can't control.

MR: Did you see any Soviet influence?

TAYLOR: You see Soviet rifles there — the Nicaraguans will buy arms from anyone who will sell to them. We went to a clinic. As a nurse, I was particularly interested, so I asked what they do when someone needs emergency surgery. They told me they take the patient to a hospital about 35 miles away. That hospital was built by the Russians. I understand the government has a small number of Soviet military advisors.

MR: What is our embassy doing there?

JAFFE: We asked the Consul that. He said he doesn't understand why they still allow him to stay.

MR: Did you have a friendly discusion with him?

JAFFE: We did not! We just asked him questions; we didn't let him make speeches at us. By the end of the conversation, some of our people were so angry they were crying.

TAYLOR: This is where I differed somewhat from the rest of our delegation. They didn't want to shake the hand of the American consul. I did. For me, non-violence is in both word and deed. He didn't *have* to meet with us, but he did. For me, one of the most telling things Mr. Fretz said was that the bill coming up in Congress to fund the Contras will be a crucial one — he said that if the bill is defeated and the Contras don't get any more backing, it will tend to demoralize them. I was very thankful he said that. It's a real indication of where we ought to be spending our energies.

BRESLOW: For me, the basic truth is this: Regardless of whether there is anti-Semitism there, or whether the elections were totally free, or the press is free, whether the economy is socialist or not — all those questions are irrelevant. The basic thing is that Nicaragua is a sovereign nation and has the right to govern itself, and the U.S. has no right to interfere there or in any other country. No country in the world has a perfect democracy. Is Nicaragua the worst, that it deserves the full wrath of the U.S.? Is Nicaragua any worse than the 30 or 40 dictatorships that we give our support to?

JAFFE: I would add only that as Jews we need to remember that our history teaches us not to be silent about atrocities no matter in what cause they are committed. The Contras don't just attack and kill people. Before they kill their victims they do awful things to them.

MR: It's a kind of terror?

BRESLOW: Exactly! Since the revolution, 8,000 Nicaraguans have been killed by acts of terrorism. How can we call the Contras "freedom fighters"?

MR: What do you plan to do now?

BRESLOW: I'm getting a slide show together and I'd like to speak to Jewish groups about our experience in Nicaragua.

JAFFE: My main reason for going was that I want to do organizing around this whole issue in the Jewish community, from a Jewish prespective.

TAYLOR: Witness for Peace has three groups a month going to Nicaragua now. We are also helping to organize the "Pledge of Resistance" movement to get American citizens to say to our government that its policy in Nicaragua is wrong, and that if the U.S. invades Nicaragua, we will not be silent, as in Grenada. The Pledge of Resistance says: "By announcing ahead of time a coordinated plan of massive resistance, we hope to *prevent* the invasion in the first place." I wish that sort of thing could have happened in Germany in the thirties against Hitler. (Since her return Taylor has spoken at two synagogues and a Jewish "Y" in Philadelphia.)

April, 1985

Odyssey of a Nazi Collaborator

By CHARLES R. ALLEN JR.

S INCE 1973, the name of Tscherim Soobzokov has appeared on several of the U.S. Immigration and Naturalization Service lists of "Suspected Nazi War Criminals Living In The United States."

This year, Soobzokov filed a libel suit for $10 million against the author and publisher of a book subsidiary owned wholly by the *N.Y. Times* and against Doubleday, a major publishing house, its distributors, Literary Guild, and others. In a separate suit, he also seeks damges from America's largest TV News network, CBS.

His suits mark the only time since 1951, when the issue of Nazi war criminals living in this country first emerged, that a person so accused has taken such an action. He avers in his suit that he has been libeled as "a Nazi war criminal... who served with the *Einsatzgruppen* or similar irregular forces... and had executed Jews, Communists and others. [and] had participated in the murder of 1.4 million Jews on the Eastern front." (T. Soobzokov, Plaintiff, against Blum, et al., Verified Complaint, Index #1927/77, County of Nassau, N.Y., pages 10, 32, 36).

In the book *Wanted!,* its author has a fictitiously named character "tell himself" that Soobzokov was "an *Obersturmfuehrer,* a first lieutenant in the SS..." during 1941-1943 in the USSR *(Wanted! The Search For Nazis In America* by Howard Blum, Quadrangle/The N.Y. Times Book Co., N.Y. 1977, pages 30-79).

Soobzokov's attorney has targeted in on this assertion, for which there is no documentation.

In an aptly titled article, "Is An Ex-Nazi SS Officer Getting Away? The Trouble With Howard Blum's *Wanted!" (Soho Weekly News,* New York, June 1, 1977) Richard Steiger indicated that Soobzokov might succeed in his suit and be dropped from further INS investigations.

Scoring *Wanted!* as "neither carful nor thorough nor original," Steiger asked some 20 authorities familiar with the Soobzokov case whether they thought "Soobzokov is a war criminal?" The collective answer "would be yes," reported Steiger but, he ruefully told me recently, "this ex-SS officer might just be getting away with more than murder."

Steiger's remark is insightful. The Soobzokov matter has indeed become important, Regardless of the deficiencies of *Wanted!* (see this writer's

65

review, JEWISH CURRENTS, April, 1977), should Soobzokov win a settlement of any kind, the now broadening struggle to secure a resolution of the question of Nazi war criminals in our midst will suffer a serious setback.

It was not until Soobzokov filed his suit against *The Times, et al.* that I began to take a deeper interest in him.

The general facts about Soobzokov have been known to specialists in the field for several years. He came to the United States in 1955 on a Jordanian passport, although he is a Circassian from the North Caucasus. After moving to the Circassian community in Paterson, N.J., he worked his way into a county job as inspector of its purchasing department, and has been a ward activist with the local Democratic machine.

He is close to the local Congressman, supposedly "delivers" the Circassian vote on election days and otherwise has been but a little more conspicuous than the other very minor figures comprising the more than 100 individuals now on th INS war criminals list.

But he no longer is so minor. Since the suits, several organizations (some of them Jewish) have tried to take the offensive against Soobzokov, particularly in view of the INS charges.

But the *Paterson Daily News,* some Teamsters locals and the offices of U.S. Congressman Robert A. Roe unfailingly come to his support.

The local Circassian community apparently is cowed by Soobzokov despite allegations of fraud and pay-offs involving Social Security payments leveled against him over the years. He appears to exercise some kind of hold not only in Paterson but in certain circles in Washington.

Why has this been so? Is it in any manner related to the charges of war criminality against him? And just what can be said with certainty about those charges?

Tscherim Soobzokov laid out his past when he filed, in English, an "Applicaton for Immigrant Visa and Alien registration" I-230237, on April 6, 1955 (Visa Application on file in the U.S. State Department).

He declared under oath that he was born on Jan. 1, 1918 in the village of Tachatamukai, Krasnodar, in the North Caucasus region of the USSR. Krasnodar is the ancient city in the north-west corner of the Transcaucasus, hard by the Black Sea.

His family names indicate they are of the ancient people, the Adyge, known as Circassians. Most were Sunni Moslems. His Moslem name — Abdel-Karim Showabzoqa — appears on the visa application.

While designating himself an "agricultural engineer," he was actually a peasant farmer. Until 21 years of age, he led a wholly uneventful life. Then he was drafted into the Red Army, "where," he wrote, "I served from 1939-1942." Although stating his service records (routinely required of a visa applicant), were "unobtainable," he has frequently boasted among fellow Circassians of having been "a Red Army officer."

66

He also stated: "I was arrested by the Soviet authorities in 1940 for about two months and a half under pretext of political offense and was later released and pronounced innocent of the charge, in Smolensk" (Visa App.).

To this point, his own statements reveal the following: he was a reservist, not on active duty during 1939-1941. Had he been on active duty, according to Soviet legal authorities I consulted, he would have, when arrested in 1940, faced extreme jeopardy for a serious economic crime not only from civil courts but also from the military, which would have added long prison terms of its own.

It is probable then that he was arrested on suspicion, according to this legal source. Such arrests, short imprisonments on grounds of possible pro-Nazi activity and release were not unusual. He has often boasted to his fellow Circassians here about his early, outspoken anti-communism (common enough among Moslems in the Transcaucasus).

Shortly thereafter he was called up for active duty when Germany invaded the USSR on June 21, 1941.

He claims to have served in the Red Army until 1942. We can even pinpoint the date when, in 1942, he went over to the Nazis and how he did so.

After "lightning swift" strikes by the Nazis, into the Crimea and the North Caucasus, Kransnodar fell on Aug. 12, 1942. Soobzokov went over to the Germans either from a POW (Prisoner of War) pen or as an outright deserter at or about the time of the fall of Krasnodar.

Two questions must now be asked: What was it like when the Nazis invaded the North Caucasus? And — in the context of this answer, what options were open for Soobzokov?

The answers to both questiona are clear. We know exactly what Nazi forces took Krasnodar: The Army's 11th, Group South; *Waffen SS* Divisions, *Viking* and *Totenkopf* (composed entirely of former guards of the earliest concentration camps of Hitler Germany). Local police and other collaborators formed punitive units from the Ukraine and Crimea; and two emigre former Tsarist Circassian generals were assigned the specific task of raising collaborators for an "anti-Bolshevik" force in the North Caucasus. During the Civil War in the 1920s they had fought against the newborn socialist state. (see *The House Built on Sand* by Gerold Reitlinger, N.Y., 1960, esp. ch. 9, and *Russia At War* by A. Werth, N.Y., 1964, pages 564-585, from analysis of Nazi plans to "decommunize" the Caucasus.)

And then of course they were the dreaded "special task forces," the *Einsatzgruppen,* entrusted with mobile killing operations.

Einsatzgruppe D, made up of some 300 *SS* killers, swept the North Caucasus and Crimea from 1941 to 1943 in close support of the Army and *Waffen* SS.

Einsatzgruppe D was made up of five sub-units, *Einsatzkommandos* 10a, 10b, 11a, 11b and 12; in turn each had its squads, called *Sonderkommandos*.

Documentation shows that *Einstzkommando 10b* and its *Sonderkommando* specifically operated in the Krasnodar area. (Several authorities attest to this but see especially *The Destruction of the European Jews,* by Raul Hilberg, N.Y., 1961, ch. VII, pages 177-256.)

It is important to keep clearly in mind the composition of this genocidal hurricane that raged through the North Caucasus for nearly two years. We shall see how it fits precisely with the crucial points of Tscherim Soobzokov's own journeys during World War II.

It was this Nazi juggernaut that Soobzokov joined, becoming a fascist collaborator. "[I] was 1943-1944 *with* the German Army in the North Caucasus," he declared on his Visa Application. Moreover, this Nazi collaboration is a part of the charge appearing after Soobzokov's listing by the INS as a "Suspected Nazi War Criminal Living in the United States."

Once more, Soobzokov himself provides us with leads and insights into his past, including the specifics of his *only option — under those admitted circumstances* available to a collaborator.

I have underscored Soobzokov's unwitting admission of having been "with" rather than *in* the German Army. It is accurate. At that time, the Nazi Army was not officially taking in local collaborators. Nor was the *Waffen SS,* nor the *Einsatzgruppen.*

Thus Soobzokov was *not* in any of these German elements. To this degree, therefore, charges made by Howard Blum in *Wanted!* that he was, between 1941-1944, are inaccurate. But Soobzokov very much was *"with"* the Nazi armed forces as a collaborator with the enemy of his own country.

In what capacity, therefore, did he collaborate with the Nazis? Again, we know the sharp, limited options he had at that time. From the start of their invasion, the Nazis planned to and did make use of collaborators. At first, however, their use was strictly unofficial: the fascist's racial doctrine of "pure Aryans" would not permit official employment.

This impediment especially applied to the Caucasus, where Moslems were predominant. It was only after their disastrous defeats began to pile up that the Nazis started to rationalize official employment of all kinds of collaborators, none of whom remotely qualified as "pure Aryans."

We shall take these collaborating elements from the North Caucasus region in the chronology of their appearance and show how it matched the odyssey of Soobzokov at every crucial turn from the time of his going over to the Nazis until the very end of the war in 1945.

First there were the so-called *Hiwis (Hilfsfreiwillige)* or "voluntary helpers." At first they performed menial tasks on the front and in the rear for the Nazis. Quickly, however, they began to be worked in systematically by both the Army and the SS in combat, subversion, sabotage and terror operations.

Reitlinger, in his *The House Built On Sand* (pages 300ff) describes the *Hiwis* as "renegades" who "wore German uniforms but were not officially part of the *Werhmacht* (Army)." He notes: "It is impossible to decide when and where the German Army first employed Russian prisoners and deserters as 'voluntary helpers.'" But, significantly, among the first was "an anti-Partisan militia" made up of collaborators "from the Caucasus and Cossack deserters."

These "anti-partisan" units were used by the Nazis to inform on neighbors and join the endless efforts to hunt them down. Reitlinger adds: "By the winter of 1941-42, many of these *Hiwis* [acquired] a sort of combat status."

The first of the *Hiwis* to take on this status was called the North Caucasus Legion. Its ranks consisted primarily of "Moslem mixed-nationalities," according to Werth (work cited, pages 573-580) — Chechens, Ingushi, Karachis and — Circassians recruited largely from the Krasnodar region. Suffice it to point out here that the exact origins of Soobzokov are confirmed.

The North Caucasus Legion wore German uniforms, with officer insignia and a distinctive patch of horses heads. Many years later, a witness *for* Soobzokov in his libel suits would describe exactly the uniform which Soobzokov wore as a "Caucasian army officer because of the shoulder patch depicting several horse heads." (Affidavit, Fatima Celik, Nov. 20, 1976, Cty, Passaic, N.J.)

Reitlinger tells us that at first the 2 Hiwis did not "officially exist and could not be mentioned in dispatches." Therefore this accounts for the "unavailability" of his records of early service *"with* the German Army" by Soobzokov.

Then the German General Staff, in cooperation with the SS elements along the Eastern Front, began, in its own words, "to fill in the gaps" on the front lines both in combat and genocide operations with 2 Hiwis units (like the North Caucasus Legion) and referred to them officially as "Foreign Armies," putting them on a level with the collaborating fascist legions from Hungary, Romania, Italy, Spain and elsewhere in Europe's Axis bloc.

Thus we know, by his own admissions, that Soobzokov was *"with* the German Army." As we have shown, this must have been as a member of a 2 Hiwis unit — the North Caucasus Legion — later part of "Foreign Armies."

From the North Caucasus Legion elements were taken to form yet another Foreign Armies experiment: The Bergmann (Mountaineer) Battalions, first a creature of the Army's *Abwehr* (Intelligence) and later absorbed by the SS.

After it was formed in Oct., 1941 by what Reitlinger brands as "that gifted mass killer" of Jews, Theodor Oberlander (a Nazi war criminal who ultimately became an official of the West German government), the Bergmann Battalions superceded the North Caucasus Legion.

A series of carefully documented Polish studies disclose fully the role of the Bergmann Battalions and other Foreign Armies that fought and murdered with the Nazis (see *Oberlander: A Study in German East Policies* by A. Drozdzynski and J. Zaborowski, Warsaw, 1960.)

"The Bergmann detachment," write the authors of *Oberlander*, "was composed of POWs of various Caucasian nationalites... [It] went into action in combat, sabotage-subversion..." The authors cite a Nazi battle document: "Its task was to carry out 'special actions' [i.e., executions] in mountainous terrain and to incite tribes, towns and similar actions" in the North Caucasus (p. 102).

Werth also writes of Bergmann in his *Russia at War* as a "savagely anti-Bolshevik and counter-revolutionary" force, more Nazi than its Nazi masters.

Reitlinger too takes note of Bergmann Battalions as "recruited out of the POW camps in the North Caucasus where an array of tribes... [among them] the Circassians of Krasnodar" which "extended welcome" to the invaders (work cited, pages 300ff). Soobzokov, it will be remembered, is from Krasnodar.

The Bergmann Battalions too did not "officially" exist at first "but had to be camouflaged as special duty units working with the *Wehrmacht* since it could not be admitted officially that Red Army men served in the German front lines" (Reitlinger, p. 293). Then on April 20, 1942, states Reitlinger, "the order was issued for the creation [officially] of separate national legions for the main Caucasian races" (p. 306).

Shortly afterwards, all such forces were discontinued — *except* the Bergmann Battalions, which "had fought well on the Terek River Front" in the North Caucasus. Bergmann's 1st Battalion, according to Nuremberg Doc. PS-477, was raised, it should be noted, "from the Circassians from Krasnodar."

We know from the captured Nazi documents that Bergmann's 1st "filled in the gaps" of the genocidal coordination of the Army and the SS's *Einsatzgruppe D* doing "combat and execution duties." The Bergmann 2nd Battalion engaged in sabotage and terrorism (informing, mass arrests, round-ups for slave labor, etc.).

To sum up: the circumstances of objectively ascertained fact and Soobzokov's own testimony are too coincidental to be anything other than a logical account of who he was and what he did: his place of birth and rearing, Krasnodar; his national origins Circassian, Adygei; his Nazi collaboration "*with* the German Army"; and the *only* possible such service in the North Caucasus with, respectively, 2 Hiwis, North Caucasus Legion, Bergmann/Foreign Armies.

Let us now examine the specifics of the genocide that occurred in the North Caucasus, where he admittedly collaborated "with the German Army."

As Hilberg shows conclusively in his study (in which reliance is placed wholly on Nazi documents), the very "indigenous collaborators" which we have dealt with to this point — 2 Hiwis, North Cauccasus Legion, Foreign Armies and Bergmann elements — "joined [with the Army and SS] for the complete annihilation of the remaining Soviet Jews" preceding and during the very period when Soobzokov was "with" the Nazi Army. Currently Soobzokov denies that he or "my peoples" had anything to do with genocide of Jews.

Consider, however, just a few examples that Hilberg documents; note location and time of the genocides; note which elements carry them out:

• In a combined operation of the Army's Secret Field Police (GEP— *Geheime feld Polizei), Einsatzgruppe D* and the Bergmann Battalions, the fascists gloated on Feb. 18, 1942 "that almost 10,000 Jews have now been killed in Simferopol," Crimea. "Local Caucasus volunteers" also aided.

• Escaped Jews handed over to the "Local *Kommandanturen* and *Gendarmaries* and.... *Sonderkommando 10b...* for 'special treatment.'"

• During March, 1942, *Einsatzgruppe D* recorded 3,358 Jews, 78 Gypsies and 375 Slavs killed in North Caucasus sweeps especially around Krasnodar.

• July 16, 1942, with the assistance (informers and executioners) of Bergmann units, "*Einsatzgruppe D* killed the Tati (Mountain) Jews from the Caucasus, who had been resettled in the [area] by the American Joint Distribution Committee." (All citations, Hilberg, pp. 240-256).

Werth, also, records "the specific German practice of exterminating the entire Jewish population...[as in] *Krasnodar...* with [SS] gas wagons which killed 7,000" (work cited, p. 702). Werth, himself an eyewitness, wrote that the savagery toward the Jews, especially in the North Caucasus region, "was too nauseating" to describe.

Reitlinger, also, adds to the voluminous testimony of anti-Semitic genocide in the Caucasus where "it seemed that against [*Einsatzgruppe D*] and their renegade Russian helpers, no one could do anything."

Contrary to their own Moslem doctrine, the "renegades" of Bergmann and other collaborators from the "mixed Caucasian nationalities" took special pleasure in murder of the very young, old, infirm and insane, as the following indicates:

• "In Sept. 1942... they emptied the hospital at Stavropol, and gassed all the patients. Just before Christmas they removed the tubercular children from a sanitorium near Mikoyan Shakar... On 29th Sept. [Rosh Hashona], the occupation of the Caucasian watering places Piatygorsk, Essentuki and Kislovodsk was celebrated by a round-up and registration of all Jews, including many members of the evacuated staff and students of Leningrad

University. A few days later, 2,000 Jews were shot in an anti-tank ditch at Mineralny Vody" (Reitlinger, work cited, p. 301).

• In Jan., 1943, the Soviet offensive in the North Caucasus began. This of course did not lessen the anti-Semitic frenzy of the various Caucasus collaborators *with* the Nazis. "Even in January," Reitlinger writes, "during the general evacuation, they were still gassing the inmates of *Krasnodar* hospital in daily batches until the capture of the town by the Russians" (emphases added).

Soon the Soviet drive took hold. The Nazis were driven pell-mell out of the North Caucasus, across the Crimean Peninsula, up north and west to the Ukraine and Byelorussia. "The most active collaborators naturally followed the German Army in its retreat to the North," writes Werth. The grandiose plan — developed in constant consultation with the Grand Mufti of Jerusalem, then in Berlin — to capture the Caucasus "with the help of the Caucasus mountaineers" (Bergmann, *et al.*) was over.

Behind them, the fascist genocidists — the Army, *GEP,* the 2 Hiwis, Foreign Armies, North Caucasus Legion, the Bergmann Battalions, *Einsatzgruppe D.,* German Nazis and Caucasus collaborators — left some 325,000 innocents put to a racist death. "The vast majority," *Einsatzgruppe D's* comander, SS Lt. Gen. Otto Ohlendorff, was to testify at Nuremberg, "were Jews" (Nuremberg Doc. PS-2620).

Among the "most active Caucasus Collaborators" fleeing with their Nazi masters was our Tscherim Soobzokov: "In 1943-1945 [I] moved with the retreating German Army," he wrote on his Visa Application.

All the preceding is instructive in demonstrating the inherent pattern of fabrication and cover-up which Tscherim Soobzokov has consistently engaged in. Consider, nevertheless, another example, his own words uttered many years after the genocidal sweeps noted above, on the nationally syndicated "The MacNeil-Lehrer Report," WNET-TV, Ch. 13, New York, on Feb. 2, 1977:

"I had to laugh... I was supposedly rounding up Communists and Jews. For your information... in our territory there were no Jews whatsoever. We had a Jewish colony about 300 kilometers [away] who were living with our people where I never went at that time or after or before! They [Jews] were saved like as in heaven. Our people, neither I, neither anyone of my ethnic group ever had anything to do with the Jewish people for the reason they were never our enemies!"

At every twist and turn in their retreat, those very forces in flight continued to commit systematic murder. At Slonim in the Ukraine and Rachovich, Byelorussia, the archives show, they perpetrated foul murder, marked always by a lust for Jewish victims.

The documents also show these same collaborating forces were involved in mass atrocities at Buzov, Romania on June 6, 1944 and, later, in Hungary.

72

I have singled out these specific places and dates for one purpose: there are in the files of the INS today several affidavits placing Soobzokov at each and every place, including the date of June 6, 1944, as a "Caucasian officer" wearing "a German uniform."

By this date, 1944, the Bergmann Battalions had been taken over by the SS for use by both the SS and the Army. (The commander of Bergmann had an itch for power that exceeded his grasp. After he had insisted on enlarging his Bergmann Battalions with other nationals from the Soviet Union, Heinrich Himmler, head of the SS, had him sacked.) The SS chieftain then shrewdly absorbed Bergmann Battalions into his command while at the same time continuing to treat them officially as Foreign Armies. Reitlinger points out that this move was part of Himmler's ambition for the SS to supersede the Army itself.

Thus Soobzokov was still *"with"* the German armed forces as part of "Foreign Armies." Even though the Bergmann Battalions were largely under the control of the SS, they were all still attached to the Army. He was not yet in the SS during 1944. (This fact will shortly be seen as a key to unravelling further his journey as a Nazi collaborator.)

Soobzokov has himself provided evidence for his presence at the places indicated along the line of the Nazi retreat, 1943 to 1945.

He was to tell the *Paterson* (N.J.) *Daily News* July 16, 1974 that he was "a semi-enforced transportation laborer" in both Romania and Hungary in the Spring of 1944. "We were not exactly forced to go there," he said, "but we didn't have any choice." Such a claim is nonsense. There were no "semi-enforced" laborers for the Caucasus with the Nazis in their retreat. Such Caucasians were Nazi collaborators; all the others were in slave labor bondage, concentration camps, dead or back in the USSR.

In the INS files there are additional allegations that place Soobzokov "in a German Army officer uniform, with Caucasian insignia" in, consecutively, Italy, the south of France and Poland during the remainder of 1944. As far-fetched as it may sound — Caucasians fighting in Western Europe! — the evidence supports amply such a possibility.

By the Spring/Summer 1944 the long-delayed Second Front had opened, along with Allied advances up Italy and into the south of France. In desperation, the Nazis had diverted forces south in an attempt to arrest these massive incursions.

The Polish studies already referred to document the presence of *Waffen SS Viking* and *Totenkopf,* remnants of *Einsatzgruppe D.* Foreign Armies and remnants of Bergmann at all of these points, fighting as consolidated units and used as bilateral elements of both Army and SS. That is, the whole of the very genocidal power, intact structurally, which had decimated the North Caucasus when one Soobzokov had been *"with"* them, was operating in Western Europe.

Reitlinger also confirms this crucial aspect: "... *[in Italy]* where men of Central Asia fought in German uniforms... against a Japanese regiment in American uniforms."

In the meantime "a third complete 'voluntary' division was created from the *[North] Caucasus Legions* for service *in the south of France. ... [Among]* the 'volunteers' in the West... the *Caucasians* and the *Cossacks were still a majority.. kept in separate battalions... attached singly to German (Army/SS) regiments"* (p. 347, emphases added).

I have italicized the pertinent evidence illustrating once again how Soobzokov has been glibly covering up his personal presence as a Caucasian collaborator while confessedly *"with* the German Army."

Furthermore, many of these very Caucasian collaborators did fight to quell the Warsaw Rising of Aug. 1 to Oct. 1, 1944. Again as consolidated units, they fought on assignment to the notorioius Erich von dem Bach, Chief of the Anti-Partisan SS Forces. During some 60 days, these Nazis exterminated 300,000 Polish citizens.

Documents testify that *"Traces of the Bergmann... 'particularly distinguished itself during the suppression of the Warsaw Rising'..."* (Note, T. Oberlander, to H. Frank, March 1945, cited by Drozdzynski and Zaborowski, work cited, p. 103. Also see supportive evidence in: T. Cyprian and J. Sawicki, *Nazi Rule In Poland, 1939-1945,* pages 219-233, and *Poland Under Nazi occupation* by J. Gumkowski and K. Leszczynski, pages 179-219, reproduction of documents.) Moreover, affidavits in possession of the INS today place Soobzokov personally at the Warsaw Rising.

Now we come to the evidence which proves that Soobzokov has falsified his past, both as a Nazi collaborator, self-admitted, and as a participant himself in the Holocaust.

On April 11, 1973 the (West) Berlin Document Center (⁻ BDC) — operated by the U.S. State Department — unearthed a highly important document. It was the German original of a Personnel Roster of the *Waffen SS* ordering the transfer of *"Former Officers, Foreign Armies"* to *"the aforementioned Waffen SS Units Effective, 1 Jan. 1945."*

On the face of the first page of the 2-page order was a hand-written date of unknown origin: *"March 13, 1945."*

On page one of the Transfer Order, SS, fifth line up:

"As Waffen-Obersturmfuehrer (Waffen SS/First Lieutenant), Soobzokov, Tscherim, born, 1 Jan. 1918, Assigned, Effective, 4 Jan. 1945 to, Kauk. (Caucasus) Waffenverb. (Caucasus Armed, Waffen SS) der SS."

The *Waffen SS* Transfer Order was signed by a Major-General. *There are 12 "Former Officers, Foreign Armies" taken from the indigenous collaborators out of the North Caucasus and transferred to the Caucasus Waffen SS. Most appear to be Sunni Moslems.*

Accompanying the document itself was a letter of analysis by the BDC's director, Matild E. Holomany, who commented as follows (emphases are on face of original letter):

"... Regrettably, we have no other records on SUBJECT [Soobzokov] in our collections. However, we searched records of other individuals listed on the enclosed document who were also taken over by the SS under similar circumstances as SUBJECT and assigned to the same unit... We discovered several files of similar cases. Judging by the internal evidence of those records... the *following deduction can be made:*

"*a)* SUBJECT was a *former officer of the Red Army* who was *either captured by the German forces or deserted to the Germans.* It can also be assumed that SUBJECT held the equivalent rank of a *First Lieutenant in the Red Army.*

"*b)*... it can be assumed that SUBJECT at no time was in the regular German Army.

"*c)*... it can be assumed that SUBJECT prior to his official takeover by a regular *Waffen SS unit,* 4 Jan. 1945, was not assigned to regular units of the *Waffen SS* but rather *performed services with such organizations such as SS Bandenkampfverbaende, SS Einsatzgruppen or similar irregular forces."*

The document and analysis require comment. I have already demonstrated that both the general historical context and the internal evidence, based exclusively on the sworn testimony of Soobzokov himself, more than support the general contentions of the BDC analysis.

Consider: the name in the SS document, identical; birth date, identical with that of 1955 Visa Application; dates of Red Army Service and admitted collaboration "with the German Army in the North Caucasus" fit my own analysis and the BDC conclusions precisely.

Consider: rank equivalency in transfer from Foreign Armies to SS; preclusion of official German Army enrollment, independently verified by historians cited

Moreover, the document proves my own demonstrations that Soobzokov was *not* in the SS at any time before his transfer order into *Waffen SS* of Jan. 1, 1945.

Finally, the double-usage by both the Army and the *SS* of 2Hiwis and Foreign Armies (Bergmann) is exactly illustrated by the literal instructions of the SS Transfer Order: *Soobzokov is taken out of Foreign Armies and, officially, put into the Caucasus Waffen SS.*

Within this context, he most certainly participated as a minor Nazi collaborator, self-confessed, in an as yet personally unspecified way in the Holocaust itself.

Now comes Soobzokov's own slip, which proves fatal to his entire fabrication. In his libel suit against *The N.Y. Times, et al.* Soobzokov tries to explain away the *Waffen SS* Transfer Order and roster.

Newsday Feb. 25, 1977 summarized his suit's contentions: "Soobzokov says that he was enrolled in a Circassian unit of the *Waffen SS* that existed only on paper. He says this was done by a Circassian general who wanted to help [Soobzokov] get out of Germany and back to Hungary to rejoin a Circassian refugee group."

According to Soobzokov's libel suit, "... General Kucuk Ulugai was opposed to the Soviets and his mission in Germany was to form a North Caucasian unit to fight the Soviets but he had becme disaffected with the Germans and had formed mainly 'paper' military organizations... mere 'paper' rosters" (Soobzokov libel papers, p. 11).

Soobzokov sought out "Ulugai's" aid because he happened to be a friend of "the plaintiff's wife's family."

This "Circassian General" then supposedly makes Soobzokov a fictitious *Waffen SS* First Lieutenant; manufactures a bogus "SS identity card and [officer's] SS uniform" complete with phony travel orders — all of which enabled Soobzokov to move about freely, no questions asked.

"Under this protective guise," supplied by this "Circassian General," swears Soobzokov, "[I] could rejoin [my] group of Circassian refugees" in Hungary "where [I] could protect them until the end of the war... several months later" (pages 11, 12, 13).

Soobzokov's account, if somewhat tortured, sounds neat. Except that it is utterly false.

In the National Archives of the United States, the Modern Military Affairs section houses an enormous mass of Nazi documents. There are some two dozen frames, containing more than 30 SS documents, in the original, which tell the true story of "this Circassian General" on whom Soobzokov places so much of his story.

Who was he? How much "disaffection" toward the Nazis did he have? How much credibility can be extended to his purportedly making up "paper" SS organizations? (The data about "this Circassian General" are found in the U.S. Archives' "Records of the Reich Leader of the SS and Chief of the German Police, Reichsfuehrer SS und Chef der Deutsche Polizei; PESS Microfilm, Group T-175," Serial 163-164, roll 165, F#2-698484 et seq, from which the following evidence has been gleaned.)

The Circassian General's name is specifically Kucuk *Ulagay.* He immediately went over to the Nazis upon their invasion of the USSR. He commanded the collaborating unit, the North Caucasus Legion (*"chef der NK Verbandes,"* head of the North Caucasus Anti-Partisan Legion, collaborators with *Einsatzgruppe D*).

Ulagay was an *"SS Standartenfuehrer"* (a full SS Colonel), often decorated for his "distinguished service" — in SS atrocities throughout the Caucasus Crimea, The Ukraine, Italy, south of France and the Warsaw Rising of 1944.

76

He personally led the retreat westward of the North Caucasus "Military Collaborators," as the U.S. prosecution at the Nuremberg war crimes trials described the units which Soobzokov admittedly accompanied, as we have seen, "with the German Army."

Ulagay was charged with war crimes by the Soviets in 1943. He was on the "wanted" list of all the Allies by 1944.

In 1944, Ulagay occupied offices in Berlin of the *"National Kommittee fuer der SS"* as its executive director. He reported daily and directly to Himmler himself (*"Betr: NK SS Einheiten.... zu Der Reichsfuehrer SS"* — Exchange: North Kaukasus SS Units... to the National Chief SS).

His task during 1944-1945 was to integrate all *"Nord Kaukasische Legiones Truppen und Soldaten in Freiwilligen Verbanden"* into the *"Kaukausischen Waffen SS,* of which Ulagay was a top commander.)

In a "Top Secret" memo to Himmler by his Aide ("One Copy Only!"), Ulagay is praised for the "quick and efficient" way he has moved to effect such integration. ("RFSS," work cited, F#2-698503, Nov. 16, 1944.)

By Dec. 27, 1944, another "Top Secret" SS memo on *"Nord kaukasische Fragen"* shows that "SS Standartenfuehrer Ulagay has completed the integration into the SS of the NK Anti-Partisan elements from the *Wehrmacht* and *Hiwis* [collaborators] down to the level of *Unteroffizier* [sergeant] of all North Caucasus soldiers." ("RFSS," 164/165, F#2-698484.)

Ulagay's efforts were so appreciated that a Christmas holiday party was planned in his honor. Schnapps and other delicacies were to be served. A Himmler deputy enthused: *"Oberst (Colonel) Ulagay ist ein gut Kamerad."* Thus SS Standartenfuehrer Kucuk Ulagay, acknowledged benefactor of one Tscherim Soobzokov!

However, let us take Soobzokov's tale strictly on his terms: that he goes under this "protective guise" as a fully accredited, uniformed *Waffen SS Obersturmfuehrer* to Hungary on March 13, 1945.

But consider the historical facts of the chronology of the defeat of Hungary: Oct. 20, 1944, Red Army smashes across eastern borders; initial offensive rapid to the west. By Dec. 27, 1944 Budapest is surrounded while the remaining Soviet forces sweep past the city. Budapest falls Feb. 13, 1945. Before March 1st, the Red Army punches to Austrian/Czech borders. By early to mid-March all of Hungary is held by Soviets. (For chronology, see Werth, pages 1064ff; dates provided author by the Embassy of the People's Republic of Hungary to the U.S.)

I asked a senior archivist at the War Crimes Documentation Center in the German Democratic Republic this past summer to assess the known data and my analysis. He summarized as follows:

"This Soobzokov's own admission is that he was in an SS Circassian unit only if it existed on paper. On no other basis than that, he is established as anti-Soviet.

"That he was in Germany, not Soviet-occupied at the time, trying to get back to his Circassian refugees while at the same time getting away from both Nazis and Soviets to the safety of Hungary simply won't wash.

"At the time Soobzokov claimed, namely, March 13, 1945, all Hungary, and most assuredly all those parts holding any Circassians were firmly in the hands of the Soviets.

"No admitted anti-Soviet Circassian wearing an SS uniform with SS credentials, even phony, would have made it. There would have been immediate arrest, quick trial and certain death. So you see, this Soobzokov is making it up."

Soobzokov's lawyer has complained about the abuse his client has suffered. He loudly asserts that no less a personage than Simon Wiesenthal and "the War Criminals Section of the Anti-Defamation League" have all given the accused Nazi war criminal "a clean bill of health" (WNET-TV, Feb. 2, 1977).

Simon Wiesenthal has since, through intermediaries to me, denied "any such imputation." Dr. Lawrence Lishnick, head of the European Affairs desk of B'nai B'rith's ADL told me Sept. 8, 1977: "We don't have a so-called War Criminals Section. That's his lawyer's invention. Moreover, we don't give out 'clean bills of health' to anyone here. That's outrageous!" (The ADL has been so angered by Soobzokov's falsehood, that it has demanded a correction by WNET-TV.).

And Soobzokov's attorney also said on the same WNET-TV program, in denying that his client participated in "any atrocities" near Krasnodar: "... the mayor of Edepsukay #1 gave a statement to the Immigration and Naturalization Service of the United States stating, first, that Mr. Soobzokov was never near the place where the three individuals were executed. Second, the mayor said they were not executed by the Germans but were executed by their own people for excesses committeed by them under Sviet rule."

On Aug. 11, 1977, I interviewed the chief of the INS Special Task Force on Nazi war criminals. I read to him the full text of Soobzokov's lawyer's claim regarding Edepsukay #1.

This INS official said: "That's totally false. We never have had a man over in Russia. No statement of any kind was given to the INS, or the State Department, which did query the USSR on Soobzokov. Can you imagine any Soviet mayor making such a statement today?

I then asked whether Soobzokov's further claim that "the US has ended its investigations, as there is no evidence to substantiate the allegations" against him was accurate.

"Also false," he replied. "His case is still wide open. What we need now are eyewitnesses from over there [USSR]. And let me tell you, they [Soviets] are very helpful and are looking. This case is far from over."

78

The Soobzokov matter is in fact ongoing. His suits against *The Times, et al.* are still at the pre-trial stage.

Shortly after my interview with the INS, a grand jury convened in New York City to consider possibly criminal fraud in connection with Social Security payoffs. Tscherim Soobzokov is involved.

A source close to this latest development told me that also under consideration are Soobzokov's purported employmen, as a low-level CIA agent in the Middle East during the 1950s and his relationship to the Tolstoy Foundation, an emigre group shown to have been a CIA conduit in the past and Soobzokov's sponsor in coming to the United States in 1955.

Moreover, the details of yet another Soobzokov involvement have surfaced. Soobzokov, it is now alleged, has for some years been working as an FBI infromer among his own Circassian community in Paterson, N.J. The FBI refused comment when queried about this allegation. However, under the provisions of the FIA (Freedom of Information Act), I shall pursue this question vigorously. Soobzokov is not the only accused Nazi war criminal living in the United States reported to be or proved to be associated with both the FBI and the CIA, as other journalists and I have demonstrated. Perhaps this lead may account for the hidden powers that such an insignificant figure as a Soobzokov apparently enjoys.

The odyssey of Tscherim Soobzokov, admitted Nazi collaborator, war time traitor and one-time *Kaukausier Waffen SS Obersturmfuehrer* and listed among "Suspected Nazi War Criminals Living In The United States" by an agency of the U.S Government has not yet ended.

December, 1977

[Soobzokov died of wounds from a bomb attack Aug. 15, 1985 by unknown perpetrators, but attributed to elements of the Jewish Defense League and Jewish Defense Organization. The United Press International and Jewish Telegraphic Agency wire services carried Charles R. Allen Jr.'s categorical condemnation of such "terrorist attacks" as "illegal, immoral and stupid." The bombing remains an "open" F.B.I. case — *Editor*, Feb. 1, 1987.]

The New "Rassenscience"

By KAREN SACKS

THERE has been a resurrection of pseudo-scientific racism, elitism and sexism in the last decade. Together, these "isms" are called Social Darwinism. Social Darwinism explains the state of the world as the outcome of a struggle in which biologically "superior" cultures, races and individuals eliminate or subjugate their inferiors. In all Social Darwinist schemes the fittest people are white, male and well-to-do; and the best culture is industrial capitalist.

Social Darwinism has a long and dishonorable history. Its roots go back to the industrial revolution: in Thomas Malthus (1766-1834), who first raised the specter of too many people and advocated letting the poor die of poverty; in Herbert Spencer (1820-1903), who made the first full theory of benign neglect and women's biological inferiority; in the Comte de Gobineau's (1816-1882) creation of superior and inferior races; and in Francis Galton's (1822-1911) hopes of sterilizing the "inferior" people.

Yet Social Darwinism blossomed only in the 20th century, when it shaped national policy on a large scale in Europe and America. Thus it is important to know what the Social Darwinists claim and why it is unscientific; to know how their ideas shape policy, and why their pseudo-science is repeatedly revived and has so much influence.

First, who are the Social Darwinists and what do they say? The recent wave was led by University of California Prof. Arthur R. Jensen's claim that black people had fewer "intelligence genes" than white people and therefore it was pointless to use public funds to improve schools in black communities. He was echoed by electrical engineer William Shockley, who advocated sterilization of black women on welfare because they were stupid. They were followed by Harvard Prof. Richard Herrnstein, who insisted that the rich were rich because they inherited, not money, but superior genes from superior parents. A fan of Shockley, he too worried about "genetic enslavement" of the better people by the unrestricted fertility of the masses.

Garrett Hardin and Stanford Prof. Paul R. Ehrlich meanwhile were claiming that Third World people were going to engulf the wealthy white part of the world unless they were somehow stopped from breeding. Konrad Lorenz, a high academic official of Nazi Germany, resurfaced with the "novel" thesis that humans are naturally aggressive, and that war is therefore inevitable and moral; "might makes right" became natural law.

80

Lionel Tiger and Robin Fox asserted that human society is a pecking order of men with "the best" at the top, from which women are and should be excluded because they are genetically inadequate to form the relationship necessary for social decision-making.

Most recently zoologist E.O. Wilson pasted these (and others) into a "new synthesis" which he calls sociobiology. It asserts that human behavior is genetically programmed, that society is really a battle among men with women's fertility as the prize. The genetically best men win by passing on their genes; so too do superior cultures. Women are walking wombs and men are the actors. This does not exhaust the list.

Despite their claims to originality, they differ very little from earlier Social Darwinists of the eugenics movement in the United States and from the Nazi "race science" tutored by the same American movement. The eugencis movement was the organized political form of Social Darwinism in the 20th century up to and through World War II. It was aimed at preventing the proliferation of "bad stock." It preached that "feeblemindedness," poverty, alcoholism, criminal tendencies, insanity, susceptibility to tuberculosis, epilepsy, "moral degeneracy" and so on were inherited traits that were harmful to society. Southern and Eastern European immigrants, the Italians, Jews, Slavs and Hungarians, as well as American Blacks and Mexicans were all inferior races which threatened to out-breed and overwhelm the superior "Nordic" Americans.

Eugenicists directed their efforts to developing "objective" methods of distinguishing the good from the bad, the "smart" from the "feebleminded," restricting immigration of the latter, and preventing the reproduction of hereditary "defectives" who were already in the United States.

The first step, the development of an "intelligence" test, was taken by Lewis Terman, Henry Goddard and Robert Yerkes. All set out to prove that the new European immigrants as well as black and Latin people were basically inferior beings. In his book, *The Measurement of Intelligence,* in 1916, which introduced and explained the Stanford-Binet test, Lewis Terman (1877-1956) wrote: "The fact that one meets this type ['dull' as measured by the Stanford-Binet test] with such extraordinary frequency among Indians, Mexicans and Negroes, suggests quite forcibly the whole question of racial differences in mental traits will have to be taken up anew and by experimental methods."

Terman claimed that then "there will be discovered enormously significant racial differences in general intelligence, differences which cannot be wiped out by any scheme of mental culture. Children of this group should be segregated in separate classes. They cannot master abstractions, but they often can be made efficient workers. There is no possibility at present of convincing society that they should not be allowed to reproduce. They constitute a grave menace because of their unusually profilic breeding."

Eugenicists also claimed that the rich were rich because they were smart, and that workers were poor because they were dumb. Henry Goddard (1886-1957), speaking before a Princeton University audience in 1920, put it this way: "As for an equal distribution of the wealth of the world, that is equally absurd. The man with intelligence has spent his money wisely and saved until he has enough to provide for his needs in case of sickness, while a man of low intelligence, no matter how much money he would have earned, would have spent much of it foolishly and would never have anything ahead. It is said that during the past year the coal miners in certain parts of the country have earned more money than the coal operators [sic]. Yet today when the mines shut down for a time, those people are the first to suffer. They did not save anything although their whole life has taught them that mining is an irregular thing..."

Goddard gave an early version of the IQ test to immigrants at Ellis Island in 1912. He concluded from it that well over 80% were feebleminded. To be precise, 83% of the Jews, 80% of the Hungarians, 79% of the Italians, and 87% of the Russians. In 1917, the U.S. Government asked Col. Robert Yerkes to administer the IQ test to all World War I draftees. Col. Yerkes published the results which, very predictably, claimed that Southern and Eastern Europeans, blacks and Latins were all more or less equally stupid.

The IQ test transformed a folk notion, "feeblemindedness," into a "scientific concept": "intelligence." The IQ test, then, rather than a measure of people's "intelligence," was a measure of the class and race biases of the test makers. Nevertheless intelligence tests were a very important part of a campaign to restrict immigration and to sterilize, legally, so-called udesirables.

Agitation for sterilization laws and for restricting immigration became the scientific and political mission of eugenicists. The Eugenics Research Association was a most influential body of psychologists and biologists including Yerkes, Goddard and Terman, under the leadership of Charles Davenport and the Association secretary, Harry Laughlin. Davenport, together with the patricians Henry Fairfield Osborn (1857-1935), founder of the American Museum of Natural History and the Bronx Zoo) and Madison Grant (President of the Bronx Zoo) formed the Galton Society in 1918. It was to be a racist and anti-Semitic anthropological association to rival the professional American Anthropological Association, which under the presidency of Franz Boas (1858-1942) had little respect for such views.

It was *Passing of the Great Race* (1916), by Madison Grant (1865-1937) that created races for Europe: the superior Nordics (later called Aryans) and the inferior Alpines and Mediterraneans. The point of the book was that inferior Europeans, especially Jews, should not be allowed into the United States. Robert Yerkes, through the National Research Council, awarded Carl Brigham the support to produce his *A Study of American Intelligence* in 1923. Brigham used Yerkes' army IQ data to conclude that Nordics were smart while non-Nordics were not, and that unless immigration were cut off and inter-breeding stopped, the collective intelligence of America would go to hell in a handbasket.

He concluded: "But the decline of the American intelligence will be more rapid than the decline of the intelligence of European national groups, owing to the presence here of the Negro. The steps which should be taken must of course be dictated by science and not by political expedience. Immigration should not only be restrictive but highly selective. And the revision of the immigration and naturalization laws will only afford a slight relief from our present difficulties. The really important steps are those looking toward the prevention of the continued propagation of the defective strains in the present population."

American eugenicists were great admirers of Nazi Germany. The admiration was reciprocated: Hitler's expert on race, Eugen Fischer, wrote a laudatory preface in 1937 to the German edition of Grant's second book, *The Conquest of a Continent* (1933). Lothrop Stoddard, Grant's protege, visited Germany and Hitler in 1940; he returned and wrote calmly, "Inside Germany, the Jewish problem is already settled in principle and soon to be settled in fact by the physical elimination of Jews themselves from the Third Reich." And, finally, Hitler's infamous Eugenics Law was a close paraphrase of the Eugenic Research Association's Model Sterilization Law.

All this was no more science than hushpuppies are dogs. Nazi science and eugenics have been thoroughly discredited. Unfortunately claims by the current crop of Social Darwinists that they are creating a new science have confused a fair number of people. We need to make sure that it does not take another holocaust to make us see things clearly.

Arthur Jensen's 1969 acrticle, "How Much Can We Boost IQ and Scholastic Achievement?", in the *Harvard Educational Review* was among the first, and most pernicious, of the new articles. It can serve to illustrate some of the current ways that Social Darwinism is not science. A scientific argument needs to begin with a sound premise, to define its terms, to deal with real things and to show the relationship between cause and effect. Jensen's article does none of these things. I will summarize the outline of his argument and show why it is not science.

He claims (1) IQ tests measure intelligence; (2) identical twins reared in different environments had basically the same scores on IQ tests, proving that heredity is more important than environment in determining intelligence; (3) black children score lower than white children on IQ tests;

(4) therefore black people are less intelligent than white people; they have fewer "intelligence genes"; (5) thus there is no point in putting money into schools in black communities.

Jensen's argument rests principally on IQ test scores and on studies of identical twins. Both Terman's original test and subsequent IQ tests have been discredied as independent measures of anything. Likewise, the twin studies are suspect, and the most important of them, those of psychologist Sir Cyril L. Burt (1883-1971), were exposed as fraudulent last year.

First the IQ tests. Even their greatest fans admit that they cannot define intelligence. What then is the standard for determining what is "high" and what is "low," what is a "good" question/answer and what is a bad one? In short, how are test questions and scales made up? The answer, from Binet and Terman, is that questions were included if children who were judged by their teacher as "good students" could answer them.

Terman, his associates and successors, also made another critical assumption: that "intelligence" was not equally distributed among the populace, that most people were fairly dumb, some were very dumb, and only a few were smart. Thus, questions which everyone could answer correctly were thrown out, as were questions on which good students did not do well. In short, IQ tests *results* were and are determined by the biases built into constructing the tests: that the school's successes are the intelligent, that intelligence is unequally distributed in society. When we add Terman et al.'s racist and elitist biases it is hardly surprising to discover that well-to-do whites score highest on IQ tests.

IQ tests then are a tool in a vicious educational circle: to those who have good middle class schools, shall be given; and from those in under-staffed and overcroweded schools, shall be taken. IQ tests then are no independent measure of anything. If the testers do not define intelligence it is quite impossible for them to make a scientific statement about who has how much of it.

Jensen's second point is that this non-thing he calls intelligence is inherited; that there are intelligence genes; and that whites have more of them than blacks. In this, Jensen displays a pathetic ignorance of elementary genetics. Genetic differences within a species are governed by different forms (alleles) of the same gene, not by different numbers of genes. More serious though is the fraudulent nature of the only twin studies which control for environmental variation, and which are thus the foundation for Jensen's argument that intelligence is inherited. These "studies" were exposed by the *London Times,* Oct., 24, 1976 as totally fabricated.

Behind the trappings of science then, Jensen's argument is simply racist propaganda against affirmative action in education and emplyment. As such it has been forcefully denounced by individual scientists, by

84

professional associations like the American Anthropological Association and the Eastern Psychological Association, and by concerned citizens as well. But Jensen was simply the first in a new line of "scientific" propagandists of racism, elitism and sexism, all of whom celebrate the existing social and economic order as genetically ordained and unchangeable. It is the same old eugenic song in a new key for the '70s.

Each of these new theories is being criticized on the same grounds as Jensen's theory has been criticized: First, instead of relying on real evidence about how people act they rely on stereotypes — that workers and black people are dumb, while rich white people are smart; that women want to be dominated and that men want to dominate; and that people, mainly men, are aggressive, therefore war is inevitable.

Second, they insist that behavior is determined genetically, but they haven't the slightest bit of evidence to support that claim. Social Darwinists do not do genetic research; they often display gross ignorance of genetics; and they postulate whatever behavioral genes are needed to support a particular argument. Third, the construction of Social Darwinist argument is faulty because each part is faulty: unexamined things (genes) are claimed to cause unverified behavior (stereotypes) by unpostulated mechanisms. The argument is as unscientific as claims that spacemen built the pyramids.

It was not long before critics also pointed out that these theories were thinly disguised justifications for racism, sexism, imperialism and attacks on working people. They were dangerous not simply because they were wrong, but because they advocated — successfully — genocide, and various forms of slow death. Hitler made racism the official science of Nazi Germany. By 1945 an estimated two million people had been forcibly sterilized, most of them for "feeblemindedness." This "science" also justified killing six million Jews and five million non-Jews who resisted their own oppression by the the the Nazis.

In the United States the eugenicists were very influential in the move to restrict immigration and to legalize forced sterilizations. Variations of their Model Sterilizations Law were enacted by 30 states and Puerto Rico before World War II. By 1968 some 65,000 people had been forcibly sterilized under these laws, more than half of them because they were alleged to be mentally retarded on the basis of an IQ test.

In restriction of immigration from Southern and Eastern Europe, racism combined with anti-working class sentiments. Immigrants had been recruited by industrialists to keep wages low. But employers began to change their minds as their workers, foreign and American-born alike, organized and fought back. Instead of docile cheap labor to the captains of industry, workers became dangerous. Using the IQ data from World War I draftees, eugenicists like Stoddard, Osborn and Brigham "proved" that the foreign workers were inferior. They then went on to lobby among the politicians and the college-educated for cutting off immigration of all these "under men" as Stoddard called them. They succeeded with the Immigration Act of 1924. And some of the eugenicists later agitated for its use in keeping out Jewish and European refugees from Hitler.

Among today's Social Darwinists, the racist William Shockley advocates sterilization bonuses for poor black women. Along with Herrnstein and Jensen, Shockley claims that poor people are dumber than rich and have more children; hence allowing them to reproduce will lead to "genetic enslavement." Shockley's work has been dismissed by geneticists and other scientists of the National Academy of Sciences as "unworthy of serious consideration by a body of scientists," although Nixon's top scientific advisor, Edward David, supported Shockley and publicly berated the National Academy of Sciences for its stand.

Jensen opposes upgrading schools in the black comminity. A 1970 *Life* magazine story gave full play to Jensen's influence in the White House. Daniel Moynihan, then a Nixon advisor, claimed that "the winds of Jensen were gusting through the capital at gale force." Jensen had two scientist-politician friends in the White House. Moynihan, in a sexist version of racism, blamed black people for their poverty and oppression by claiming that they had inferior families — female headed — and hence reared inferior children. This theme was amplified by Edward Banfield, Nixon's urban advisor, who claimed black and Hispanic people made slums. His urban program is an up-date on Spencer's and Malthus' "benign neclect."

Sexist policies, by which the government seeks to control women's reproductive lives, have become increasingly central to racist programs. Forced sterilization with state and federal blessing has been an increasingly common practice on poor and minority women. An estimated 100,000 to 150,000 poor people have been sterilized annually under federal programs. Many women on welfare have been threatened with being cut from the program, denial of medical assistance in pregnancy or denial of abortion, unless they agreed to be sterilized right after the birth or abortion. Perhaps the most genocidal attack within the United States has been aimed at native Americans. A recent investigation by Dr. Constance Uri, a native American physician, has shown that perhaps as many as 42% of native American women of child-bearing age have been sterilized, most involuntarily under the Bureau of Indian Affairs controlled medical "care." This past summer the newspaper *Indigena* reported that as many as one-third of all Puerto Rican women and one-fifth of all married black women in the U.S. had been sterilized.

The "population explosion" eugenicists, Garrett Hardin and Paul Ehrlich, have advocated more global plans to sterilize the poor and non-white of the whole world. Indeed, Hardin was claiming, in his biology text, right on the heels of World War II, that intelligence was inherited, that the world's population was finite, that the "feebleminded" have more children than the "smart" and should be sterilized, while the smart should be encouraged to have more children.

Paul Ehrlich has popularized "kill the people, save the earth," as one school child put it. He calls for tax laws to discourage having children; for making abortion legal when approved — ominously — by the *doctor,* not the woman; and for federal funding of biomedical research into population restriction rather than death control. And indeed the lion's share of American funds for health care overseas is allocated in this way.

Though the new eugenicists favor abortion and birth control as well as sterilization, they are not feminists for they want control over women's reproductive lives to be vested not with women themselves, but with government. And they call for coercing the poor and the non-white not to have children, by any means possible. The old eugenicists wanted white and well-to-do women to be mothers of the superior race. And Theodore Roosevelt echoed them in his complaints about "race suicide." Among the new eugenicists only Garrett Hardin has clearly echoed this view — so far.

Why does Social Darwinism so consistently influence government policy? The answer is embarassingly simple. It is fabricated mainly by the rich and powerful, funded by them through their foundations and prestigious universities, published in their outlets, all to serve the needs of the very same rich and powerful.

A favorite pose taken by the new eugenicists is to claim that they are being persecuted for their new and unorthodox views. In an ad to that effect in the July, 1972 *American Psychologist,* they likened themselves to Galileo and other persecuted scientists. There is a flaw in the analogy that Jensen, Herrnstein, Hardin and the rest of the ad's signers make. The scientists to whom they liken themselves were persecuted by religious and governmental powerholders. By contrast today's Social Darwinists are *protected* by the political and academic establishment and attacked by the scientific and lay "grass roots" — quite a different predicament from Galileo's.

Research in the social and biological sciences is seldom given media coverage. But the Social Darwinists are consistently publicized favorably. Jensen's work has been carried prominently in *U.S News and World Report, Time, Life, Newsweek, Fortune,* the *N.Y. Times,* and *The Wall Street Journal,* while Shockley was featured in *U.S. News* and a variety of TV talk shows. When Herrnstein's article was published in the *Atlantic Monthly,* Eric Sevareid used it to tell a national TV audience that the government should now rethink equal educational opportuinity.

In 1973 *Fortune* reviewed Jensen's article-made-into-a-book. Allen Chase, in his *The Legacy of Malthus,* calls it "the making of a pseudofact 1971-1973." He juxtaposes Herrnstein's claim based on Jensen's numerology ("Jensen concluded — as have most of the other experts in the field — that the genetic factor is worth about 80 percent and that only 20 percent is left to everything else.") and *Fortune's* amplifications of it into "well known fact" status: ("A search of the scientific literature from one end to the other reveals no serious challenge to the view that differences in I.Q. are largely hereditary.") with the following note: "In the only sampling of the opinions of American psychologists, made in 1970 by the sociologist R.W. Friedrichs of Williams College, over two-thirds (68%) 'either disagreed or tended to disagree' with Jensen's thesis that genetic factors are strongly implicated in the average Negro-white intelligence difference."

Thus heritability of "intelligence" is a "well known fact" that is neither fact nor well known. With a little help, *Fortune* turned an old lie into a new truth.

The latter day Social Darwinists are highly rewarded for their work. Moynihan went from Harvard to the White House to the UN to the Senate. Banfield went from Harvard to the White House. Jensen was made a fellow of the American Association for the Advancement of Science Feb. 24, 1977. And Hardin is the editor of *Science,* magazine of the American Association for the Advancement of Science.

Why are Social Darwinists cultivated? The nation has been in a recession for almost a decade. Public and private employers have fired employees, driving up unemployment and the need for public assistance, increased prices and taxes, slashed governmental services and given away our tax money to bankers and bondholders. Both the working class and sectors of the middle class might unite with black and Hispanic fellow sufferers to resist all this. It is a divide and conquer strategy also directed at women. Forced sterilization and denial of women's right to abortion attack poor and minority women's control over their childbearing lives. But such policies also deny that control to white and non-poor women who could protect their rights by joining with minority and poor women.

Eugenics has never been a truly mass message, since in one or another way it attacks not a minority but probably a majority of the populace. Emanating in polysyllables from prestiguous universities, published in the magazines, newspapers and textbooks of the "educated," it is a seduction of those who are or hope to be in a position to succeed economically. The message is that those who make it are the deserving few; they are biologically predestined. And it urges victims who dream of joining the elect to become accomplices in repression or in fascism. The old eugenics helped underwrite Nazi genocide. It began with "scientific" discussions about why Jews, Eastern Europeans and/or black people should be exterminated. Let us nip the new eugenics in the bud.

February, 1978

88

Stalin Dissected

By MAX GORDON

JOSEPH Stalin was born in Gori, Georgia, Dec. 21, 1879, just 100 years ago. Few individuals have had so massive an impact on the course of history.

In my view, the overall impact has been tragic. But this, as well as other complex questions concerning Stalin's seemingly contradictory role, continue to be debated among both socialist revolutionaries and academic scholars. For while his monstrous crimes have been disastrous for socialism, during the years of his rule the USSR emerged as a great power, the economy was socialized, the fascists' bid for world domination was crushed and the stage set for great Soviet technological advances. Whether and to what extent Stalin's leadership contributed to these achievements, or whether they were accomplished despite him, is a matter of much controversy and is perhaps a judgment that can never be rendered, since there is no way to determine what would have happened without him.

But, as described below, the record is clear that economically, politically, socially and morally Soviet socialism was profoundly hampered and distorted by Stalinism.

To pose a few of the complex questions about Stalin's role: What was the actual extent of Stalin's crimes? Does the phenomenon known as Stalinism embrace only the crimes? Were these crimes, or Stalinism, a necessary accompaniment to socialist construction in the USSR? How could the phenomenon have arisen in the USSR's victory over Nazi Germany and what was Stalin's contribution? Was Stalinism a necessary or inevitable outgrowth of the system of proletarian dictatorship constructed under Lenin's leadership? What have been the consequences of Stalinism for the USSR, and for world socialism? How enduring are these consequences?

The literature on Stalin is, of course, enormous. My discussion here relies most heavily on the carefully documented studies of two Marxist — Communist — scholars, both dissidents, and the personal memoirs of two former Communists who, after dedicated service in behalf of the USSR, suffered 10 years each in the Gulag, the prison labor camps. The studies are Roy Medvedev's *Let History Judge,* completed in 1968, published by Knopf, 1971; and Jean Elleinstein's *The Stalin Phenomenon,* initially published in France in 1975 and in England by the left wing publishers, Lawrence and Wishart, in 1976. Medvedev, a historian, was expelled from the Soviet Communist Party after he wrote the book, which is based on the many Soviet publications, records, documents, memoirs and first-hand testimony that followed the revelations of the 20th and 22nd Soviet Party Congresses in 1956 and 1961; unpublished in the USSR, it initially circulated as *samizdat* literature. Elleinstein, a leading French Communist intellectual, is critical of his Party's leadership for the slow pace of destalinization. The two personal memoirs are Leopold Trepper's *Great Game* (McGraw-Hill, 1977), an autobiographical account by the organizer of the USSR's leading anti-Nazi espionage ring in Western Europe (the "Red Orchestra"); and Lev Kopelev's *To Be Preserved Forever* (Lippincott, 1977), the work of a leading Soviet dissident, most recently expelled from the Party in 1968, still, like Medvedev, living and active in Moscow. [Kopelev now lives in the West. — *Ed.*]

Stalinism has come to mean an explicit historic phenomenon, a malformation with essential features distinct from those of the formative years of the Soviet state and world communist movement; it cannot be equated with socialism any more than fascism can be equated with capitalism. Medvedev defines it as a personal despotism, sustained by mass terror and worship of the despot (or the cult of the individual). The record reveals that the mass terror, Stalin's crimes, was even more extensive, more incredibly evil, than exposed by Soviet leaders at the 20th and 22nd Party Congresses. Khrushchev and his associates were concerned primarily with the crude frameups of masses of Communist leaders and members, and with the damage to the nation as a whole. They did not deal with the cruelties visited on non-communists, such as the peasantry — poorer peasants as well as kulaks — in the early 1930s. Even within the limits of his concern, the facts are worse than Khrushchev reported.

Yet Stalinism encompasses other things as well. It profoundly influenced the method of governing party and states; the party's, and the world movement's, ideological and methodological outlook; Soviet natural and social sciences; its art, literature, psychology, ethics; the relationship between workers and peasants, and of both to the operations of the economy; the treatment of national minorities including the Jew; and Stalinism did incalculable damge to the world's perception of socialism. As Kopelev puts it, only after years in prison camps for having protested Red Army raping, looting and killing of German civilians during the advance into Germany, was he able to free himself gradually from the "sticky web of dialectical sophistry and syllogism" which was Stalin's hallmark and which could "transform the best of men into villains and executioners."

To deal with some specifics. In the early years after the Revolution, debates among Bolshevik leaders were sharp, animated, frank and free. Policies were arrived at through controversy. The clash of opinion,

90

Trepper recalls, "gave the Party its conhesion and vitality." Lenin was often outvoted in leading Party bodies, and the idea of penalizing someone for opposing him was inconceiviable. The concept that debate cease after a decision was taken did not exist. When in 1921 the Revolution was threatened by White armies on all sides and by mass starvation and the 10th Party Congress banned factions as a temporary measure, it initiated a free-wheeling discussion bulletin for expressions of opposition opinion.

Under Stalin anyone with a differing opinion, even if loyal, was a political *criminal,* a "deviationist objectively in the service of the enemy." As early as 1925 Stalin was charged with using his position as the Party's General Secretary to assign critics to posts far from Moscow. At the 14th Party Congress that year Lenin's widow, Krupskaya, assailed the emerging Stalin pattern of removing opposition members from important party posts and of demanding public renunciation of opposing views once a decision is taken. From 1929, when Stalin gained almost total power over the party machine, even Old Bolsheviks dared not oppose, or even discuss, his decisions.

Trepper recalls that you spoke "only to your trusted friends, and even then with trepidation. With everyone else you recited the official litanies from *Pravda.*" Even the forms of party leadership were abandoned. Until 1927 Party Congresses were held yearly or every two years. In the ensuing quarter century, just three Congresses were held; there were few plenary Central Committee sessions, and even the political bureau rarely met after Stalin had seized full power. Collective rule had given way to a single dictator who ruled by fiat.

Though Stalin is long gone and party rule has been largely restored at the top, a neo-Stalinist tendency that demands blind discipline and unquestioning submission to leadership persists in the USSR and in some communist movements abroad.

A second specific Stalinist feature: Lenin and the Bolsheviks considered dictatorship against the former ruling classes as essential to the preservation of the revolution. Their violence was directed against coounterrevolutionary forces warring against the regime. When in 1920-21 the desperate economic and military situation led some erstwhile supporters to revolt, the regime did suppress these revolts. But Lenin insisted upon the exceptional nature of the measures taken and demanded otherwise "unwavering adherence" to the rule of law.

Stalin's practice was to consider the proletarian dictatorship as force uninhibited by law and that this applied to the entire transition period from capitalism to communism. The concept of revolutionary legality was contemptuously cast aside as "rotten liberalism," and rampant lawlessness became the hallmark of the dictatorship despite the camouflage of the 1936 "Stalin Constitution."

Third, until 1921 Mensheviks and Left Social Revolutionaries were

91

represented in the Soviets. Leninist theory did not envisage a one-party state. These parties were banned in 1921 after they participated in uprisings against the regime. In 1923, after Lenin was removed from the scene by illness, the 12th Party Congress decreed that the dictatorship of the proletariat could be exercised only through the dictatorship of the Communist Party. Whatever Stalin's role in this decision, in the ensuing years he precluded all reexamination of the monolithic party issue. In typically syllogistic fashion, he proclaimed that since parties reflect classes and there was now one class in the USSR, there was no need for more than one party.

Fourth, Lenin was profoundly troubled by the perils of bureaucracy that he saw developing. Thus, he fought for independent trade unions as essential for the protection of workers' interests against the "bureaucratic distortions" of the workers' state. Under Stalin, bureaucracy, unchecked, ran rampant. Unions were reduced to handling nonessential individual problems.

Fifth, Lenin considered anti-Semitism, and all forms of racism and chauvinism, counterrevolutionary and to be relentlessly fought. Stalin treated minority peoples in the USSR brutally. He became increasingly anti-Semitic, and in his final years was uninhibitedly so.

Sixth, Lenin repeatedly admitted error. He recognized that in the light of the USSR's poioneering socialist role, its cultural backwardness, the inexperience of its leaders and its struggle for survival, mistakes were inevitable and needed serious collective study for their lessons.

Stalin, by stifling debate and suppressing consideration of alternative approaches to his own mechanistic solutions, enhanced error. But no one could point out his mistakes, much less undertake to learn from them.

Finally, Lenin recognized that the Revolution had to surmount sectarianism, a widespread and dangerous disease of socialist movements. He welcomed the support of former anti-Bolsheviks, other parties and their members, former tsarist military and civilian officials and bourgeois specialists, provided they refrained from counterrevolutionary activity.

In sharp contrast, Stalin was suspicious of, and hostile toward, all these elements. Whereas Lenin carried through the rule that political leaders not interfere with military specialists during the Civil War, Stalin had to be removed as a political commissar on the Southern Front for such repeated, and costly, interference. Later he was to persecute bourgeois specialists, as well as former Menshevik and Socialist Revolutionary leaders who had long accepted the Revolution. The tendency to characterize as an enemy all who do not see eye-to-eye with the party became widespread in the communist movement and persists in some places.

Stalin, a Bolshevik leader but by no means preeminent in 1922, became the CPSU's General Secretary early that year. Newly-created, the post was viewed as an administrative one and Stalin was expected to bring some order into party organization. But this included cadre assignment and Stalin made shrewd use of this power to advance his personal position, while weakening those he considered rivals or opponents. The sharp divisions in the leadership following Lenin's death facilitated his power moves.

Lenin, in his last year, had several run-ins with Stalin and strongly criticized him on several specific grounds. Ironically, in the light of Stalin's later reputation as the Leninist expert on the national question, some of the sharpest critiques involved serious charges of "great Russian" arrogance on Stalin's part, despite his Georgian origin.

Ironically, too, Lenin declared a failure the Workers and Peasants Inspection, an agency under Stalin's charge designed to control bureaucracy, on the grounds that it had itself become a huge, badly-organized bureaucracy. Late in 1922 Lenin warned, from his sickbed, that Stalin had accumulated too much power. In a series of "testaments" to the 12th Prty Congress set for March, 1923, he again warned against Stalin and urged his removal from the General Secretaryship. He placed the testaments in sealed envelopes labelled for opening in case of his death His intent was to present them personally otherwise. During the Congress, however, he was alive but in a coma. The Congress thus did not learn of the testaments. By the next Congress in 1924, which knew of them, Stalin was able to exploit the struggle for leadership between Zinoviev and Trotsky to consolidate his position.

Lenin's New Economic Policy (NEP), introduced in 1921 to replace the primitive "War Communism" of Civil War days, permitted the country to recover from the terrible famine and devastation broutht by seven years of imperialist and civil wars. With industry virtually wiped out and agriculture producing less than half of 1913, Lenin knew that socialization required a certain level of production attainable only under conditions of private ownership of at least small business and farms. NEP, in his view, would need to function for a few decades, with socialization to take place gradually through persuasion and incentives, not administratively by force.

From 1923 to 1928 productive forces developed with some rapidity. While kulaks and middle peasants, small industrialists and merchants prospered particularly, the Bolshevik state controlled large industry, finance, transport and foreign trade, as well as the state apparatus. The Trotsky-led opposition pressed for rapid industrialization through intensified exploitation of the peasantry, but Bukharin and Stalin had the support of the bulk of the party in defeating this. As Medvedev observes, Stalin's later crimes did not mean that he was always wrong or that all struggles in the 1920s were simply power struggles; genuine issues of socialist construction were involved.

But the outcome permitted Stalin to oust from key positions or expel from the party large numbers of the Trotskyist opposition. He was able to gain support for this because the basic policies he upheld against the opposition — the need to "build socialism in one country" and maintenance of the alliance under NEP of workers and peasants — were widely backed by party leaders and membership. But his measures against the opposition meant the destruction of inner-party democracy, even in the top leadership. These measures led later to physical destruction of party opponents.

In 1927 a poor harvest resulted in a huge shortfall in grain collection. A crisis threatened and the 15th Party Congress in December agreed to a temporary increase in requisitions, amid strictures against harsh collections measures. But immediately after the Congress Stalin sent instructions throughout the party for ruthless, forced requisitions and suppression of all opposition. He then proceeded to put over a program of rapid, forced, industrialization and forced collectivization. Bukharin and other Bolshevik leaders opposed Stalin on the grounds that his program threatened the workers' and peasants' alliance, would alienate the middle peasants who comprised the peasant majority, and would require massive terror against the people and the party. They argued, too, that the material base and trained personnel for effective collectivization and rapid industrialization were as yet inadequate. Experience tragically proved them right.

Bukharin also feared Stalin's political direction. He foresaw that Stalin's thesis of heightened class conflict as industry and collectivization advanced would mean mass repression, and he protested against the replacement of collective party leadership with Stalin's personal leadership. Privately, he predicted that Stalin's course would lead to a blood purge, that Stalin would "subordinate everything to his lust for power," and that "he knew only vengeance and the stab in the back..."

Thus at least some top Bolsheviks were aware of the direction Stalin was taking before 1930 but were powerless to stop him. He had gained the support of the former opposition since he had taken over — in exaggerated form — their policy of rapid industrialization. By attacking his opponents, including Bukharin, as siding with the kulaks and capitalists against socialism and industrialization, he isolated and destroyed them.

He also collided with Bukharin, who headed the Communist International, over the speed of development of the world economic crisis and its political effects. Stalin, operating through the Soviet delegation to the Comintern, led it to adopt a program based on expectation of imminent world revolution, thereby making Social Democracy and reformist trade unions — "social facism" — the main enemy, since in his sectarian concept they were the main obstacles to communist-led revolution. Bukharin, more sensitive to the fascist danger, was removed from the Comintern in 1929.

94

After they were already in motion the CP's Central Committee approved Stalin's plans for moving against the kulaks, speeding industrialization and collectivization, and imposing central planning early in 1929. Whereas there has been undemocratic and repressive practices earlier, what occurred afterwards was so vastly different in scale as to represent a qualitatively different social phenomenon. It was neither foreordained nor an inevitable consequence of Leninist policy. Bukharin's position certainly reflected Lenin's program far more accurately and was a possible alternative.

The initial collectivization target was 8,000,000 hectares under cultivation in 1930. Stalin, without consultation, upped it to 30,000,000. By the end of 1929 kulaks were being deported *en masse,* armed struggles were developing, party officials were assassination targets and thousands were arrested for attacking these officials.

Stalin launched the slogan of "liquidation of the kulaks as a class," but since the definition of kulak was vague, many middle peasants were included in the subsequent wave of deportations. Panic-stricken peasants killed their stock, farm work was partially paralyzed as millions were forced into collectives and the countryside was in chaos.

By 1933 over 15,000,000 households had been collectivized, as kulak liquidation continued. But livestock numbered no more than half that of 1929; the harvests of 1931 and 1932 were disasters, and the USSR stood on the birnk of famine in the winter of 1932-33. Large numbers did die of starvation in some areas, many died while being transported and many were executed. Cholera and typhus epidemics carried off many thousands more.

Trepper, recounting some of the terrible hardships suffered by deported peasants, reports that according to rumor the collectivzation drive cost about 5,000,000 lives. Unprepared for collectivization, materially and ideologically, Soviet agriculture has never fully recovered.

Stalin aslo upped industrialization targets unilaterally and arbitrarily after careful plans had been worked out. This upset balances and resulted in enormous waste. Buildings were constructed but could not be equipped; machines were built that could not be used for lack of raw materials, etc. While the first five year plan was an achievement, it was far short of goals, though this was not reported at the time.

Meanwhile, the cult of personality was assiduously being developed with millions of small busts, pictures, encomiums of every kind. A Russian tradition of the "Little Father" was intensively exploited, but the cult's spread did not stop at Soviet borders; it became a phenomenon of the international communist movement and bred little cults in other parties, as in local parties in the USSR.

Though Stalin had enormous power, he had still not eliminated all possibility of challenge to his control of the party apparatus. A few Politburo members retained some independence and would have removed him if they could. A handful of leaders was expelled form the party in the early 1930s for private discussion of plans for his removal and reestablishment of collective party leadership. Stalin wanted a public trial and execution, but the Politburo refused. In late 1932 and 1933 Stalin also staged trials of party leaders of the Ukrainian, Armenian and Central Asian Republics, as well as many university people, charging them with bourgeois nationalism; apparently they had resisted his centralizing tendencies. The forced labor camps and zones were filling up with hundreds of thousands of prisoners.

At the 17th Congress in 1934, Stalin appeared in supreme control. Extolled extravagantly by all speakers including former opponents, his policies were unanimously approved and he was given a blank check. Despite this apparent subservience, 1,108 of the of the 1,966 delegates were later executed, including 98 of the 139 elected to the Central Committee and at least five of the 15 members of the presidium (two others died mysteriously).

Why? Later records suggest substantial underlying opposition to Stalin's policy of terror and a desire to replace him with Kirov, Leningrad party chief who delivered the Politburo report to the Congress. Stalin's enormous popular prestige probably precluded this. In the elections for the Central Committee, Kirov's name was crossed out by only three delegates; Stalin's, by 270. He received the lowest vote, but this was not told to the Congress.

Several former opposition leaders were elected to the Central Committee and changes in party rules placed strong emphasis on inner-party democracy, sharply restricting the powers of the General Secretary. Elleinstein observes that the Congress' outcome appeared to have been a compromise in a struggle between Stalin and the Party.

Soon after the Congress, Kirov was assassinated. Khrushchev later suggested Stalin's responsibility, and both Medvedev and Elleinstein indicate NKVD culpability. NKVD Commissar Yagoda, himself on trial in 1938, declared he had instigated the assassination. Though he named others as havaing ordered it, he could not have accepted such an order from anyone but Stalin.

In any case, Stalin seized the occasion to launch the terrible blood purge of 1936-38. Medvedev estimates, and others accept this, that some 5,000,000 were sentenced to prisons and labor camps, and 400,000 to 500,000 executled. Long before it was over, Stalin had eliminated all potential critics and opponents; he had established absolute control over the party with the NKVD as his tool. His own people, thoroughly

96

committed to him personally, occupied all key posts throughout the party and NKVD.

A few public trials of prominent Old Bolsheviks were staged during the purge period. Absurd confessions were wrung from them by a combination of physical torture and psychological pressures. Both Trepper and Kopelev, who were later subjected to the process, describe it in graphic detail, as have many hundreds of accounts by victims published in the USSR after 1956. The public was thus confronted with the signed confessions of veteran revolutionaries, long known as Bolshevik stalwarts, that they had been agents of the enemy. What else could the public believe? Kopelev writes that he for one never believed then that Trotsky or Bukharin were Gestapo agents and he did not think Stalin believed it. But he regarded the purge trials as an expression of some far-sighted policy designed to discredit all political opposition. A besieged fortress, the USSR could permit no vacillation or doubt; but since inner-party differences were too complex for the masses, the opposition had to be so discredited as to be hated by the people.

In fact, the purge massively weakened the USSR. Victims included party secretaries at all levels down to the lowest, masses of leading technologists, educators, scientists, diplomats, historians, mathematicians, philosophers, writers and artists, almost the entire Komsomol leadership, party leaders of the trade unions and nearly all the Autonomous Republics. Trepper notes that thousands of communists perished before firing squads singing the Internationale and shouting their faith in the Revolution.

The Red Army was decimated. Three marshals out of the military's five — including Marshal Tukhachevsky, head of the armed forces — 13 of 15 army commanders, 57 out of 85 corps commanders, 110 out of 195 divisional commanders and tens of thousands of lesser officers were executed or deported to labor camps. Nuremberg Trial testimony and information gathered by Trepper indicated that Hitler's decision to attack when he did was motivated by his determination not to give the USSR a chance to train a new officer corps.

The chief of military intelligence was summoned, with other officers, from the Spanish battle front and executed. Trepper's highly effective espionage network in Western Europe, including Berlin, suffered because of the inexperience of the men who replaced the executed General Berzin. The military, Trepper maintains, was decimated because it was the last organized force independent of Stalin's will.

The mass repression heavily affected foreign Communist parties and leaders caught in Moscow. The Polish Party was disbanded in 1938 and its leadership executed. The same fate befell the three Baltic parties (before absorption into the USSR), and leading members of the Yugoslav, Bulgarian, Korean, Chinese, Iranian and Indian CPs. Bela Kun, legendary leader of the 1918 Hungarian Revolution and a top Comintern figure, perished, as did several German and Italian Communists who were refugees in Moscow.

The Palestinian Party leadership (then all Jewish), sent to Kiev University to study, was destroyed; one survived after 21 years in the Gulag. Several leaders of the Biro-Bidzhan party were destroyed, and the Jewish institutions they had developed were dismantled.

Not only the principals were victims of the repression. In many cases their families, including grown children, were affected. At the 22nd Congress in 1961, it was charged that Stalin, abetted by Molotov and Kaganovich, was responsible for these terrible massacres. Elleinstein observes, however, that it is hard to imagine that other Politburo members — Khrushchev, Mikoyan, Zhdanov, etc. — were unaware of what was happening and thus share some of the responsibility. The implication is that the country as a whole may have been unaware of it. A few public trials were held of top leaders, but the vast majority were either tried secretly or not at all and no. reports of their arrest appeared in the media. Disappearances were simply reported as removals or replacements.

The destruction of the Red Army's trained cadres was in effect only one service Stalin rendered Hitler. Resistance to the Nazis' seizure of power in 1933 had been greatly weakened by the sectarian policies imposed on the Comintern in relation to Social Democracy. The Popular Front tactic, advanced initially by the French, Spanish and U.S. parties, was adopted by the Comintern in 1935 only after a year's internal struggle, capped by Dimitrov's joining it after his release from a Nazi jail. Stalin evidently held back.

The Nazi-Soviet Non-aggression Pact was doubtless justified by the obvious intent of the West to push Hitler into war with the USSR. Not justified, however, were the secret clauses on territorial changes at the expense of Poland, Romania, the Baltic states and Finland. During the pact period, Stalin gave Hitler huge amounts of needed food and raw materials, halted Soviet criticism of fascism and levelled his main attacks on Britain. The Comintern was directed to do likewise, at a terrible cost to Communist Parties everywhere, particularly in the West.

Moreover, the USSR did not use the respite to prepare militarily. Production generally, and arms manufacture in particular, stagnated as a result of the purges. The Finnish War demonstrated the effects of the military purge. Top replacements, appointed for bureaucratic reasons, proved totally unfit.

Trepper's espionage center informed Stalin long before the Nazi invasion the date on which it would occur, the troops involved, the plan of attack, etc. He, Medvedev and Ellenstein tell the now well-known story of Stalin's receipt of all this data from Richard Sorge, the Soviet master spy in

Tokyo's German embassy, from agents in Berlin, from Roosevelt and Churchill, and even from sources in the German Embassy in Moscow. Stalin insisted the reports were all British plots to divide the USSR from Germany. The air attache to the Soviet Director of Intelligence left Moscow a few hours before the invasion with a message from Stalin to Trepper expressing amazement that a man of Trepper's intelligence should be so intoxicated by British propaganda.

When the Nazis invaded, Soviet armed forces were not on alert and Stalin refused for hours to believe the attack had occurred. Incredibly, no contingency plan to meet such an attack existed. The cost of the first weeks of war to the USSR was incalculable. Most planes were destroyed on the ground in the first few hours. Whole armies were surrounded and decimated, often because Stalin refused to approve orders to retreat so that they could be preserved.

Typically, he insisted that not one inch of Soviet soil be surrendered. Soviet soldiers took an oath not to be captured alive. Where they broke out of encirclement and made it back to Soviet lines, they were often arrested as German spies. Where captured and later freed, they were arrested for not having committed suicide. In both cases, sentences were heavy. During and after the war, these arrested amounted to several million.

As is known, in six months the Nazis had taken much of the Soviet's west, were besieging Leningrad and were 15 miles from Moscow. The advance was initially disastrous for the Soviet economy but more than 1,500 large factories were effectively transported to the Far East. By 1943 the Soviet arms industry was able to outpace the Nazis in several vital areas. As Elleinstein suggests, the underlying development of education and socialism — despite Stalin, Medvedev maintains — was having its impact. While Soviet resistance was inspired by patriotic appeals, it was equally stimulated as a revolutionary struggle in defense of socialism. Both elements were embraced in rallying the people.

Stalin's virtual paralysis during the first days of the war has been widely reported; he is said to have suffered a nervous breakdown. Though he quickly recovered and assumed the role of commander-in-chief, his leadership was important as symbol but not for its military substance. Khrushchev's indictment of his military role, Medvedov writes, has been confirmed by hundreds of memoirs. The great Soviet victory, which resulted in the crushing of fascism was a tribute to popular heroism, at least in part doubtless inspired by loyalty to the socialist society. The contribution of Stalin's symbolic leadership was undoubtedly considerable, though the extent cannot be determined.

Stalin had called off the terrible blood purge in 1939 because of the severe damage to the economy. But the purge did not cease entirely. Thus, Soviet military advisers returning from Spain continued to be victimized.

During the war, the labor camps were emptied of needed military men and technicians. But their places were taken by soldiers who had escaped encirclement or had been freed from Nazi prison camps, as well as by Volga Germans, Kalmuks, Crimean Tatars and several other peoples whose Autonomous Republics had been dissolved. Elleinstein estimates that some 2,000,000 of these peoples were thus incarcerated. After the war, those who had had contact with the West — diplomats and intelligence agents — faced long internment. This was Trepper's fate.

Stalinism emerged from the war intact. Hailed by the Soviet media as "the greatest man of all time," Stalin continued to control party and country through the ministries of State Security and Interior. Every citizen, institution and organization, including every foreigner, was under daily scrutiny. The security apparatus still sent to labor camps "enemies of the people" without public trial; since 1943, sentences could run to 20 years. There was no party apparatus — even the Politburo no longer met — to offer even a formal check to Stalin's arbitrary power. Even top figures continued to disappear, without trial, and sometimes even without notification to anyone. This was the fate of the nation's top economist and planner, Voznesensky.

With Stalin using Russian nationalism as a power tool, the communists of non-Russian republics again became targets of repression. Hundreds of thousands of Georgians, Ukrainians, Latvians, Lithuanians, Estomans and citizens of the Central Asian republics were sent to the camps. As is well-known, the CPs of Eastern Europe were also controlled by the Soviet security police and copied Stalinist repression. The staged trials of leaders of these parties, aping Soviet trials, were evidently designed to prevent a repetition of Tito's independent stand.

In 1946-47, Stalin and Zhdanov launched a witchhunt against intellectual and cultural figures. One result was the arrest in 1948 of leaders of the YIddish theater, and the charge of a pro-American Jewish conspiracy. Simon Lozovsky, long the head of the Red International of Labor Unions, and outstanding Yiddish writers and members of the Jewish Anti-Fascist Committee were arrested and eventually executed Aug. 12, 1952 as part of this alleged conspiracy. This reflected an anti-Semitic upsurge after the war which Stalin appears to have encouraged. He began to exclude Jews from the party and government apparatus. After the Jewish Anti-Fascist Committee arrests, Jews were barred from the diplomatic service and judiciary, and secret quotas were instituted in educational and scientific institutions. In the campaign against "cosmopolitanism," Jewish schools, theaters, newspapers and magazines were closed down.

In the last years of his life, Stalin's anti-Semitism was uninhibited. As is known, he planned a mass deportation of Jews to remote areas of the Far

East. With the initiation of the "doctors' plot" at the end of 1952, thousands of Jews were expelled from hospitals and medical schools as a "prophylactic measure." Books by Jews were removed from publishers' lists and even medications developed by Jewish doctors were banned. In some places Jews were physically attacked. Medvedev supplies a list of Stalin's anti-Semitic manifestations; it is long. It is also a measure of the huge distance that Stalin had travelled from the Leninist origins of the revolution.

The economic changes in the USSR since Civil War days have been striking, particularly in the face of the terrible destruction wrought by World War II. Though in 1953 the population, primarily because of the loss of 23,000,0900 in World War II, was less than in 1940, production in various strategic industrial items, had more than doubled. But agriculture lagged, with grain production actually lower and cattle only marginally higher. By the mid-1970s the USSR had caught up with, or outstripped, the U.S. in steel, coal and oil output, while still lagging badly in consumer goods and agriculture.

The exaggerated emphasis on heavy industry at the expense of human needs was evidently one effect of Stalinist practice. Because of this practice generally, the economic potential of socialism has been only partially realized. The destruction of personnel and the associated disruption of economic development has been recounted. Perhaps more pervasive and enduring, the supremacy of administrative decisions minimized economic stimuli and denied a corrective role to the masses particularly the unions. Thus the economy could be mismanaged, towns badly run, collective farms poorly administered since decisions were often made by incompetent, irresponsible, corrupt bureaucrats with no checks on their power. Accountability for effective results was absent after 1929. The check on bureaucracy proposed by Marx and Engels after the Paris Commune and put into practice by Lenin — official salary levels equivalent to workers's, universal suffrage with the right of recall — had disappeared by the early '30s. There was no autonomy for enterprises and planning had become extremely bureaucratic.

On top of this, no schools of management, finance or commerce were set up under Stalin, and political economy was taught under police supervision. The Stalinist system led to a denial of economic laws, and often to the substitution of personal caprice to acceptance of reality in planning. The results achieved in the face of such formidable obstacles suggest the potential for socialism if rationally run. While many things have changed in the USSR since Stalin's death, profound Stalinist manifestations remain; they include the promotion of anti-Semitic propaganda.

101

Obviously, foes of socialism have been able to exploit the bloody cruelties, the dictatorial rule, the mismanagement of the economy, the deprivation suffered by workers and peasants, and the spread of anti-Semitic propaganda. Since for many years the USSR was the only socialist country* it was easy to equate socialism with Stalinism. As both Medvedev and Elleinstein note, however, while Stalinism had its roots in the unique circumstances of revolutionary Russia — the emergence from Tsarism, the lack of democratic experience or traditions, the illiteracy and absence of culture of the people, the devastation of war and civil war, the violence of the White Terror and inescapable response with Red Terror — there was nothing necessary or inevitable about the Stalinist phenomenon. Alternative courses were possible, just as Hitler's rise out of the bourgeois democratic soil of the Weimar Republic (with all its democratic experience and tradition) was not inevitable. Evidently just as capitalism can exist in different political forms, so too can socialist economies. As indicated earlier, Stalinism was a sharp departure from Leninism in many ways. The individual's role cannot be discounted.

Stalin's impact on Communist parties elsewhere was deadly in ways already indicated. Many of these parties are striving, in varying degree, to cast off its effects. All of them have to contend with resistant members or with deeply ingrained Stalinist features. Those mislabelled "Euro-communist" have gone furthest as they seek to shed the monstrous dogmas, the rigid formula-thinking of Stalinism, and aim to restore the Marxist vision of a genuinely democratic socialism — politically, economically and socially — and one that is guided by a humanist ethic.

In the USSR cultural backwardness has generally been eliminated, thereby creating the conditions for the eventual eradication of Stalinist bureaucratic methods. There are signs of gradual change in that direction and socialists need to pay some attention to these. But many Stalinist rationalizations persist and the efforts to rehabilitate him have by no means died, either in the USSR or elsewhere. Certainly, in developed countries with democratic traditions, the USSR can in no way serve as a socialist example, as was once projected in Stalin's concept of "socialism in one country."

October, 1979

---

* For simplicity's sake, I refer throughout to the USSR as a socialist country, as do Medvedev and Ellenstein with reservations. I consider that while the economy is socialist, the USSR lacks the democratic and humanist values associated with a socialist society.

102

Growing Old

By *BILLIE PORTNOW*

Youth, large, lusty, loving — youth full of grace, force, fascination.
Do you know that Old Age may come after you with equal grace, force,
fascination.... — Walt Whitman

Dishonor not the old, we shall all be numbered amongst them.
— Ben Sirah in the Apocrypha

GROWING old is something we all want to do but nevertheless fear. The fear is rooted in social attitudes which glorify youth and devalue age, and stems from the realization that aging is often accompained by deteriorating conditions, lowered status and powerlessness.

But history has taught us that weakness can be overcome when the powerless unite. (Gray Power" has become part of our vernacular.) We had a recent indication of this when the Reagan administration attempted to make revisions in the Social Security Act, which would lower benefits and reduce the number of recipients. Though food stamps were cut, school lunches reduced, CETA programs emasculated and college tuition increased, the proposed cuts in the Social Security program met with such fierce resistance that the Administration was forced to retreat on some of them. While cuts in disability, survivor and burial benefits are already creating a great hardship for many, the Administration *was* prevented from trimming benefits from early retirees and abolishing minimum benefits for those already receiving them (although workers coming into the Social Security system now will have no required minimum payment). All this was accomplished through unity, militancy and *sheer numbers.*

Almost 25,000,000 people in the United States (one of every nine) are 65 years and older. In 1900 this age group constituted 4.1% of the population. Today it is 11.2%. Between 1900 and now, the 75 and over population has increased from 29% of the elderly to 38%. (This group is often referred to as 'old-olds' to distinguish it from the 65-75 group, the young-olds.') Among Jews, the 65 and over group constitutes 14-15% of the total Jewish population and 40% of this group are 75 and over. Jewish longevity and declining birthrate are responsible for this higher mean age (35) than the general population's (30).

The increased number of older Americans is accounted for by the high birth and immigration rate at the turn of the century and the greater

103

longevity due to medical, scientific and social advances. In 1900 the average life expectancy was 47. Today it is 73 and for those who have already reached 65 the average life expectancy is 81. The elderly are the fastest growing segment of the population. For the first time, the number of Americans over 60 is greater than the number of children up to age 10 or youths from 11-19. While 85% of the general aged population live not far from close kin, this figure is probably lower among the more mobile Jewish population, some of whom have migrated to the Sun Belt.

These demographic and societal shifts portend profound changes in the structure of our society. They accentuated the urgency of the third decennial White House Conference on Aging (WHCA) held in Washington, D.C. Nov. 30 — Dec. 3, 1981. The 1961 and 1971 WHCA spawned Medicare, Medicaid, the Older Americans Act and other legislation. The 1981 WHCA was charged with making recommendations for the development of a national policy on aging.

Fearful that such recommendations would not coincide with its present national policy of cutting human services while increasing military expenditures, the Reagan administration and the Republican National Committee are accused of the last minute addition of from 200-400 delegates favorable to them and packing committees with their supporters (which may account for this writer's failure to get an accurate tally of the delegates — though it's safe to say there were over 2,000 voting delegates and 1,500 official observers). This tactic brought them only partial victory because resolutions which could not pass in the stacked committees were reintroduced and passed in other committees. Furthermore, the resolution on Social Security which was passed by the stacked Committee on Economic Well-Being created such an outcry that it had to be amended.

The original resolution called for the preservation of "the traditional means for financing Social Security, the payroll tax... and that the use of general revenues would jeopardize the fiscal integrity of the Social Security funds." After the intervention of former Sen. Claude Pepper, requested at the "open mike" session convened by the Leadership Council of Aging Organizations representing 15 million people, the following was added: "To oppose strongly any reduction in benefits being paid to current Social Security recipients and to recommend strongly that Congress and the Administration make every possible and fiscally reasonable effort to maintain no less than the real protection which Social Security provides to all participants."

Fortunately, when the Reaganites were stacking committees, one of those passed over was Committee #11, "Concerns of Older Women," which made some of the most far-reaching recommendations for the advancement of the well-being of older people. It was in this committee that many of the resolutions were presented that could not get through the stacked committees. Some of the 33 resolutions passed called for "balancing [sic] the defense budget and social programs," giving women Social Security credit for years devoted to child bearing and rearing, giving 50% of a worker's pension to surviving spouse, a "Bill of Rights for Older Women" and a "recommendation to require the ratification of the E.R.A. through the leadership of the Federal Government."

This was the first WHCA to deal with the special needs of older women. Old age disadvantages women more than men. The poverty rate for older women is about 65% higher than it is for older men. More than one out of every two women in the U.S. can expect to be a widow at age 65 or over (two of every three women 75 or older) and one third of all widows live below the official poverty level. Over 80% of retirement-age women have no pensions and half of presently-employed women are in jobs with no pensions. Only 2% of widows get their husbands' pension benefits. In addition three quarters of all nursing home residents are women.

This last fact brings up an issue which was raised in more committees of the conference than any other. Seven committees called for tax incentives and community services to "assist families to maintain and support their elderly members at home or in the least restrictive settings." Our aging population has created the phenomenon of the middle-aged child. One third of present 60-year-olds have at least one living parent. This has often caused a crushing dilemma for middle-aged children. Just when they have finished raising their own children who are out of the house and the parents can live a life of their own, they are saddled with the care of elderly parents. Or they may be sandwiched between the incapacitated and/or senile parent(s) and their adolescent children, whose lifestyle they are trying to understand and adjust to. Often the female care-giver is widowed or divorced, creating an economic hardship. As with child abuse (see my "Children in Trouble," JEWISH CURRENTS, Jan., 1980), the ensuing frustrations are often a cause of elderly abuse, which is occurring with alarming frequency.

The Intergenerational Relations Project of the American Jewish Committee (AJC) has developed a program designed to heighten family understanding and support for the frail aged. They cosponsored 19 community conferences, organizatonal programs and individual workshops throughout New York City, including a seminar for legislative assistance on advocacy and entitlements for their aged constituents. These programs are discussed in a booklet published by AJC, "The Aging Parent," which deals sensitively with this problem and is a valuable guide to resources available to adult children and their aging parents.

The need to reward and not punish those "who maintain and solidify family bonds across generational lines" (Alvin Toffler in *Third Wave*) is acutely felt by Black people, whose aged have traditionally lived with their relatives. An example of this punishment is the one third reduction of

105

Supplementary Security Income (SSI) benefits when a recipient is living with others. The Black Caucus at the Conference, which had held three regional mini-conferences (in Detroit, Atlanta and L.A.), recommended against such reduction "when aged, blind or disabled recipients live in the household of another," otherwise they "may wind up in institutions at a much higher public cost than if they could have been maintained in a relative's home," and the Health Care Committee of the Conference endorsed "in-home care as a viable alternative to institutional care with appropriate changes in Medicare reimbursement policy to accomplish this." Respite care should also be provided for the temporary relief of care-givers.

While the family is "the number one staker of older people in America" (Robert Butler of the National Institute of Aging), the 5% of the aged who live in institutional facilities covered by Medicare and Medicaid add up to over 1,000,000 persons. The Reagan administration is now preparing to relax the strandards governing these facilities. This is an "encouragement to... allow mistreatment, maltreatment and neglect to rear its ugly head once again," said Lloyd Nurick, executive director of the New York Association of Homes for the Aging. It is to be hoped that action supporting the recommendation of WHCA for improved long-term care will help to defeat this latest manifestation of Reagan's deregulation craze.

Among the institutions covered by Medicare and Medicaid are voluntary nursing homes under Jewish auspices. In response to the poignant cry in the Book of Psalms (71:9), "Cast me not off in time of old age; when my strength fails, forsake me not," and to the Talmudic reference, with exquisite delicacy, to the senile, "Even the man who has forgotten his learning must be treated tenderly' (Ber. 8b; Bab. B. 14b), American Jews have since 1870 established a network of homes and services for the elderly. The approximately 100 U.S. homes affiliated with the Association of Jewish Community Nursing Homes have the highest standards in the country. They are considered pacesetters in many respects, including the achievement of greater community involvement.

Health concerns were expressed in a number of committees, many of them calling for a national comprehensive health program. Lacking from the many health recommendations were those dealing with the patronization of the elderly by hospitals and doctors and the hasty diagnosis of "senility" when the patient may be suffering from other problems, including a drug side-effect.

High on the list of concerns at the conference was the wide area of economies encompassing income maintenance, job opportunities, job training, pre-retirement planning, etc. Over 15% of elderly live below the poverty level. The income of older Americans is about half that of the under 65 population. Older women are the poorest group in the country.

These depressing facts can be multiplied from two to three times for older Black Americans. Most of the income of the elderly poor is derived from sources such as Social Security, SSI and public assistance. Therefore recommendations were made at the conference to raise these benefits to the poverty level and above and to set age eligibility for certain minority groups in accordance with their lower life expectancy. Since the elderly are the largest group of the population living on fixed incomes, they are most affected by inflation — hence the resolution to keep Social Security indexed 100% to inflation.

A most popular demand was the abolition of mandatory retirement and age discrimination in employment. Unfilled decent-paying jobs — particularly in middle-management — could be assumed by older workers if there were no age barriers. Age discrimination leads to such absurdities as young actors portraying old men while talented older actors remain unemployed, and agencies on aging run by young people. Sudden firing of an older worker often breaks most of his/her social ties; therefore there is the need for partial retirement and training for work in the community on a volunteer or part-time basis. Such work can include "adjunct teaching" in the school system, which would put them in contact with young people.

The need for such contact was expressed at the conference in its call for the development of inter-generational programs. This writer has long been an advocate of greater interaction between the generations (See my "Sustaining the Family," JEWISH CURRENTS, March, 1981). When I was growing up, there were no senior citizens, elderly, aged, young-olds or old-olds. What were "the old folks" to some were to us our *bubbes* and *zeydes*. There was no suburbia with its homogeneity of family age, size and income — with nary a wrinkled face in sight. The old folks were integrated into the family and society, and aging was regarded as a natural process. On my block, everyone had a *bubbe*. If she was not the parent of your parents then she was the parent of your neighbor's parents. There were enough *bubbes* to go around — to make *ingberlach* (ginger candies) on Passover for all to share, to tell stories of happenings *"in der heym"* (in the old country) and to take us all in tow to *shul* on Purim to razz Haman with our groggers.

Today's generation of grand and great-grandparents "have seen more changes than any generation in the history of the world," said the late Margaret Mead and can therefore play an important role in transmitting their values and traditions to the young. Maggie Kuhn, founder of Gray Panthers, enlisted two young people to help care for her mother and brother. After their death, this living arrangement continued "and now in my intergenerational house... there are nine of us and we range in age form 22 to 75. We have a marvelous new family that provides the kind of support and loving care that each of us needs." Instead of separated child day-care, youth and senior centers, why not an intergenerational community center? At the New York Jewish mini-conference before the WHCA, participants questioned the wisdom of separate White House Conferences on youth and aged and stressed "commonality of purpose in supporting the family." (Other Jewish mini-conferences were held in Florida, New Jersey, Ohio and California.)

The fact that New York has the largest concentration of Jewish aged (over 65) in the world warrants a closer look at their status, as revealed in a study by JASA (Jewish Association for Services for the Aged), affiliated with the Federation of Jewish Philanthropies of New York, which partially funded this study. Jewish aged constitute 13.1% of the Greater New York Jewish population. Of these 21% live at or below the poverty level (which corresponds to the general aged population of Greater New York).

The New York study further informs us that the proportion of Jewish elderly in long-term care is higher than that of the general elderly population. Jewish elderly are a more educated group. Of the Jewish males 30% had at least some college education compared to 10% of the general elderly. Future Jewish aging population "will increasingly be an educated one, representing professional and managerial classes in our society. Their income level and capital assets will be greater than prior generations of the elderly." It's estimated that 37% of the students attending the Institute for Older Adults of the N.Y.C. Community College are Jewish despite the fact that the programs are deliberately located in non-Jewish areas to attract less educationally oriented older cirtizens.

Of Jewish elderly 40% live alone in N.Y.C. compared to 29% of others and 33% of the national elderly population. Living with spouses are 45% (same as general population) and less than 10% live with children or relatives (16% for total population). The Federation of Jewish Philanthropies and its affiliates, independent Jewish communal agencies and more than 60 senior citizen centers serve more than 100,000 elderly and their families annually with the help of government funding. More government assistance wil be required in the future. As the report states, "The role of government has become fundamental to ensuring the well-being of older people."

But the Reagan administistion seeks to *reduce* the role of government. However, many recommendations contrary to this approach were passed at the WHCA. Much action, education, organization and legislative lobbying will be necessary for needed recommendations to become law.

Other resolutions dealt with crime (and the amelioration of one of its causes — youth unemployment), housing (subsidized housing at affordable prices) and a cabinet-level Department of Aging. The Research Committee's resolution to coordinate research on aging in U.S. with that of other nations can be implemented this summer at the forthcoming World Assembly on Aging in Vienna. The U.S. Senate voted to give early consideration to the more than 600 recommendations sent to it from the conference.

Despite strong protests and threats of a walk-out by the conferees, the administration-appointed leadership ruled that all resolutions be submitted to the plenary session as a package for a single vote of approval or disapproval. (A precedent for this was set by the Reagan administration in reference to the single vote in Congress on the budget.) This compelled the conferees to vote on resolutions which contradicted each other. For instance, on Social Security: one resolution called for annual cost of living increases and another for semi-annual increases; there was a resolution for and another against the use of general revenue funds for Social Security if necessary; one for raising benefits to the poverty level and another for 10% above the poverty line, etc., etc. Some of these conflicts may be resolved when the recommendations approved by voice vote are mailed to the conferees in the form of a referendum.

The WHCA was preceded by 10,000 local forums, 58 statewide conferences (including territories and the Navajo people) and 42 mini-conferences on special issues and ethnic groups, but their deliberations were not adequately reflected at this most undemocratic of White House conferences because of no open debate and failure to split committees into sub-committees as promised. This was strongly protested by Dr. Dolores Davis-Wong, president of the National Caucus and Center on Black Aged, who charged the administration was trying to "control and railroad" the conference. The House Select Committee on Aging is being asked to investigate the politiciziation of the conference by the White House and the Republican National Committee in polling delegates to find ones sympathetic to the Reagan program and stacking pivotal committees with them and adding delegates to the conference.

However one assessses the White House Conference on Aging — whether it's deemed a victory for the Reaganites, the liberal forces or a draw — one cannot doubt that it helped erase the negative image of older Americans and establish them as a potent political force in the coming decade.

May, 1982

Mama

By REGINA P. KRUMMEL

I SEEM to recall
Perhaps a blank, white sheet
recollection

Of you as very happy
Alive — running in the wind
Blowing your hair across your eyes.

But Mama, it is an ache
Of desire
For *my* youth
I remember

You have been an unsmiling
Memory of stalwart stubborn
Implacable determination

To feed and to control
To keep a oneness of a
Tattered family

Eating in shifts
Grabbing for sustenance.
Never laughing in the rain.

After Poppa died
Back then in the fifties
The age of silence and neglect

I seek to feel your anguish
You would never say it.
I seek to know your pain
Of fractured limbs and broken bones
And filmy eyes — unseeing.

I feed you lumps of grey and green
     and sugared yellow
You sit an ancient infant
Barely moving — a fleeting smile
At the liturgy of youth.

"I'm your *machashafe*
Remember, your Raisele, the *meshugene*
From Poppa's village
Or was it Pinsk?"

Did I ever grow up for you
An adult woman?

Will I be forever the evil, little
     witch of the home
Keeping the family lights aglow
So we'd never burn out?

I feed the glop to your mouth
And feel a sense of joy that you
     are fed.

But, mama, where are you?
Where have you gone?

Hidden in that gray head
Slumped in a knotted sheet?

March, 1985

The Match *(Story)*

By JOHN SHERMAN

POPPA moved his head back on the pillow. I leaned close. "My watch," he whispered with an effort. "The nurse."

When the nurse brought it Poppa tilted his grayed short beard toward me. He wanted me to have the watch. My fingertips felt the patina of its simple gold case. It was still going. The nurse had been winding it. I checked the time with my wrist watch. It was almost five o'clock. As I held the watch the long, heavy chain slipped through my fingers and the bar at the end swung back and forth. I pressed his hand, limp on the worn bedcover, to thank him. His eyes smiled acknowledgement. His fingers were cold.

This was the same chain he wore on his vest in our old album picture. It had been taken at the time of his marriage in 1902. At 33, Poppa, wide forehead, balding, bright thoughtful eyes, firm narrow chin and sensuous lips, was almost debonair, with his selvage-edged vest and trim down-curving mustache. He did not look then like the Hebrew scholar and teacher that he was. Only a certain inward concentration of the eyes gave a hint of his distant Hasidic background. Momma, a buxom, handsome woman of 27, looked straight out at you from the facing page, her swept-back hair accentuating an elusive severity in her demeanor.

My thoughts returned to Poppa. In the ebbing light he looked not much different from the picture of 40 years ago. His beard hid the emaciation of his cheeks, and the fire was gone from his eyes but they still held the same serene contemplation. The eyelids dropped intermittently but his raspy breathing continued. I took a gulp from the bottle of brandy I had brought. The doctor had said Poppa could have whatever he wanted, and I knew he liked brandy. But he couldn't drink any now. Not anything. I took another gulp and walked out of the room down a corridor to the waiting room.

In an uneven circle sat a dozen of our relatives. Dominating the scene loomed my uncle, Shimon Berner, grown wealthy from his successful business. Shimon Berry Clothes was a big name. Florid and portly, his usual authoritative manner appropriately subdued. He was recounting anecdotes about Poppa. He remembered, he said, the Saturday afternoons he used to spend with Poppa at the synagogue in Boro Park a few years back discussing Talmud or a *blettel Gemora*. He enjoyed those sessions, he said, because Poppa had "such a good head" and his comments were "always to the point."

112

Uncle Shimon's three sons were there too. They had often made a great to-do about their liberalism but used to bait Poppa in discussion about the Bolshevik revolution. Poppa had accumulated an arsenal of information about the Soviet Union. For the past 10 years he had confined his reading to material about the "hope of the future" as he called it, in English, Yiddish and Russian newspapers and periodicals. He would brook no criticism whatever of the Soviet government or its ruling party. They had only to raise a small objection to some action or position or condition in his beloved "new world for man" to provoke him to violent polemical defense. Driven to exasperation by their taunts, he would end in a mock gesture of spitting on the floor.

"Ptuh," he would say, with a jerk of his head toward the floor. "You are such ignoramuses. Why don't you find out the facts? You are afraid. You like your soft beds too much." They would smile and tell him to take it easy. For them it was a game.

My aunt Surah, Poppa's sister, had also come. She spoke of Poppa, her older brother, as generous, introspective and reserved, even as a youth. She remembered, she said, how strongly he resisted the importunings of the *shadhun* for him to marry Momma. It was only when she, Surah, had urged him to agree that he consented. It was the thing to do for a young man like him "who was not getting younger," she had told him. And besides, Cloora was a pretty, healthy girl "from a nice family." There had been some problem but it had been resolved. Aunt Surah was very much like Poppa: they were loved and respected by all who knew them. It was she who had told me that Poppa was named Yitzhak after their grandfather, who had been named after his grandfather, the famous Berditchever Rebbe Levi-Yitzhak.

I listened for a while, then walked back to the small room where Poppa lay. After another gulp of the brandy I sat down again in the chair beside his bed. He was breathing with more difficulty. His eyes were closed. Dark sockets in his face, they gave it an ascetic other-worldly quality. In the dusk I saw him again as he bent over the *Himish* with me when I was a boy of five, patiently correcting my halting translation into Yiddish; then as he chanted and sang the *Hagada* during the Passover seder while I, a little tipsy from the wine, accompanied him; and later as he stood at the *bimah* of the small syanagogue that was fetid with the odors of the congregation. He was called on during the minor holidays to do the *shakhris* before the regular cantor took over for the *mussaf*. The cantor always seemed to sing with much more feeling than Poppa, who would race through the liturgy almost perfunctorily.

Momma, in those years, spent many days lying down. A heart condition debilitated her for long periods. It had developed immediately after she gave birth to me at the end of a long and difficult time in labor. I couldn't remember Momma ever holding me in her arms or kissing me. She appeared in my memory as a large woman bent on molding me to some unfathomable design, resentful when I resisted and sternly pleased when I complied. Especially clear were the arguments between Momma and Poppa, often about me.

While they listened I would be reading from the *Daily Forward* a chapter of the humorous serial about Moishe and Yenta Telebenda and their son Pinyah. Momma would interrupt to say, "You see, he's spoiling him, letting him read all those crazy stories instead of studying the books he brings home from *heder*."

Poppa would say "*Gott in himmel,* Cloora, a child can't keep his nose in those school books all the time, like Moishe says, can't you see? And besides, it's only a story."

But the beginnings of an argument would be there and it would last until Poppa slammed the kitchen door and walked out into the store behind which we lived in three tiny rooms.

Sometimes the wrangling that began with a small matter would turn to more fundamental issues. It might start with a complaint by Poppa that he couldn't eat the meat Momma had served because it was too tough for him to chew with his dentures. Momma would remind him that there was not enough money to buy more tender cuts and intimate that was because Poppa was such a poor businessman. That was true. He would insist on selling the merchandise in our little dry goods store at a set amount above what he had paid for it, no matter how much higher the wholesale price rose later during the big war. "I refuse to be a profiteer," he would shout, leave the table and stalk out as Momma burst into tears.

Or Momma would charge that the newspapers he read, *The Call, The Appeal to Reason* and later *The Freiheit* especially, were sacrilegious and corrupting. Poppa would talk to her of *mentchlichkeit* and the desirability of change in the "lousy system" that tolerated, even fostered, so much misery. More and more often, as the years went by, he would grow angry and vehement, attack Momma's simple religious faith, and religion in general, as one of the major causes of man's submission to intolerable exploitation. Eventually he stopped going to the synagogue except on High Holy Days. But at home he continued to *daven* every morning. Finally, after I had grown up and moved out of the house, Momma, resigned to the situation, ceased offering any resistance and turned, in failing health, almost entirely to her *tehina* and her thoughts of the afterworld.

There came the day when I was called to their house because Momma was very close to that world for which she had been longing. I sat beside her then as I was sitting now at Poppa's bed. She was mumbling indecipherable words between moans. Poppa was standing close to me, looking down at her. His face bore no expression. He seemed tense, expectant.

114

Momma called to him faintly, "Itzik."

He bent over close to her, his tie hanging just beyond her chin. Suddenly, out of some last residue of strength, she took hold of his tie with both hands and tried to pull his head down to her. Startled, Poppa jerked himself away. Only a flicker of distaste crossed his face. A hoarse, rasping sound came from her throat as her upper body shook in one convulsive tremor, then sank back deeper into the pillow. That was her last breath.

Freed of his duty to care for Momma and the unspoken restraints imposed by her, Poppa began to become involved in the American radical movement. But the Soviet Union was still the most important thing in his life, and he grew fiercely defensive at any criticism of his Socialist Fatherland and its leader Stalin. I remembered with sadness his great hurt when I questioned the validity of reported purges of Jewish individuals and the elimination of Jewish institutions under Stalin.

"Lies, all lies," he had shouted. "Where did you read it? In a capitalist paper. How can you believe such stories? You should know better." I had not pursued the matter. When Soviet newspapers confirmed the reports but charged the victims with "bourgeois nationalism" and "crimes against the state," even "plotting with a foreign power," he would say, "'You see, they're criminals and get what they deserve. It's not because they're Jews." His trust was complete, unshakable.

As I looked now at his tortured face, I remembered how pleased he was at my own increasing involvement in the movement and our frequent political discussions. I thought of the time I had asked Poppa how he could reconcile his having carried out all those religious activities despite his staunch political beliefs and the atheism he freely expressed to anyone but Momma. She had known about his ideas but did not dispute him after the first futile clashes.

"That's a good question, Yankel," he had said, and turned away. His eyes, clouded with apologetic defiance, asked me to let the matter rest. And so I did.

He had the same answer when I asked him how Momma had endured his apostasy. But he added, "She was a good woman, honest and strong in her beliefs. It was not her fault she got sick. I respected her till the end."

With this memory in my thoughts I glanced over at Poppa. He was still breathing heavily. It was getting darker outside. I looked at his watch. It was still going. I got up, took another slug of brandy and went back to Poppa. I pressed the switch to turn on the light and took his hand in mine. With a fearful shudder he sat up and, his eyes closed, began to flail his arms about as if warding off the *Malach Hamoves* that had come to take him.

I ran into the corridor for the nurse. She came running.

"Poppa," I cried to her, long repressed tears now flowing from my eyes. "He's dying. I know it now."

She didn't stop to quiet me but strode into the room. I continued down the corridor to the waiting-room. The relatives knew when they saw me what was happening. I walked away from them and stood looking out the window through my tears. I felt closer to Poppa than I had ever before. After a while I went back to him. There was an oxygen mask on his face. I took his hand again and looked at his cold worn fingers. The nails were getting blue. I stared for a long time. They turned more blue. Strangely there came into my mind that last question I had thought of. How could he have reconciled those opposite ideas for so many years? I felt his hand twitch, looked up and saw his lips move. I stood and bent closer. Barely audible, as if he had known what I was thinking, he murmured, "It was agreed."

April, 1980

The Trial *(story)*

By LOU WAX

JUST as we were finishing supper the farmer Ahrun came bustin' into our room and said, "Beneh, we're in trouble! The sheriff just came with Mrs. Klebanoff and he's in the new bungalow talkin' to Mr. Men-dell and Mr. Klebanoff right now! Beneh, be careful! He's a pistol expert!"

And he scrammed out and Ma jumped up and locked the door with the hook and eye and grabbed her rolling pin and stood before the door.

I just sat there and looked at Pa. Pa just sat there and looked at Ma and then he said, "Rosie, where are you creepin'? Put down that *volgerholtz* and let him come in."

Ma did like Pa said but I could see right off she was starting to worry and Pa took another drink of his tea and then he got up and opened the door. I got out on the porch and Pa stood in the doorway and soon along came the farmer Ahrun and Mrs. Klebanoff and between them they had a man as big as Pa with a badge on him like a real sheriff, and a gun in a leather thing hanging from his belt and bullets all around the belt.

"That's no sheriff, Pa," I said right out loud. "That's the man that sold me a lousy fishhook for one whole cent! His name is Mr. Perkins."

"That's him!" Mrs. Klebanoff hollered. "He's the cockroach that put my husband on his back, scratched and drowned and burnt to pieces and murdered! He murdered him with huckleberries!"

"Which one?" the sheriff said.

"Him!" she said, pointing at me. "The big Cossack killed my brother, Mr. Men-dell!"

Mr. Perkins had one hand on the handle of his gun but it was in the leather thing hanging from his belt and he didn't pull it out. He just looked at Pa and Pa looked at him and Pa didn't look scared or anything. He had a couple of wrinkles on his forehead and I think he even smiled a little bit, but I'm not sure.

Mr. Perkins then took his hand off his gun and said to the farmer Ahrun, "This the feller that rode the Laird's hoss?"

"Yes, Judge," the farmer Ahrun said. "He's my friend Beneh. Please Judge, I'll be responsible for him."

"Ahrun," Mr. Perkins said, "you see this badge?" He pointed to his badge. "Right now you address me as 'Sheriff.'"

117

"Excuse me, Sheriff," the farmer Ahrun said. "I'll be responsible for my friend Beneh. He's a good man."

Mr. Perkins said, "Tell him he can't go around here beating up people. This is not Russia."

"No," Pa said. "This is not Russia."

"You speak English?" Mr. Perkins said.

"Yes," Pa said.

Everybody on the farm came a-running up to see what was going on and were all standing off on one side, off the porch. I said to myself it's a wonder the hoss Jake don't come over to take a look because he always gives Pa at least one visit every weekend since Pa rode him, and Pa has to rub his nose and say a couple of words to him and chase him back to his private field. A couple of times Pa didn't come out when Jake came over and neighed and Jake got right up on the porch and knocked on the door with his foot.

So who came trotting over to take a look for himself on account of the Sheriff's model T Ford making a racket before the motor was shut off? Jake!

The second Jake saw the sheriff and the gun on him he laid his ears back and went up on his hind legs and gave a big whistling holler with his front feet waving all over the place.

The sheriff snapped his gun out of the leather thing fatser than lightning and he had it in his hand pointing at Jake.

"Shtick fehrd! Shtay!" Pa sang out loud and jumped between the sheriff and Jake, and Jake came down and stood up straight but he was still lookin' at Mr. Perkins and his gun, and his ears were laid back.

Pa took a step toward Jake and Jake reached out his nose to Pa and Pa rubbed him on the head and along his nose between the top of his head and the end of his nose, and then Pa took Jake's ears and pointed them up where they belong and slapped him on the neck and said, *"Shtay! Du shtick fehrd!"* Pa then turned around to Mr. Perkins and said, "Holster your gun."

Mr. Perkins put his gun slow back into the leather thing, looking at Jake all the time and Jake was now standing like a statue with his head up and a big curve in his neck, with muscles, and was watching Pa.

Pa then said to Mr. Perkins, "We were having tea."

Mr. Perkins took one long look at Pa and then said, "Don't mind if I do."

Pa pointed toward the door of our room and we all got on the porch and I was going in first but Pa grabbed me right by my hair and I stopped where I was and Pa had his hand on my head till Ma went in first and then Mr. Perkins, and then he let me in and Pa came in last.

The farmer Ahrun kept everybody else out because he stood in the door and Ma put another cup of tea on the table for Mr. Perkins.

"How about a cup of tea for me, Ma?" I said.

"You drink your milk," Ma said.

"Aw Ma!" I said. "You're givin' Mr. Perkins tea and he don't even belong here! I belong here and I can't get nothin' but lousy milk!"

"Labe," Pa said. "You drink milk!" I took one look at Pa and I drank my milk and I kept my mouth shut.

Nobody said anything but just drinking tea and then Mr. Perkins said to me, "Sonny, what is this about a fishhook?"

I looked at Pa and Pa nodded his head at me and I said to Mr. Perkins, "Your lousy fishook bent when I hooked a catfish!"

"A big one?" he asked.

"Yeah, so big!" I showed him with my hands.

"What were you using for bait?

"A big dead stinky worm," I said. "And he got away because your lousy fishhook bent!"

"You come down to the store and I'll give you another fishhook free," he said.

They finished the tea and Mr. Perkins said, "I'm the Judge in these parts too, besides being the Sheriff. I believe we can get all straightened out here without taking you all to town. I thank you for your tea, Ma'am," he said to Ma and Ma dipped her head.

"I'll set up my court right on the porch and we'll get this over and done with so I can get on back home," Mr. Perkins said.

We all went out on the porch and Mr. Perkins took off his badge and he took off his belt with the gun on it and put it on the porch under a rocker and he sat down on that rocker and said, "Judge Perkins will now hold court and all witnesses line up here off the porch and the accused stay on the porch in these two rockers. Pull up those two rockers, boy," he said to me, "and drag another one over here for your Ma."

That's what I went and did and everybody was off the porch and watching to see what was going on and Jake was still standing like a statue where Pa left him and was looking right at Mr. Perkins.

Mr. Perkins said, "I can't hold court with a hoss as a spectator. Can't we get rid of the hoss?"

The farmer Ahrun went to get Jake but Pa said, "Ahrun, *shtay!*" and the farmer Ahrun stopped dead and stood where he was. Pa then went over till he stood in front of Jake and he rubbed Jake's nose again and said, *"Shtick fehrd! To your field! Langsahm!"*

Jake turned right around and went trottin' off with his head up in the air and didn't even look back at Pa.

"He's good with hosses," Mr. Perkins said.

Ma piped up for the first time and put in a lick for Pa. "He's a good husband, too," she said.

"Hmm," Mr. Perkins said, looking straight at Ma. Then Mr. Perkins said, "I call this court to order and hereafter I will be addressed as Judge

Perkins and 'Your Honor.' All defendants will remain on the porch. All witnesses off the porch. You, Ma'am," he said to Ma, "may remain on the porch with your men." Ma dipped her head at Mr. Perkins.

Mrs. Klebanoff said, "Why should they stay on the porch higher than we when they are all murderers!"

"You address me as 'Your Honor,' Mrs. Klebanoff," Mr. Perkins said. "I'm the judge here and in my judgment they stay on the porch and you and all witnesses stay on the ground beneath us."

What was she batting about? When we sat down we were all the same height as everybody standing off the porch.

"We'll start with the young 'un here," Mr. Perkins said. "What's your name, Sonny?"

"Labe," I said.

"Labe, you are charged with all kinds of stuff here, and you're on trial too, in a manner of speaking," Mr. Perkins said to me.

"Me!" I said. "Whad'yamean I'm on trial! I'm too young! You can't trial me!"

"You call me 'Your Honor,'" he said to me. "Understand?"

"Yes. But what does it mean?"

"It means I have honor and I'm going to give a full measure of justice to all concerned."

"If you have so much honor, Mr. Perkins," I said, "then how come you sold me that bent fishhook?"

"The catfish bent it and not me," he said. "I told you I'd give you another one free. Now you call me 'Your Honor.' Say it."

"Your Honor," I said. "But your lousy hook lost the biggest catfish I ever almost caught!"

"On with the case," Mr. Perkins said. "We'll take testimony from the youngsters first against the defendant Labe, as to his character and general behavior. Who's got a complaint against him other than the Plaintiff, Mrs. Klebanoff? Anybody?"

Itzik stepped out and said, "Me! I got plenty complaints against this East Side Cockroach!"

"Call me 'Your Honor,'" Mr. Perkins said.

"Your Honor," Itzik said, "that cockroach rode me like a horse and held me by the ears for reins!"

"So what?" I said.

Mr. Perkins looked at me, and I said, "So what! Your Honor."

"What did *you* do?" Mr. Perkins said to Itzik.

"We chased him, Your Honor."

"Who is 'we'?"

"My friends. Moish and Chaim and me."

"Who caught him?"

120

"Moish grabbed him 'cause Moish is the fastest runner, Your Honor," Itzik said.

I said, "He ain't faster than me, Mr. Perkins. He's just faster than these other two *klutzes.*"

"Your Honor," Mr. Perkins said.

"Your Honor," I said.

"What is a *klutz?*" Mr. Perkins asked.

I said, "A *klutz* is a *zhlub.*"

"A what?"

"A nothin' runner, Your Honor," I said.

"Oh," Mr. Perkins said. "What else?" Mr. Perkins said to Itzik.

Emma piped up and said, "I wanna be a witness."

"Emma!" I said. "Why don't you take yourself and your red hair out of here!"

"Speak," Mr. Perkins said to Emma, "and you," he pointing to me, "keep quiet."

"Labe is the best kid on the farm," Emma said and showed all her teeth at me, "but, he's afraid of girls. 'Specially me!"

"You're a red-headed liar, Emma!" I said. "And I ain't afraid of nothin'!"

"Nothin' but me!" she said.

"Order in my court!" Mr. Perkins said. He pointed at Itzik and said, "What else?"

Itzik said, "That louse Labe runs around with a snake twenny-five feet long and makes it bite people all over the place. And if he didn't keep runnin' away from me all the time I'd knock his brains out the second I'd lay my hands on him!"

"Liar!" I hollered. "I'm gonna tear those big ears off your head right now!" And I started off but Pa grabbed me by the seat of my overalls and said, "Sit."

How do you like that! That lousy big-eared fat Bronx liar! He was lyin' a mile a minute!

Mr. Perkins said, "Now everybody keep quiet until I give permission to speak. Mrs. Klebanoff," he said. "What happened?"

"What didn't happen," Mrs. Klebanoff said.

"Not 'what didn't happen,'" Mr. Perkins said. "what *did* happen?"

"This little murderer," she said, pointing at me...

"No name-calling in this court," Mr. Perkins said.

"He took my husband Mr. Klebanoff into the woods and buried him in a place with quicksand and hung him on barb wire and got him so burned and torn and dirty and so *tsibruchen,* he came home *kahm a lebedicker!*"

"What's that?"

121

"He came home completely dead and ready for the coffin!" Mrs. Klebanoff said.

"Can you explain to this court how this boy could do all this to your husband, a full grown man?" Mr. Perkins said.

"He is not a boy! He is a devil straight from hell!"

"Mrs. Klebanoff," Mr. Perkins began but that's as far as he got because Emma hollered out, "He is not!" and Ma said, "No! Don't you call my Labe names, you..." and Ma started off her rocker for Mrs. Klebanoff and found Pa standing right in her way. Pa just stood there.

"Rosie," Pa said, "sit down." Pa's voice had the command.

"Labe," Mr. Perkins said, "what happened with Mr. Klebanoff?"

"Nothin'," I said. "And he didn't give me the ride in the Reo Flying Cloud!"

"Why should he give you a ride in his car?"

"Why? 'Cause that's the only reason I took him to point out the huckleberies to him! That's why! He said he'd drive me all the way to Phillipsport and back to the farm. Just point out the huckleberries! That's what Mr. Klebanoff said!" I said.

"Did you point them out?" Mr. Perkins said.

"Sure I pointed them out," I said. "You ask Mr. Klebanoff! He was right on the barb wire fence when I pointed them out and I said to him, 'Look! Mr. Klebanoff! There are the huckleberries!' "

Mr. Perkins put his hand over his mouth and cleared his throat a couple of times and then said, "Hmmm! Now the case of Mr. Men-dell. Mrs. Klebanoff, what were the charges?"

"This Cossack hit my brother Mr. Men-dell and almost killed him!" Mrs. Klebanoff said, pointing at Pa.

"Why?" Mr. Perkins asked.

"Because he's a murdering Cossack animal!" she hollered.

Pa jumped out of his rocker like a bullet and grabbed Ma who was just taking off, hollering, "I'll close her lying mouth for her! Just let me get one hand on her hair!"

"Mrs. Klebanoff!" Mr. Perkins hollered. "This is the last time you will call names in this court for free. The next time you will do any name-calling you will be in contempt of this court and it will cost you five dollars per name called! Now why did Beneh hit Mr. Men-dell?"

Mrs. Klebanoff said, "For nothing!"

Mr. Perkins looked at Pa and Pa looked at Mrs. Klebanoff with his eyebrows raised. And Ma sat there with her mouth open.

"And this Cossack said he'd drag my husband Mr. Klebanoff by the feet all over the whole farm!"

"Hmm!" Mr. Perkins said. "You got anything to say for your defense, Beneh?"

"No," Pa said.

"Did you hit Mr. Men-dell?"

"Yes," Pa said.

"Did you threaten to drag an incapacitated Mr. Klebanoff through the farm by his feet?"

"Yes," Pa said.

"Why?" Mr. Perkins asked.

Pa shook his head and said nothing.

Ma now got up and pointed a finger at Mrs. Klebanoff and said, "This female dog spit on my Labe!"

"Rosie," Pa said. "You will sit in your rocker and not say one more word. Only the men in this family will speak."

I couldn't believe my ears. I said, "Pa! You mean *me!*"

Pa nodded his head and he smiled a little bit and reached over and gave my ear a little tweak.

I stood up and said, "Judge Perkins. Pa didn't do nothin' to Mrs. Klebanoff when she spit all over my face and on my head too!"

"What did you do, Labe? When she spit all over your face and head, what did you do?" Mr. Perkins said.

"Pa said, *'Shtay!'* And that's what I was doin'."

"*Shtay?*"

"That means stand where you are and don't move!" I said.

"And she spit on you and you *'shtayed?'*,"

"Yeah. And Pa didn't do nothin' cause he don't hit grownup women, not even Mrs. Klebanoff!"

"Go on," Mr. Perkins said.

I pointed to the side of my face and one part of it was a little black and blue and I said, "And then Mr. Men-dell gave me a wallop and knocked me flat!"

"While you were *shtaying?*"

"Yeah. And then Pa gave it to him. Pow! Pow!"

"Hmm," Mr. Perkins said. "Is this true? Anybody?"

The farmer Ahrun said, "It's all true, Your Honor."

Everybody else nodded except Mrs. Klebanoff.

"One minor point," Mr. Perkins said. "Why did Beneh say he'd drag Mr. Klebanoff by the feet through the farm?"

"'Cause Mr. Klebanoff was cussin' Ma!" I said. "You shoulda heard him in the swamp!"

"What did you do as one of the men in your family when you heard Mr. Klebanoff cussin' your Ma?" Mr. Perkins said to me.

"I hit him with a hunk of dirt, right in the head, and then I didn't listen," I said.

"You told your Pa?" Mr. Perkins said to me.

"Yeah. But not all of it 'cause Pa would kill Mr. Klebanoff!"

"Did your Pa drag Mr. Klebanoff by the feet?" Mr. Perkins asked me.

"Nah!" I said. "Ma chased him into our room for supper."

"She chased your Pa?" Mr. Perkins asked me.

"Sure she chased Pa," I said. "She chases the heck out of Pa sometimes."

Mr. Perkins got out of his rocker and stood up and bowed to Ma and then he sat down again.

He sat there for about two minutes and didn't say anything and nobody moved and then he got up and said, "Everybody will rise and stand for the verdict and decision of this court."

Ma and Pa and me got up and faced Mr. Perkins and everybody else was standin' anyway so it didn't make any difference to them.

Mr. Perkins got out of his rocker and stood up and bowed to Ma and then he sat down again.

Mr. Perkins said, "By the authority vested in me, this is the considered judgment of this court. Re Men-dell:

"The defendant was justified in defending a member of his family against unjustified attack, particularly since said attack was made upon a minor, said Labe. Do you, Beneh, wish to bring suit against Plaintiff Mendell for attacking your boy, Labe?"

Pa said, "No."

"This part of the case is dismissed," Mr. Perkins said. "For the cussing out of the defendant's wife by Mr. Klebanoff, the defendant would have been justified in dragging Mr. Klebanoff through the farm by the feet. Since same had not been done, do you, Beneh, wish to bring suit against Mr. Klebanoff for said cussing?"

Pa said, "No."

"For spitting on said Labe, there has been no compensation from Mrs. Klebanoff. Does the defendant wish to bring suit? I mean you, Labe," Mr. Perkins said to me.

"I don't wanna bring nothin'," I said.

Mr. Perkins continued, "For the fulfillment of part one of contract to point out huckleberries to Mr. Klebanoff, and for the unfulfillment of second part of said verbal contract, to wit, one ride in the Reo Flying Cloud to and from Phillipsport as a passenger, this court orders Mr. Klebanoff or his representative to give said Labe one ride from this farm to Phillipsport and therefrom returning via same route back to this farm; said order to be accomplished and completed tomorrow morning. This court will be here to witness that said court order is properly executed in fulfillment of part two of said verbal contract."

"Yaay!" I hollered. I was gonna ride in the Reo Flying Cloud touring car with the leather seats. My can! My own private can was gonna sit right on the tan leather seats of the Reo Flying Cloud!

124

Pa said, "No."

"Aw, Pa!" I said.

Pa said, "Labe! *Shveig!*" and I closed my mouth with a snap. Pa's voice had the command.

Mr. Perkins looked at Pa and he took a pretty good look at Pa, and then he looked at me and said to me, "Labe. This court is giving *you* the option of riding in the Reo Flying Cloud if *you* want to. Speak up, boy."

I kept my mouth shut and looked at Pa.

"Tell him to talk up, Beneh," Mr. Perkins said.

Pa nodded at me and I said, "No."

Mr. Perkins' face busted into a smile and he said to me, "Scared of your Pa, huh, Sonny?"

"No, Mr. Perkins," I said. "I ain't scared of nothin'. But it's like the hoss Jake. He ain't scared of Pa. But if Pa tells him to do somethin' there's no argument 'cause he figures Pa knows what he's doin' better than him. And he likes Pa, that's the main thing!"

"You like your Pa, boy?" Mr. Perkins said.

I didn't look at Pa but I looked straight at Mr. Perkins and I felt my face go all red and said, "Yeah. But I never tell him that because we don't talk about it. But I like my Pa. And I like my Ma too!"

By this time my face was on fire and I could feel it burnin' and just then Emma sang out, "And he likes me too!"

"Never!" I hollered back.

"Order in my court!" Mr. Perkins said and I shut up and so did Emma.

"All cases dismissed," Mr. Perkins said, and he got up to go.

Ma said, "If you'd care for a little something to eat, Your Honor?"

"I thank you, Ma'am," Judge Perkins siad. "But my Missus is waiting with my supper. And if I get back too late, she'll chase the heck out of me, too. Goodbye." And he gave Ma a pretty good smile. And then he picked up his gun belt and slapped it on him fast like he was used to doing it with his eyes closed. He stood there looking at Pa and Pa stood there looking at him and Mr. Perkins didn't say nothing and Pa didn't say nothing but their eyes were talking. Then Mr. Perkins took off with the farmer Ahrun, but first Mr. Perkins reached over and gave me a tweak on my left ear just like Pa! How do you like that!

January, 1984

Compassion and Criticism

By ITCHE GOLDBERG

ONE hundred years of modern Yiddish literature* is not an isolated cultural date in the life of the Jewish people. We are not evaluating a literature which had no previous existence and then suddenly appeared. We are marking an important stage in the 3-4,000 year development of our people's culture. The predecessor of modern Yiddish literature was not only the Haskala literature, not only the Hasidic tale, not only the Yiddish works created during the centuries before Mendele, not only the writings in other languages; the Bible itself and the post-biblical literature are the primal soil from which modern Yiddish literature sprouted. Modern Yiddish literature is a rung in the national ladder of our people's culture, a rung without which the ladder is not a ladder.

That's not all, however; that's only in the national depth. In the universal breadth, modern Yiddish literature would not have been possible without Cervantes and Gogol, without Hugo and Chekhov, without Dickens and even without Thomas Hooa — without the critical and social humanism of the 19th century and its forerunners.

We have before us, therefore, a cultural phenomenon which summed up millennial cultural values, which transformed them into the idiom of our own time and into the language in which our people lived, which selected and adapted these values to a new social conjuncture, poured the old wines into new bottles and at the same time was in step with human progress and the humanism of the 19th century.

Mendele learned from the ancient prophets as well as from the great critical realists of the 19th century such as Dickens or Hugo; he was even familiar with Fielding; Winchevsky translated Thomas Hood, Bovshover — Emerson.

In the wisest, most subtle and most compassionate manner, modern Yiddish literature — especially its classicists, who set the tone for the future — not only registered the experience of our people, but gave expression to its psyche and to its folk wisdom, to the specifically Jewish manner of responding to the world, to our unique way of breaking through from

* 1864, when Mendele Mokher Sforim's *Dos Kleyne Mentshele* appeared, is considered as the "birth year" of modern Yiddish literature. This essay was written on the centennial occasion in 1964.

126

darkness to light. The classicists not only summed up this national experience but also elevated it to the universal. They not only registered a definite epoch, they caught the timelessness of the epoch. For that reason, their works carry the breath both of continuity and durability, of yesterday and of tomorrow.

What were the actual currents that flowed in that literature and which filled it with so many national juices and so much social substance that it became one of the most effective forces of reeducation in Jewish life? What did that literature contain that was able to fortify the Eastern European Jewish community where it was born, and make it the center of the cultural configuration of our people for the last hundred years? (In our context, "Eastern European" includes the North American Yiddish culture, which is part of our modern Ashkenazi cultural sphere, and also the creations of the East European Jewish immigrant in many other countries.)

Let us, in the traditional Jewish manner, try to answer our question with another question. What kind of literature would be most useful to the oppressed, bewildered Jewish folk masses of that time, caught in the vise of historic events, persecutions and transformations — what kind of literature did they need? The people needed education, a sense of self-dignity, self-belief, a feeling of faith in the world, despite the injustice and the wrongs dealt out to them. Further: the people needed to be liberated, to be freed form the bonds that held them back, to be rid of medieval encrustments, to be helped to a rebirth, in order to face the approaching changes and transmutations. In short, the people needed to be loved, to be educated, to have planted within them hope and faith and a feeling of their own worth.

And that is what the Yiddish classicists brought to the Jews — as though history itself had ordered it; for not always do cultural forces mature as quickly and as precisely as the need of the people demands. Not every people that liberates itself, that faces a great historical transformation, is so quickly provided with the necessary cultural tradition, that its raw material had ripened in the viscera of generations deep in the cultural recesses of the Jewish people. Whatever the reasons for it, the simultaneous appearance of Mendele (1836-1917), Sholem Aleichem (1859-1916) and Peretz (1852-1915), is a historic phenomenon which testifies to the exceptional creative potential of the people and to the whole scope of Yiddish creativity over a 100-year period.

What were the currents which flowed in that literature, which vivified it, which watered the tragically bleak wilderness of Jewish life in the mid-19th century?

The mainstream that flowed in that literature, constantly refreshing and warming the shores and the waters themselves, was the great stream of humanism. The primary tone of Yiddish literature, that which expressed the essence of the folk psyche, was love for the human being, faith in the human being. Without these two essential elements nothing remains but some books describing the Jewish way of life in the 19th century. That is not yet a literature, certainly not a Jewish literature. The love, along with the faith, expressed itself in various gradations — from the sweet sentimentality and the lachrymosity of Jacob Dinesohn (1856?-1919) to the active humanism of I.L. Peretz, which takes the side of the human being, which storms not only the earth, but the very heavens to lift man from privation, suffering, ignorance and despair.

At the very center of modern Yiddish literature stands the human being. "I will have compassion for the human being" — that is the leitmotif of the first Yiddish classicists which has remained, in its general contours, the leitmotif of that literature for 100 years.

This compassionate humanism is a complicated ideological and psychological phenomenon. It stems from the premise that if the human being is the crown of all life then literature must serve him, take his part and oppose those who torment him. The outcry of protest against wrong, which runs through all of Yiddish literature, from the "Tax Collector" by Winchevsky (1856-1932) and Peretz' "Don't Think the World Is a Saloon" to "The Wedding in Fernwald" by Leivick (1882-1962) and *Shadows of the Warsaw Ghetto* by Feffer (1900-1952) and *War* by Markish (1895-1952) is the kettledrum in an orchestra that is never still, a drum that often drowns out the violins with its blasts and never lets the musicians or the audience fall asleep. There is a great unrest in Yiddish literature because there is an unrest among the people, because there has been an unrest within the human being throughout the generations ever since Mendele's *Dos Kleyne Mentshele** appeared in 1864.

"Don't think there is no law and no judge!" expostulates Peretz. 'Brother Workers, Awake!" pleads Edelstat (1866-1892). "It will not be forgiven!" warns Bergelson (1884-1952).

But this alone — the protest against wrong — is still not enough. The social explosion and the protest, by themselves, did not yet make great literature. Often it becomes necessary not only to free the human being from a cruel and evil environment, but to free the human being from himself. Joseph Bovshover (1872-1915),** a talented poet, but the child of an age which oversimplified complex events, saw them in only two dimensions — black and white — believed that we need only to "rip out the thorns" and the flowers will bloom of their own accord. Mendele, Sholem Aleichem and Peretz do not yet see any flowers. They see buds, they see seeds, they believe that the flowers themselves must first be nurtured to life. It is not enough to free Mendele's lame Fishke*** from his rags — he will still remain a cripple and a stammerer and a beggar. It is not enough to free Mendele's Binyomin**** from his illusion of the "Red

128

Jews" (the Ten Lost Tribes) — he must be shown not only where to go; first he must be taught to walk. And in order to be able to walk, he must overcome his fear of taking a step; he must *believe* he can walk.

The Jewish folk in the mid-19th century were culturally stuck in the seventeenth. The underbrush of generations had to be cleared away from their consciousness in order for them to take a step into the 20th century. It was necessary to free the dwellers of the *shtetlach* (and the cities) from their backwardness and fanaticism, from the ropes that held them back. Modern Yiddish literature was thus not only a national educational tool of historic significance, but also a process of liberation which, with quickened tempo, helped to transform a medieval people into a differentiated, variegated, self-aware national organism.

Compassion and love were only one expression of this literature. Coupled with those went a liberating, conscious self-criticism. Yiddish literature sharply criticized the cruelty of the social order, of national and social oppression, but at the same time it just as impartially criticized the internal backwardness, the fear of going forward. However, while the criticism of the external conditions stemmed from hatred of malevolence and injustice, the criticism of the internal welled up out of a pure love of the people and the human being. This internal criticism was not a mild rebuke or a mere pretext of criticism. It was sharp and unrelenting.

True, had some of Mendele's works (or Sholem Aleichem's) been written by non-Jews, they would have been described — and justly so — as anti-Jewish, if not anti-Semitic. But this hypothesis is itself false and can lead only to fallacious conclusions, a non-Jew, a whole galaxy of non-Jews, great artists all, would have been incapable of writing even one page of *Fishke* or *Benjamin the Third* or *Menachem Mendel* — let alone *Tevye der Milchiger.*

(For that reason the current fad of labeling Mendele Mokher Sforim a Jew-hater is in itself a piece of foolishness and malice, as for example the Israeli writer who asserted that Mendele exposed "the soul of the cow, the frog and the bed bug." A similar bit of "wisdom" is repeated by another Jewish writer in America who, in a letter to the *N.Y. Times,* describes Sholem Aleichem as a sort of primitive folk-artist and asks the "goyim" this innocent and refined question: "Can a *folk-writer* really be a great genius?")

---

* In English: *The Parasite,* translated by Gerald Stillman (Thomas Yiseloff, 1956).
** The last 16 years of his life were spent in the State Hospital in Poughkkeepsie.
*** Fishke — *Fishke der Krumer (Fishke the Lame),* translated by Gerald Stllman.
**** Binyomin — Benjamin of *The Travels of Benjamin the Third,* translated by Moshe Spiegel.

The criticism of Jewish life by the classicists arose out of profound love. It was a conscious process of building up a sense of self-worth of a folk-mass which, over the generations, had been kept in ignorance, dehumanized, violated, persecuted. Only the belief that one could lift up and improve the human being, that the human being carries within himself the seeds of his own salvation, nourished the national criticism levelled by the classicists. Their intent was to liberate, to seek out the spark of Man and God from beneath the rags. Mendele wants to free the prince who had been transformed into a mare, the human being who had been made into a beggar. But in order to free the prince and the human being, one must first *see* them under the horsehide and underneath the begger's rags. More than that. Fishke the Lame is not even a prince, but inside the beggar slumbers a purified *mentshlekhkayt* capable of a rare, exquisite love.

Had it not been for this direct belief in the human being, the collective expression of criticism by the classicists would have been malicious and hostile, and would not have accomplished much. But thanks to this faith, their social outcry against external and internal wrongs becomes a cultural phenomenon of such historic-national scope that it is comparable to the collective protest of the biblical prophets on behalf of their tormented people. It was not a matter only of justification, of saying "this is good" about Man as he is. It is difficult, in truth, to glorify the Tuneyadevker, the Kasrilik — Fishke or Menachem Mendel. It was, however, a matter of *anticipating* the human being, of envisioning him as he *would* be, freed from the grip of oppression and degradation, dehumanization and despair.

"I am constructing worlds," says Peretz, "worlds that are more beautiful, better, where he who had been trod upon like a worm has now become a mentsh, a decision maker..."

To go a bit further: Yiddish literature is full of liberating self-mockery. This self-mockery represents a stage of inspired sitting-in-judgment upon oneself. Menachem Mendel would have been no more than a caricature, a scoffing portrayal of a hapless Jew who deserts his wife and children to chase after impossible get-rich-quick schemes. But a Menachem Mendel who *judges himself* becomes almost a tragic figure, a man who is caught in the pincers of a life that he cannot overcome, conditions that grind him down and dehumanize him, who struggles desperately and yet manages to keep himself from drowning.

The critic Baal Machshoves once said that Menachem Mendel is the "Jewish *meshugas* in the form of a petty tradesman." That evaluation is too narrow. It is not merely a *Jewish meshugas*. The madness is not necessarily a Jewish one. It is rather the historic Jewish embitteredness, the Jewish tear and passion against wrong (see some of the *slichot* written during the middle Ages), the Jewish grasping at straws of hope in order to stay alive, the ability of the folk to survive by every impossible method and expedient, the habit of the *folksmentsh* to judge himself when he starts losing the "image of God" (more correctly, the image of Man), even the ability to sustain oneself with an invented *bitokhn* (faith), with an illusion, seduced by a concept, anything, but to keep oneself from going under. This self-mockery, this self-judgment, when supported by an enduring faith, is personified by *Tevye der Milchiger*. Tevye is only one step removed from Menachem Mendel, but first the warts had to be scraped off Menachem Mendel in order to arrive at Tevye.

This is not a collection of accidental themes, but a consistent, self-conscious and purposeful style created by the classicists. The style? A synthesis of a punitive father and a loving, consoling mother. the result is a literature which moves on a double rail; not love alone, but love paired with criticism; not realism alone, but a lyrical, yet critical, realism; not anger alone, but good-humored or even harsh rebukes which are intended to help the one being punished; not skepticism alone (because of all the troubles in the life around us) but skepticism mixed with faith. Even when the literature slides into sadness, as it often does with Sholem Aleichem, it is still sadness paired with the confidence that somewhere a better time awaits; not laughter alone, but a gentle ripple of laughter that can be used *instead of* tears. This *laughter instead of tears* became one of the most subtle and unique creative expressions of modern Yiddish literature, an expression which has almost no equal in any other literature and which was not limited to its master creator Sholem Aleichem, but found expression in every generation that followed him — in Moyshe Leyb Halpern (1886-1937), in Moyshe Kulbak (1896-1940) in Itsik Manger (1901-1969), in Moyshe Nadir (1885-1943), in Itsik Kipnis (1896-1974), in Dovid Bergelson (1884-1952).

True, Mendele did not materialize out of thin air, but he turned Yiddish literature inward, into the people, and made out of it a mass literature and out of the Yiddish language a refined cultural instrument, because without Yiddish that literature would have been impossible.

Isaac Meir Dick (1841-1893), whose hundred thousand booklets circulated during the 1850s; Eliakum Zunser (1835?-1913), whose song-poems sweetened the mouths of the people; *Hefker Velt* by Isaac Ber Levinsohn (1788-1860), *The First Jewish Recruit in Russia* by Aksenfeld (1787-1866), *Serkele* by Shmuel Ettinger (1801-1856) — all these were important milestones in the long and difficult process, lamps on a dark, unpaved road. Critical realism, although often primitive, was already fermenting and hatching among the Haskala writers.

But the mass reader did not appear until the classicists did. This signalled the beginning of a new national consciousness, a new maturing process which influenced and helped to shape Jewish life.

Sholem Aleichem's "every-day Jew," Peretz' "plain Jew," the Jewish artisans of David Pinski (1872-1959), Edelstat's "brother workers," the intellectuals of H.D. Nomberg (1876-1927), the countless *folksmentshn* of

Sholem Asch (1880-1957) — all of them moved into Yiddish literature to stay. "Your humble servant" took off his shoes and made himself at home in Yiddish literature — not as in his father's vineyard — as the Yiddish saying goes — but in the heart of the reader.

The values which they created were thoroughly national and secular, progressive and humanist. Deep-rooted in the history and tradition of the people, they breathed with modernity, with a vision of the future (often fresher than some of today's Jewish writers who get lost in mysticism and demonism). These were not mere *apikorsim* (skeptics), they stormed the heavens in order to elevate the human being. Hillel Zeitlin once said: "Peretz *does* have a heaven — but there is no God in it." Maybe. But that he wanted to raise the human being up to heaven — *if not still higher* — of that there can be no doubt.

The three classicists were the tuning-fork which set the tone for an entire literature. They were not only the foundation — the cellar — but the pillars of the building as well, and they have remained so until today.

(Incidentally, the labor poets in America sing in the same key. The thread of "love of mankind" runs through Morris Winchevsky, Joseph Bovshover, David Edelstat, Morris Rosenfeld (1862-1923). Leon Kobrin (1872-1946) evaluated this correctly when he said that the writers of his generation were creating in America *"something out of nothing,"** in order to drag the people out of their "greenness," their confusion, their misfortune and their hopelessness.)

And this is how the wheel turned: Thanks to this literature, the people grew more mature, but the founders never grew old. Humanism and the drive for justice, which has lived within the Jewish people ever since the days of the prophets, found a new idiom; it put on not only the clothing but the flesh and blood of the new times.

And the tone positively held. It almost never ceased, despite frequent detours and loss of direction. One could not simply remain standing before Mendele's broad canvasses, where the features of the characters were not always clear or sufficiently individualized. But the tone was never lost. The second generation after the classicists inhaled the rare maternal quality of Abraham Reisin (how far removed was Reisin from the first clasicists?); they breathed Asch's faith in man's divine spark, Bergelson's often elegiac, sorrow-filled defense of man, even Nomberg's helpless anger — the *nigun* (tune), in new conditions and more differentiated, was not lost. The shtetl, like a poor, barefoot child, followed them all and sought redress — from Mendel's Kabtsansk to Bergelson's Rakitne, to Izzy Kharik's "Shtetl, be gone," to Moyshe Nadir's "Narayev, crown city of my life" — all variations on a basic theme of human redemption.

* In Hebrew *"Yesh Meayin."* The allusion is to the creation of the world.

132

The same happened with *Di Yunge* in the U.S., who needed to bring order into the reckoning with the New Country, who wanted to peel off the covering of confusion and despair, and preserve the kernel of human dignity. This was true of Morris Rosenfeld's sweatship worker and Leivick's ragpicker, of the bewildered intellectuals of David Ignatow (1885-1954) and the Goerek Street dwellers of Opatoshu (1886-1954), and it was true of the lyrical poems of Mani Leib (1883-1953) and Joseph Rolnick (1879-1955), which sought to understand and raise up the human being, of the Jew, Joshua, of I.J. Schwartz (1885-1971) who became "Josh" in Kentuck and carried his grandfather's tradition with him into the Southland, and it was true of Moyshe Leib Halpern's war against the city of granite and steel, and of Moyshe Nadir's self-mockery because otherwise a person could dissolve in his own tears in this new land.

Variations, variations on a basic theme, which all hummed the same melody, the same motif: how shall we redeem the lost "little man"? And here too, as on the other side of the ocean, the themes of national and social redemption flowed together.

And this basic tone held in the Yiddish literature of Poland between the two world wars, in the Yiddish literature in America of the same period, in the breathtaking creativity in the Soviet Union before 1948.

Make no mistake. Wherever our literature lost this basic tone, that is, getting to the universal through the national Jewish idiom, there it had no substance. But as collective creativity it very rarely lost that tone, almost never. Take, for example, the national character of Soviet Yiddish literature; not only Bergelson and Der Nister, who wrote earlier, but also Kulbak and Feffer, Kharik and Halkin (1897-1960), Markish and Godiner (1893-1942), Kvitko (1892-1952) and Hofshtein)1889-1952) — none of them would have been possible without Mendele and Peretz or Reisin — and more deeply, without the Jewish Bible. Kharik drank from the spring of Reisin, Kulbak from Sholem Aleichem, Markish from Peretz, Mendele and Bialik, Halkin from the Bible as well as from the Revolution. It is myopia not to see the great *national* significance of Soviet-Yiddish literature, and especially its inseverable rootedness in that tradition.

The struggle for the continuing rebirth of the people — and the people is constantly being reborn — is artistically reflected in Yiddish literature. The tradition of the classicists pulsates unceasingly. When the years of the worst, most tragic experience came, when it was necessary to mobilize anew the spirit of the people against its deadliest enemy, fascism, our literature again came to our aid, raised us anew to our great *kiddush hashem* (sanctification of the Name) and to superhuman heroism. *The Song of the Slaughtered Jewish People* by Yitzkok Katzenelson (1886-1944) and *Notes from the Warsaw Ghetto* by Emmanuel Ringelblum (1900-1944) and Feffer's *Shadows...* and "Never Say" by Hirsh Glik

133

(1922-1944) — through all of these one could again hear Sholem Aleichem's "*a mentsh is a mentsh*" even when he is caught in the deranged, murderous claws of facism.

In Leivick's *Wedding in Fernwald,* in which he declares that "after Dachau we must say yes to life"; in Feffer's *Shadows...,* the youngster wrapped in the ghetto flag soars on, never falling; in Markish's Gur Aryeh (hero of *War*), who crawls out of a mass grave because "the massacred community sent him out to be the unrolled megilla of disaster," and in the lines of Sutskever, like God's tears — in all these one can hear the old *nigun* of the classicists.

The factories in the Lodz ghetto, where the Germans forced Jews to work on Nazi uniforms, were called "resorts" by Germans. And what song did they sing inside these "resorts" and about these "resorts"? A song that begins with the lines, "So wild is the roar of machines in that resort, I often forget I exist, in that roar..." This is not parody but a re-singing of Morris Rosenfeld's "So wild is the roar of machines in the sweatshop..." (written in New York in 1890s).

So that is our *yikhus,* our tradition, and the clamor of generations that began one hundred years ago when, in the Odessa newspaper *Kol M'vaseyr* the first installment of *Dos Kleyne Mentshele* appeared, written by one Sholom Yaakov Abramovich, who insisted that his people call him Mendele Mokher Sforim (Mendele the Bookseller).

What of the future? Not of Mendele — he can take care of himself. But of our grandchildren and their descendants? Will they experience and be enriched by this wonderful stream of love that human beings have for each other and for the world, for justice and redemption, for the fight against wrong, against malevolence — the love so well represented by Yiddish literature?

Can we stride into the future without those values? What are they — mere books? pages out of old texts that once had a meaning only for us?

If I believe in a future that will be an orchestra of peoples — in which every instrument is of equal importance — then I cannot imagine the Jewish violin, or violincello, without the continuity of that literature. (And continuity means both the writing in Yiddish and the repouring of its values in depth into other languages, including Hebrew.)

Without that continuity, not only one string, but the whole instrument will be out of tune.

February, 1984

A Silver Dollar's Worth of Eggs *(story)*

By RUTH LEVIN

WE lived in a small house on Peabody Street in Dallas, Texas. The years were somewhere in the late 1930s and early 1940s. I was around nine or 10, the oldest of three children.

The kitchen, at the rear of the house, looked out on the alley. The alley, lined with tumble-down shacks and bright long cars, was fascinating with its dark noisy people, its strange smells, its focal point of white adult fears. The alley was the short cut for me to the Kroger market on the far side of the block. Forbidden to my white playmates by their parents. The alley was also the short cut to my knowledge of life.

Brownie, our fox terrier, ruled the back yard, which was enclosed by a high wooden fence. A southern dog, her vicious bark echoed down the street whenever a Negro walked in the alley. Since our back yard was actually part of the alley, Brownie barked incessantly, except when she was giving birth. My mother refused to give up her dog despite the white neighbors (or maybe because of them). She spent much time washing her long black hair and freshening and cleaning the only good dress she owned so that when summoned to court she could look classy before the judge and any other non-Jews present. The possibility that the judge might be Jewish couldn't have crossed my mother's mind.

Inside our house my mother and father had a bedroom, separated by French doors from the living room. The French doors were a refinement that definitely did not go with the rest of the environment. My brother, sister and I shared a room, about the size of three telephone booths, but not as high. However, we had a dining room. The dining room might better have been used as a bedroom, but then we would not have had any place to put all the people my father invited to the house.

Poor, rich, friend, stranger, famous, infamous, it was all the same to him. He liked good company. If he went to the synagogue for evening prayers he would return with any visiting stranger, or with the Rabbi and his wife. My mother not only kept a strictly kosher home, which meant that the meat was slaughtered in ritual fashion, but meat and milk were never served together at the table, nor even eaten together at the table. We had two different sets of dishes, silverware, pots and pans. The only sea-food we ate had scales. My mother observed most of the other rituals as well. Sometimes I had the feeling that one side of my mother *was* meat and the other milk, and it was hard to tell which side was up.

On the other hand, my mother knew of my alley life and let it be, just as I

135

knew she cracked that unbreakable code by eating at the same table with her Black friends. Always referring to them as *"shvartze,"* to their face and her children's, she nevertheless never used that term in the presence of white people. She served her Black friends whatever she gave herself, and commiserated with them as she did with herself. She was always surprised at the similarity of the problems.

Sometimes when there was not enough for us, let alone someone else, they brought the food. Then they ate from wax paper or paper napkins, with newspapers covering the kitchen table and any exposed counters, so that table, dishes, house, would not be contaminated by non-kosher food. My mother managed to convey that this was the not an anti-Negro prejudice but a religious one. To them that religious prejudice seemed not only acceptable but admirable. Had someone not pulled the shades in the kitchen or in the front room when they were together, both she and they would have been marked for life. As it is, they were anyway.

My father spent a good deal of time at the synagogue, where he did not get paid, and little time at his job, where he did. Aside from praying and studying, he conducted a choir, arranged chairs and cleaned the place if the old *shamas* whose duty was, fell ill or was too tired, and in general lent moral and voice support to the Rabbi when he was not violently opposing him on some important issue. All issues were important to my father. He was also the makeshift cantor.

My father found strangers irresistible. They were additional fodder for his think and talk mill. If he went downtown into the heart of Dallas on the rickety Irvy trolley, he would return with guests located by his generous spirit and agile fertile mind. When we had food, they ate: roasted chicken, groats in rich gravies, light fluffy potato pancakes, noodle *kugel* high as the top of the stove, hominy and apple fritters made in the Jewish manner, carrot-sweet potato *tzimmes,* eggfilled cakes and steaming coffee, or strong tea with a hard candy to suck when it goes down. If we were fantastically lucky or had rich guests who had been generous, there might be brandy to lace the coffee or strong *kimmel,* and something special for children.

When we did not have food, the guests shared the small amount of too-sweet wine my mother made and a piece of dark bread and butter.

At times my mother wept. "You take from the mouths of your children," she would accuse my father bitterly, "they don't have to eat and you give to strangers."

My father, exhilerated from the religious or political discussions, glorying in the richness of thought, feasting and satiated on words, ideas, philosophies, would answer: "Rabbi Hersh used to say 'On meeting any man be the first to extend greetings, and be a tail to lions rather than a head to jackals.' Man is meant to share whatever he has and whatever he is."

"And what if he has nothing and three hungry children? What did the good Rabbi say about that?"

His answer was always the same. "God will provide."

In the mornings of those years my father was often the first one to rise. Someone in the congregation was sick or dying or saying *kaddish* and he was needed for the early morning *minyan.* Actually my father liked to see the rays of light begin to spread across the sky, liked to find for himself the first hints of the rising sun, to see the stars disappear as the lights appeared.

When the alarm went off he would shout "ahoy!", his crashing baritone causing the small wooden house to vibrate. Three children would plunge into the parental bed screaming "Ahoy, ahoy." Our day would begin with hilarity and a story. Sometimes it was the three pigs and Little Red Riding Hood, sometimes tales from the Talmud, either translated or changed by my father, sometimes stories of beautiful flowers that turned into people and devils that were made of vegetables; sometimes people who turned into shimmering colors and danced through walls up into the sky, or whose souls became birds of glorious plumage and soared with translucent joy across the world into heavenly arms, but always dramatic. The gestures were all-engrossing and the range of voice was wide. My father, earlier in his youth, had been in the Yiddish theatre, and he fancied himself an actor, which indeed he was in many ways. Certainly he had chosen his role in life and played it to the hilt.

My father never returned to the house empty-handed. If he had a dime he would buy a cheap bottle of perfume for my mother, or a real flower; if he had enough he might buy something for us children. If he had nothing, he would sail into the house, paper hats on his head that he had folded out of newspapers, paper birds in his pockets, and if he had a handkerchief, a fascinating knotted mouse that he would make dance. "It is not my doing," he would laugh, as that knotted handkerchief jumped and hopped, "it is the prophet Jeremiah come to see how everyone is. Welcome to the exalted visitor."

Welcoming the Sabbath was the high point of our week. On the Sabbath my father did not work at all. If he had it would have meant that he could not act as cantor, could not go up on the *bemah,* that platform in the synagogue on which sits the holy ark that houses the scrolls of the Torah. In honor of the Sabbath everything was scrubbed, including us. Whatever special we had for the week was saved so that the Sabbath meal (Friday evening) would be the week's memorable one. In our house we did indeed welcome the Sabbath as a bride.

After anointing himself with soap and water in the afternoon of Friday, my father would begin to work his voice and himself up to what he considered the proper Sabbath pitch. Sometimes in the tiny kitchen where my mother was cooking and fussing for the evening as well as for the next day, since she did not cook on Saturday, slipping and sliding on newspapers she put down after she had scrubbed the floor so that it stayed clean for the Sabbath, sometimes out in the yard if the weather was too beckoning, his plain small black yarmulke on his head, his jigger of whisky already warming his throat, my father would begin to sing. As he worked on the *Lecho Dodi,* the *Mizmor Shir L'yom Hashabbas,* the *Alenu,* and the many other parts of the service he loved so much, our alley would begin to join him. As he cried, pleaded with the Lord, begged, promised, praised, exalted, his voice shifting, changing, falling, rising, weeping, his baritone running all the ranges of a human voice and then some, the alley would pick up the rhythms and melodies and more and more voices joined in.

When the alley really began to swing, my father would suddenly burst forth in English — "The righteous shall spring up like a palm tree; he shall grow tall like a cedar in Lebanon. Planted in the house of the Lord, they shall blossom in the courts of our God. They shall still shoot forth in old age; they shall be full of sap and green; to declare that the Lord is upright; he is my rock and there is no unrighteousness in him." As sundown began to approach, the Negro blues, mingled with the Jewish blues, could be heard all over South Dallas.

If I make my father out to be a saint, I have no such intention. He was not. There were times when we did not have enough to eat and it was the black alley, not his synagogue, that helped feed us. There were times when not his singing voice, but his screaming, furiously angry voice, could be heard over South Dallas, and the crockery would break as well as our hearts, while my father gave vent to his violent erratic temper. His strong feelings of right and wrong and good and bad cascaded over, rather than merely spilled over, on to his family, and we were not exempt from the moral and ethical rigors he imposed on himself or others, no matter how impossible or irrational they could be proved to be. My father knew his children to be the best, and any deviation from that myth of perfection that was his personal image was dealt with accordingly. Every facet of everything seemed to matter to my father and passed under his emotional scrutiny with equal weight.

The violence of his temper accounted in part for my father's too frequent periods of not working. Always changing jobs, he thought the next one would be the perfect set up for him, where everything would be as it should be and he would stay, and we would be forever well fed and happy, My father, that unbelievable optimist, who wept and wailed to the Lord, but laughed and danced to his fellow men, insisted you never looked down at your feet, you held your head high and looked up. He could always find something up there that seemed to delight him, though he was never able to hold it, touch it, reach it, taste it or smell it. When my mother, in her moments of despair, would point out how everyone had more than we, my father could always find someone who had less, and this, of course, made it all right, in his eyes anyway. His personal despair came not from not having but from not being understood or not giving.

138

Hand in hand with his temper came a peculiar ability to be his usual self once he had exploded, regardless of who had been seriously wounded by the shrapnel, and how they still suffered. No sooner had his hand finished with the strap for what he considered some horrendous deed — these could run the gamut from dashing into the street after a ball and not looking to see if a car were coming, talking back to my mother, not wanting to go to Hebrew school, whispering about the Rabbi behind his back, not making an A on English recitation, to not working sufficiently hard at penmanship so that the script on the blackboard came off second best to the writing done at the desk — his fury evaporated, and it was as though none of this had happened.

Unfortunately it had, and our inappropriate reaction to his restored self was hard for him to understand, just as he could not fathom why his wife, after having been berated and humiliated, after exchanging dishes, pots and pans all over the house, could not smile and make up after my father felt relieved. His friends in the alley understood this, however. It was to the alley he went in his moments of excruciating need as did we all, despite Brownie's objections.

One day, shortly before the coming of the Jewish New Year, my father went to the synagogue, and came home with Yisroolikel. Yisroolikel and his Uncle Gershon.

It was the custom to hire an outside cantor of some special or unusual talent for the High Holidays, Rosh Hashona and Yom Kippur. This established the fact that our synagogue was keeping pace with all the other synagogues in Dallas, which were doing the same and assured the loyalty and pleasure of our congregants, as well as payment of their dues for the coming year. Though they might leave the synagogue during the lengthy full days of prayers, walk around, visit other houses of worship, they would feel that they were being sufficiently looked after at their own synagogue, as well as entertained, and they would keep their membership with us. The solemn days would be emphasized not only by the choir worked up into a frenzy by my father, but by this particular professional cantor as well.

Yisroolikel, billed as the boy wonder of New York, arrived accompanied by his ever-watchful, high-hatted, black-frocked, snuff-smelling, black-bearded, grey-*peyesed* uncle. Two weeks of more than wine-intoxicating pleasures began at our house.

Yisroolikel's highpitched tenor was the perfect companion for my father's voice, and Yisroolikel's educated, impossible, narrow-minded, experience-resistant long-suffering uncle, was the perfect companion for my father. Once the uncle had ascertained exactly how kosher our household was, by asking innumerable questions, poking into shelves and cabinet, calling the Rabbi several times as well as the kosher butcher, it was immediately settled that they would take all their meals and spend their free time with us. This despite the fact that my mother wore no *sheitel,* the traditional wig that Orthodox Jewish women wear.

At 19 or 20 Yisroolikel had a round egg-white face, devoid of any whiskers and smoother than any girl's, large waterfilled brown eyes that hung limp inside his round heavy glasses and thick shining lips which he constantly licked with a nervous darting pale tongue. His tenor, despite its reediness, was soft and soothing. When he sang, lifting this high sweet voice, when it embraced the ancient prayer, when he appealed to and beseeched the Lord in all the words, wails and melodies Jews have used from ancient days to the present, he transformed and transfigured those assembled in the synagogue. With radiant faces and one voice the singing of the congregation rose to join his in their appeals and petitions to the Lord, in their gratification and thankfulness for the continued gift of life and its joys.

My mother, pleased and flattered that Yisroolikel and his uncle were our guests at table, could not reconcile the cantor who so moved her and the congregation with the quiet boy who thanked her when offered food, though he did not, in the orthodox fashion, look directly at her since he was unmarried and she was a woman, and who smiled as sweetly as one of her own children when he sang grace. He was, despite his thin frame, a hearty eater, and this did my mother's motherly heart good. She served awkwardly and stiffly, making a wide skirt around the old uncle, whose habit of gesturing broadly with his arms portended spilled platters if one were not careful.

My father, master of this house, where everything shone with holiday cleanliness, holiness and love, and food was, for once, abundant, proud of the delicious meals his wife was serving, proud of her silent respect and delight as she went in and out tending to needs, pleased with his children who could sing with honored guests and read the *sidur* fluently as well as answer a question now and then about Rashi or the Pirke Avos, was in his element.

Sometimes when the old uncle and my father became so involved in a discussion they were clearly transported to another place. Yisroolikel and I, with my mother's blessings, would sneak out and walk around South Dallas, many times starting our walk through the alley. Yisroolikel, a product of northern ghettos and frenzied streets, was fascinated by the alleys.

No one, least of all I, thought to tell him that according to the code he was not supposed to walk through the alleys, and he was certainly not supposed to find them interesting. We stole away in order to avoid the younger children. Had they spotted us and called attention to our going on a walk together, the uncle would not have allowed it, and Yisroolikel

140

would again receive the lecture about the company of girls and women. There was no doubt that I qualified as a girl but there were indications that I would soon be considered a woman. The sex itself, not I, seemed to be the danger to Yisroolikel.

A day after Yom Kippur I awoke to a shouting household which also contained the uncle and Yisroolikel, early though it was. My mother, angry and red faced, looked as though she had been crying. My father was shouting. He was shouting so loud I could not tell what he was shouting about, or at whom for that matter. Yisroolikel, pale and shaking, managed a smile at me as I came into the front room, a smile that barely interrupted the nervous darting of his tongue. Uncle Gershon's snuff had spilled all over his beard and there it hung.

No one seemed concerned about school. Neither was I.

Upon seeing me, my mother, too, began to scream. "Not with my little girl," she shouted, "there will be no *shidachs* with my little girl."

The love that I always saw or sensed, that integral part of the anger when my father quarreled and raged at my mother, was nowhere to be seen or felt. My mother was angry, angry in a much different, more potent, way than I had ever seen. For the first time in my life I thought of my mother as formidable.

As soon as I had scrambled into clothes, my mother sent Yisroolikel and myself out for a walk, despite my rumbling stomach that had not breakfasted, and with a warning glance at Yisroolikel and a wicked glance at the uncle who had started to protest. I was so fascinated by those changing expressions on my mother's face I was reluctant to take the walk.

"What's the matter with everyone?" I asked.

"Rivka," he said, "will you remember me?"

"You know I'll remember you. How could I forget you? Anyhow, you'll be back sometime."

"I don't think so."

His white fluttering hands began to fumble through his pockets.

"Are you looking for Jeremiah?" I asked.

It did no good. Yisroolikel had no sense of humor anyway and he was especially grim that morning.

What he did find was a silver dollar. When he gave it to me he kissed the top of my head, having first removed his glasses. Tears suddenly rolled down his smooth cheeks and he looked as though he had a stomach ache. Without the glasses his large liquid brown eyes had no confinements and for a minute I had the sensation of being immersed in them, as in a ritual bath.

"This is all I have," he said, "except for what is in my heart. I want you to have it to remember me by."

"Don't remember my voice," he whispered, "don't remember my

discussions. Remember me. Will you look at it sometime and think of me?"

I had begun to feel strangely shy and did not know what to do. I took the silver dollar.

It was very worn. On one side, only the outlines of the eagle were visible, though the leaves around it were still raised and could be felt. It was impossible to read the date.

On the other side it was hard to feel anything. The coin was completely smooth. I knew that In God We Trust was written somewheres on the silver dollar but I could not find it.

"I've never seen a silver dollar before," I said.

"Keep it, keep it," he shouted. "Don't spend it and think of me."

It was with pain that Yisroolikel reached for my hand. Before that day he had never touched me.

"Yisroolikel, what is the matter?" I asked again.

"Remember me, remember me," is all he said.

When we returned, whatever happened had been settled. Some of the signs were still scattered about, but the uncle, my father and my mother were in the kitchen. My sister and brother were happily eating in the dining room.

Yisroolikel and his uncle left our lives. I put my silver dollar under my pillow and every day I looked at it and thought of Yisroolikel. Sometimes I even heard him — that beautiful voice and those so-much-felt prayers.

Other Jewish holidays came and Passover came and April came. The Jewish New Year and Yisroolikel were further and further away. My birthday came. The hot Texas summer began without a spring. Things were not so good at our house. My mother was unwell; though Jeremiah made the handkerchief dance it was without its fantastic joy; there were no pennies for ices.

One day the silver dollar disappeared. I searched the bed and under the bed. I accused my brother and sister of hiding it from me. When I went to my mother she told me how foolish it was for me to have a silver dollar lying under my pillow when we did not have enough to eat, and how like my father I was. She had bought a silver dollar's worth of eggs and they would last us for a long time.

"You've sold Yisroolikel," I wept, "you've sold Yisroolikel."

That early evening, in our alley, Lorallee-May and I exchanged panties. I had always wanted "sexy" black ones, and she had always wanted "white folks'" ones. Her mother gave in to my teasing and let me taste a pork chop. It made me violently ill for three days.

Even without the silver dollar I have remembered Yisroolikel.

March, 1978

142

Yom Kippur in Montana

By JESSE BIER

HERE where the light, the light
crashes with breaking beauty on the yellowing
leaves of the quaking aspens, the mountains still
ache with summer, a golden hush
holds in the blue steeps before onslaughts of winter.
I am burned with the gold,
am fled up the blue steeps into the very eye of the sun,
am the sun itself in the blue steeps.

Sawtooth mountains tilt below, Colorado goes under,
Texas slips sideways — into what Gulf —
Florida shimmers, the Keys — to what kingdom — disappear
and the sea flows phosphorescent.
Afric shores gleam,. Maraketch, and everlasting sands,
Khartoum and O! Egypt,
The Negev, dwarf olive trees, and then Jerusalem,
minarets and synagogues, bazaars, a wall,
streets of sudden turning, cries, hubbub
there, where I come into my own.

But here,
in sentimental citizenry with everybody else, I am this
American: polyglot, always home-yearning:
for Israel, *my* Ireland, *my* ol' sod, *my* old country.

But I cannot speak the Hebrew in the streets,
my tongue cleaves or stutters. Stranger in that homeland,
soul-slain upon those alien hills.

Yet heart-speaking, lifted over voids.

Spetember, 1984

143

40 Years Later — But Not Too Late

By MORRIS U. SCHAPPES

ONE thing leads to another, and all actions have antecedents, but the action of the Faculty Senate of the City College of the City University of New York taken March 19, 1981 all began April 13, 1980. On that sunny Sunday afternoon, I set foot on the campus of the City College for the first time in 40 years. From 1921 to 1941 I had virtually lived on that campus: first as a student at the Townsend Harris Hall High School (the preparatory school for the City College), then as an undergraduate, and from 1928 to 1941 as a member of the English Department. For over 25 years I had continued to live very near the College; often on a Sunday while I was teaching there, Sonya and I would stroll on or through the grounds. In 1941, however, I was one of over 40 teachers and staff members driven off the campus as a result of the anti-Communist witch-hunt conducted by the Rapp-Coudert Committee of the N.Y. State Legislature. Because I was the conspicuous "red" on the campus, and because I refused to be an informer, I wound up serving 13½ months in state prisons, a full-fledged felon (so that to this day I cannot serve on a jury, or drive a car — or own or work in a liquor store).

During those 40 years since 1941 I had made no vow not to step onto that City College campus, but somehow Sonya and I strolled in other directions on Sundays. A knot of resentment grew within me until I knew, consciously, that I would not go onto that campus again until I was invited to do so for some official function. And for April 13, 1980 I had such an invitation: to witness a ceremony — the unveiling of a plaque to the 13 teachers, students and alumni of City College who had been killed in Spain fighting Franco fascism. For such an occasion, I had agreed to return. The City College would be the first in the USA to have such a memorial plaque, with the names of all the 13 and a definition of the cause for which they had gone abroad to die — the first in the world perhaps. I felt I belonged there again.

The project that led to the unveiling of the plaque had begun on Dec. 13, 1977, when I attended a small meeting to launch a drive to raise $25,000 for a scholarship fund the interest on which would be awarded annually in the name of the 13 who had died as volunteers in Spain, and $1,000 for the bronze plaque designed by Maximilian Vogel. The project was the happy brain-child of Dr. Irving Adler, City College '31, himself once a brilliant teacher of mathematics in the New York high schools who had been ousted as part of another witch-hunt. With free tuition at the City College abolished by the Rockefeller governorship, Adler conceived the idea of simultaneously serving Alma Mater and memorializing the Spanish Vets, many of whom he, and we who joined him, knew personally.

Well, in two years, our handful had raised $34,000 and the money for the plaque. The College Administration had arranged to have us make the unveiling in the Lincoln Corridor of the Main Building (most appropriate for the Veterans of the Abraham Lincoln Brigade), and with the Acting-President of the City College, Dr. Alice Chandler, as one of the speakers. (See "The Editor's Diary," in our issues for May and Nov., 1978 and June, 1980 for details.)

It was not without emotion that I entered the marble-floored, lofty, long, stately Lincoln Corridor, on which my classrooms and my office in the English Department had once fronted. Some 350 people had turned out for this unveiling. There were 16 Veterans of the Abraham Lincoln Brigade, comrades of the 13 fallen. There were some fellow-victims of the Rapp-Coudert Committee attack: John Kenneth Ackley, who had been the Registrar of the College when the axe fell; the historians Philip S. Foner and his twin, Jack Foner, the first now Professor Emeritus of the Lincoln University and the latter Professor Emeritus of Colby College; David Goldway, now Professor of English at a State University college in Farmingdale, N.Y., and Jesse Mintus, who had worked in the Registrar's office, now retired after a career in the business world that he hated and then as administrator of a mental health facility that brought his social conscience into play. There were others, whose jobs would not be made more secure today if I identified them as victims of a witch-hunt of 40 years ago.

With Irving Adler presiding, the program went smoothly in that thronged corridor, with standees along both sides. I was seated in the front row, among the committee members, speakers and special guests. In her address as Acting-President, Dr. Chandler, a Professor of English before she became Provost and then Acting-President, spoke very well. Responsive to the spirit of the occasion, she pointed to the mission of the College now, serving Black and Hispanic students as it had once served Jewish students who were poor immigrants or the children of such immigrants.

Then it came time for Phil Foner to speak. He was the only one on the program who had been teaching at the College during the Spanish Civil War, and had been a colleague of the two teachers killed in Spain — Alfred "Chick" Chaikin and Ralph Wardlaw. When Phil had written to me

145

asking for suggestion of things he might say, I had responded with several, including: "If Wardlaw and Chaikin had not been killed in Spain they would undoubtedly have been fired from the College by the Rapp-Coudert Committee like the rest of us." And Phil, in the course of a historian's analysis of the Spanish Civil War, did just that: "They would have been dismissed in 1940-41, along with over two score anti-fascist teachers (myself included), all victims of the Rapp-Coudert Committee, premature victims of McCarthyism." And he called on Ackley and me for bows. In the audience there was a sudden intense brief hush.

When the ceremony ended after some fine addresses by the Lincoln Vet and University of Pittsburgh History Professor Robert C. Colodny and by Pulitzer Prize winning biographer Joseph P. Lash, there was a crackle in the air. There was milling around, there was crowding around the plaque, there was a sense of reunion. Colodny had hit it perfectly when, in his speech, he turned solemnly to Dr. Chandler and said, "By these official proceedings, you have restored the integrity of the national memory, you restored these heroes to the American people." When the Lincoln Vets who had given me a lift to the College were ready to take off, I went — all of us aglow with the success of the event in legitimizing the Spanish Vets on such a college campus, I with a private warmth that this had been achieved on a campus on which the Rapp-Coudert Committee had once wrought its academic havoc.

It wasn't until the following Saturday, when I made my weekly telephone call to Ken Ackley, that I learned that something else had happened on April 13 that might start a new chain of events. It seemed that Dr. Chandler had been hard hit by Foner's pointed remark that Wardlaw and Chaikin, had they lived, would have been fired too. She had gone over to Ackley when the ceremony ended, had told him she was only a girl of six when the Rapp-Coudert Committee was operating, but that in her parents' home the words Rapp-Coudert were "dirty words"; she knew nothing else — and what was it all about? Ken told her a few of the facts. On leaving him, she said that, before she left City College June 30 to take up her new post as president of the State University of New York at New Paltz, perhaps she would "have some fun" and see whether she could do something about this. Was this a polite way of disengaging herself, or was she serious? And how much could she do between April 13 and June 30?

Early in May, I think it was, I received a phone call from a Dr. Stephen Leberstein of City College. Dr. Chandler had asked him to look into the operation of the Rapp-Coudert Committee for her. He had been digging into the archival material available at the College and wanted to interview me. The next Wednesday I took a few hours out of my one day a week that I set aside to work on the rewriting and updating of my history of the Jews in the USA, to go to the College to meet Dr. Leberstein. He turned out to be

146

an administrator in the Provost's Office and responsible for some of the College's new efforts at worker education. A student activist leader at the University of Wisconsin in the 1960s, he had obtained his doctorate in history there with a dissertation on the French labor movement at the turn of the century. He had never heard of the Rapp-Coudert Committee until now and was appalled at the witch-hunt.

Steve explained that at the moment he could not be as thorough in researching the material for Dr. Chandler as he would like to be. So I supplied as much information as I could. He then interviewed Ackley at his home, and later David Goldway too. He soon had a paper with the evidence to convince Dr. Chandler that she should petition the Board of Higher Education (now the Board of Trustees of the City University) to recognize the injustice it had done to all those who, having tenure, had been dismissed after "due process," and to those who were forced to resign or simply not reappointed since they had no tenure.

Her first step was to have Dr. Leberstein present his memorandum to a session of the President's Cabinet, consisting of the heads of all the various schools that now make up the City College. Only one person present had ever heard of the Rapp-Coudert Committee before hearing the Leberstein report; Prof. Arthur Tiedeman of the History Department was of the class of '43 and remembered it vaguely. He was to succeed Dr. Chandler as Acting-President when she left June 30. The Cabinet too was favorably impressed with Leberstein's paper and agreed with Dr. Chandler that something should be done to set the record straight.

Dr. Chandler left the College on June 30, 1980 before she could put her name to any official action, but Leberstein was determined to carry on. At the College he organized the support of sympathetic colleagues, among them Haywood Burns, Dean of Urban and Legal Programs, and began intensive work on the research with Barbara Caress, an urban historian now teaching at Baruch College. She too in the 1960s had been a student activist — at the University of Chicago.

The more they studied the record the more they were convinced that, as Leberstein wrote in his 25-page paper, "The investigation marked a new era in the repression of political dissent in this country, and resulted in a major attack on the academic freedom of the faculty of the municipal colleges." He also noted that of those fired, dropped or resigned, "None was ever officially charged with any misuse of his office as a teacher or with any other matter of professional competence and conduct."

To me it was an inspiration to witness the zeal and dedication with which Steve worked. What was most significant to me, and to others of us who were soon drawn into consultation, was that it was not we who were "self-servingly" conducting this new struggle but people of another generation, who had known nothing of the Rapp-Coudert Committee. Yet

147

these new administrators and scholars at the City College, who knew none of us victims personally, were impelled by their own social consciences not only to see that an injustice had been done but to feel personally committed to doing something about it, even if it was 40 years after.

As a first step Leberstein proposed that the Faculty Senate at the City College, consisting of representatives of every department totaling about 90 members, pass an appropriate resolution. Preparing a draft resolution, he took it, with his supporting memorandum, to the Executive Committee of the Faculty Senate. There it was referred to the Academic Freedom Committee for its recommendation. Duly that Committee decided unanimously to recommend to the Faculty Senate that this resolution be passed. The Senate was to meet March 19, 1981. Two weeks before that date each Faculty Senator received a copy of the memorandum and the resolution.

Would there be opposition and a debate? The faculty Senate consisted of people with a wide range of socio-political views. Would a climate of opinion in which neo-conservatism was in full cry be a context unsuitable for such an action by the Faculty Senate? At its meeting on March 19, when the chair of the Faculty Senate, Prof. Barbara B. Watson of the English Department, called for discussion of this resolution, no one rose to speak. When she put the resolution to a vote, it was passed — with one dissenting nay from a professor in the Sociology Department. On this issue of academic freedom and constitutional rights of teachers, unity had been established.

Worth recording is the full text of this "Resolution on the Rapp-Coudert Victims and on the Repression of Political Dissent":

"*Resolved*, that the Faculty Senate of the City College expresses its profound regret at the injustice done those former colleagues on the faculty and staff of the College who were dismissed or were forced to resign in 1941 and 1942 as a result of the investigations carried out by the Joint Legislative Committee to Investigate State Monies for Public School Purposes and Subversive Activities, popularly known as the Rapp-Coudert Committee, solely on the basis of their political associations and beliefs, and their unwillingness to testify publicly about them; and be it further

"*Resolved,* that the Faculty Senate states its determination to safeguard for the College community those fundamental American rights of association and speech, without which a citizen is deprived of his rights, and without which intellectual discovery and discourse is not possible; and be it further

"*Resolved,* that the Faculty Senate requests that the Board of Trustees consider the matter of this injustice with a view toward obtaining an official resolution of regret and a pledge to safeguard in the future the

148

Constitutional rights of the faculty, staff and students of the University."

Noteworthy is the fact that this resolution looked not only to the past in attempting to redress a wrong but to the future, committing the Faculty Senate to warding off possible violations of academic freedom and constitutional rights in a Reaganized neo-conservative atmosphere. The resolution was eventually transmitted to the Board of Trustees by the new Acting-President, Prof. Arthur Tiedemann. And to each of the surviving victims, Prof. Watson sent an official letter, with a copy of the resolution. When the text of the resolution was printed in the April issue of the *Newsletter of the City College,* the entire City College faculty and staffs learned of the action. The New York metropolitan press, however, which had so zealously in 1941 spread on its front pages the news of our hearings, trials and dismissals, was not yet interested in this reversal of judgment.

As the news spread in the College a train of consequences began to emerge. It so happened that the English Department had been, 40 years ago, the one with the greatest concentration of targets of the Rapp-Coudert witch-hunt. Five of us in the department had been ousted: Arthur Braunlich and Seymour A. Copstein (who died in 1979 and 1977), David Goldway, Arnold Shukotoff and I. On the few occasions when Steve Leberstein had invited me to the College for consultation and we had gone to the Faculty Dining Room for lunch, he had seen to it that two or three faculty people were also present to meet me, among them Prof. Edward Quinn of the English Department, a Shakespearean scholar. Dr. Saul N. Brody, chair of the English Department, was co-chair of the Academic Freedom Committee of the Senate that had recommended the resolution. And so things began to happen between the English Department and me. On March 28, a few days after the Faculty Senate action, I received a telephone call from Prof. Barry Wallenstein, whom I had met once a few years ago in some other connection. He explained that the College was preparing a small anthology of pieces by "distinguished alumni" of the College about their College experiences. The book, which he was editing, was to be used by the College for promotion, — and would I please supply something of mine for the book? Irving Howe was to be in it, and some other writers... Did he think that an account of how, in 1936, the head of the English department came into my classroom for the first time in eight years, caught me reading Shelley, thought I was quoting Marx, and tried to fire me — would such a tale be appropriate? He thought it would, but I suggested he consult his colleagues about it. A few days later he called again: everyone had agreed that account would be quite suitable — and could I please have it in by the end of May? Well, overburdened as I am, now that I was suddenly turned from an outcast into a Distinguished Alumnus, I managed to write up that story, sent it in May 6, and was assured it was accepted for publication.

At lunch one day late in March, Prof. Quinn asked whether I could accept an invitation from the English Department to attend the Department's annual Awards and Prizes ceremony, at which over $10,000 is given out to students. This was something new. In 1927 and 1928, when as an undergraduate I had won certain English Department medals, there was no ceremony (the medals have since then been stolen by whoever burgled our apartment some 25 years ago). Wanting to meet the English Department and curious about this new ceremony, I readily accepted the invitation.

Therefore on Thursday, May 14 I arrived at the College by 3 P.M. Steve met me at the elevator, which took us to the Webb Room in the tower of the Main Building (now renamed Shepard Hall) where he introduced me to Prof. Brody. We chatted. I told him what the English Department had been like in 1928 and the '30's, until our efforts through teacher organization had won a tenure system (until the late '30's all appointments were for one year only) and a democratic structure that provided for a department curriculum committee, a committee on appointments and promotions, election of department chairs — history that neither he nor anyone else in the department had ever heard of. At one point, Dr. Brody excused himself, and returned in a moment with the Program for the awards ceremony — and an envelope. Would I mind presenting one of the awards to a student? What award, to whom? The Tuck Award, of $200 — to Mr. Nashid Al-Amin. I agreed.

As the ceremonies were about to begin, I took a seat at a table with three Black students. There were about 100 people in the room, English faculty members, college administrators, winners of the 23 awards and prizes and their friends. Prof. Quinn came over to introduce me to a man at an adjoining table: Prof. Brooks Wright of the English Department. He remarked that my former student, Marvin Magalaner, until recently a member of the Department, had often spoken to him about me. And then the proceedings began. The award I was to present was tenth on the list, so I settled down to listen.

Late in his opening remarks, Prof. Brody said that the Department was glad to have with it on this occasion a man who had been a member of the department over 40 years ago and had, together with others in other departments, been dismissed for allegedly being a communist. He noted that recently this man had been teaching at Queens College and that for many years he has been editing the magazine JEWISH CURRENTS. He indicated that later in the proceedings I was to present one of the awards, but called on me now for a bow. I stood up. There was applause, more applause — and then suddenly everybody was standing up, applauding. I was overwhelmed — glad that I didn't have to make the award presentation at that moment.

150

The first award, a fellowship of $3,000, was to be presented by Prof. Brooks Wright. In ironic solemnity he explained that the magnitude of the award required due pomp, and so he was going to present the award in Latin — which he proceeded to do, to an occasional titter. His fine Harvard Latin then was ceremoniously rendered into Engish by Prof. Arthur Zeiger (whom I had met some 30 years ago when he was writing a doctoral dissertation on Emma Lazarus). And so it went, award after award to men and women, among them many Blacks, reflecting the changed student body. There was good humor, laughter and joyous applause as the winners stepped up for their prizes. I had been debating with myself: should I or should I not, should I or should I not? And then it came my turn to make the presentation.

Award envelope in hand, I stepped into the center of the room. I indicated that it was a poignant pleasure to be invited back by the English Department after exactly 40 years of separation; that in the 1930s there were only four or five prizes, none of them in cash; that since Prof. Wright had made his award in Latin it would perhaps be appropriate for the editor of a magazine named JEWISH CURRENTS to make this award in Yiddish — and proceeded to do so: *"Es iz far mir a grois fargenign ibertsugebn dem priz fun $200 tsu Mr. Nashid Al-Amin."*

Amid some laughter and much applause, a tall, sturdy Black student stood up and came forward. As I handed him the envelope, we shook hands, shook and shook, to mounting applause. Soon after that the ceremonies ended and broke up into "Champagne Reception." When I asked Mr. Amin what his plans were, he told me he was going to work for his master's degree in Communications at the City College, aiming for a career in journalism. He wanted to know — what was this magazine I was editing? I offered to send some specimen issues to his home in the Bronx — which I did the following day.

Several faculty people came over to express their pleasure at hearing Yiddish again after so many years and a couple were gratified that they could still understand what I had said before I had translated it. Apparently my bit of *hutzpa* had not been taken amiss.

Within a half hour, the reception was thinning out — and Prof. Brody and I drifted together again. He told me he had not yet been born when the Rapp-Coudert Committee was doing its work and had never heard of it until the matter came before him on the Faculty Senate Academic Freedom Committee. It had occurred to him to ask his parents, who had in those years been Jewish workers, whether they knew anything about the Rapp-Coudert Committee . "And they did," he said, "and they gave me an earful about the whole dirty affair." So both Dr. Alice Chandler and he had parents who knew about the Rapp-Coudert Committee attacks on the colleges! This point was underlined when I learned that Leberstein's father-

151

in-law, Charles Kagan, a Jewish worker, had also been aware of the case at the time, and that the parents of Prof. Caress were City College and Brooklyn College graduates of the Rapp-Coudert days. Parents' experience, apparently, had not been entirely lost.

After a few moments, Dr. Brody suddenly said, "Look, Mr. Schappes, would you be able to come back to the Department to teach a couple of courses?" What had sometimes in these 40 years been a fantasy of mine was becoming a reality! But I was sober. No, I explained, much as I might like to accept such an invitation, I could not, for the same reason that, in 1977, I declined an offer to resume my Adjunct Professorship in the History Department at Queens College after having been "let out" in 1976 because of the budget crisis. At my age, I thought I should rather devote the day or day-and-a-half I spent in teaching my courses in American Jewish history at Queens into working on a rewriting and updating of my long out-of-print history of the Jews in the United States. Dr. Brody understood, but persisted: "Can you give us *something* that would not take much of your time — even for one session?" So we left it at this: if he could get together a few students for it, I'd be glad to come onto the campus for a one-session seminar on Emma Lazarus...

Another coincidence was to round out that day for me. When I came home, Sonya handed me a letter that had arrived that day — the official notification from Prof. Barbara Watson enclosing the text of the Faculty Senate Resolution and adding, "It is a great personal satisfaction to me to be able to inform you of this action..." May 14, 1981 was indeed a red-letter day for us.

During all this period, the action of the Faculty Senate had been all but blacked out as far as the public was concerned.

On May 19, the issue was coming up again in another forum. The City College Faculty Senate had sent its resolution to the Faculty Senate at other colleges that had been affected by the Rapp-Coudert inquisition: to Brooklyn, Hunter and Queens Colleges, and to the City University Faculty Senate.* After minor semantic changes, the resolution was adopted by the University Faculty Senate. Now the Board of Trustees had two of its constituent bodies asking for action to redress the old injustice. Again the press ignored the story.

* A word here is necessary about the possibly confusing names, the College of the City of New York (CCNY), the City College and the City University of New York (CUNY), not to be confused with New York University, which is a private institution. Here is history on a pinhead: The Free Academy was established by the N.Y. State Legislature in 1847, ratified by a public referendum in 1848 and opened its doors in 1849 as the first free public college in the country (and the world). In 1866 the name was changed to the College of the City of New York, and in 1929 to the City College. At the time of the Rapp-Coudert Committee operations, there were four municipal colleges in New York: City, Hunter, Brooklyn and

Then it occurred to Steve and Barbara that if the story was not seen by the press as "news," perhaps it would be receptive to a "historical piece." They submitted an article to the Op-Ed page of the *N.Y. Times,* where, after much negotiation with the editor, it appeared June 2, 1981 with the head, "40 Years After Firings." Following a thumb-nail sketch of the tactics of the Rapp-Coudert Committee and the press hullaballoo it provoked, Caress and Leberstein noted the action of the Faculty Senate of March 19 and said, "The issue awaits the board [of trustees'] action."

One passage in this Op-Ed article aroused considerable curiosity. The authors had written: "The firings ended some promising careers. One scholar changed his name and, after the 1952 episode of repression, went to Cambridge University, where he was knighted for scholarship." Who was this academic knight? Well, in 1941, when he was simply not reappointed to the City College history department because he had no tenure, Moses Finkelstein had been for some time the executive secretary of the American Committee for Democracy and Intellectual Freedom, headed by the great anthropologist at Columbia University, Franz Boas (1858-1942). Changing his name to Moses I. Finley (probably after a past president of City College from 1903 to 1913, John H. Finley), he completed his doctoral work in ancient history at Columbia University and obtained an appointment at Rutgers University. There late in 1952 another red-hunt blasted Finley out of his teaching post. In England, however, Finley's Marxism was no barrier to academic distinction; he in a few years established a reputation defined as "the foremost expert on ancient slavery — as on Greek and Roman social and economic history in general — in the English-speaking world" (Harvard historian E. Badian, reviewing Finley's latest book in *N.Y. Review,* Oct. 22, 1981).

It so happened that Sir Moses I. Finley coincidentally made the news columns in the *N.Y. Times* May 10. On May 9 he was scheduled to be awarded an honorary doctorate at the Syracuse University commencement. When he arrived and learned that Secretary of State Alexander M. Haig, Jr. was also to be awarded an honorary degree at the same time, despite extensive protests from faculty and students, Finley anounced to the press that he was refusing to attend the ceremony. "All

Queens. In 1961, the City University was constituted of all the four-year Senior and two-year Junior or community colleges, now numbering 17, plus the Graduate School. Now in 1926, the Board of Higher Education had been created to govern City and Hunter Colleges — and all the municipal colleges born after that date. In 1980, the BHE had been reorganized and enlarged as the Board of Trustees of CUNY, its members appointed by the Governor and the Mayor. It was this Board of Trustees that the City College Faculty Senate had urged to act, since it was the predecessor Board of Higher Education that had dismissed the victims of the Rapp-Coudert Committee.

honor to Sir Moses" was the private toast of those of us who knew him in his City College days.

The next hurdle, and the decisive one, was the Board of Trustees of CUNY. After all, it was not the faculty at City College that had unjustly fired us, or forced us to resign, or failed to reappoint us. It was good to have the sentiment of the Faculty Senate as expressed in its resolution of March 19. But redress of injustice, to be at all meaningful, should come from those who had perpetrated the injustice, or at least from the institutional successors of that body, the CUNY Board of Trustees. Two months had passed, without the Board having paid any attention to the Faculty Senate request. Now that the University Faculty Senate had acted, would the Board be more responsive?

We hoped the June 2 article on the Op-Ed page of the *Times* would stimulate the Board to act. At the same time, there was a possibility that conservative or reactionary forces on the Board or outside might become alarmed and press the Board to reject the proposed resolutions.

This possibility was sharpened on June 19 by an incident that occurred at the 50th anniversary dinner of the City College class of 1931. Some of us had been thinking that it would be good for the Board to know that its favorable action on the resolutions would be well received in City College alumni circles. One of the Rapp-Coudert victims, Jesse Mintus of the class of '31, took it upon himself to seek out the president of that class and to arrange that he call on Mintus to read the resolution and propose that the audience present endorse the action of the City College Faculty Senate. When Mintus was called to the dais and read the resolution, up jumped Prof. Lewis Feuer of the Philosophy Department of the Virginia Polytechnical Institute and State University with an amendment: that the Board of Trustees also be urged to ban all secret political societies on the campus! The Class President and MC, fearing a controversy that would upset the festivities, fumbled for a moment for a proper procedure — and then announced that he would proceed to the next event on the program. Had the MC put the resolution to a vote, the probability is it would have been passed overwhelmingly, but one sudden irrelevancy injected into the scene by a Feuer, apparently an advocate of free speech for all except..., had derailed the proposal. Would Feuer, or others, mobilize to try to spike the resolution when it was considered by the Board?

When nothing was heard by the date of the Trustees' June meeting, a telephone call yielded the information that the Trustees had not yet received the resolution of the City College Faculty Senate. A subsequent telephone call by Trustee Herman Badillo succeeded in having the chancellery locate the resolution. Then interminable "due process" was started.

Finally we learned that the Board was to act on Oct. 26, 1981. Would

154

there be opposition at the prior public hearing? Colleagues from the City College Faculty Senate were prepared to speak at the hearing — but when no one had asked to speak against the action, their names were withdrawn and the hearing was cancelled. Because the public, by law, is allowed to attend the meetings of the Board of Trustees, I telephoned as many of the surviving victims as I could reach. The following came to the Board headquarters for the occasion: John Kenneth Ackley, the registrar of the College when he was ousted; Jesse Mintus, who had worked in the Registrar's office; Anne Bernstein, widow of Dr. Paul Bernstein of the Biology Department, their sons Jonathan and Peter, who had flown in from other cities for this occasion, other members of the family and the Bernsteins' old friends, the artist Philip Reisman and his wife; and Minnie Motz, whose husband, Emeritus Prof. of Astronomy at Columbia University Lloyd Motz, could not attend because he was teaching at that hour at the New School.

Leberstein and Dean Haywood Burns had tried to get permission for me to read a statement to the Board. But the Board's rules prohibit anyone but a member of the Board from addressing it. A satisfactory substitute, however, had been arranged: my statement was to be read to the Board by the Secretary before the vote was taken. And so it was. When our item on the long agenda was reached, the Honorable James P. Murphy, the Queens banker who is chairman of the board, asked whether Prof. Schappes was present. When I stood up, he explained that my statement would be read and thus become part of the proceedings in the minutes. That was an unforeseen advantage we had not counted on. Sight-reading a statement he had not seen before, Martin J. Warmbrand, secretary of the Board, read my text, perhaps less fervidly than I should have, but effectively. At the end, from the Board members and the CUNY officers and staff present, there was a tremendous well-sustained burst of applause. A couple of Board members who had not seen me when I first stood up asked the chair to have me stand again. This time Ackley and Mintus at my side stood with me, to more applause. The chairman put the resolution to a vote — which was unanimous, to more applause. And that was that — 1941 to 1981.

Finally, my associate-victims and I stole out of the Board meeting room. There was a round of congratulations -- and Steve, for whom no chore was too small and no courtesy too minor, drove Ackley and me to our homes. And so it was morning and evening of another day...

Despite the efforts of the CUNY public relations office, the *N. Y. Times,* which in 1941 had regarded the Rapp-Coudert proceedings against us as front-page news, printed nothing. Only the *N. Y. Daily News* of Oct. 27 had Sheryl McCarthy's account, headed, "City U issues apology/ to Red scare victims." The City College student weekly, *The Campus,* carried a news story on Nov. 2. In its Dec. issue, the *City College Alumnus* published a fine article by Leberstein and Caress and the full text of my statement.

What does it add up to? Well, the harassment, persecution and prosecution waged against us was not merely personal, and so our victory in exacting an apology, no matter how belated, is not only personal. Profound democratic principles and constitutional rights were involved in 1941 — and are now in 1981. The fact that the Reagan administration is bent on repression did not deter Dr. Chandler and Dr. Leberstein and their conscientious associates from waging their protracted struggle nor did the untoward climate of opinion prevent a victory — a victory that we hope will make it that much harder for repression to make its way again onto these campuses. During this very period, in fact, there were three other instances of redress of academic injustice, although not on the same wholesale scale as ours. The *N.Y. Times* May 31, 1981 had a story from Portland, Ore., "College Apologizes to Professor for 1954 Dismissal" — in which Reed College trustees apologized to Prof. Stanley W. Moore for having dismissed him for refusing to discuss his political affiliations with the House Committee on Un-American Activities.

On June 7, 1981, the *N.Y. Times* carried a very short story from Los Angeles, "5 Teachers Dismissed in 1950's/ Ruled eligible for reinstatement" — in which a Superior Court judge ruled that the late David Arkin (father of the actor Alan Arkin) and five other school teachers dismissed in 1953 for refusing to discuss their political affiliations should have been reinstated, possibly with back pay. And then Aug. 1 the *N.Y. Times* reported that Barrows Dunham of Temple University in Philadelphia, a Marxist philosophy professor fired 28 years ago for refusing to testify before the House Un-American Committee, was reinstated with a $9,000 annual pension. One conclusion I draw from such developments is that no struggle for social progress is ever totally lost — or, for that matter, permanently won. That is what is meant by the old saw, "Eternal vigilance is the price of liberty."

I have been asked, what about your criminal conviction as a felon for refusing to name names and be an informer — is this affected in any way by this apology from the CUNY Board of Trustees? Not legally, I guess, but morally there is a relation. At my trial for perjury (in denying I knew any other communists at City College) I had as a character witness the great teacher of philosophy at City College, Morris Raphael Cohen (1880-1946 — see my interview about Cohen in our issue of July, 1980). He had explained to me privately that he understood what I was doing because, in the Tsarist *shtetl* in which he had been born, there was a saying, "It's no use to tell the truth to the police, because they wouldn't know what to do with it." And so Cohen swore in court that I had the highest reputation for veracity, although I had refused to give names to the Rapp-Coudert Committee. The Board of Higher Education then fired me after my conviction — and for my convictions. Now the successor to this Board wakes up to the fact that it had been an invasion of my academic freedom and a subversion of my constitutional rights even to ask me about my political affiliations or associations. So it seems that, if you ask foolish — or forbidden — questions, you get foolish — or unresponsive — answers, which were ruled perjurious. Was it not Shakespeare — but not in *The Merchant of Venice* — who said, "The law is an ass"?

Statement by Morris U. Schappes

I THANK you for your courtesy in reading my comment, on behalf of the victims of the Rapp-Coudert Committee and of the then Board of Higher Education, on the resolution you have before you.

In the span of a single life, 40 years is a long time to wait for justice to be done, or rather for injustice to be admitted. So long that for about one third of our some 40 victims your notable action comes as a posthumous redress, nevertheless fully valued by surviving members of their families. Your action, no matter how late, vindicates our faith in the democratic process.

For us it is almost a matter of poignancy to find that, 40 years later, an entirely new generation of administrators, faculty and staff at the City College, learning for the first time that a wrong had been done to former colleagues whom they did not know personally, decided that it was their duty to attempt now to right that old wrong. It was Dr. Alice Chandler, then Acting-President of the City College, who almost accidentally stumbled upon the facts of what had happened when she was but a girl of six, and was moved speedily to set in motion the process that, after 18 months, has resulted in the action you have just taken. It was she who charged Dr. Stephen Leberstein to study the record of those events and prepare the memorandum of facts that later became the basis for the resolution recommended by the Academic Freedom Committee and adopted by the Faculty Senate of the City College and then by the University Faculty Senate of the City University of New York. It is to Dr. Chandler, Dr. Leberstein and their associates that we, and also you members of the Board of Trustees, owe the impetus to your formal recognition of the injustice done to us.

But it is not only for what your action means to us individually that we greet and applaud your resolution. In these times particularly it is of no small public significance that a Board as responsible and distinguished as yours "pledges diligently to safeguard the constitutional rights of freedom of expression, freedom of association and open intellectual inquiry of the faculty, staff and students of The City University." I say in these times

157

because today the rumble of repression is again heard in our land. Why, the very New York State legislature that some 40 years ago spawned the Rapp-Coudert Committee and its train of ill-consequence has this year rejected a bill to repeal the Feinberg Law, which, although the Supreme Court of the United States has declared it unconstitutional, is still on the statute books of our state. The vote on May 21 was 59 to 48 *against* repeal in the State Assembly. The reason for such willful flouting of the constitution, as given by one Assemblyman, was that the Feinberg Law might need to be reactivated in the future! Your Board of Trustees, which only recently had to redress the grievance of those it had wronged because of the Feinberg Law, is thus alerted from Albany to the possibility of the repetition of this tragic history, this time as farce. In these times, therefore, your action today, as it becomes known to academe and to the general public, will fortify the resolve of others who cherish the constitutional rights of our country to the point of being willing to fight and sacrifice for their protection.

Finally, while we accept in good faith your recognition of the injustice done to us, we cannot forget the still unrecorded harm done to us. Careers were wrecked; families were disrupted; suffering of all sorts — economic, academic, social — was widespread. Even in the armed forces of our country in World War II, in which a goodly number of us served honorably, the Rapp-Coudert tag on our names was a source of suspicion, harassment and, most distressingly, a barrier to rendering our country the full sevice of which we were capable. Yet the calibre of these men and women who 40 years ago were wrongfully dismissed, or forced to resign, or not reappointed was such that many had the resilience to build second careers, some of them of high distinction. Nor did we abandon our social concerns because of our private woes. Sometimes it took decades to break through the barriers set up by the Rapp-Coudert Committee — but it was done.

One of us had to change his name, leave the country, and then established such a reputation as an ancient historian in England that the Queen knighted him and he is now Sir Moses [Finley]. Another [Dr. Lloyd Motz], having been a past president of the New York Academy of Science, recently became Emeritus Professor of Astronomy at one of New York City's eminent private universities. A third [Arnold Shukotoff] changed his name and occupation to become a widely recognized musicologist. A fourth [Dr. Philip S. Foner] has published some 40 books in American history, is an Emeritus Distinguished Professor of a university in Pennsylvania and is currently a Distinguished Visiting Professor at a university in New Jersey. A fifth [Sidney Eisenberger], a chemist, won a first prize of $10,000 for an essay entitled "We are the Founding Fathers of the Future" in a contest sponsored by the Smithsonain Institution and a

158

famous bank as part of the Bicentennial of our American Revolution. A sixth [Dr. Jack Foner] has just retired as a Professor Emeritus of History at a university in Maine. A seventh [Maxwell Weissman] went abroad to become an M.D. and is now Director of Public Health Services in a nearby state. An eighth [David Goldway] is about to retire as a Professor of English at one of our State University of New York colleges. A ninth [David Cohen] heads an institute in one of the colleges of our City University. A tenth has just earned the signal honor of being selected by the Jewish Book Annual of the National Jewish Welfare Board as one of five American Jewish writers whose birthdays next year are worthy of public notice in the Jewish book world; on this roster, Barbara Tuchman's 70th and our Rapp-Coudert victim's 75th brithdays are to be celebrated. And last, one [Dr. Saul Bernstein], a biologist, had to change his name, retool and finally became the president of a sizable machine tool company in New Jersey.

Had we not been driven from our beloved campus of the City College, these achievements and others might well have been effected for the direct benefit of the City College community. For every one of us has been, according to our varying talents, a useful and productive citizen of our republic. Now too, today, we stand ready to support the City College and the City University in "diligently safeguarding the constitutional rights of freedom of expression, freedom of association and open intellectual inquiry..."   Morris U. Schappes

April, 1982

Personal and Political: Prison Recollections

By MORRIS U. SCHAPPES

THIS past year, you probably know, has been for me and my associates of 40 years ago, a year in which, while we looked at the reality around us, and looked ahead to see how we could change and improve that reality, we also had been compelled to look back upon that old struggle because of the unexpected but not unfought for development that led the institution that had fired over 40 of us 40 years ago to apologize to us formally and publicly for the injustice done to us and for the violation of our academic freedom and constitutional rights. Of the 40 or so I was singled out for preferential treatment as a perjurer in the first degree because I refused to be an informer. I therefore served 13½ months in jail in The Tombs and in New York State's prisons, Sing Sing, Dannemora and Walkill. Now about my jail experiences there is the little book, *Letters from The Tombs,* published by the Schappes Defense Committee, with an introduction by Richard Wright, in 1941, while I was out on bail pending appeals to the higher state courts. But about my prison experiences I have never written — and there is a reason for that.

Some of you here knew or will remember that outstanding lawyer, Carol Weiss King (1895-1952), whose many successful arguments of immigration cases before the U.S. Supreme Court helped shape immigration law and practise and made the American Committee for the Protection of the Foreign Born an outstanding progressive defense agency. Well, shortly after I was released on parole from Walkill Prison in Dec., 1944, Carol Weiss King invited Sonya and me to her home for dinner. Carol King had been part of that battery of radical lawyers that counseled us in our struggles in and out of court against the Rapp-Coudert Committee witch-hunt — and Sonya and I were delighted to have this invitation. Carol King was a lovely hostess, served a splendid dinner — of which I have not the slightest recollection. But one thing Carol King said to me that evening I have never forgotten. "Morris," she said, "don't make a career of your prison experiences." Perhaps she thought that, having written *Letters from The Tombs,* I was about to follow it up with another book of prison life. I had no such intention because I had already, while in prison, begun my studies in American Jewish history. But her injunction has ever since inhibited me, not from talking about my prison experiences privately to friends (and that not too often), but from writing about them.

Now, however, 40 years have passed. In these past 18 months I have had to recall the events of 1940 to 1944 in such a way that — well, today I am ready to go public with a few of these experiences, those that seem to have a social significance.

Now it so happened that I received my order to surrender to serve my sentence of 1½ to two years in state prison on Dec. 19, 1943 at about the same time that I received the galley proofs of my book, *Selections from the Prose and Poetry of Emma Lazarus,* which was being published by the Cooperative Book League of the Jewish-American Section of the International Workers Order. So Sonya and I spent the evening and part of the night before I surrendered romantically proof-reading my book, which came out during my imprisonment. Next day I was transported to the first stop on what was to turn out to be a prison-tour of duty that encompassed the best and the worst in New York State.

At Sing Sing, after my official induction as No. 102-800, I found another reception awaiting me. Some here will remember the trade union leader of the Laundry Workers of the Amalgamated Clothing Workers, Alex Hoffman. Well, he had just been released from Sing Sing, where he had been incarcerated for actions arising out of a laundry workers strike, by a pre-Christmas pardon from Gov. Charles Poletti. Learning from the press tlhat I was about to be checked into Sing Sing, Hoffman had arranged with two men serving life terms to "take care" of this radical "professor" who had refused to be an informer. So Mischa, a first violinist in a famous orchestra who had killed a girl in what the French call a "crime of passion," and Louis, whose crime I no longer remember, took me in tow, had me eat at their table, and lent me books from the clandestine circulating library the prisoners had managed to found. The first book lent me was Maxim Gorky's vivid and inspiring account of how, in the USSR, the White Sea-Baltic Canal had been built by prison labor as a project for building socialism. The Sing Sing Jewish chaplain, Rabbi Jacob Katz, lent me Mordecai Kaplan's *Judaism as a Civilization.* Both opened my eyes, but in different directions.

Comes Christmas, a particularly miserable time in any prison here because the separation from family is most acute, and of course the prison authorities not merely allow Christmas cards freely to come in but also offer the inmates a Christmas dinner. I am on the chow line; my plate is already full — with turkey, cranberry sauce, potatoes, gravy, all commingling on one metal plate, but I still have to get dessert. The man dishing out ice cream digs into his can routinely, comes up, sees me, calls out, "Why, Mr. Schappes! Wow, I was a student at City!" And down he lunges into the ice cream can for a second scoop, both of which, *far grois gedila* (for great joy), he slaps on top of — my turkey and gravy. This City College alumnus was not the only one who, during the depression, had responded to Mayor Fiorello H. LaGuradia's call to college graduates who could not find professional work or any jobs to join the city and state police on correctional forces.

That same Christmas, I was to learn later, Christmas vacationers at the nearby Fred Briehl's farm also had me on their minds. Fred Briehl, the farmer, was a member of the State Committee of the New York Communist Party, and supplemented his small income by taking in vacationing boarders at comradely prices. Mindful of my presence at nearby Sing Sing, they all signed a statement of encouragement and solidarity, and sent it to me. If the Warden was impressed, it was not in the way my well-wishers had intended. So on Jan. 22, as I was at work in the prison print-shop (printing, in the Russian revolutionary tradition, was a highly desirable craft to learn), I was suddenly taken by two guards, returned to my cell, and told I was being "boated out," that is, transferred to another prison.

I was scared, and I was frantic, because Sonya, who had visited me every week, was due to come that afternoon and I could imagine her reaction when she was told I was not there. Soon my lifer friends turned up at my cell to explain that I was to be on a "boat" to Dannemora, a maximum security prison in Plattsburg, near the Canadian border, a place dreaded as the Siberia of United States, or at least of N.Y. State, prisons. I had to pack all my belongings into one duffle bag, including books that had been sent me and passed by the prison censor. Carl Sandburg's six-volume life of Lincoln was a particular problem, and I gladly accepted Mischa's offer to send it to me at Dannemora — which he did.

At 11. P.M. that night, all of us on the transport to Dannemora were lined up. My right hand was handcuffed to the left hand of a Black prisoner. Heavy leg-irons on my right ankle were attached to heavy leg-irons on the Black man's left ankle. Unless we kept in step we would chafe each other raw. Our line hobbled up an incline to the Ossining railroad station, where we waited for a midnight train for an all-night journey. The January wind from the Hudson was mean. I was cold, cold and scared, wondering what had happened to Sonya. Suddenly behind me, a low voice, "You're the professor?" I turn my body without moving my legs. He adds, whispering, "My name is Scalise. Don't worry, Mischa said I'm to take care of you, professor. Don't worry." And he vanished. George Scalise was a notorious mobster, who

162

had been at Sing Sing for a few years and, like me, was being "boated" out.

In the train my Black companion and I shared one of the cross-seats, with a guard opposite us. The Black man had already been at Dannemora. Knowing what awaited him, he was scared of particulars; I was just generally frightened. The ride was long; conversation was short. After a few hours, I noticed my companion was squirming in his seat. He was sweating in the cold. "What's wrong, man?" No answer. "Anything I can do?" No answer, just squirms and squirms and pain writ large on his face. Finally, he let it out: He had to go to the toilet; he was afraid of me; what would I do if he, Black, had to sit and shit while I, handcuffed to him and with leg-irons binding us, had to stand there? I hurried him painfully to the narrow train toilet and hovered over him perforce while he relieved himself. His gratitude was embarrassing, but the incident was infinitely and permanently illuminating.

For I had studied the "Negro Question," as it was then called, intensively. In fact it was through my study of the Negro question that I became interested in the Jewish question as a Marxist, and was thus rescued from the cosmopolitanism into which I had lapsed as a student at the City College, with its pervasive atmosphere of deracination, deculturation and "melting-pot" pressures. So I knew about the "special character" of the Negro question; I knew that equality of opportunity was not enough for a people that had been enslaved and then Jim-Crowed into a position of inferiority out of which it would emerge only by special consideration; I knew all this theoretically and intellectually. But the experience with this Black prisoner stripped away totally the idea that we were equal in fact even when we were shackled to one another; he had a fear of forcing me to take him to the toilet that I should not have had in the reverse situation. So, if in JEWISH CURRENTS my advocacy of affirmative action and even of preferential treatment seem to you to have a special fervor it is because my political and moral conviction is continually reinforced by the memory of this experience: that handcuffs and leg-irons did not make us equal.

Dannemora was a fearsome place. It had been built during the Civil War to house Confederate prisoners-of-war. I was put into a small, dim cell with only a bucket for a toilet and with half-inch-thick vertical bars on the door. Both The Tombs and Sing Sing were palatial and modern in comparison. Within a half hour after I got into my cell, however, a figure appeared at the door. "You're the professor?" "Yes." "Scalise sent this." And he slips through the narrow aperture between the thick bars a large, round, metal container designed to slip through just this aperture — a can of soup! And then he pushed through the bars another object — a copy of the *N.Y. Herald Tribune!* That's how

Scalise took care of the professor! That's organization, I thought to myself admiringly — I, who thought I knew something about organization. Let me add at once that I met Scalise only once more at Dannemora (or anywhere else): in the infirmary one morning we were accidentally seated side by side, waiting for the doctor. There Scalise lamented to me that his being in prison was less hard on him than on his poor, old mother...

At Dannemora, even when, after a week of processing as No. 28-305, I was placed in the new building, with a large cell and inside toilet, the atmosphere was one of total intimidation. You never walked 10 steps alone. You were marched to the shower (once a week), marched to the movie theater, marched to the dining room, marched — and always on the double, with guards always at your elbow. The guards wore high-necked uniforms, hats with visors, and carried guns on their hips and sticks in their hands. Iñ the dining-room, you sat at narrow metal tables, ate on the double (no talking allowed), while at strategic places on a mezzanine there were guards with machine guns trained on us below. In the movie-theater, too, on either side of the projection booth, there were machine guns pointed at our backs.

But Sonya came to visit me every week, an all-day train ride to Plattsburg, an overnight stay in the home of Rabbi and Rebbitzin Shoenfeld, and then an hour opposite me with a glass barrier between us and a speaking-tube for intimate communication. On her first such visit, between bravely restrained tears, she told me that the lawyer Joseph Brodsky (1889-1947) had accompanied her to Albany to demand my transfer out of Dannemora. The prison officials told them about, and showed them, a *post-card* addressed to me, signed Earl Browder (obviously a forgery), in which Browder instructed me to organize the guards into a union and strike the joint at Sing Sing as soon as possible. Brodsky roared with laughter and indignation.

After four weeks — tough weeks — at Dannemora, I was transferred by two guards in an automobile to Walkill State Prison at New Paltz, a minimum security prison, where I did the remainder of my time.

Prison-wise convicts spoke with contemptuous envy of Walkill as a "country club" — which it wasn't. But the Warden at Walkill had a Ph.D. from Teachers College and had been Commissioner of Education in Puerto Rico. On his staff, there was a professional social worker. Your room was small and the windows were small but unbarred, and your door was wooden, and unlocked. You could shower whenever you wished. You ate from china, not metalware, and your cutlery included knives. The tables were wide and wooden — and you could talk to the man opposite you. The guards wore open-collared uniforms and carried neither guns nor

164

sticks. The chapel was a pleasant room that guards did not enter; if they wanted you, they knocked on the door and called you out. There was a basketball court, and as soon as the other inmates saw me perform there, I became a human being as well as "the professor."

After two weeks on the road-gang in the February cold as No. 3249, I was assigned to work as the inmate clerk to the Kitchen-Keeper, a Sergeant with an Irish name. When Sonya came to visit me every week, we were allowed to embrace at greeting and parting; we sat side by side and could hold hands. The one guard for the several couples in the visiting room was not intrusive.

Incidentally, have you perhaps wondered why I have been repeating that in each of these prisons, even in distant Dannemora, Sonya exercised her *right* to visit me every week? It is not only because her visits were infinitely supportive for my morale and wellbeing; of course they were that — and frankly I do not know how I would have fared without them. There is another reason. In our April issue, on p. 47, in my monthly half page on Jewish life in the Soviet Union, I included this little item: "Jan. 4 the mother of Anatoly B. Shcharansky was allowed to see her imposined son for two hours behind a glass partition for the first time in 16 months." I raged inside when I typed that item. There is no humanism of any kind, much less a socialist humanism, in a regime that prevents a prisoner from having any visit at all for 16 months, and in which there is no channel for the family of the prisoner publicly to protest such inhumanity. From an Argentinian tyranny I can expect such treatment as a Jacobo Timerman got from his sadistic, anti-Semitic jailers. From Soviet prison authorities I have a right to expect the humanism that pervaded Maxim Gorky's account of the building of the White Sea-Baltic Canal with prison labor. I do not expect, and I cry out against, the treatment being dealt out to Shcharansky and others like him.

But to return to life at Walkill State Prison in New York. There was a library into which you could go. (At Sing Sing and Dannemora, the library was the place from which books were brought to you.) So I enter the library. The civil-service librarian sees me and blurts out, "Schappes!" It was my City College classmate, H.R. Rudolf of the Class of '28. He was more embarrassed than I was. This "in" of mine with the Librarian, however, made it possible for me to get a Yiddish newspaper. Since the *Morgen Freiheit* was not allowed in and the *Forverts* I did not want, Rudolf ordered the *Tog* for my reading pleasure, and approved my importation of Nathaniel Buchwald's book, *Teater,* and Itzik Feffer's *Haimland,* published by the YKUF. I guess it was fortunate I was too poor to go to Harvard or Columbia, whose alumni were not likely to turn up as guards at Sing Sing or librarians at Walkill...

My clerical work for the Kitchen-Keeper was easy, and I spent much time reading my *Herald-Tribune,* which I preferred at the time because Walter Lippmann's columns on foreign affairs were more to my taste. At one end of the huge kitchen, which had an employee as chief cook and inmates working with him, there was this large metal-meshed cage, which served as storehouse for supplies and office for the Kitchen-Keeper. Each meal was tasted by the Major before being served (and it did not take me long to notice that the Major, instead of being served the food we inmates ate, was handed what he personally had ordered.) After each meal, the Sergeant, the Major and the Cook would gather in the cage. The Cook would bring a pitcher of coffee and there was always a cruller or piece of cake around.   After my first breakfast as clerk to the Kitchen-Keeper, I was at my work-place in the cage, reading my *Herald-Tribune* when the Cook walked in with his pitcher of coffee and — . The Sergeant called out to me — "Hey, Schappes! Want coffee? Help yourself." They seemed surprised when I replied, "No, thank you," and returned to my *Herald-Tribune.* After lunch and after the last meal, at 4. P.M., this dialogue was repeated. When the Cook and Major left, the Sergeant came over to me, mad. "Who do you think you are? Too stuck up to have coffee with us? You're here doing time, and don't you forget it."

My answer, when I could break in, was: "No, Sarge. That's not the point. You expect me to have coffee with you with the inmates out there in the kitchen looking on, wishing they could have coffee too. What would it take for the Cook to make a pitcher of coffee for his crew out there as well as for you and the Major?" The Sergeant said nothing. Next morning, the Cook put out a pitcher for his crew before he brought one in to our cage. And when the Sergeant called out, "Coffee, Schappes?" Schappes had coffee.

Well, word got around among the inmates that Schappes was a good guy, a right guy, even though a professor. But they missed the point too. For I was acting out what I had been taught, what I had learned from my studies of Marxism and Leninism by the book: that communists were to have special responsibilities, not special privileges, under socialism, and here I was simply trying to pattern my life under capitalism on such a vision — a vision worth going to prison for if necessary, a vision that did not envision that in a state run by a communist party there would be, among other privileges, special stores for the party and state bureaucracy.

In the Walkill kitchen there was another incident worth mentioning. I always ate with the other prisoners in the dining room (except for that coffee in the Cage). I was always first on the chow line, since I could take my place there from the Cage as the doors to the dining room were

166

being opened to let the others in. One day at noon at lunch, the big meal of the day, the main dish was liver, beef liver. I took my tray with a big slab of liver and vegetables to a seat, and started cutting the liver; then I started sawing the liver. No go; I think only a power saw could have cut that liver. I took my plate and walked clear across the length of the dining room to the Major, who was in the rear. Men at the tables arleady and men on the chow line stopped to look at me. To the Major, who was also amazed, I held out my plate, with the words, "Major, I cannot cut this liver."

Taking my knife, he tried it himself. Then, trembling with fury, he hurried to the chow line and ordered the serving stopped. The inmates were ordered back to their rooms; the Cook was ordred to prepare another meal. And 45 minutes later, the men were called back to the dining room and served something edible. Meantime, in the Cage, the Major was giving me the bawling out of my life...

Now what about Jewish life at Walkill State Prison? The Jewish chaplain was Rabbi Herbert I. Bloom (1899-1966) of Kingston, N.Y., a sweet man, a historian who had written a first-rate book on the Jews of Amsterdam in the 17th century (which I later used in my work on New Amsterdam Jews). I joined the congregation of about 25, but with the stipulation that while I would attend Sabbath services I would not pray. The services, by the way, were not conducted by Rabbi Bloom, a Reform rabbi. There was an inmate named Friedman, who had been ordained (obtained *smiha*) at the famous Slobodka Yeshiva in Poland. I think he was a swindler and a bigamist, but he was an orthodox Jew and would not attend a service conducted by a Reform rabbi. So Rabbi Bloom agreed to have Friedman conduct the service, after which Rabbi Bloom gave a short sermon, and then held private conferences with each inmate to see what he could do to help him. The rabbi was particularly friendly to me. In fact, after I got out and we opened the School of Jewish Studies, I persuaded Rabbi Bloom to teach a course for us in post-Talmudic literature.

One day I asked Friedman whether he would teach me Hebrew. All I knew of Hebrew was the little I remembered from my *bar mitzva* instruction — almost nothing. Friedman agreed and Sonya sent me the two-volume text book then used in the New York high schools, *Elements of Hebrew,* by Simha Rubinstein, published in 1936 by the N.Y. Bureau of Jewish Education. In prison Friedman worked in the tailor shop. But every day I would walk into his room, which adjoined mine, for a Hebrew lesson. We stipulated that he would use his Ashkenazic pronunciation, but I the Sephardic pronunciation indicated in the text.

Of course the authorities knew I was studying Hebrew with Friedman, and so did the Episcopalian chaplain. One day, Friedman tells me that that chaplain had called him into his office, to tell him that, in order to rise in the Episcopalian ministry, it would be well for him to study Hebrew. Would Friedman therefore teach him Hebrew? Friedman's answer was that he was doing time, and if the chaplain would get the Principal Keeper to assign Friedman to teach the chaplain Hebrew, Friedman would be glad to do so. But the chaplain knew he could not get the P.K. to make such an assignment, so he appealed to Friedman with "But Friedman, you are teaching Schappes Hebrew, why not me?" To which Friedman replied, "Ah, sir, but Schappes is an inmate!" So now I had status (*yihus*), I was an inmate!

Comes Rosh Hashona, 1944, at which time I had been at Walkill about eight months, and it occurs to me to try something else with Friedman. I knew that prison authorities set a great deal of store by religion. They think it's good for the inmates and many prison-wise inmates to join several congregations, including Christian Science. Now about a half mile down the road from the main building at Walkill there was a pond, which we could see from our elevation. Remembering how, when I was a boy on East 10th Street, I used to see the Jews on Rosh Hashona go to the East River to *tashlich* (the ceremony of emptying your pockets of sins into the water), it occurred to me that it would be a wonderful thing for the Jewish congregation of Walkill to demand the right to observe this religious commandment. So I persuaded Friedman to ask the Principal Keeper for permission for the congregation to go down to the pond for this ritual, and to show the P.K. where in the good book *shtait geshribn* (it is written) that this is a necessry part of the Rosh Hashona observance. And if previous congregations had not asked for this observance, that was not Friedman's fault, and he, Friedman, was an orthodox Jew, not this Reform kind, and so on. Well, the Principal Keeper agreed!

I must admit that only about 14 of our congregation had the nerve to go through with it. But on that Rosh Hashona morning, the 14 of us lined up, with Friedman and me at the head (with the rest of the prisoners lined up at the unbarred borders of the institution, looking at us in amazement), and, with one guard in front and one in the rear, we marched down that road, breathing deeply, basking in the autumn sun, striding to the pond according to the Laws of Moses.

At the pond, Friedman, in all his glory, uncorked a prayer so fervid and so loud that it could have been heard in the next county, or maybe in Albany, or Washington, or in the heavenly realms to which Friedman had directed his chant. And then we marched back to Walkill State Prison — and I assure you modestly that, had we wanted to, we could have had a mass conversion to Judaism of all the Christian denominations there. What, a religion that can get you out of prison for an hour to walk to a pond, etc., that's a religion for you! But Friedman did not believe in conversion — and we all had our hands full that day answering the questions of our fellow-inmates.

One day the Warden called me into his office, as he had done several times before, because he had had very few college teachers as his wards. On occasion he would even lament to me how frustrated he felt because the prison bureaucracy did not allow him to make the reforms in the prison regime that he had hoped to make. This time he showed me a book he had just received and asked me to read it. The book was by Nicholas S. Timasheff, assistant professor of sociology at Fordham University, and was entitled, *Religion in Soviet Russia 1917-1942*, published in 1942 by the Catholic house of Sheed & Ward. I said to myself, on the boss's time (that is, while I am doing time) I'll read the book, although I had immediately marked it as a book by a Russian White-Guard scholar of whom I'd be instinctively leery.

Well, the book was an eye-opener. Basing himself primarily on Soviet sources, Timasheff described a two-week conference called by the Soviet Academy of Historical Science so that the Bezbozhniki, Yemilian Yaroslavski's League of Militant Atheists, could be hauled over the coals as petty bourgeois atheists, as anarchist atheists and not Marxist atheists. At this conference early in 1939 the Marxists demonstrated that the Militant Atheists were ahistorical, condemned Christianity as a whole and in its entirety without regard to the historical fact that the introduction of Christianity into the Kiev Rus had historically marked an advance, and that therefore the work of the Militant Atheists was unsuccessful because it was non-Marxist. The spokesmen for the League of Militant Atheists accepted the criticism of the Marxist historians and promised to change their approach — but it was not long before the League was dissolved.

Now this whole ideological struggle was news to me. It had not been reported in the *Daily Worker,* or *The Communist,* or *Inprecorr* or any other Soviet or communist publication in English — all of which I read extensively. And I, a Marxist scholar, had to learn about it from a book by a White-Guard Russian pressed upon me in prison by a Warden. Perhaps here was born in my mind a certain caution in approaching Soviet and communist sources in English — a caution that possibly they were not revealing all that needed to be known about Soviet life and practices. From this caution grew, under changing circumstances, the critical posture I now have towards all such writings. For me the five-pointed Star of Socialism has not been dimmed by the blunders and crimes committed and still being committed in its name, what with anti-

169

Semtitism being propagated by official communist and Soviet publications. But the Star of Socialism, in my vision, must include room for the Star of David — and the stars of all nationalities — too.

It was in prison that I began to do some of the secondary reading for work on my history of the Jews in the United States. Dr. Joshua Bloch (1890-1957), Chief of the Jewish Division of the New York Public Library, having noticed my scholarly work on Emma Lazarus, suggested to Rabbi Ben Goldstein (1902-1953), who from his pulpit in Alabama had dared support the Scottsboro Case (and therefore later had to change his name to Lowell), that he send me books on American Jewish history — which Rabbi Goldstein did, much to my delight.

Then on March 14, 1944, I received in prison a copy of the printed volume of my Emma Lazarus selections. About that time I was also beginning to get the *Tog* — and there I came upon H. Leivick's Act II of his play, *Der Ness fun der Varshaver Getto.* (The Miracle of the Warsaw Ghetto). The *Tog* with Acts I and III never got to the Walkill prison library (and I must confess that to this day I have not read those missing acts). But I did translate Act II into English, as well as a few poems by Itzik Feffer (published later in the *Chicago Jewish Forum* and in our pages).

Therefore in the fall of 1944, as my parole release date was nearing, I arranged to have a Jewish Cultural Evening in the Chapel. With a couple of inmates, I rehearsed a reading of Leivick's Act II (with men reading the women's parts). Came the appointed evening, and most of the Jewish inmates gathered in the Chapel. First came a reading by four of us of Leivick's Act II. Then I read from the poetry and prose of Emma Lazarus. Then we adjourned not to *gedekte tishn* (tables with table cloths) but to a snack of a couple of cans of SPAM bought in the commissary! And a good Jewish cultural time was had by all — at least by me!

My first work reflecting my initial studies in American Jewish history as well as my prison experiences, was my long poem, *Time Done!* I think Rabbi Bloom unofficially got that to Sonya for me. It was published in the *New Masses,* Dec. 18, 1945, after I had safely completed my parole period.

I trust I have not conveyed the idea that I had a good time in prison. It is not that I have forgotten the dark aspects of that year, the loneliness, the separation from Sonya, family, friends and comrades, the crudeness all around, the longings and sometimes the anguish. But I was determined, as a way of fighting the system, to make the most of my time there, because if there is anything I hate it is to waste time — our most precious possession, It is not true that "walls do not a prison make," because they do. But it is what can be done behind those walls that is significant. I did what I could — facilitated by Sonya, family, and a movement continually concerned,

170

and in a society sufficiently democratic so that the concern could be made manifest.

I had valued democracy, democratic rights, before I was imprisoned. I was one of those who took almost literally Lenin's hyperbolic cry that "Socialist democracy is a thousand times more democratic than bourgeois democracy." I believed it as a True Believer. So not a thousand; let it be a hundred, or ten times. That it could turn out in practise to be *less* democratic than bourgeois democracy in countries calling themselves socialist and led by people calling themselves communist was an experience that came late and sadly. If my vision of socialism now stresses democratic rights, forms and institutions as the essence of socialism, my prison experience laid a basis for a perception that was slowly, slowly, to mature.

I realize that in this overlong discourse I have said very little about JEWISH CURRENTS itself, but I hope you will consider what I have said not irrelevant to it. This, however, is the character and these are some of the principles I brought to JEWISH CURRENTS. They may help explain some of the grievous errors we made — and they may also perhaps help explain our ability to recover from the mistakes after 1956 and their serious consequences of isolation from the Jewish community.

I know that your splendid out-pouring of solidarity here today is not only about me as a person; I see it as a symbol of my work with the magazine all these past 36 years. JEWISH CURRENTS is now the largest sector of the progressive Jewish movement. JEWISH CURRENTS can and must expand.

You have given freely today. We shall be coming back to you, again and again. The spirit, the enthusiasm displayed here must not evaporate. This is not a nostalgic binge, although I have talked about the past. As the old City College seal has it: *Respice, Adspice, Prospice.* We look back (for experience and wisdom); we look around us (for clarity and analysis); and we look forward — forward, past Reagan and Haig, past the new right, the old right, the all-right, past Podhoretz and his crowd, to a vision of what humankind can make of a world — of peace, of brotherhood and sisterhood, of amity and community of peoples, of the good life. Together, only together, can we go forward.

September, 1982

171

II: Israel and World Jewry

Beth Hatefutsoth in Tel Aviv

By NEIL SALZMAN

THE State of Israel is the house of Jewish reintegration. *Beth Hatefutsoth* is the institution committed to the memory, preservation and understanding of the disparate Jewish cultures, languages and histories during the past 2,500 years. Those were the years of the Diaspora, the scattering, the fleeing, the expulsions, the taking of refuge, the struggle of Jews to preserve their identity and consciousness within dominant societies, cultures and religions. And ultimately the Jews of the world Jewish communities sought integration within the societies in which they lived without total assimilation. It had never been easy. It is still a challenge; and there are those who believe it was and still is impossible.

I always felt some special pride driving our pilgrim car, our *coche,* the Seat 124 D, with the big "E" for Espana emblazoned on the back. We had driven from Mallorca to Piraeus, 2,000 miles, and then the ferry from Greece to Haifa. New York Jews, Yiddish-speaking Jews, driving down Derech Haifa along a different Mediterranean shore from the *playa* of the Puerto de Soller, the Costa Brava or the Cote d'Azure. I took a left up to the campus of Tel Aviv University.

The building is modern glass, formed concrete overlaid with dressed stone — but the most arresting thing for me was the beautiful typeface used for the Hebrew words *Beth Hatefutsoth* writ large to the right of the entrance: בית התפוצות

And we began, up the flight of stairs from the busy lobby.

Many histories of the Diaspora mark its beginning with the ninth day of the Hebrew month of Ab, in 70 C.E., the day of the destruction of the Second Temple by the Romans. And there in the entryway, copies of the huge tumbled stones of the Temple, and behind, a copy of the Arch of Titus, the triumphal monument erected in Rome to commemorate the destruction and sacking of the city of Jerusalem, complete with the Roman legionnaire marching away with the sacred Temple Menorah. That arch still stands in Rome; the Dome of the Rock and the Al Aksar Mosques rise on the Temple Mount. Christianity and Islam, offsprings of ancient Judaism, are central realities of the Diaspora, often decisive in shaping the

172

Jewish experience. They do and will continue to shape it as well as the future of the State of Israel.

Faces. "What Is a Jewish Face?"

That was the caption above a dozen projection screens, two feet by two feet, and on each a Jewish Face. And every 10 seconds in random sequence the image changed: another face, another Jewish face. It was all of humanity, *all* of humanity. There was no question. And I was immediately moved to tears: the dark Arab face of the Yemenite Jew; the long beard and *shtreiml* of the Eastern European Hasidic Jew; the bright face of a fair young girl with golden hair, windblown; a dark-eyed young man, strong face, chiseled features. From Italy? Greece? Persia? A Sabra? They are all chosen well: eyes bright with the fire of life and each with its joy, distinct and individual. The Jew is everyman.

A *viglied.*

A lullaby drifted through the hall that led to a series of rooms. They housed the Jewish traditions of life: birth, circumcision, childhood, Bar Mitzva, learning, prayer, marriage and death. The lullaby, a Yiddish song I had heard only a few times before, like the faces, reached deep inside me in an instant. We went back to *Beth Hatefutsoth* two more times in our short month in Israel, and that elusive melody has come to symbolize all I saw, all I experienced in that extraordinary place — the sweet lilting tune and the words expressing all the mother's love, the joy of life, and at the same time, deep sadness and pain, the struggle for life of the *shtetl* Jew that is my father and mother, their fathers and mothers.

Everything in the "museum" is instructive, didactic, intended to teach and inform about the life of the Diaspora. The unifying thread is simply the people who call themselves Jews, who share some part or variation of that identity, that consciousness. There is much at *Beth Hatefutsoth* about Judaism: its rituals, ceremony, obligations and responsibilities. The rites of passage through life were institutionalized in ancient Israel, and through the Bible and Talmud they have been codified. But in all the Jewish communities of the world, differences have evolved. They may be as subtle as the phrasing of the melodic *nign* that accompanies a particular prayer: sung one way in one village and another way in a neighboring *shtetl*. On the other hand, the differences may be radical: the Ashkenazic versus the Sephradic rite; the Misnagdic adherence to the word of the Talmudic *halakhah* (law) versus the Hasidic embrace of the ecstasy of emotional mysticism; or the even more divisive split of the Karaites, who rejected the Talmud in toto and remained the Children of the Text (Bible). They were not even considered Jews by the Tsarist police.

But there are more profound differences than those found in the practice of the rituals of Judaism. The differences are racial, ethnic, cultural, linguistic and customary. Even the historic consciousnesses of the Jewish communities of the world are different. Only the events that *preceded* the very first exile of the Jews at the hands of Nebuchadnezzar in 586 B.C.E. — the Babylonian Exile — are for the most part universally accepted. The task which *Beth Hatefutsoth* has undertaken is nearly the universal history of the last 2,500 years — wherever on the face of the earth Jews have found a home, however temporary so many of them tragically happened to be. That is the scope of the museum, formallly named The Nahum Goldmann Museum of the Jewish Diaspora.

Because of the ambitiousness of the undertaking, *Beth Hatefutsoth* must be more than a museum. It must be more than room after room displaying artifacts, shards and memorabilia. It must also be a library, a storehouse of the available information about all the communities throughout those 25 centuries. For the Jews whose ancestors lived for 40 generations in Damascus and in this generation fled for their lives to Israel, *Beth Hatefutsoth* must be and is a repository of the experience of those 40 generations: the heritage of the Damascan Jew, the source of his mother tongue and the crucible of his consciousness as a Jew, a Syrian and a human being. He may now be a citizen of the State of Israel but he is more, and any denial of those other dimensions of his inheritance is both an escape from reality and an attack on his being. The Syrian Jew, the Polish Jew, the American Jew, the Yemenite Jew, they may all reach for the touchstone of their own past.

During each of the three visits we saw both school children and large groups of solidiers dressed in their fatigue greens, and like nearly every random group of Israelis, their faces were as varied as those we had seen on the screens at the entry way. And for them *Beth Hatefutsoth* has another vital function. Consider the Syrian Jew who fled as a child to Israel and now bunks with the son of German Jewish refugees during his stint in the I.D.F. (Israel Defense Forces). Who is this stranger who also calls himself a Jew? The museum has to be a school; it must teach in striking terms and convey the complexity, diversity, richness, universality and the tragedy of the Diaspora experience for all Jews and gentiles alike. And wisely, the artifacts are not allowed to sit in exhibition cases gathering dust. They speak out — some of them literally, in the animation of masterful dioramas, sculpture, paintings, film, slides, dialogues, debates. Even the computer information storage banks, which have been used for amassing data on Jewish communities thgroughout the world, have been made available as a pedagogical tool, testing the visitor or pouring out the available information on the smallest Jewish settlement in the far reaches of nowhere.

Beyond the color slides and music of a dozen different Jewish marriages is a short display on the theme of relationships: peers, parent-child, man-woman, brother-sister, adult-old age, the very young and the very old. Again, the diversity of the Diaspora is explored while emphasizing the common values of compassion, justice and respect nurtured by Biblical and Talmudic tradition.

There is a wonderful section on the "Community," which examines the social, religious, economic and political institutions of the Diaspora. And though, throughout the world, variation clearly exists, the common communal needs prescribed by Judaism are apparent: alms for the poor, houses of study, the ritual slaughterer, the *mikveh* (ritual baths), the burial society, orphanage, the scribe and the rabbinate. Nearly an entire floor is devoted to the beautiful scale models of representative synagogues around the world: Venice; Newport, Rhode Island; the Altenschul of Prague; Dura Europus, one of the oldest; Toledo; Amsterdam; Worms; Cochin, India; modern suburban America; the wooden synagogue of pre-Holocaust Russia and more.

Each distinct, each out of a separate archtectural tradition, and yet each is a synagogue, with its *bimah* (central reading platform), its arc — the sacred place where resides the *sefer torah,* the holy torah. The models are more than studies in the exquisite reproduction of reality in precious minuscule. Just as the question "What is a Jewish Face?" is answered with the diversity of all humanity smiling out twice as big as life, the models of the synagogues, to the scale a tenth, a hundredth the size of life, are a testament to the varied cultures of the Diaspora. Common Jewish values were planted deeply in the rich soils of a dozen nations, and there the holiest of houses were built in the tradition of their gentile neighbors; the holy songs influenced by the native folk melodies; and the same is true of the foods, clothing, language, modes of livelihood, art, thought and daily life. All this, while maintaining an identity: "I am a Jew."

At *Beth Hatefutsoth* generalizations are not sufficient; something of substance must be said about as many of the major Jewish communities of the Diaspora as possible. And there begins a chronological search into nearly 20 such communities, using all of the tools of theater, art, pedagogy, data retrieval systems and the tasteful magic of modern audio-visual techniques.

An example: In the 13th century, Benjamin of Tudela (northern Spain) set out on a journey circling the Mediterranean Sea. His journal of those travels is a rare document of that era, one of the most informative and colorful accounts of community after community. And as a Jew, Benjamin took special note of the state and condition of his co-religionists wherever he went. He was animated by the very same spirit that has built *Beth Hatefutsoth.* A little alcove is devoted to a pictorial and narrative presentation of the journal, amply enriched with direct quotations from the pen of the author himself. Simply put, it is an animated cartoon with an accompanying recorded narration. The audience can choose either a Hebrew or English rendition (the languages of all the displays). It is done with humor, artistic taste and creativity, and all the while, a map traces the path of Benjamin's travels. A child of six or grandfather of 96 would have no trouble understanding the experience of that brave and perceptive traveler of 700 years ago, nor the life of each of the Jewish communities he described, from Rome to Baghdad, Jerusalem to Cairo.

It is worth noting some eras of the Diaspora to which special attention is given. There are no surprises for someone who has read any brief survey of Jewish history.

The Babylonian era of the Talmud and the academies of higher learning at Sura, Punbeditha and Nehardia are shown. The famous debate between Saadiah Gaon and the Exilarch, the chief of the Jewish community, is presented as a dialogue between two men, each supporting one of the two positions: Saadiah's, the immutability of law, law above those in positions of power; and the Exilarch, that those invested with power are the sovereign interpreters and formulators of the law. Here the Jew is seen within Bayblonian society but as part of the nearly autonomous community of his co-religionists. The theme of Jewish autonomy is explored elsewhere: in the Poland of King Casimir the Great in the 17th century, and under the Umayaad and Abbasid Caliphs in Spain and Baghdad.

The interaction between the Jews and the Greeks has had a great effect on all of Western civilization, and in the extraordinary Hellenistic city of Alexandria, *Beth Hatefutsoth* explores the final tragic confrontation and destruction of what had been the largest concentration of Jews in a single city in the ancient or medieval worlds (surpassed for the first time perhaps by the Jews of Warsaw in the 19th century). The era of the Pale of Settlement is also a major focus, with emphasis on the socio-economic sources of anti-Semitism in the Slavic lands.

One goes on to view the Jew within Roman, Islamic and Christian society in Italy, North Africa, Spain, France, England, the Germanies and the great haven in Holland, to which the remnant of the generations of Spanish Jewry fled after their expulsion in 1492. And also the settlements under the Ottoman Turk, in Istanbul and Thessalonica, where Spanish surnames were to be found in abundance until the modern catastrophe of Nazism, which nearly extinguished the last flame of every Jewish community that came within its maniacal power.

During my three visits I don't recall any specific reference to the Falashas of Ethiopia in the permanent exhibit. I have since learned from the Museum newsletter, Feb., 1980 that a "Mini-Exihibit" entitled "The Jews of Ethiopia" was on display at *Beth Hatefutsoth* for several months in

1979 consisting of "60 color slides on the life of the Falashas in Ethiopia taken during the past 10 years as well as photographs from the collection of Dr. Jacques Faitlovitch (1881-1955), the outstanding Polish-born researcher who 'discovered' the Falashas in the first half of the century." *Beth Hatefutsoth* also has as part of its video-film library, a 30-minute color film by Meyer Levin, called "The Falashas — Jews in Ethiopia." The museum has clearly concerned itself with the Falashas, but their apparent absence from the readily visible, permanent collection, indicates some equivocation of their acceptance as a *bona fide* community of the Diaspora.

Near the end of the sequence of presentations on separate Jewish communities, a sparse room has been set aside with a number of TV monitors; surrounding them are seats, with earphones. One can watch three 20-minute documentary films, each an autobiography narrated in the first person, Jewish lives in an Eastern European *shtetl*, Fez and Thessalonica. All abstractions, historical generalizations and phraseology are swept away; in their place, the lives of three Jews, born, raised, educated and involved in the life of their town. They are individuals with very different perspectives on life and their purpose in it, both as Jews and in their consciousness as Pole, Moroccan and Greek. The scenes appear to be taken from family albums for the most part, though in the Polish film I recognized many of Roman Vishniac's striking photographs. The three lives taken together, the startling differences, the overriding similarities, the moving universality of both their Jewishness and their humanness, make these films a highlight of the museum.

All three of these communities have been nearly destroyed. The Nazis killed almost all the Jews of Warsaw and Thessalonica, and the vestige of Jewish life in Poland and Greece hardly suggests the once vital culture and community. The persecution and recriminations following the creation of the State of Israel have virtually ended any chance for normal Jewish life in Fez and dozens of other Arab towns and cities from Morocco to Iraq. Those Jewish populations, some thousands of years old, many having origins which long pre-date the arrival of Islam, have had no choice but to flee to Israel. In those Arab cities from which they fled, little remains of the Jewish community.

The Diaspora experience suggests many more questions than there are answers available. The most basic of these is simply: "Why did it happen? Why did Jews find their way to every last coner of the earth?" Christian dogma, popularly accepted and officially approved until the pronouncements of the Second Vatican Council in 1964 under Pope John XXIII, in large part explains why. The Christian world held the Jews responsible for — guilty of — the crucifixion of Jesus after they rejected his messianism. The Diaspora and the incalculable persecutions through those

177

2,000 years were viewed as God's punishment, and many under that banner carried out the cruelties and barbarities in His name. There can be no understanding of the world dispersion of the Jews without insight into anti-Semitism, ancient, medieval and modern; its social, economic, psychological and political dimensions.

Exhibits in a museum, even using the creative techniques of *Beth Hatefutsoth*, can only begin to suggest answers to such complex issues. Instead, a great hall of memorial has been built to house the *Scroll of Fire*, a book with a leaf for each week of the year, each recording one of the tragic martyrdoms of the Diaspora, a brief sentence or two, a suggestion of the pain and the agony. The sound of a horn quietly echoes between the stone walls, and suspended from the high ceiling, imprisoned in layer after layer of black steel bars of diminishing thickness, burns the fire, the *ner tomid,* the Eternal Light. There can be no understanding of the Dispersion without empathy for its pain as well as its joys.

The joys are varied and manifold: room after room is devoted to the creativity of those 2,500 years. A half dozen distinct languages evolved through those generations, and with each a vital body of literature. Yiddish, Ladino, Aramaic and then the rebirth of Hebrew as a vernacular language in Israel. Case after case, exhibit after exhibit: newspapers in half a dozen alphabets and 20 languages to chronicle the course of Jewish life, and books to match from an equal number of publishing houses around the world. And what was the work of the Jew? What did he or she do to earn a livelihood? To what end were those energies devoted?

Beth Hatefutsoth tries to suggest the "contribution of the Jews." But like the dozen books I have come across that try to enumerate and identify the deeds and the men that were "Jewish," it appears trite and has the smack of petty boasting. I am convinced that it is more a problem of the limitations of space and time than one of attitude and philosophy. Far more effective was an exhibit of three contemporary generations in three different Jewish families. It is a portrayal that suggests another critical question: What is the future of the disparate Jewish communities in the generations to come? What will be the bonds of Jewish cohesion in the absence of ritual observance and synagogue membership?

The final rooms, devoted to the struggle for and realization of the State of Israel, are at least a partial answer to those questions. The ingathering of the exiles is one of the most remarkable human dramas in modern times. All of those peoples of diverse races, languages, nations, cultures and outlooks, thrown together, and most, tragically not by choice but because Israel represented the only available refuge. With the existence of the State of Israel, the Diaspora will clearly never be the same.

I am a Jew of the Diaspora. All Jews are, except for the sabras born after 1948. And in a most important sense they too are the children, not of Judea or Samaria, Saul, David or Solomon of those ancient times, but of the experience of the Diaspora. Whether with pride, shame or in seeming oblivion, they, as all Jews, wear the cultural vestments of those 2,500 years.

Months after we returned to Soller, my 11-year-old son ingenuously said, "You know what I like best about Israel? *Beth Hatefutsoth*." The museum is a success because it demonstrates and teaches the affirmation of life and what it means to be a Jew under the best and even under the worst conditions. That struggle for life is the inspiration of the Jewish experience. It is a struggle shared by all humanity.

May, 1981

There Is a Breira

THE thunder produced by major Jewish organizations and periodicals through malicious attacks on Breira — the organization founded in 1973 to advocate a program of peace in the Middle East as an "alternative" to the lack of motion towards an accommodation with the Arab neighbors on the part of the Israeli government — helped make the first Membership Conference of Breira a greater success than anticipated by its leaders.

Held Feb. 20-21 at the 4-H Center in Chevy Chase, Md., the Conference unexpectedly attracted more than 300 members and was indeed hardworking and generally well-organized. It was highlighted by a certain brilliance of intellectual and devotional approach that this writer has seldom met in the hundreds of conferences he has attended.

The participants were young people in the overwhelming majority, in the 20's, 30's and early 40's — many professionals, teachers, rabbis and graduate students. Breira is a coalition aiming to win Zionists and non-Zionists, religious and secular Jews to its program — but the majority present were Zionists and religious Jews, and in the main progressive-minded.

The survival of Israel was a dominating factor in all the discussions.

The attacks on Breira by Jewish leaders, the *Jewish Week* and the vicious McCarthyite pamphlet *Breira, Counsel for Judaism,* by Rael Jean Isaac, clearly lie in their teeth when they accuse Breira as being partisan only to the Arab cause and "traitors" to Israel.

Israeli Major-Gen. (Ret.) Mattityahu Peled, representative of the Israeli-Palestinian Peace Council, in his speech stated that the attitude of the Jewish Establishment in the USA is that American Jews should not be "subject to the debates that are taking place in Israel." He pointed out that "it is not really opposition to discussion because the *hawks* get a warm welcome here."

There were 12 Educational Seminars, which anyone could attend, and five Policy-Making Commissions, one of which all members chose when registering. Such seminars indicate the interest of Breira in Jewish affairs at home and abroad: Israeli Economy and the Social Gap (dealing with the Oriental Jews and the Israeli Arabs and their special problems); West Bank: New Voices, New Options; Jewish Education; Diaspora-Israel

180

Relations; Arms, Security and the Nuclear Deterrent; and U.S. Foreign Policy.

In the seminar on "How the Jewish Press Works," it was heartwarming to hear one man, with our Sept. 1976 issue in his hand, say, "My wife gave me this magazine, which I never saw before. It's the September issue and has an editorial on Entebbe. And already back in September this magazine made an analysis that could very well be adopted by Breira." He then quoted two paragraphs from the editorial. (A few hundred copies of JEWISH CURRENTS were distributed — as were many other journals — and one could see it being read by many present.)

The five Policy-Making Commissions were of key importance as truly democratic opportunities to mould the resolutions presented to the plenary session. The Commissions were: Quality of Jewish Life, Diaspora Involvement in Israeli Society, Israel-Diaspora Relations, Peace in the Middle East (which I attended) and U.S. Policy in the Middle Eeast.

Since Breira's position is so brazenly misrepresented by defenders of Israeli government policy, it is important to cite the resolution on Peace in the Middle East:

"Breira believes that peace is possible only if major and mutual concessions are made by both sides of the conflict.... We believe that Israel cannot achieve a secure and lasting peace without: (1) a willingness to negotiate on the basis of the June 4, 1967 borders with such rectifications of those borders without which Israel's Security would be clearly and substantially affected. An indication of this willingness would be the immediate cessation of Jewish settlement of the occupied territories. (2) A recognition of the Palestinians' right to national self-determination including, should the Palestinians so choose, a state alongside Israel in the territories from which Israel withdraws. In this regard, we call upon the Israeli government to enter into negotiations with a recognized and authoritative representative body of the Palestinian Arab people, not excluding, on the basis of mutual recognition, the Palestine Liberation Organization."

The resolution later says, "We take note of indications that certain Arab countries and Palestinian leaders are willing to recognize Israel's right to exist. We call upon these, as well as other Arab spokesmen to publicly acknowledge and confirm these indications and, further, to clarify that they recognize Israel's right to exist as a sovereign Jewish state within secure borders. Such recognition is essential for successful peace negotiations."

The keynote address was given by Major-Gen. (Ret.) Mattityahu Peled. He brought greetings from the Israeli Council for Israel-Palestinian Peace, organized Dec. 1975 with the participation of 130 leading intellectuals of Israel. Breira maintains a close relationship with the Israeli Council and

181

Peled had just finished a rather rocky 22-day tour of the United States. Rocky because the Establishment organizations exerted great pressure on the Jewish community to prevent attendance at his meetings. Still, he did meet with hundreds of people.

In a quiet, unassuming style, Peled stated that the PLO began to review its position in 1974. In 1975 it was clear a process of moderation was taking place. The Israeli government refused to take notice of the new developments in the PLO — and this failure spurred the organization of the Council for Israel-Palestinian Peace. The Council issued a Manifesto March, 1976 with 10 points. In July the Council received word from the PLO that it is interested in talking. PLO felt the Council's Manifesto could serve as a basis for discussion. Peled stated that the Israeli government, when consulted, saw nothing wrong in such a meeting.

Peled said: "We learned there is indeed a profound development in PLO." Significantly, PLO informed the Council that it is ready to make peace with the idea of the existence of Israel. Peled stressed that the Council's position (and Breira's) is that the PLO must amend the Palestine Covenant before discussions can go ahead.

The keynote address concluded with the admonition that Israel cannot stand aside as an impartial observer. Israel can play an active role by approving developments that are constructive and suggesting rewards for further progress toward genuine peace with Israel.

Irving Howe, author of *World of Our Fathers,* in a caustically humorous speech explained that he is not a member of Breira but accepted the invitation to speak because of the attacks against Breira by the Jewish Establishment, which fears dissenting opinion like the plague.

As expected, the big brains of the Jewish Defense League had a scraggly picketline of young people for a time on the sidewalk in front of the 4-H Conference Center. They bore signs with such sweet slogans as "Death to Breira Traitors," "Not One Inch of Retreat," "There is No Palestine," "Peled Go Home," "Sinai is Jewish," and so on and on.

While the Conference members were at dinner, the JDL'ers succeeded in evading the security men and broke into the lobby right outside the dining room, shouting "PLO Must Go!" again and again. The Breira leadership appealed to those present to remain seated and let the security police handle the situation. The JDL'ers caused some damage to typewriters and furniture but were finally pressed back to the sidewalks outside the hall.

The majority present were shocked to find that the executive committee had agreed to allow a speaker from the JDL 10 minutes at the Mock Press Conference (where the members ask questions of the leadership) following dinner the next evening. This was done in the name of "dialogue" with those we disagree as well as agree with, explained the Chairman of the Conference and of Breira, Rabbi Arnold Jacob Wolf. His agreement to the

182

speaker did not show lack of courage but of judgment because Rabbi Wolf, Hillel director at Yale, is a man of great courage to maintain his position with Breira under the pressure exerted against him.

The speaker for the JDL was one of its national leaders, a Bonnie Peacher, who immediately anounced that one of the prime objectives of the JDL is "to get Breira" by any means necessary. She said that the "JDL believes every inch of land is Jewish land given to the Jews by God" and that "Breira represents a greater threat to the Jewish people than anyone else."

The JDL incident was a minor flaw in a Conference which reflected the coming of age of a most vital and important organization in Jewish life — Breira.

The leadership of Breira deserves commendation for organizing and conducting such a rewarding Conference. Its position on Middle East Peace and on the problems of the Diaspora are harbingers of changes that will have to take place if there is to be an Israel—Arab peace, with justice for both sides, and if Jewish life in the USA is to break with the conformism, fear of healthy dissent and check-book dominance that stifle it today.

April, 1977

To Our Friends Who Support the PLO: an Open Letter

By MORTON STAVIS and ANNETTE T. RUBINSTEIN

THE object of this letter is not to urge that you discontinue supporting the PLO. Our purpose is rather to suggest that you build on your support of the PLO to influence it in directions which are most calculated to achieve its fundamental objective, namely, a Palestinian state.

Essentially, we shall be outlining an approach not much different from that which many of you have urged on progressives like ourselves in our attitude towards Israel. For some years, because of our concern that Israel survive, we have indeed been striving to change the policies of that state towards Palestinians. Because of the dramatic changes within Israel which we shall describe in this letter, it is now urgent for you to do comparable work within the PLO.

We assume that you share our view of the ultimate resolution of the Israeli-Palestinian issue — the two-state solution, a Palestinian state existing peacefully alongside the Jewish State of Israel, basically the partition idea promulgated by the UN in 1947 — and that the only useful question is when and how this solution will be achieved. Obviously the sooner and the more peacefully the better, so that the Israeli and Palestinian peoples may move together towards achievement of the economic and social advances for which both yearn.

If you still harbor the view that somehow the State of Israel can be made to disappear, then this letter is not directed to you; yet if you read on you will understand why we believe that the practical consequence of your position, if adhered to by the Palestinian leadership, would prevent your major objective, the creation of a Palestinian state.

The two-state solution is today, even more clearly than in 1947, the only answer to the otherwise intractable confrontation between Israelis and Palestinians. To be sure, during the 1930's and even until 1947 there were some leading Jewish figures and also political parties in Palestine who urged a bi-national state for the entire area. Continuous violent confrontations with Palestinians whose leadership had bitterly fought

184

against growing Jewish presence made it obvious that a single state would merely set the stage for a bloody civil war.

Andrei Gromyko stated the conclusive argument for partition before the UN in 1947. Referring to the general support of partition within the UN, he said:

"This can be explained only by the fact that any other possibility of solving the Palestine problem seemed unrealistic and impractical. I refer also to the possibility of establishing a single Arab-Jewish independent state with equal rights for Jews and Arabs. A study of the Palestine problem... has indicated that the Jews and Arabs in Palestine do not want to and are unable to live under one rule. The logical conclusion of this is that if the two peoples residing in Palestine — each with deep historic roots in the country — cannot live together within the same framework, the only thing left to do is to set up, instead of one state, two states — an Arab and a Jewish one...

"Those who oppose the partition of Palestine into two independent democratic countries contend that such a decision aims at injuring the Arab population in Palestine and the Arab countries. The Soviet delegation cannot agree with this point of view. The partition proposal is not aimed against the Arabs... On the contrary, in the view of the Soviet delegation, it intends to benefit the basic national interests of the two peoples, in the interest of both the Arab people and the Jewish people."

It is pointless to belabor the refusal of the Arab peoples to implement the partition plan of the UN. The fact is the Israelis accepted it and achieved statehood. The Arabs rejected it and brought about first the 19-year-long occupation of the West Bank and Gaza by Jordan and Egypt. The tables turned in 1967 and for the past 12 years it is Israelis who have prevented a Palestinian state from coming into being. But no matter who is obstructing the creation of a Palestinian state, fundamentally partition remains the only plan presenting a chance for peace and for the achievement of the national aspirations of *both* peoples.

How is the elusive two-state solution to be brought about? Discussions of the Israeli-Palestinian conflict almost invariably involve digging up past claims or pointing out present wrongs to establish that both sides have rights and that neither side is blameless. There was Deir Yassin, but also Hebron; villages in Lebanon are being bombed and innocent persons are being killed while athletes in Munich and airline passengers in Lod Airport were also slaughtered. There are endless disputes about the alleged denial of human rights to Palestinians in the West Bank and Gaza, and equally heated discourses about the security threat to Israel by the PLO as necessitating Israeli occupation. The tales of horror suggest no solutions; they merely underscore the need for finding a solution.

The solutions offered generally come to, "Why doesn't Begin do thus

185

and so?" or "Why doesn't Arafat make such and such a pronouncement?" These seem to presume that a single action or statement by one leader can elicit a hoped-for response from his counterpart and voila! an instant resolution.

It should by now be clear that any such approach leads to a deadend. Mr. Begin and his political supporters do not believe in a two-state solution. More than 30 years ago Mr. Begin led the unsuccessful opposition to a Zionist acceptance of the partition plan and he has not modified his views since. No one we know can say with certainty how Mr. Arafat and his close supporters really feel about a two-state solution. But regardless of their personal feelings, they are so hemmed in by the delicate political balance within the PLO, and so effectively imprisoned by years of their own propaganda calling for the destruction of Israel, that even if they believed a two-state solution was appropriate, they would probably not be able publicly to state that position to their constituency.

In our view, the starting point for any serious discussion of an approach to peace must be not the actions or pronouncements of political leaders but rather political movements among the people — Israelis and Palestinians. We suggest that there is an historic opportunity at this time and in the immediate future to resolve this bitter conflict.

Within the past year and a half there has developed in Israel a broad-based mass movement directly confronting the Begin government and the other political forces within the State of Israel that are opposed to an accommodation with the Palestinians. The Peace Now movement includes many groups of varying ideas all seeking such an accommodation. Every element of the Peace Now movement opposes the government's settlement policy in the West Bank and Gaza; there is considerable support for a two-state solution, and many are searching for a formula acceptable to the people of Israel by which negotiations with the PLO can be undertaken.

Recently this Peace Now movement undertook the responsibility of communicating with Jewish people in the Diaspora to explain why the Begin policy is unacceptable and threatens the State of Israel. Peace Now representatives have visited Jewish communities in practically every major city in the United States, as they had done in Europe, meeting with Jewish rank-and-file and leadership to urge a break in the hitherto uncritical support of the Begin government's policies. And they are succeeding. The beginning of a change in the position of American Jews is well illustrated by the comment of Theodore Mann, president of the Conference of Presidents of Major Jewish Organizations, in Montreal last Nov., "... The present Israel cabinet is beyond the consensus within the American Jewish community and maybe in Israel."

Despite the fact that the PLO and most of the Arab world have attacked the Camp David agreement, there is no question that the Israeli Peace Now movement grew out of Mr. Sadat's visit. When he went to Jerusalem and said plainly and convincingly that he accepted Israel's existence (thus far the only Arab leader to do so since the creation of Israel in 1948), he started a train of consequences which led directly to the peace agreement and now to the steady withdrawal which will eventually require the removal of Jewish stettlements from that area. These agreements were achieved despite Mr. Begin's reluctance and the campaign promises he had made only six months before. His hand was forced by massive peace demonstrations in Tel Aviv which, in terms of percentage of population participating, made the American peace demonstrations during the Vietnam War seem comparatively puny.

The simple fact is that Mr. Sadat offered the Israeli people what they have always striven for: recognition and peace. This offer, regardless of the doubts raised by some Israelis, aroused such an overwhelming response within the Israeli people that Mr. Begin had to move towards accomodation with Egypt even against his wishes and against the program of the political party which put him into power.

The Peace Now movement in Israel showed extraordinary strength during the negotiations with Egypt, but while it is able to mount huge demonstrations against new settlements in the West Bank and Gaza, it cannot *at this time* call for the evacuation of those areas by Israel military forces because the PLO has not given the signal which Mr. Sadat gave — an assurance of the acceptance of the State of Israel in a form and with an earnestness which the Israeli people can find believable. In the present posture of the PLO, Israelis have some reason to consider that withdrawal from the West Bank and Gaza would simply give the enemy a chance to move rocket emplacements closer to urban centers.

What a response would be forthcoming from the Israeli people if the PLO leadership were to state clearly and unequivocally that it is willing to accept the State of Israel and thus allay the fears of the Israeli people with respect to their own security! An overwhelming political pressure for peace would take shape within the Israeli body politic and the Israeli political leadership would be forced — exactly as it was with respect to the Sinai — to yield to the wishes of the Israeli people, vacating the West Bank and the Gaza Strip in exchange for peace.

It is argued by some PLO supporters that because of ancient historical affinity the Israeli people simply could not, in a peaceful way, do for the West Bank what they did for the Sinai. Opinion polls in Israel as recently as Sept., 1979, some time after the Camp David agreement, show that by a large majority the people understand that peace is not possible without a settlement with the Palestinians. Beyond that, the Israeli Peace Now movement, having forced Mr. Begin's hand in the Sinai, has shifted its focus to the West Bank, and the physical evidence of Israeli popular opposition to the government's settlement policy has been as large as it was when its attention was directed to Egypt.

The scenario for peace from the Israel side is thus clear and the political machinery for achieving peace is discernible. Reassured of their security, the Israeli people would readily once again accept the two-state formula which they accepted from the UN in 1947. But this scenario at present still appears to be an impossible dream. The leadership of the PLO doubtless understands the dynamics of public opinion in Israel, yet it refuses to address the essential audience — the people of Israel — to show that it understands their concern for security and their own nationhood. Such an address would certainly permit the Peace Now movement to call for withdrawal from the West Bank and Gaza. Instead the PLO leadership has embarked on a brilliant world-wide diplomatic campaign, speaking to everyone but the Israeli people. Recently some West Bank mayors ready to attend the *New Outlook* symposium in Washington, D.C. met such intimidation that they withdrew.

PLO statements so far focus entirely on the theme of recognition for the PLO and negotiation with it. Of course peace will require negotiation with the PLO. But exclusive concentration on that procedure rather than on the *content* of negotiations seems to emphasize concern about political leadership among the Palestinians rather than about a basis for peace between Israelis and Palestinians. Beyond that, some of the recent statements by PLO leaders, in their subtleties and nuances, seem designed to discourage any idea that the PLO would ever accept a two-state solution; naturally these undercut the Israeli Peace Now movement.

For example, the Rev. Jesse Jackson reported that Mr. Arafat is flexible because he does not seek "to exterminate Jews." Many Jews, in or out of Israel, must read that as a reaffirmance by the PLO leadership that it *does* want to exterminate the *State of Israel.* The excitement generated by the Middle East travels of important American Black leaders, following Andrew Young's resignation, quickly evaporated when it became clear that PLO leaders were not prepared to give the unambiguous statements, sought by the Black leaders, accepting the existence of the State of Israel. Every time a PLO representative makes what appears to be a conciliatory statement it is directed to an American or other foreign newspaper or politician — never to its own constituency or their allies (and Israelis read these statements very carefully); their pronouncements continue to be brutal. Thus on Jan. 1 the PLO representative Hani el Chasan declared on Radio Iran: "We derive our main support from the Iranian Revolution and Khomeini. In five years we shall proclaim a Palestinian government and in 15 years we hope to destroy Israel... It is our hope that the leaders of Iran and Palestine will enter Jerusalem arm in arm."

The current strategy of the PLO leadership seems rooted in the idea that

Israel can be so isolated and pressured (even by the United States) that it will have to sue for peace with the PLO on any terms, without the minimum assurances of security its people must demand.

The strategy will not work. There are limits to the pressures that Israel's friends can impose, oil or no oil. Recent developments involving those with whom the PLO had allied itself will significantly affect the PLO's image within the United States. Thus the Iranian turmoil, which is likely to have long-term impact, has undoubtely made Israel's concern for its own security much more meaningful not only in Israel but among most Americans. The Palestinian people themselves are the best proof of how a determined group dedicated to nationhood can outlast and overcome any amount of external pressure.

Although the PLO leadership is, at present, either unwilling or unable to address the concerns of the Israeli people and its Peace Now movement, there is a wide spectrum of opinion among the Palestinians, including many of those within the leadership of the PLO, who recognize that just as Israel needs peace with the Palestinians in order to secure its existence, so the Palestinians need peace with the Israelis in order to achieve their statehood. For more than 50 years — antedating the creation of the State of Israel — Palestinian policy has been controlled by those who refused to recognize the legitimacy of the rights, first of Jewish people, and then of the State of Israel, in any part of Palestine. It is pointless to reargue that issue. As of today, Israeli statehood exists and cannot be wished away. The vast bulk of the Palestinian people must understand the reality of Israeli statehood. Similarly, the majority of the Israel people must understand that, whatever may have been the situation previously, the Palestinian people has now achieved a national consciousness which will not rest until it comes to fruition in statehood.

The problem for the Palestinian people then is no different from the problem for the Israeli people: How can Palestinians move their own political leadership so as to bring about acceptance of a two-state solution, which is the only way the Palestinian people can achieve their statehood. Rejection of partition in 1947 prevented a Palestinian state from coming into being. Such rejection still stands in the way.

We cannot ignore differences between political forms, nor can we dismiss the terrible impact of assassination as a political weapon. Nevertheless the Palestinian people have to move their own political leadership, as the Israeli people are doing with respect to their own leaders. It is, of course, presumptuous for outsiders to tell any political group how to conduct its internal battles; yet with due deference we suggest that those Palestinians and supporters of PLO who agree that the two-state solution is the only answer should at this time re-evaluate their tactics. Because of

189

developments within Israel, the time may have arrived when it is appropriate to take a public stand to move the leadership.

The potential for interaction between the Palestinian and Israeli peoples makes it even more clear that the time has come for open debate on this issue within the PLO. The Israeli Peace Now movement is by its *actions* sending clear signals to the Palestinian people. Were the signals to be reciprocated, not by mere phrases but through PLO action — the visible initiation of open debate within the PLO concerning parallel action with the Israeli Peace Now movement and the necessity of a two-state solution — the Peace Now movement in Israel would acquire even greater impact which, in turn, would strengthen similar forces within the PLO.

It is not slogans, rhetoric or word formulae that are involved. To be sure, rewriting the PLO Covenant would be decisive, but obviously that will be the *result,* not the beginning, of a change within the PLO. What is needed within the Palestinian movement now is the initiation of open discussion and debate, and serious consideration of relating to the Israeli people, and acceptance of partition.

That is where you come in. You can help induce that debate. The PLO has turned to progressive forces throughout the world seeking their support. The *quid pro quo* for such support should be a willingness to listen to outside voices, and if, as we assume, you yourself support a two-state solution, you ought to be urging the PLO to take positive steps to debate it openly and finally accept it.

We have been saying to the Israelis that a policy that does not address the problems of the Palestinians is not a viable policy for the Israelis. Should you not be making the parallel point to the PLO? Uncritical support of the Israeli government encourages Israeli intransigence. You should realize that blank check support of the PLO has exactly the same effect on that organization. There are signs, few but significant, that some Palestinians of considerable standing within the PLO are ready for the public debate which is required. At the recent *New Outlook* symposium, the large audience was much moved by constructive statements by Raymonda Tawil. She, and every effort of hers to generate public debate within the PLO on the need to accept a two-state solution, should receive your outspoken support.

The time for you to bring your influence to bear is now. Political activity in Israel is obviously heightened by the weakness of the present government and the elections scheduled for next year. If the present opportunities are missed, if the most promising peace movement in Israel's history is frustrated, if its people are forced to return to the view that "we have no choice," if the Israeli militants and expansionists remain in political power because of the people's fears for security, both the Israelis

190

and the Palestinians will have lost a chance to enjoy peace and separate statehood in the foreseeable future.

The history of the Middle East conflict includes a sad litany of missed opportunities, of the failures of political leaders to respond to signals from their counterparts. It would be tragic if this were repeated now when people are in motion — and when it is the people, not their leaders, who are signaling.

March, 1980

Kahane on a Rampage

By W.S. (WILLIAM SHNEYER)

IF the Arab intransigents ever needed documentation of the invalid generalization that "Zionism" is inherently expansionist and of the impossibility of achieving a compromise solution to the Middle East conflict, these books by the peripatetic Meir Kahane would be a gold mine.*. They present a repetitious distillation of the clerico-fascist ideology of this commuting demagogue which has been repudiated by the majority of Jews and by Zionist organizations both in the U.S. and in Israel. The books also abound in typographical errors and unattributed and undocumented quotations.

Kahane cloaks himself in *Ahavat Yisroel* (love of Jewry) as people chosen by G-d (MK spelling) for a unique role in history to whom "... normal rules of nationhood and statehood do not apply..." (p. 15).**Based on "divine revelation" he declares that "... there never will be such a thing as a 'Palestine' people or state. The Land of Israel, Eretz Yisroel, is the land of the Jewish people, and no one else's, in all its historical boundaries" (p. 21). Anybody who thinks otherwise and believes that there can be peace between Israel and its neighbors is "either a fool or a knave" for "... there will be no peace between Jews and Arabs so long as there remains a Jewish state of *any* kind no matter how small" (p. 26). As far as the Arabs are concerned, all they can do is "... ask to be allowed to live in Eretz Yisroel, but they can expect nothing more than that" (p. 24).

In line with his infamous support of U.S. intervention in Vietnam, Kahane sees as the greatest danger to Israel the growing movement among Israeli youth, students and other circles to support the right of Palestinian Arabs to self-determination alongside the Jewish state of Israel. He accuses this movement of "helping the enemy" just as the U.S. peace movement did, according to Kahane.

Kahane wants Israel "... to hold on to every inch of the land they liberated in 1967..." (p. 22). Moreover, he calls for a crash program of Jewish settlement in the occupied territories, including the heart of the major Arab cities such as Hebron, Jericho, Gaza and Ramallah, and for an organized campaign to induce Israeli Arabs to emigrate.

Our Challenge—The Chosen Land, by Rabbi Meir Kahane. Chilton Book Co. Radnor, Pa., 1974, 181 pages, $7.95. *The Story of the Jewish Defense League,* by Rabbi Meir Kahane. Chilton Book Co., Radnor, Pa., 1975, 338 pages, $7.95.
** Quotations are from *Our Challenge* unless otherwise noted.

192

In the tradition of the reactionary Revisionist wing of the Zionist movement, whose ideological heir Kahane is, he reserves his most vicious invective for the Left in the U.S. and in Israel. He blames all the social problems of the 60's and 70's in the U.S. on the New Left and warns against similar "danger" in Israel. He demagogically exploits the national nihilist tendencies in the New Left in order to attack the entire secular sector of the Jewish people. Kahane would destroy the historically democratic, pluralistic structure of the Jewish community both in the U.S. and Israel to advance the "only true Jewish" ideology as revealed to him.

Progressive Jewish secularists will not surrender to Kahane the exclusive right to *Ahavat Yisroel*. Their commitment to the survival of the Jewish people has grown and matured over the last three decades as a result of the tragedy of the Holocaust and the establishment of the State of Israel. They have outgrown the early vulgar atheistic tendencies and, while remaining secular in their philosophical outlook, have learned to understand the positive unifying role played by the Jewish religion during the years of dispersion and persecution as well as its contribution to the development of ethical values that are universally accepted.

Kahane attacks the educational system in Israel for not inculcating Israeli youth with his concept of the Jews as the "chosen people" and not teaching them "... that Jew-hatred is a *halakha dorot* (an eternal law)..." (p. 78). He rejects class struggle among Jews as divisive. Yet nowhere does he state how he proposes to solve the social problems in Israel.

The concept of Jews as a world people is anathema to Kahane unless it is based on religion, the Torah and the divine origin of the Jewish "nation." According to him the Jewish nation was created by God at Sinai. At the same time the Jews were given an "irrevocable title" to the entire land of Israel from Lebanon and Euphrates to the sea. Because of this gift the establishment of the State of Israel was pre-ordained and it would have risen without a Balfour or a League of Nations or a United Nations.

He denigrates the role of the predominatly secular pioneers who built the Israeli kibbutzim and institutions. Contrary to Kahane's thesis, it is very doubtful that the State of Israel would have been born without the basically secular Zionist movement, without the Haganah and the Palmach, It is historically dishonest for Kahane to lump toghether the heroes of the Warsaw Ghetto, the anti-fascist Jewish partisans of World War II and the Haganah with the reactionary Irgun terrorists for whose anti-Arab chauvinism Israel is still paying dearly.

All Jews outside of Israel, according to Kahane, are still in exile and in dire danger, "... for so long as one gentile lives opposite one Jew, the possibility of a Holocaust remains" (*Story,* p. 5). He performs some fancy gymnastics (in line with his American superpatriotism) not to deny that

193

Jews are loyal citizens of the countries they live in. At the same time he maintains that it is the obligation of every Jew to go to live in Israel. The problem of anti-Semitism in the U.S. receives a typically insidious Kahane treatment. He foresees the danger to the future of U.S. Jewry because "America is today a troubled land torn by racial passions and hatreds" (p. 123). He expects the Jews to become "... the major target of embittered masses of Americans" (p. 123). He sees such Jews as Jerry Rubin, Abbie Hoffman and Henry A. Kissinger being blamed for the defeat of the U.S. in Vietnam. On p. 124 he sees the Jews already being blamed for everything from the decline in social, moral and ethical values to the generation gap, spread of pornography and the change in sexual standards.

Yet Kahane does not attack the John Birchites, the Liberty Lobby, the Saxbes and the General Browns who would make Jews the scapegoats of U.S. social ills. He attacks the liberal Jews for being too prominent in the civil rights and the anti-Vietnam war movements, thus making themselves targets of the anti-Semites. One would expect the supermilitant Jewish "Defense" Leaguer to call for an all-out struggle against the anti-Semites in the U.S. Instead his only prescription is to run away to Israel in a mass emergency Aliya.

One wonders how this defeatist attitude toward anti-Semitism in the U.S. sits with those young people who have joined the JDL primarily because of their desire to act militantly in behalf of the Jewish people. Their experience over the past few years should have taught them that militancy alone is not the answer. What is needed in addition is clarity in defining the enemy, the allies and the goals. Kahane's hysterical exaggerations do none of these.

The story of the Jewish Defense League repeats and expands all of the by now familiar positions of Kahane and his JDL. The only basic addition is his claim of credit for moving the Jewish "Establishment" organizations into activity on behalf of Soviet Jews and the Jewish poor in the U.S. Unfortunately there is some substance in his claim.

This magazine has pointed out from the early days of JDL's unwelcome appearance on the Jewish scene (see Robert Marcus, Jan., 1970 and W.S., Sept., 1971) that there is a gap between the leadership of the major Jewish organizations, which is often chosen on the basis of the size of financial contributions they make, and the much less affluent majority of American Jews. The need for eliminating this gap and democratizing the Jewish community structure still exists.

There is one "achievement" that Kahane could possibly brag about but does not. That is the fact that, over the past few years, many Jewish organizations, while denouncing Kahane's tactics, have moved considerably to the right and have allowed the traditional coalition between Blacks and Jews to deteriorate. It is only lately that, spurred by the

194

economic crisis and isolation of Israel, new efforts at revitalizing this coalition have begun.

If Kahane and his ilk had a chance to become the dominant force in Israel, the present disproportionate influence of clerical forces would become even greater. What would happen to dissenters under that kind of regime can only be surmised. Kahane gives a clue by the labels he pins on those religious Jews who do not accept his interpretation of the religious law *(halacha)*. They are either "ignoramuses" (p. 162) or "empty heads" (p. 163). The revered Dr. Abraham Joshua Heschel is "...one of the great theological frauds of our time..." *(Story,* p. 260). Not to speak of those who are not religious at all and are "psychopathic leftists and pseudo-intellectuals" (p. 165). Shades of the Middle Ages! Kahane wants Israel to recognize that the Jewish people has a "holy character" and to incorporate this "holiness into itself" (p. 170). To prove this, *mezuzot* should be affixed to the public gates — even in predominatly non-Jewish areas!

What a mockery of Judaism and the prophetic tradition is Kahane's statement that "Our youth must be imbued with *Jewish* concepts..." which are "... not to be determined by liberalism or democracy or progressive circles" (p. 171). Arrogance growing out of Kahane's chauvinist nationalism has no bounds as witnessed by his statement on p. 173: "The Jewish people and state are not just one more people and state — they are spiritually greater than all the rest. We are not simply one more little, superfluous nation, but the heart and the reason for the world."

What a contrast between this nationalism gone wild and the humanist tradition of progressive secularists! They take second place to nobody in the feeling of pride at the resilience and the will to live exhibited by the Jewish people throughout its long history. Yet they know that not everything in Jewish life is positive (Kahane and the Jewish Defense League are obvious contemporary examples). Building upon the democratic humanist essence of Judaism, the Jewish people in most countries (including the U.S.) have always participated in numbers disproportionate with their percentage in the population as a whole in movements for social justice and progressive change. They will continue to work for creative survival of the Jewish people as an equal among other peoples and for a secure, independent Israel within negotiated and recognized borders.

It is a tribute to the good sense and the greatness of the Jewish people throughout the world that Kahane's suicidal prescription for an expansionist, militaristic, clerically dominated Israel and inner-oriented, isolated Jewish communities in the rest of the world have been rejected.

July-August, 1976

The Soviet View
of the Arab-Israel Conflict

By A.B. MAGIL

THERE is more than one Middle East conflict, but certainly the major and most persistent one is the Arab-Israel confrontation. A Soviet book on this conflict, especially one by a member of the USSR Academy of Sciences, could be an important contribution. Unfortunately, "could be" in this case fails to reach its target. *Anatomy of the Middle East Conflict* contains little "anatomy" in the sense of serious analysis, and is not even good journalism despite the author's considerable experience as a *Pravda* correspondent in several Arab countries*. Primakov draws on a large number of secondary sources to support the standard dogmas of Soviet anti-Israel policy. However, to his credit, though strongly anti-Zionist, he does not resort to the frenetic, mindless anti-Zionism that is the staple of so many Soviet publications and is often thinly disguised anti-Semitism. In several passages he condemns anti-Semitism, though he associates it exclusively with capitalism in general and Nazism in particular. It is sad that such minimal virtues in a writer from the first country of socialism need to be pointed out.

Primakov rightly views the Arab-Israel conflict as having internal and external causes. The internal causes are for him a tale of villains and victims: "Israel with its expansionist policy" versus "the Arab people of Palestine and the Arab countries in general." The external causes involve primarily the policy of the United States, "which has directly backed Israel's policy of expansion." He adds, more to the point, that the U.S. "is using the Middle East conflict in its struggle against the region's national liberation forces and world socialism."

Certainly there is much to criticize in the policies of Israel's various governments toward the Palestinian Arabs and the Arab countries. The term "expansionist" is in my opinion justified when applied to the 1956 invasion of Sinai and the creeping de facto annexationism pursued since the Six-Day War of June 1967. But contrary to Primakov's assertion that

---

* *Anatomy of the Middle East Conflict,* by Y.M. Primakov, tr. from Russian by H. Vladimirsky. Nauka Publishing House, Moscow, 1979 (Russian ed., 1978), 330 pages, indexed, $3.60.

196

the drive for additional territory became an article of faith of David Ben-Gurion and his colleagues as soon as the UN partition resolution was adopted, Don Peretz, an American political scientist who has been critical of Israeli governmental policies and has written sympathetically of the Arab situation, has stated: "Before June 4 [1967] only the Herut wing of the Gahal party [Begin's wing] made acquisition of territory beyond the 1949 armistice frontiers part of its ideology and dogma. Now, only the... Communists and Mapam, a leftist-oriented party in the coalition government, have taken a stand against retention of some occupied regions" ("Israel's Administration and Arab Refugees," *Foreign Affairs,* January, 1968).

After a capsule account of the early conflict between political Zionism and the Arab people of Palestine — a conflict in which undoubtedly great injustices were done to the Arabs — the author notes the creation of the State of Israel on the basis of the United Nations partition resolution of Nov. 29, 1947. However, Primakov amputates his own country's history by excluding the details of the crucial, perhaps decisive role played by the Soviet Union in the birth and survival of Israel. Only toward the end of the book does a hint of this appear: "... the Soviet Union recognized and supported the right of the Jewish population of Palestine to self-determination in 1948." Primakov makes no mention of Andrei Gromyko's eloquent address at the United Nations, March 14, 1947, in which Gromyko rooted the rights of Jews for "a state of their own" in the failure of the Western states to protect the very life of the Jewish people during World War II.

We are then told that after the partition resolution was adopted, "armed clashes began throughout Palestine in December 1947." How did thay begin? Who began them? Silence. Walter Laqueur, whose *A History of Zionism* (Holt, Rinehart and Winston, 1972) is cited favorably by Primakov in another context, tells us that in response to the UN resolution, "the Palestinian Arabs called a three-day protest strike, and *Jews in all parts of the country were attacked"* (p. 582, emphasis added). As is well known, bands of armed Palestinians, incited by the pro-Nazi Grand Mufti of Jerusalem, as well as "volunteers" from other Arab countries, attacked Jewish settlements to prevent implementation of the UN resolution. With the departure of the British and the proclamation of the State of Israel on May 14, 1984, a large-scale invasion was launched by the armies of five Arab states. It was a war not only against newborn Israel, but against the unborn Palestinian Arab state projected in the UN resolution.

Not content with suppressing this vital piece of history, Primakov seeks to plant in the reader's mind a totally different idea. He turns to the memoirs of the reactionary British general, John Bagot Glubb (Glubb Pasha), who created and commanded Jordan's Arab Legion. Glubb relates an alleged talk between another British officer of the Arab Legion and an

197

anonymous Haganah officer about the fact that the territory assigned to Israel would have virtually as many Arabs as Jews. The Haganah officer is quoted as saying that "a few planned massacres would eventually help to get rid of the Palestinians."

The author follows this scurrilous hearsay with examples of Zionist "terrorism," including the massacre in the Arab village of Deir Yassin perpetrated by Menachem Begin's *Irgun Tsvai Leumi* and the Stern Gang. Primakov knows or should know that the Irgun and the Stern Gang were outcasts from the Zionist movement whose atrocity was condemned by the responsible Jewish leadership. However, in documenting his thesis that in the Arab-Israel conflict all virtue is on one side and all vice on the other, Primakov does not make a fetish of accuracy.

And so we are treated once again to the threadbare myth that the Jewish authorities drove hundreds of thousands of Arabs into exile. According to Primakov, this was official policy and "it had been planned." He cites various writers, mostly British. Yet how explain the report of the London *Economist* of Oct. 2, 1948: "... the Jewish authorities... urged all Arabs to remain in Haifa and guaranteed their protection and security... Various factors influenced their decision to seek safety in flight... by far the most potent of these factors was the announcement over the air by the Arab Higher Committee urging all Arabs in Haifa to quit. The reason given was that upon the final withdrawal of the British, the combined armies of the Arab states would invade Palestine and drive the Jews into the sea."

I was in Israel in the latter part of April 1948, when the exodus of the Arabs almost overnight assumed massive proportions. I can testify that many Israelis were shocked and that the authorities did appeal to the Arabs to remain. This does not mean that non-official Israelis bear no responsibility for what happened. Certainly the Deir Yassin massacre was a factor in the exodus. And there were instances (I learned of one such occurence) where individual Israeli field commanders, in occupying Arab villages, brutally demolished homes and drove their occupants away.

The defense and survival of Israeli statehood involved the occupation of considerable territory that had been assigned to the Arab state whose formation was blocked by the Arab aggressors. Primakov cites as evidence of "expansionism" the decision of the Israeli government to include this territory in the State of Israel. It is true that Israel's leaders welcomed the opportunity provided them by their enemies, but this does not alter the fact that they had accepted the much smaller area proposed in the UN resolution and that the expanded borders resulted from aggression not by Israel, but by the reactionary Arab regimes. Here too the author finds it necessry to suppress Soviet history: in the UN debates the USSR opposed all efforts to roll back Israel's borders.

Complementing Primakov's suppression of Soviet history is his suppression or distortion of U.S. history in relation to Israel. It is not true

198

that what he calls "Israel's policy of expansion" has always been backed by the U.S. During the first Arab-Israel war, the plan of UN mediator Count Folke Bernadotte to *contract* the area allotted Israel by the UN, depriving it of three-fifths of its territory including the Negev, received Washington's blessing. As late as 1955 Secretary of State John Foster Dulles, according to a column by the well-informed Alsop brothers (New York *Herald-Tribune,* Dec. 30, 1955), demanded of Israeli Foreign Minister Sharett territorial concessions in return for $50 million of arms for Israel. The Alsops reported that Sharett "furiously replied that apparently Dulles wanted to destroy Israel."

Nor did the U.S. support Israel's 1956 aggression against Egypt in alliance with British and French imperialism. On the contrary, for different reasons the U.S. and the USSR, acting along parallel lines, brought the fighting to a halt within a few days and forced Israel to disgorge the Sinai territory it had swallowed.

Primakov does concede that "the United States did not take part in, and did not support the tripartite (British-French-Israeli) aggression that had been conceived to reestablish foreign control of Suez." His account of the 1956 Sinai war is reasonably objective. Unfortunately the same cannot be said for the book as a whole. Is it possible to understand the Arab-Israel conflict in simplistic one-dimensional terms while ignoring or minimizing the obdurate Arab refusal to recognize Israel's right to exist, the threats to destroy Israel, the countless terrorist attacks on men, women and children?

In all fairness it should be said that *Anatomy of the Middle East Conflict,* in part of one chapter, does criticize Arab anti-Israel propaganda and actions, and in this respect it is more balanced than the Soviet press. The chapter bears the curious title, "Israeli Leaders' Utilization of Extremist Appeals Against the State of Israel," which indicates the tilt of the author's concern. Much of it is in that extenuatory spirit. Yet it is refreshing to read in a Soviet publication:

"International public opinion is quite right to condemn acts of terrorism against Israel's civilian population. Grenades going off in buses, the 'massacre in Munich,' and the taking of schoolchildren as hostage bear no relation whatsoever to the just struggle for the rights, including that of self-determination, of the Palestinian people and, on the contrary, make that struggle a lot more difficult and alienate many people."

Primakov adds that Soviet representatives have argued with Palestinians and "on numerous occasions sharply criticized those Palestinians advocating further terror." This chapter section, however, seems like an afterthought and is not integrated into the book as a whole or into the author's general approach to the Arab-Israel conflict.

The Six-Day War of 1967 posed a problem for the Soviet author: to condemn Israel as the aggressor without ignoring the provocative statements and acts of the Arab leaders, particularly Nasser. "In 1967," writes Primakov, "Tel Aviv was trying to exploit the situation prior to its attack as much as it could, especially the irresponsible statements by the Palestinian leaders of that period and the Egyptian troop concentration in Sinai. Although this troop movement was in answer to Israeli threats against Syria, Tel Aviv was cunning enough to portray it as a prelude of an impending Egyptian invasion of Israel."

The facts do not support this picture of Israeli cunning and innocent, if tactless, statements and actions by Egypt. The trouble did start with Syria, and the threats, raucous in tone, plus numerous terrorist attacks, came from the Syrian side. Egypt and Syria (and the Soviet Union) charged that Israel had moved troops to the Syrian border threatening to invade. But UN Secretary General U. Thant stated on May 19, 1967: "Reports from UN Truce Supervision Organization observers have confirmed the absence of troop concentrations and significant troop movements on both sides of the [Syrian] line."

Moreover, the Egyptian government took actions which appeared to be preparatory for an attack on Israel: it dismissed the UN force in Sinai which for ten years had acted as a buffer between the two countries; it moved 80,000 troops into Sinai to confront Israel and to occupy the strongpoint of Sharm el-Sheikh; it closed the Gulf of Akaba and Strait of Tiran to Israeli shipping; it made a sudden military agreement with Jordan. All this was accompanied by a drumfire of highly bellicose statements by Nasser and the Syrian leaders. "Taking Sharm el-Sheikh meant confrontation with Israel," said Nasser in a speech on May 26, 1967. "Taking such action also meant that we were ready to enter a general war.... There is complete coordination of military action between us and Syria... The battle will be a general one and our basic objective will be to destroy Israel." (Quoted in Menachem Z. Rosensaft: *Not Backward to Belligerency: A Study of Events Surrounding the "Six-Day War" of June, 1967,* Thomas Yoseloff, 1969, pp. 33-34).

Primakov states: "The Israeli Leadership had no doubts that the steps taken by Egypt were no more than a display of force and that Nasser really did not want a war," and he cites an interview with Itzchak Rabin, then the Israeli Chief of Staff, affirming that Nasser's moves were not meant to instigate war. Rabin made his statement months after the event with benefit of hindsight. The Soviet Union was evidently sufficiently concerned about Nasser's intentions to send its ambassador to see him at 3 A.M. to request him not to initiate hostilities. Certainly a responsible government had every reason to take at face value Nasser's aggressive moves and the threats from Cairo and Damascus, and to act accordingly.

Nasser's miscalculations had tragic consequences, not only in the casualties on both sides, but in the occupation of the West Bank and the Gaza Strip, the subjection of more than one million Palestinian Arabs to alien rule, the stimulation of Israeli and Arab chauvinism, and the exacerbation of all problems to the flashpoint of a new armed conflict: the Yom Kippur War of October 1973. For that conflict, in which the Egyptians made some limited gains, Primakov blames the intransigent Israeli occupation policy and its support by the U.S. It is a view with which I agree — differing from the stated position of JEWISH CURRENTS — even though the Arab side was also not without blame for the impasse after 1967.

A large part of *Anatomy of the Middle East Conflict* is devoted to American Middle East policy. The author sees the U.S. as being attracted not only by the magnet of oil, but primarily by strategic considerations: the area's "importance in the confrontation with the Soviet Union and its role in the U.S struggle against the anti-imperialist national-liberation movements." His discussion of the evolution of this policy begins in the 1950s, when the U.S. commitment to Israel was still limited. The various shifts in Washington's relations with the Arab governments in the effort to entice them into an anti-Soviet bloc; the Eisenhower Doctrine and the 1958 armed intervention in Lebanon; the increased American political, economic and military support for Israel in the 1960s as a strategic base for countering the anti-imperialist trends in certain Arab countries and for extending U.S. influence in the Middle East; the successful seduction of post Nasser Egypt — all this traces a history essential for understanding the Arab-Israel conflict. There is no doubt that the Israeli government lent itself to U.S. objectives in the Middle East and elsewhere, thereby widening the gulf between it and some of its Arab neighbors.

However, the Arab "anti-imperialist trends" bear closer examination. The reactionary regimes that made war on Israel in 1948 were overthrown in Egypt, Syria and Iraq, and eventually replaced by governments that were more progressive and that opposed imperialist domination of the Middle East. But one thing remained unchanged: their hostility to Israel and refusal to recognaize its right to exist. The fact is that the *anti-Israel obsession subordinated and in time largely eroded the anti-imperialist trends,* though it would be a mistake to regard them as entirely extinct.

Primakov cites a well-known passage by Lenin: "The bourgeois nationalism of any oppressed nation has a general democratic content that is directed *against* oppression, and it is this content that we *unconditionally* support." And Primakov adds that Lenin also pointed out that there exists simultaneously in bourgeois nationalism a reactionary element. Then why have Primakov and Soviet propaganda in general idealized Arab nationalism and failed to criticize its reactionary side, among whose manifestations are the denial of Israel's right to exist and efforts to extinguish that state by force?

The Soviet author finds it necessary to fudge "anti-imperialist" Syria's

201

role in the bloody Lebanese events in 1976, noting that "Lebanese progressive forces and the Palestinians began making several accusations against the Syrian troops, one being that the Syrians stifled their (Lebanese and Palestinain) initiative just when there was a sharp activization of the right Christian units, which had received help from Israel." Why does Primakov hide behind accusations made by others? He knows of course that the Syrians, defending the rightwing Christian forces, massacred the Palestinians and bombed their refugee camps.

And he goes even further. He speaks of "Iraq's path to socialist orientation" — this about a government that hangs Communists and Jews! This is on the same dismal theoretical level as Khrushchev's discovery of "socialism" in Egypt — with the Communist Party outlawed and many of its members in jail. Primakov too, discussing Egypt in the mid-1970s, writes of "a retreat from the socialist orientation to the restoration of capitalism as its dominant economic mode." What actually had happened in Egypt, Syria and Iraq, as well as in other Third World countries, was the development of state capitalist enterprises through nationalization of banks and certain other large firms, plus creation of new government-owned projects. Socialism it was not, as Nasser's successor, Anwar el-Sadat, demonstrated when he reversed many domestic reforms, broke with the Soviet Union and aligned himself with the U.S.

In contrast to his idealization of Arab nationalism, the Soviet author treats Zionist nationalism as unmitigated evil: "... Zionism had never had and does not have two sides... it is reactionary left, right and center." He does not explain how he squares this dictum with the fact that he presents approvingly no less than five quotations from Dr. Nahum Goldmann (1895-1982), former president of the World Jewish Congress and for decades one of the leaders of world Zionism, as well as favorable references to Arieh Lova Eliav, former general secretary of the Labor Party, General Mattityahu Peled and other Zionist Israeli critics of government policy.

Anatomy of the Middle East Conflict also gives a false picture of the Zionist role in World War II. It states: "In the Second World War the Zionist movement was outside the active struggle against fascism; there are no known instances of the Zionist movement mobilizing the masses to struggle against German fascism or forming groups to fight alongside the Resistance in Europe... Several thousand young men from the Jewish communities in Palestine were recruited to serve in a Jewish brigade which was part of the British army, but the Zionist leadership told them that their main job was not to fight but to 'expropriate' weapons for the Haganah."

It is not my purpose to defend Zionism, of which I have been an opponent throughout my adult life, but to defend the truth. The truth is that, according to Laqueur's *A History of Zionism* (p. 535), shortly after the war began, 136,000 young Palestine Jews volunteered for military service. Also, according to the same source (p. 488), members of Zionist youth movements in eastern Europe "played a leading part in the resistance to Nazism. Many died." The truth is that Zionists in April 1943 participated in the heroic Warsaw ghetto uprising, whose leader, Mordecai Aniliewicz, was a socialist Zionist (the Israeli Kibbutz Yad Mordecai is named after him).

The truth is that with the outbreak of the war, the president of the World Zionist Organization, Dr. Chaim Weizmann, requested the British to support formation of a Jewish brigade within the British army. Opposition by high civilian and military officials delayed agreement till Aug., 1944, and the Jewish brigade "saw action in Italy towards the end of the war" (*Ibid.,* pages 540-541). And the truth is that after a proposal of the Zionist-controlled Jewish Agency, Palestinian Jewish commandos, including the legendary martyred Hannah Senesh, were parachuted into Nazi-occupied Bulgaria, Rumania, Hungary and Slovakia to organize Jewish resistance.

Turning to more recent events in the Arab-Israel conflict, Primakov is totally negative toward the Camp David accords. The agreement which led to a peace treaty between Egypt and Israel and withdrawal of the Israeli armed forces from Sinai is for him a betrayal of the Palestinian cause and of the interests of the other Arab countries. For Sadat, who replaced fantasy with realism, this agreement meant recovery of the vast Sinai territory and lightening the arms burden that was draining Egypt at a time of serious economic distress. For Begin, exchanging territory for peace with Egypt meant neutralizing Israel's most formidable foe, thereby fracturing the hostile Arab front, without any clear commitment to exchanging territory for peace in regard to the West Bank, the Gaza Strip and the Golan Heights.

I believe Primakov is wrong in attacking the agreement between Israel and Egypt. After 30 years of intermittent bloodshed that cost both sides thousands of lives and millions in economic resources, this agreement represents a historic breakthrough. However, the book's criticisms of the second Camp David accord on autonomy for the West Bank and the Gaza Strip are on target. From the outset I regarded this part of the accords as a fraud, though I did not anticipate that Prime Minister Begin would so quickly confirm my view. Certainly in the elaborate "autonomy" minuet that Sadat and Begin conducted with State Department sponsorship, the Egyptian leader and Washingon demonstrated the hollowness of their commitment to the "legitimate rights" of the Palestinians. Yet if, instead of isolating Egypt, the other Arab countries and eventually the PLO had joined the Camp David process and sought, together with the Arab population of the occupied areas, to add flesh and blood to the autonomy agreement, there might have been a different story to tell.

There is no doubt that one of the objectives of the Camp David accords, shared by all three partners, was to exclude the Soviet Union from exerting

203

influence toward a comprehensive settlement based on Resolution 242. I believe that the one-sided Soviet anti-Israel policy and reliance on not too reliable Arab governments (as exemplified by Egypt) facilitated this objective.

There had been growing trends in the Carter administration toward pressing for overall settlement and resumption of the Geneva Peace Conference. This led to a joint U.S.-Soviet statement on Oct. 1, 1977, favoring a comprehensive settlement that would embrace such problems as withdrawal of Israeli armed forces from occupied territories, resolution of the Palestinian question to assure "The legitimate rights of the Palestinian people," and "establishment of normal peaceful relations" based on recognizing the sovereignty, territorial integrity and political independence of all states involved. Dr. Nahum Goldmann blamed "the Jewish Lobby" for thwarting implementation of this declaration (*New Outlook,* Oct., 1979, p. 9). One should also blame certain influential people in the State Department and the National Security Council — and not least, Sadat's journey to Jerusalem the following month, which transformed the situation and converted the U.S.-Soviet statement into a dead letter.

If one assumes that without Sadat's dramatic journey, progress toward implementing the U.S.-Soviet declaration would have proceeded without hindrance, one is assuming the improbable. Viewed realistically, the big plus of Camp David remains, but also the big minus. The Begin government is expanding that minus, intensifying confrontationist tactics and militarization and betraying Israel's moral values with brutalities against West Bank citizens and its own brand of massive terrorism.

The final chapter of *Anatomy of the Middle East Conflict* discusses Soviet proposals for a Middle East settlement submitted on Oct. 2, 1976, as an agenda for a renewed Geneva Conference. Except that they call for Israeli withdrawal from "all" occupied territories, whereas Resolution 242 omits the word "all," the proposals are excellent. But they do not deal with the post-Camp David situation, and Primakov seems to have no ideas of his own on that score. He is right in maintaining that "the unresolved Palestinain question is blocking the road to a fair and lasting peace in the area." A public opinion poll published in Nov., 1981 showed that 59.9% of the Israeli people believe that no comprehensive peace with the Arab states is possible without resolving the Palestinian problem, while 23.4% believe such a peace can be attained without doing so. However, the Soviet author sees the roadblock as being entirely made in Israel.

The book notes that the PLO "made a major contribution to the search for a constructive solution" when in June 1974 its highest body, the Palestine National Council, adopted a resolution to establish a "Palestinian authority" on the West Bank and the Gaza Strip once Israeli occupation troops withdrew. The author concedes that subsequently George Habash's

204

Popular Front for the Liberation of Palestine and two other components of the PLO coalition formed the "rejectionist front," but he does not discuss what the PLO majority means by a "Palestinian authority" on the West Bank and the Gaza Strip. Does it mean an Arab state coexisting with Israel? Or does it mean a base for future attacks on Israel?

There are conflicting trends within the PLO, but Primakov fails to deal with the fact that official policy continues to reject resolution 242 and to refuse acceptance of Israel's legitimacy. It is true that such a change is extremely difficult, not only because of PLO hardliners but because the Begin government daily demonstates its determination to hold on to every inch of the occupied territories and vows never to negotiate with the PLO. The mutual non-recognition policies of the Begin regime and the PLO complement and reinforce each other. And Begin's de facto annexationism is endangering both the peace agreement with Egypt and Israel's overall security. That security is further menaced by the Reagan administration's aggressive anti-Soviet designs in the Middle East, with which Begin has been all too ready to cooperate.

The belief of the architects of Camp David that an Egypt-Israel peace would open the way to resolving — after their fashion — the Palestinian question while immobilizing the Soviet Union has proved illusory. U.S.-Soviet consensus is essential for mitigating the dangers and overcoming the passions and prejudices that feed the Arab-Israel conflict. Within Israel, within the PLO and the Arab states, as well as among American Jews and non-Jews, there are those who view a negotiated two-state agreement, with proper guarantees and safeguards, as the realistic road to peace and security. They need to be heard.

This review article was written before the June 6, 1982 Israeli invasion of Lebanon. That war of aggression with its tragic aftermath — the slaughter of Palestinian refugees by the Israel-allied Christian Phalangists — underlines the article's argument in several respects: the reactionary, expansionist character of the Begin government, whose policies menace Israel's future; the self-defeating nature of the refusal by the Arab governments and the PLO to recognize Israel's right to exist; the U.S. thrust toward dominating the Middle East in general and Arab-Israel relations in particular; and the isolation and loss of influence of the Soviet Union.

May, 1983

An Israeli Soldier's Nightmare

By ALISON B. CARB

A S I look in the mirror
an Arab stares back frozen

with glittering teeth,
black eyes
and long fingers

He smiles slowly
but does not cock his head to one side
when I cock mine.

The moon slips
through the barrack window
and beams of light tiptoe through my hair.

He squats in the corner
with a frayed leather book
clasped in sinuous fingers.
As he reads
my head falls onto my chest,
and I creep away, ashamed.

"There is an Arab in my mirror,"
I say to my commander.

He shrugs, and turns away from me.

May, 1979

Coming Home *(story)*

By GEORGE I. BERNSTEIN

IN a small cemetery at Kibbutz Bar-Lev, a frontier settlement in Northern Israel, white tarp covers the gravestone of Shoshana Dagoni, who was the daughter of my comrade, Moshe. Heavy string is tied around the tarp near the base of the stone. Moshe stands with his wife, Shulamith, at the foot of the grave. Rabbi Ariel Ben-David chants in a low, rich, bass voice a haunting melody of remembrance, a song of peace. The Rabbi's shoulders sag, his frail body bends with the weight of this peace. We have come together at an unveiling ceremony, the day when Jews uncover the headstone, a year after a death.

On another dark stormy day, a year ago, when we buried the child, the Rabbi's voice was discordant, as if vocally probing my thought that we are all jokes unto eternity. Now his voice rings with hope, a requiem of meeting, a meaning for all our Shoshanas, for our land. The chant sings for Shulamith and Moshe Dagoni; a meaning for their tears, a why for forgiveness — surely a time to forgive.

Moshe stands at attention but his head slowly lowers, his eyes close and, like a small boy, his hand gropes for the hand of Shulamit. Shulamit stares at the headstone, lips compressed, jaws set and eyes dry. It is a year, and she had not cried. I cannot bear to see her this way; I turn away, for upon her face is the chill of death.

The Rabbi continues the service with a Hebrew chant. "Sweetly slumbering, here rests Shoshana, our departed child. She is the blossom that Death broke off. Peace unto her soul."

Peace... Shalom.

Shalom, a word of many colors. It can mean peace and hello and goodbye. Oh, the chimneys, the chimneys thrust into a carbon sky. To those living only in our memories, we whisper shalom. We shout shalom as we stand vigilant in our garden and hope it will not become our graveyard. Shalom — hello, my friend — goodbye, my friend — peace, my friend.

Rain batters the tarp clinging to the headstone. The cold wind from the north eddies about the stone base. The edges of the tarp, below the string, flap like a wounded, dying bird.

In the mid-November gloom, the dark horizon fills with birds approaching us at lightning speed. Screaming F-4 Phantom fighter-interceptors profane this moment, this moment of peace. Their sonic booms dislodge my Uzi submachine gun from its resting place on a nearby

207

rock. It falls to the ground, just as it did on that cold and rainy night, a year ago, the night we lost Shoshana.

One hundred yards to the north, a barbed-wire fence divides Northern Israel from Southern Lebanon. Along the fence and parallel to it, the northen perimeter roadway follows its serpentine twisting, allowing rapid communication. The road, studded at intervals with strobe lights, is easily identified from the air as an international boundary. We lie in the wet, rocky grass, breathing quietly in the cold drizzle, listening for sounds that might betray infiltration of our perimeter.

Moshe Dagoni looks sharply in my direction, his finger placed to his lips, frowning. I carefully lift the fallen gun and cradle it in my arms, the only safe place for a soldier's weapon.

"Avram — remember our commando group in '48."

He pulls his parka firmly over his head and shivers. "Those were the days of history."

The wind dies from the north and freshens from the direction of stately Mount Hermon to the west. The cresting wind carries the salty tang of the Mediterrancean.

Moshe turns to me. "Quiet, isn't it? I can almost hear the tinkle of the Sabbath wine glasses."

A muffled cough. The snap of an ammunition clip. I jerk my gun at the ready, tapping Moshe's shoulder in silent warning. We cock our Uzis and creep forward, crouching low over the soggy earth. We crawl to the fence and move parallel to it from 60 meters. Moshe probes the barbed-wire with the barrel of his gun. I cover him. The fence has been cut. A loose strand hangs weakly from a nearby post. Moshe flips his pocket flashlight on, inspecting the fence in better light. We roll away. No shots. Footprints in the mud. I follow them for a few meters.

"Where do the tracks lead?"

"Directly southward."

There are at least three pairs of footprints, maybe more. We will need help. We follow wheel tracks but lose them in the rocky ground.

I unlimber my R.T., depress the switch, muffle my voice with a glove hand: *"Blue Leader, to Jezebel. Red Alert, Jackals on the loose. Call out the dogs. Estimate time of break-through, 1158 hours. Coordinate fix of infiltration point, 1-8 fiver. Laughing Johnny and Blue Leader are moving for intercept. Require motorized reconn to plug our patrol sector. Bring up armor to break-through coordinate. Suspect further activity. Have noted BM-21 Rocket-Launcher tracks. Re-transmit, using Code Blue priority through tango station. Terminate on Jeremiah frequency. Todah Raba Jezebel. Shalom, Shalom. Blue Leader Out."*

I snap off the unit. We move southward, tracking the prints, checking several times with our flashlights. Marauders are heading straight for

Kibbutz Bar-Lev.

We know the land. Those who lie under its blessed soil are our people, our family. In other lands, there are monuments, shrines, great buildings built by people. Our monuments have been built with blood.

We run full out, our Uzis loaded with 33 rounds of nine millimeter ammo. We have plently of spare clips. After sprinting two kilometers we sound like two wheezing asthmatics.

"Avram, I hear shooting to the south."

I listen. Muffled staccato popping of automatic small arms fire. "Moshe, we won't make it this way. Let's get off the road and take to the fields. We'll move in from the flank on their dark side."

We creep through dense foliage and marshed grass and ford a rain-swollen stream. Keeping our heads low, we race through a maze of mounds left from an archaeological dig. Now, in the open, we see tracers crisscrossing and bursting like fire-works in the sky. Sprinting to the tree line surrounding the kibbutz, we press into the shelter of a wet, jagged rock wall.

"Look to your right."

I whirl and see Elazar, the night guard, soaked in dark blood, lying at the entrance to the children's dormitory, his right arm flung in front of his head still clutching his Uzi.

The fog is creeping in; damp, heavy, swirling toward us from the olive groves. The dormitory's windows are dark. On its new concrete block walls, the brilliant red graffiti of children. The fog surrounds the dorm. The building becomes an island in a heaving sea.

Gun's bark, Muzzle flashes. Three PLO raiders, holed up in the children's dorm, are firing AK-7 Kalashnikov assault rifles, on automatic, sporadically. The villagers cannot directly return their fire for fear of hitting the children inside.

"Can't use the Uzis," I whisper, "have to go in from behind, the dark side, with the knife." Quickly unslinging our Uzis, we shove them under a juniper bush.

Moshe unsheaths his knife. He does not wish to kill. He looks at his large bony hands.

We creep through the cold dirzzle, through the foggy darkness; we edge around the sheltering tree line of dark green olive groves. We drop to our bellies, our knives between our teeth. A villager sees us in a clear patch in the fog and directs his gun fire over the roof of the dorm as a diversionary tactic. If the terrorists see us, the children are dead.

Another 40 meters, and we make it to the nearest rear window. The fog is thick here. We can barely see each other. Search light beams begin their dance through the dark, the rain and fog, seeking a partner to embrace. We wait for the light to swing away, and as the automatic fire resumes, we

209

jump through the window into the rec room. We hug the darkest corner, still, silent.

Three marauders are firing out of adjacent side windows toward the main portion of the kibbutz. Rough wood flooring creaks as the Arabs dart about their window posts. The light ascends the walls in its cyclic probes and we see the children's paintings hanging there and the chalk scribbling on the blackboard. On the floor, a piece of red chalk squashed by a heavy boot.

The light pirouettes and then we see them, the children, huddled in the corner adjacent to the gunmen's firing posts. Shoshana gathers the children about her. Each holding firmly the other's hand, she herds them to the most remote corner, away from the gun fire. She smiles and speak to each one in turn, nodding answers to their questions. Their voices are hushed and calm. Only Moshe and I are afraid.

Shoshana is thin, taller than the oldest of the children. Her hair is black and straight. It falls over her eyes and she brushes it away with her hand. Tails of her white shirt hang loosely over faded jeans. Around her neck, a small golden star of David hangs from a thin chain. Her feet are bare.

Shoshana half-turns from the children and checks the position of the enemy. As the reflected light crests across the floor, she sees first in silhouette, and then in full view, an Arab boy of 15 or 16. He stands at the centre of the recreation room. Cat-like he watches Shoshana's every move. He halves the distance between them, his Kalashnikov slung over his shoulder.

"What is your name, my fearless sabra?"

Shoshana knows that he is in command. She takes a short step toward him and answers, "I am called Shoshana. May one of us take a message to our parents, stating your demands?"

The young Arab unslings his rifle. The children begin to cry again. He places the gun at his feet, then turns to the children moving his finger to his lips.

The boy's cheeks are smooth. His chin and mouth show the hard lines of defiance. The Arab boy is as tall as Shoshana, and handsome. The muscles of his wiry body stand out in the oblique light, as it advances and recedes. he wears the camouflaged fatigues and cap of an Arab irregular. His uniform shows no insignia of country nor rank. His mission is to conquer Muslim lands from the infidel. His reward is eternity.

Achmed turns to the children and gazes at Yehudit, the smallest of them. Her white cotton dress has a floor smudge on the skirt. Then he stares at his comrades, hunched over their weapons, watching him — waiting.

He lowers his eyes... he gazes into the sun at the silhouette of his little sister Rochella, *his* rose. She plays with a brown puppy. It has large ears and a long tail. Her white dress is spotted with dark loam. Achmed's knees feel soft and warm as he kneels in his father's tomato patch. Rochella

210

giggles and mimics Achmed, as he chews on a ripe tomato. His father carefully tilts a large rusty battered British army canteen, measuring out a few drops of water for each plant. It is soon prayer time, for the bright red Israeli school bus bounces along the gravel road as it passes Rashid El Rahaman's little farm in the lower Galilee, a few kilometers from Degania. Achmed smiles widely as he hears the squealing children tormenting the old man driving, hiding behind his sunglasses and dreaming of battles fought long ago...

Shoshana stands close to Achmed; she holds her hands together, finger tips pointing upwards. In the echoing light, they are tapers of supplication transcending the room, and penetrate the fog.

In the darkness, the children rise as one, carefully stepping foward, the small ones at the rear pushing the older ones.

"Sh'ma Yisroel..." Hear Oh Israel, The Lord our God, The Lord is one... the most solemn of Jewish prayers — the confession. Then their faltering voices sing the Hatikva — The Hope. The soprano grows stronger, haunting, a song of life and a chant of death.

Anwar and Yassir keep up a steady barrage of fire from their adjacent windows. A ricochetting round hits Anwar in the face. The force of the bullet spins him around still shooting, his face covered with blood. The bullets strike Shoshana Dagoni as she prays. She stumbles, her hand extended to the Arab boy for help. Achmed catches Shoshana and sinks with her to the floor.

"You killed her! Allah will curse us all! We are dead men."

Yassir shouts, "They have shot Anwar!! Achmed, your gun! Pick it up! Quickly! Back to your post, or we *will* die."

Moshe springs from the shadows and dashes to his fallen child. Yassir fires. I break cover. I dart to the left, away from the children and hugging the blackbord, get behind Yassir. I grip my knife. Yassir fires another shot, and Moshe dives to the floor. I sink my knife into Yassir's back. He drops like a stone, his gun clattering across the floor. The round grazed Moshe's cheek, and blood flows along flesh and bone.

The tempo of the dancing search lights quickens. They weave through the rain and fog and darkness and cast a hundred shadows in the room, each moving to embrace and then retreating. I cannot distinguish between friend and foe.

Anwar darts from his post at the window and rakes the rear of the room with automatic fire. Moshe rolls away from his daughter. The bullets hit her body. Moshe abruptly rights himself after spinning behind Anwar. The pulsing, cresting, dazzling light and the blood running down his face, blind Anwar. Moshe strikes Anwar's neck with the side of his hand.

The Arab solemnly bows as if acknowledging a performance. His knees buckle and he falls; his hand reaches out for help and he clasps Shoshana's hand.

The boy, Achmed, yells, "Yassir! Anwar! Where are you? Answer me! W'allah-i-l-eazim! Answer me!"

Light and fog and rain swirl about the rec room as the children rush to the open windows and climb out. Panic-stricken, they run to their parents in the kibbutz square.

The boy, Achmed, in a frenzy, scrambles toward the rear of the rec room where the three bodies lie, body touching body. He shouts in Arabic, "The blood of Ishmael — the blood of David — mingle only in death. We all are to die, none will be left to pray. What will then happen to our God?"

Moshe and I creep back into the shadows. The Arab boy has picked up his AK-7. We must disarm him.

Achmed stands beside the bodies. His eyes roll upward. He prays, he cries, he curses. Then, with his free arm, he grabs Yassir's gun and in the shifting shadows stumbles to the front of the building. He sprints to the door. The light hits him full in the face as he runs out, shouting. The Kaleshnikovs fire wildly. The search lights, probing and accusing through the rain, take the Arab boy in a final embrace. Moshe cries out in Arabic, "Achmed, you young idiot! Drop your guns!"

The Uzis fire as one, the shots striking the young Arab. He pitches headlong into the mud. His legs twitch. He lies broken and crumpled in the mud and the rain washes over him. His eyes are open, sightless. The fog becomes his tomb.

As an animal creeps into the dark to die, so a man makes for the light.

Moshe bunches over Shoshana. He kneels beside his dead child and speaks to her. He speaks and says he is sorry he has failed her. He smooths her dark hair and wipes the blood from her face. He takes off his jacket and folds it beneath her head. I am a man who cannot cry or pray yet I must look upon other men who do so. Moshe weeps for Shoshana.

Nehemiah, our sage, taught that he who saves a single life, saves the world; he who takes a life, destroys the universe.

Moshe weeps for his child, for all the children of Zion and Jerusalem, and for the innocent ones in every age, in every land. They have a place of honor in the world to come — so it is written.

Moshe carries Shoshana out of the dormitory, through the receding fog and the rainy mist. We blame ourselves for the dead and feel guilt because we live.

Settlers avert their eyes and slowly disperse with their own rescued children. Search lights no longer point their fingers. All are guilty. Acrid fumes of death hang low over the kibbutz. I hold my handkerchief over my mouth to filter out the sour, polluted air and stifle my coughing.

Shulamit, apart from us, remains alone at the gravesite. The wind whips the embroidered silk scarf tied about her head and shoulders. Stray curls flutter around her face. Her tall thin body bends as a Hasid bends in prayer.

Her face has become a granite mask. She now resides in a sepulcher of silence. I place my arm about Moshe's broad shoulders. I envy him; he prays while I cannot. Must a father behold his children's gravesite? Moshe's long black hair is matted down by rain.

Rabbi Ariel Ben-David rests one hand on top of the gravestone and unties the string. He hesitates. Perhaps — but no — the laws of His Universe — we cannot tamper with them. He removes the trap. So it is written:

Shoshana Dagoni
13 Years of Age
A Child of Valor
Died on the 15th Day of Heshvan
In the 5733rd Year
Of the Beginning of Creation
The Lord gives and
the Lord Takes Away
Blessed is the Name of the Lord.

Moshe opens the presentation case holding his military decorations and places them on the gravestone. He takes Shulamit by the arm and guides her slowly toward the kibbutz. The wind rises and lashes at a patch of tall grass around a small white gravestone set within a cyprus grove. The wind strikes and strikes again and the branches of the trees groan. The boy's body was never claimed. Burial for the non-Jews, as prescribed by Jewish law, occurred outside the walled cemetery.

Shoshana returned to the land. The Arab boy, too, came home.

To the left, screaming Katyusha rockets from Lebanon zero in on our sister kibbutz, Boker-Dan, four miles to the south. Deep staccato booms echo through the valley as our long range 155 millimeter guns answer.

May, 1985

The Stones of Jerusalem

By I. E. RONCH

*Translated from the Yiddish
by Marvin Zuckerman*

THE ancient stones of Jerusalem
Could move a stone.
Here on this spot a prophet dreamt of later times,
When a wolf and a lamb would live in peace
When a man would not lift up a fist against another.

Here on the stones, gods preached,
And heads were split into pieces,
And warm hearts were turned into stone,
And tears of generations
Were transformed into stones.

Here lie the ancient stones,
And wait patiently to be joined into homes for Torah,
Into healing for the sick.
Stones can become a heart
That feels and is joyful.

Jerusalem — a monument of stone,
An ice-cold document
Of hot times.
Jerusalem — granite and marble,
More valuable than precious stones.
Jerusalem — stony skeleton of yesterdays
And firm fortress of today and tomorrow.

Not a grave, but a precious quarry,
To dig and mine
The soul of humanity.
To create a new humanity
Which will seek a solution,
Will strike the stone,
And hear an echo of the past,
And its own, own voice.

Stones of Jerusalem are
Epitaphs of our ancestral grandfathers and grandmothers.
Look deeply into them and you will discover a likeness:
In the veins of the stone, dried blood of your own
Submerged groan,
Outcry of joy and jubilation.

The eyes of the world
Look eagerly to the stones of Jerusalem.
The sages of the earth await
The rebirth of these stones.

The stones of Jerusalem
Could move a stone.

May, 1978

III: Soviet Jews

How My Father Last Met Itzik Feffer

BY PAUL ROBESON JR.

I JOIN with you today because the Jewish cultural tradition has always been a part of my family's cultural heritage. I can remember vividly how more than 30 years ago my father took me to a wonderful performance of Sholem Aleichem's short stories by a cast of Black and white actors and actresses.

In Moscow in 1959, at a celebration of the 100th birthday of Sholem Aleichem, Paul Robeson said: "... The life-span of Sholem Aleichem paralleled that of my father, and the lives and experiences of their peoples were also very parallel.... How interesting and how wonderful that the tender works of Sholem Aleichem are a natural part of the heritage of my grandchildren — a dear, living example of the closeness of my father's people and the folk of Sholem Aleichem."

I also join with you because Paul Robeson developed a close personal friendship with the famous Soviet Yiddish actor, Solomon Mikhoels, who was murdered in 1948 by the Soviet authorities; and with the poet Itzik Feffer, who is among those whose memory we honor today.

In 1958 my father wrote: "... I remember the great artist Solomon Mikhoels from my first visit to Moscow in 1934... I remember ... his great performance of Shakespeare's *King Lear,* and think of the appearance in Russia of Ira Aldridge, the great Afro-American actor in that same role in the middle of the 19th century....

"Mikhoels and I appeared, together with the poet Feffer, in a tremendous Peace Rally at the Polo Grounds here in New York in Ju y of 1943....

"There were several opportunities to meet Mikhoels. His was a warm, rich personality; we talked about the theatre, various cultures, the likenesses between the Negro and Yiddish musics, and the richness of the various cultures in the Soviet Republics...

"I remember him with affection, admiration and respect."

Many years ago, my father told me a dramatic story about a meeting that he had with Itzik Feffer during his 1949 visit to the Soviet Union.

216

There is another story circulating about a meeting between Paul and Feffer, which is partly mistaken. It originated in an account wirtten by Mikhoels' daughter* and claims that in 1951 Feffer was brought to see Paul from Moscow's Lubyanka Prison by two so-called interpreters.

Paul could not possibly have been in the U.S.S.R. in 1951 because his passport was revoked in 1950 and he did not travel to Europe from Feb., 1950 until his passport was restored in 1958. So the story which he told me describes the only meeting he could have had with Feffer in the U.S.S.R. after the War.

As soon as Paul arrived in the U.S.S.R. on his June, 1949 trip, he was struck by the virulent campaign throughout the press against "Cosmopolitans" and "Zionists." The tone of some of the articles reminded him of the purges of the mid-1930s. And he could sense the anti-Semitic undertones in the editorials.

Deeply concerned about the fate of many of his friends in the Jewish cultural community, Paul set about trying to make personal contact with them. After he became politely but implacably insistent, his hosts finally arranged for Itzik Feffer to come to see him. (Paul had no way of knowing Feffer had been arrested on Dec. 24, 1948).

One afternon Feffer came to visit Paul. He was unaccompanied and looked very well. They greeted each other warmly and launched into animated conversation in Russian. But Paul quickly noticed that Feffer's comments were at variance with his gestures.

Continuing a "normal" conversation, Paul responded to this "body language," and with the aid of a few handwritten words and phrases (which Paul later destroyed) Feffer "told" him a terrible story in this surreptitous way.

The room was bugged. Mikhoels had been murdered the year before on Stalin's personal order. Feffer was in serious trouble, and many of the most outstanding Jewish cultural figures had already been arrested. They would come for the rest of them soon. There was little hope for any of them, including Feffer (here Feffer drew his finger across his throat). And there had just been a massive purge of the Party in Leningrad — like the awful days of 1937.

When Feffer rose to leave, he and Paul embraced like brothers; both of

---

*Herbert Marshall, "Paul Robeson's Obituary — the Aftermath," *Bulletin of the Center of Soviet and East European Studies,* Southern Illinois University at Carbondale, #18, Fall, 1976, p. 1, who cites article in Russian, "The Murder of Mikhoels," by his daughter, Natalya Mikhoels-Vovsi, in Russian-language journal, *Vremya i My,* Tel Aviv, 1976, p. 140. This story appeared in 1974 in the French edition of *The Long Return* by Esther Markish, widow of Peretz Markish, published in Paris; translated from the French by D.I. Goldstein. This book was published in English in the USA in 1978, where the story appears on p. 172, but the date of the Robeson-Feffer meeting is given as 1950. The authentic date, as indicated above, is June, 1949.

them had tears in their eyes, because they knew that they were probably seeing each other for the last time.

Soon afterwards, Paul sang a concert in the largest concert hall in Leningrad — a "Hero-City" that had withstood a prolonged and devastating Nazi siege in which an estimated one million of its citizens perished. After he finished "Ol' Man River," the last song on the program, he announced that he would sing only a single encore — a special song he had just recently learned.

Then Paul spoke with great emotion of the deep and enduring cultural ties between the United States and the Sovet Union, of the great Jewish writer Sholem ALeichem and the Soviet and American Jewish writers and actors who were continuing his tradition. Finally, he spoke of his close personal friendship with Mikhoels and Feffer, and of his great joy at meeting Feffer again.

By now there was a hush in the huge hall. Paul took a deep breath and explained the song he was about to sing — the song by Hirsh Glick of the Jewish partisan fighters which has become the hymn of the Jewish resistance. He would sing the song in Yiddish, but first he recited the lyrics in Russian:

> Never say that you have reached the very end,
> When leaden skies a bitter future may portend.
> For sure the hour for which we yearn will yet arrive,
> And our marching steps will thunder: *we* survive!"

When he finished the song there was a long moment of complete silence. Then the entire audience responded with a great flood-tide of emotion. The ovation swelled throughout the hall in waves — rising, falling, then rising again to an ever higher intensity.

As he looked out over the audience, Paul saw an amazing sight. Many people, often complete strangers who just happened to be sitting side-by-side, turned to each other — tentatively at first — and then threw their arms around one another. Some wept openly on each other's shoulders. Jewish intellectuals and Russian Party officials alike had been seared by Stalin's machine of destruction that had consumed their loved ones. At that moment they were united by the specter of the Nazi Holocaust, and the Warsaw Ghetto Rebellion had in a sense merged with the ordeal of Leningrad during the war.

Finally, I join with you today because as a Black American I am acutely aware that the treatment of minorities by any regime is one of the fundamental indications of the justice of its rule. The treatment of the Jewish people and their culture in the Soviet Union is one of the important

218

measuring sticks of the health or sickness of Soviet society as a whole. The repression of Jewish culture over the past 40 years contrasts dramatically with its flourishing growth in the years immediately after the October Revolution and is a sign of a retrogression of Soviet culture.

Yes, there is anti-Semitism in the U.S.S.R! Yes, it has been ignored, condoned and sometimes even instigated by the official state and Party apparatus. And yes, Stalin personally, over a period of many years, was responsible for many anti-Semitic policies and acts.

One must be blind and deaf not to see and hear this evil. One must suppress memory and reason in order to keep silent.

I shall not burden you with examples and statistics. A trip to the library or, even better, the pages of JEWISH CURRENTS, will provide more than enough specific evidence.

Yet the Jewish people of the Soviet Union, in their sacrifices during the October Revolution, the Civil War and the most difficult days of building up the U.S.S.R., were second to no other ethnic group of the Russian people. Over 500,000 served with honor in the Armed Forces during the war agianst Fascism, and Jews suffered more than any other segment of the Soviet population — 2,000,000, or 40% of the Jewish population of the U.S.SR., were murdered by the Nazis.

The Soviet poet, Yevgenii Yevtushenko, wrote:

> Russians and Jews,
> One epoch raised them both.
> Breaking time, like bread;
> They share the selfsame era.
> ... Here's the basis of Leninist morality:
> That both Jew and Russian died
> In bloodiest battle
> For their common soil...

The murder of the 24 Soviet Jewish cultural leaders 29 years ago today was not only a tragedy for the Jewish people. It was especially a Russian tragedy and a tragedy for all those who believe in socialism. For these Jewish martyrs were courageous fighters in the cause of socialism, and the arbitrary terror that struck them down engulfed all the peoples of the U.S.S.R. Tyranny, like freedom, is indivisible.

After the failure of the Decembrist uprising against the Tsar in 1825, the famous Russian poet, Mikhail Lermontov, wrote the following bitter lines (in my free translation):

> ...Farewell to thee, oh unwashed Russia,
> Land of slaves and land of masters;

219

And you blue-tinted uniforms,
And you masses who obey them.
Perhaps beyond the Caucausus' rise,
I may hide from your overseers:
From the stare of their all-seeing eyes,
And from their keen all-hearing ears...

More than 125 years later, the Soviet poet Yevegenii Yevtushenko
wrote these lines in his poem, "Letter to Yesyenin" (the brilliant young
Soviet poet who committed suicide rather than betray his conscience). By
the way, I found his poem as a typewritten sheet among my father's papers,
with a hand-written request on it that it be delivered to a friend, whose
name I cannot decipher, on the evening of Nov. 12 or the morning of Nov.
13, 1958. In my own free translation, Yevtushenko says to Yesyenin:

... Dear Yesyenin ! How Russia has changed...
And I'm afraid to say it's for the better,
But to say it's for the worse is dangerous.
See what we have built in our land, and the sputniks;
But we lost along our bumpy road
Both twenty million in the war,
And millions in the war against the people.
Forget about it, having *chopped memory* off?
But where is the hatchet with which to *chop* it off?
No one has saved others like Russian have,
No one kills their very own like Russians do.
But our ship floats. When the water is shallow,
We drag Russia forward over dry land.
That there are enough scum is no disaster;
Lenin is gone. Now that's terrible...
Who says that you were not among the fighters?...
You were more a Party man than so many villains,
Who tried to teach *you* Party loyalty....

In our way, we are helping to make sure that the voices of these martyrs
will continue to be heard, and that Jewish culture will some day flourish
once again in the Soviet Union. Itzik Feffer's words, especially, speak to us
so proudly, so poignantly, with such unknowing irony, but yet so hopefully
(in Martin Birnbaum's free translation, JEWISH CURRENTS, July-Aug.,
1980):

The heady wine of generations
Has strenthened me upon my road,
The evil knife of gloom and pain

Could not destroy my treasured load
My faith, my people, nor my striving—
My spirit always rose anew
From under swords my cry was heard:
I am a Jew!...

The Maccabean rebel blood
Still courses through my every vein;
Solomon's wisdom rests with me
And Heine's smile of bitter pain.
Halevi's song is in my heart;
Spinoza's depth and outcry: Do —
Do what you will and still
I am a Jew!...

My eyes reflect the silent mood.
Of evenings when the sun is low —
Expressed so well by Levitan —
Of Russian bayonets aglow
And scythes swinging in the blue,
I am of Soviet Land a son —
I am a Jew!...

To the sycophants who would tell me to be quiet I say, "I am ashamed that it has taken me so long to raise my voice."

To anyone who would call me traitor I say: "If this be treason, make the most of it."

Just as the Jewish partisans sang, "Let us never say that we have reached the very end," let us never say that Jewish culture had reached the end in the Soviet Union. Our voices and the voices of many millions all over the world will amplify the song of these martyrs whom we commemorate today. And that song will thunder down the corridors of history: *"We survive!"*

November, 1981

Birobidjan, Soviet Jews and Anti-Semitism

By SID RESNICK

DID you know that in the Far Eastern Region of Soviet Siberia there is a Yiddish country where almost everyone speaks in Yiddish to curious American visitors? Is this a dream?

This country, of course, is supposed to be Birobidjan, the Jewish Autonomous Region in the Soviet Union, which Samuel Aronoff of Los Angeles visited in 1975 and described in his 107-page book, *Birobidjan, Soviet Jews, Two Exhibitions.* Its style, though not its occasional patches of odd English, reminds one of similar books in the 1930s, whose authors saw nothing amiss or questionable even though the Stalinist purges and repressions hung heavy over the land. Naturally, therefore, the book was hailed in *Moskovskaya Pravda* July 15, 1978 by one I. Ablamov in a review boldly entitled "Facts Against Lies."

How many Jews live in this idyllic Yiddish country? Are there 50,000— 100,000—500,000? Mr. Aronoff cites an excerpt of an undated article by Albert Axelrod of the London *Jewish Chronicle* Foreign Service which states: "The entire Jewish Autonomous Region including (the city of) Birobidjan has approximately 185,000 citizens. Of this total, perhaps 25,000 are Jews." Why "perhaps"?

The Soviet census of 1969 records that the entire population of Birobidjan was 172,449 and of these only 11,452 were Jews — or less than 7%. This was a decline from the census of 1959, which recorded a Jewish population of 14,269 or 8.8%. In the face of a declining Jewish population in Birobidjan the figure of 25,000 appears highly dubious*.

Now if the Jews in Birobidjan constitute as little as 7 or 8% of the whole population, what is the justification for calling this a Jewish Autonomus Region at all?

What about its educational system? Mr. Aronoff writes that the "Jewish Autonomous region has fully adequate school facilities that include: nurseries, elementary and secondary (high) schools and certain trade and agricultural institutes." Are any of these schools conducted in Yiddish? Do the Russian language schools in the Jewish Autonomous Region offer

---

* *Birobidjan, Soviet Jews, Two Exhibitions* by Sam'l Aronoff, Los Angeles, 1978, published by the author. 107 pages, paperback, $2.50.

courses in Yiddish or on Jewish subjects to those of their Jewish students who apply for them? Mr. Aronoff is reticent.

The author tells us that he visited a collective farm (kolkhoz) called "Behest of Lenin," which he strangely terms "a national Jewish enterprise." Its school has "approximately 300 children of which 100 are Jewish children," and he comments that "this little schoolhouse can sure be used as a model for any school — anywhere" (p. 16). Is Yiddish taught to the 100 Jewish children of this school? No! In the Jewish Autonomous Region there are no schools at all that teach Yiddish!**

This fact is confirmed in the author's interview with Lev Shapiro, the First Secretary of the Communist Party in Birobidjan: "He (Shapiro) noted, however, that a request had come from a group of 17 Jewish youths to provide a class in Yiddish in Birobidjan. This request will positively be met soon; it may lead to an expansion of this program, and undoubtedly, will include associated subjects" (p. 11).

Since these 17 Jewish youths made this request four years have gone by and nothing was done to provide that Yiddish class or to "include associated subjects."

Mr. Aronoff also reports that there is a Yiddish radio program in Birobidjan and "a fine Jewish drama theatre performing in Yiddish" and a "substantial" Yiddish section in the local Sholem Aleichem Library.

There are also two newspapers in Birobidjan, one in Russian, the other in Yiddish: Both are called *Birobidjan Star*. Mr. Aronoff met the editor, apparently a Jew, of what he described as "the Russian version of the *Birobidjaner Shtern.*"

Having subscribed to the *Birobidjaner Shtern* a few years ago, I would say that it is the Yiddish version of the local Russian newspaper. This is a good newspaper if one wants to find out how much cement or how many machine parts or stockings are produced in the local factories or what the scores are of the local athletic teams, but one will find little in it about Jewish affairs, Yiddish literature or education. *Birobidjaner Shtern* definitely does not agitate for Yiddish schools in Birobidjan, it never calls for courses in Yiddish literature or Jewish history, even in Russian, in Birobidjan, it never urges Soviet Jews or other Jews to emigrate to Birobidjan, and it never challenges or refutes the slanders of the anti-Semitic writers in the Soviet Union.

Instead *Birobidjaner Shtern* reprints in Yiddish the scribblings of the anti-Zionist propagandists in the Soviet Union, almost all of whom are also anti-Semites. Thus, *Birobidjaner Shtern* of Dec. 27, 1972 carried a gushingly favorable review by a Novosti Agency writer of V. Bolshakov's book, *Zionism in the Service of Anti-Communism,* which repeats such fables as: "Zionism aided McCarthyism and had close connections with the

Birchites and the Minutemen and other reactionaries." Apparently the writer never took the trouble to learn that Albert Einstein and many American rabbis and liberal Jewish politicians who were either Zionists or Zionist sympathizers were also opponents of McCarthyism and never had any connections with Birchites, let alone Minutemen.

Another example: In Nov. and Dec., 1974, when the American Jewish community and a few American left publications were protesting the anti-Semitic charges by the late U.S. Gen. George S. Brown that the Jews own the banks and the newspapers in this country, *Birobidjaner Shtern* took another tack. Dec. 14, 1974 it carried an article by the Novosti Agency writer K. Maslov under the headline, "What Gen. Brown Said and Why the Zionists Are Angry at Him." Maslov wrote, "Gen. Brown was right when he spoke of the strong hand of the Zionists in the United States." All that Maslov did in that article was to substitute the word "Zionists" for the world "Jews" that Gen. Brown had used, thus covering up his anti-Semitism.

Mr. Aronoff makes it appear that Birobidjan is teeming with Jews. After visiting a factory that employs 3,000 people he writes: "A great proportion of the employees are Jewish, although the plant does not keep records of nationality." If there are really less than 15,000 Jews in Birobidjan, or even the inflated figure of 25,000 Jews given in this book, the proportion of Jews in any enterprise in this Region is likely to be quite small.

Such deceptiveness about the Jewish character of Birobidjan is standard fare with Soviet apologists on this subject. A typical recent example was the news story in the *N.Y. Daily World* (Jan. 30, 1979) which in passing mentioned "Birobidjan, where Yiddish is the primary language." In an area where more than 90% of the population is not even Jewish and where Jewish children have no schools or courses where they could learn their people's language such an assertion is nonsense.

Why this continual straining to exaggerate the Jewishness of this area which has such a small number of Jews and plays a peripheral role in the Jewish life in the Soviet Union?

It is this reviewer's opinion that the Soviet government exaggerates the Jewishness of Birobidjan in order to deflect criticism that the government is soft on the anti-Semites and restricts the nationality group rights of the Soviet Jews in the matter of Yiddish language cultural activity. A more "Jewish" Birobidjan also serves as a propaganda counterweight against the State of Israel. Another reason for this exaggeration is to conceal the fact that from the *original* Soviet point of view Birobidjan is a complete failure.

Odd as it may seem today, the Soviet leadership selected Birobidjan 45 years ago to develop it as the secure base for the Soviet Jewish nationality and for Yiddish culture in the Soviet Union!

The position of the Soviet government, which proclaimed Birobidjan as a Jewish Autonomous Region in 1934, was best formulated by the then president of the Soviet Union, Mikhail Kalinin, a Russian who was especially concerned with Jewish problems. Kalinin told a meeting in Moscow on May 28, 1934:

"You ask, why was the Jewish Autonomous Region organized?... The main reason is that there are many Jews among us and they do not have a state structure of their own. This is the only nationality in the Soviet Union which has a population of three million and has no state structure. I consider that the creation of such a Region is in our conditions the only means for the normal development of this nationality. I reckon that in about 10 years Birobidjan will become the most important, if not the only guardian of the Yiddish socialist national culture...

"In the Autonomous Region of Birobidjan there will develop a great socialist construction and at the same time also a genuine Socialist Yiddish culture and those who value such a Yiddish national culture, who will want to lend a hand to the development of the Jewish Region and its socialist national culture should connect themselves with Birobidjan and assist it. I think that the Jews will be able to maintain themselves (as a group) in their own national region longer than anywhere else" (*Yidn in Sovetn Farband,* Moscow 1935, pages 32,33).

Today, when the official ideological stress in the Soviet Union is on assimilation and hence the disappearance of the Jews as a distinct ethnic group, it is startling to realize how different the official policy on this question was 45 years ago. Kalinin's sentiments are now deemed extremely "nationalistic" in those same quarters and they are no longer even mentioned.

It is apparent from the small number of Jews in Birobidjan today and from the fact that not only is there no developed Yiddish culture, but that young Jewish students have to plead for a class in the Yiddish language that Kalinin's bold and generous vision of Birobidjan as the future "guardian of the Yiddish socialist national culture" has turned into a shambles.

Despite Kalinin's agitation for Birobidjan, the Soviet government never undertook a campaign to inspire Soviet Jews to settle on a mass scale in Birobidjan, to go there to build a Jewish socialist country. What the Soviet government seemingly granted with one hand it took away with the other when it succumbed to the fear that this project smacked of what it wrongly regarded as "nationalism" and the bias in favor of assimilation took the upper hand. In addition, the Stalinist repressions and purges in the 1930s hit Birobidjan particularly hard. Many of the assigned Jewish leaders of Birobidjan were arrested and executed on false charges of espionage. As a result Birobidjan became an unsafe place, a place for Jews to stay away from.

It is a pity that political considerations far removed from Birobidjan wrecked Mikhail Kalinin's vision of 1934, a vision enthusiastically welcomed by the Jewish left movements at the time, which helped produce an enormous pro-Soviet feeling among Jews generally. However, it is quite wrong for anyone today to sustain the fiction that this vision is now a reality in Birobidjan, and this has nothing to do with the pleasant material conditions there which Mr. Aronoff noted. The title Jewish Autonomous Region for Birobidjan is, regrettably, a misnomer.

The next chapter of Mr. Aronoff's book deals with the question of anti-Semitism and the reasons why Jews are emigrating from the Soviet Union. He quotes approvingly a statement by a Soviet official and professor who assured him "that there is no anti-Semitism and no 'Jewish problem' in the Soviet Union," nor is there any "discrimination" against Jews (p. 83).

Information of complaints by Soviet Jews who have encountered discrimination in admissions to universities or to professional institutions, or who have met with discrimination in advancement in their jobs are never publicized in the Soviet press and one learns of such things only from the persons who were aggrieved or their relatives. When one hears of so many examples of such discriminations from Soviet Jews themselves as they are reported by American Jews (including progressive Jews) who have visited their families in the Soviet Union or from Russian Jewish immigrants here, including some who are not generally hostile to the Soviet regime, they can no longer simply be dismissed even if exact statistical data will never be available. One would surely have to be naive today to assume that an exaggerated politicized concern with "security" by certain authorities, or simple anti-Semitic prejudice or suspicion, or a combination of both, had not already led to many cases of discrimination against Jews in various Soviet institutions.

Such discrimination is not unprecedented in Soviet practice. During World War II the Soviet government deprived certain nationalities *in their entirety* of all their rights and their territory, such as the Volga Germans, the Crimean Tartars, the Kalmyks and certain North Caucasian peoples. The Arab-Israel conflict has become such an envenomed subject to the Soviet authorities that it is not inconceivable that Jews in general would be subject to various suspicions which in turn result in discrimination against Jews. It is also likely that such discrimination affecting Jews who may or may not have any interest in Jewish life or Israel would create greater alienation among Soviet Jews.

However, a more realistic indicator of anti-Semitism in the Soviet Union is the persistence in the past 10 years or so of anti-Zionist literature in the form of books and newspaper and magazine articles that are clearly anti-Jewish and which are not refuted in the general Soviet media or by responsible authorities. Though Mr. Aronoff does not mention this literature at all it is noteworthy that in 1975 a specific anti-Semitic article was the subject of a public protest by the organization of which Mr. Aronoff was a principal officer, namely, the Jewish Cultural Clubs of Los Angeles. The leadership of this progressive organization issued a statement on an article by Dimitri Zhukov entitled, "The Ideology and Practice of Brutality," published in a leading Soviet weekly paper, *Ogonyok,* Oct. 12, 1974. The Los Angeles statement declared: "We express our revulsion at Zhukov's article... We are deeply offended by Zhukov's anti-Semitic libels" (translated from Yiddish).

Even the Moscow Yiddish monthly, *Sovetish Heimland,* itself criticized a few such "anti-Zionist" dissertations. In June, 1973 the *Sovetish Heimland* editor, Aaron Vergelis, published an article with the meaningful headline, "Not Only Ignorance," which denounced the pamphlet, *Fascism Under the Blue Star,* by Yevgeny Yevseyev and charged that "such pamphlets mislead the reader and distort the essence of the problem": in Jan., 1974 Vergelis cited three popular "anti-Zionist" authors, V. Begun, T. Kichko and Y. Yevseyev (again) who had denigrated the Yiddish language and culture and charged them with being "deaf to what Lenin actually said" on this subject and with quoting Lenin incorrectly in their writings on the Jews; in July, 1978 *Sovetish Heimland* published the translation in Yiddish of a strong critique by Academician M.A. Korostovtzev of V. Skurlatov's book, *Zionism and Apartheid,* a crass anti-Semitic book couched in scholarly language (English translation in *Morgn Freiheit,* Oct. 15 and 22, 1978). This vicious book attributes the origin of modern racism to the Jewish religion, claims that the Jews were from ancient times a "transnational corporation" and "that in all epochs of the development of mankind the Jews fulfilled purely parasitical functions," that the Jews promoted capitalism and imperialism and "The representatives of international Zionist capital, clinging to (the concept of) the 'chosen people,' openly aspire to world domination."

To be sure, *Sovetish Heimland's* all too occasional critiques of such anti-Semitic literature are always made in Yiddish — never in Russian for the benefit of the huge Russian reading public — and are never as forthright as they ought to be. However, if anyone has any doubt as to the sick situation of this entire problem the following may be instructive. Since Sept. 1977 *Sovetish Heimland* has printed six or seven page resumes or summaries in both Russian and English for non-Yiddish readers that give synopses of the noteworthy items, whether short stories, articles, poems or editorial comments published in its Yiddish pages. Yet, the English and Russian language resumes in July, 1978 carried no mention whatever of the critique of V. Skurlatov's book, *Zionism and Apartheid,* though items of much less importance were summarized in these languages!

In order to "prove" that anti-Semitism is not one of the reasons that prompt Soviet Jews to emigrate Mr. Aronoff cites examples of the most negative types of Jews who did leave, particularly of people who were looking to get rich quick abroad.

In one instance a doctor in a Soviet city told him that when he had graduated from medical school "two of his friends (Jewish) immediately applied for emigration to Israel. He could not discover a logical reason for their action. Neither could speak, read or write Yiddish. They had never indicated an interest in anything Yiddish. Baffled, the doctor speculated maybe they thought they can benefit better financially." A year later these two doctors asked their friend to help them return to the Soviet Union. "They were just fools *(duraki),* commented the doctor" (p. 66). Here it is Jews after money who didn't succeed.

Mr. Aronoff was frequently told that many of the Soviet Jews who left for Israel or other countries fell upon hard times and wanted to return to the Soviet Union. Yet, 50,000 Soviet Jews are expected to emigrate this year! I know of former Soviet Jews who regularly speak by phone to their relatives in the Soviet Union. Presumably if things are so bad here they would tell this to their relatives and so spare them any bad experiences. Why most Soviet Jews still want to emigrate despite their knowledge of expected difficulties abroad is a question Mr. Aronoff avoids.

This reviewer shares the view that the great majority of Soviet Jews do not want to leave their homeland — despite the problems with which they have to contend — and indeed they shouldn't. Jews have made important contributions to the defense and construction of the Soviet state and to all aspects of Soviet society. They should be able to enjoy a secure future as one of the many nationalities in their homeland. At the same time, those Soviet Jews who see no future for themselves or their children as Jews in the Soviet Union and want to emigrate ought to be allowed to do so.

Mr. Aronoff's arguments that the Jews who left the Soviet Union did so for reasons that were not "logical" or that they were not "mature" or were just cranks or speculators looking for an easy life in the capitalist West sound too politically biased, if not anti-Semitic, to be taken seriously.

A more perceptive view of this troubling situation was taken by Haim Suller, managing editor of the *Morgn Freiheit* of New York, who reported upon his return from a visit to the Soviet Union in Sept., 1978:

"Jews are leaving the Soviet Union because they feel they are more and more losing the gains of the revolution. The percentage of Jewish students in the higher educational institutions has been diminishing in recent years. According to reports of new arrivals and of tourists in the Soviet Union it is becoming more dificult for Jews to enter higher educational institutions or to receive advancement in the enterprises where they work. In the period of World War II many Jews earned higher military ranks. The old Jewish generals are gradually dying out; new high ranking Jewish officers, according to all reports, are no longer assigned. There are no longer any important Jewish diplomats or important Jewish leaders in the Communist Party, even if here or there one still finds Jews in important positions, such as Venyamin Dimshitz, who is a minister and others" (*Morgn Freiheit,* Oct. 1. 1978).

The Soviet Jewish question does not fit into other familiar categories in Jewish history. Nevertheless, it has turned out to be more disturbing and vexatious than many of us could have imagined 10 or 20 years ago, let alone longer. Mr. Aronoff's booklet repeats the pleasant and official assurances that have been heard many times before, but they now are simply unacceptable.

July-August, 1979

* In 1979 the Jewish population of Birobidjan was recorded as 10,166 (or 5.9% of the population of the Jewish Autonomous Region).

** A Research Report issued by the Institute of Jewish Affairs in London in December, 1985 stated: "Yiddish became an optional subject in a few Birobidjan schools in 1980; a Yiddish primer was published in 1982..."

Soviet Evacuations in World War II

By MICHAEL MIRSKI

Question

In your Oct., 1978 issue you ran an article on Stalinism in Poland.

On p. 26, Mr. Mirski mentions that after Hitler's attack on Russia he was transferred deep into Russia.

I am very interested in learning more about the action of the Soviet government to save Jewish lives by transporting them East. Did this actually take place on a large scale; was there resentment among the populace, etc.?

Can you or Mr. Mirski supply any details?

HERBERT L. SANDERS

Glenview, Ill., Jan. 15, 1979

Reply

I am eager to answer the questions raised, basing myself for the most part on my personal observations and experiences.

On the second day after Hitler's invasion of the Soviet Union, i.e. June 23, 1941, there began in Kovel, where I resided at the time, the evacuation of the families of Soviet civilians and military officialdom. In my capacity as school inspector, several teachers of the city schools appeared before me and expressed their desire that they too be evacuated. I thereupon sent out a suitable telegraphic notification circular. Unfortunately, of the approximately 150 teachers and educators, only a group of about 10 or so responded, none of them natives of Kovel, but refugees from ethnic Poland since 1939. These included Ida Merzhan (now a well-known pedagogue in Poland), Maria Zorska, Gabriela Pausher Kleinerman-Klonovska and her husband Stefan (both now literary figures in Poland), Dr. Rudover and his wife (now in Belgium), Madame Perlmutter (now in Israel) — all Jews. This group, which left the very same day, also included my wife, my sister (all worked in the school system), my mother and our children. I, as an activist, remained in the city.

What proved to be a complicated and drawn out process was the evacuation of about 100 Jewish children, ranging in age from 8 to 16 years of age from the Orphanage. Madame Raitzya (whose family name escapes me), who headed the Orphanage before the war and had a tremendous influence on the children and the teaching personnel, was utterly opposed to the evacuation of the orphans. She argued that she remembered the Germans during World War I... Similar illusions were widespead not only among the broad strata of the Jewish bourgeoisie and petty-bourgeoisie. Even a prominent Jewish Communist activist from Warsaw left western Byelorussia in 1940, to which he had fled in 1939, and returned to Warsaw.

Two days later, i.e. June 25, when the evacuation of the Soviet civilian administration had begun, and I too began to prepare to leave the city, I made my way to the headquarters of the Division General and appealed to him for help in evacuating the Orphanage. He immediately assigned two army trucks to me. When I arrived at the orphan asylum, the mood of the children had already undergone a change. They were already sitting on their knapsacks. In addition, the bombardment of the city had instilled fear into the children, which had a decided effect on the bearing of the older ones. They threatened that if the Orphanage was not evacuated as a body, they would form a group and leave by themselves. A number of them were already at the railroad station.

The children piled into the trucks with alacrity. Madame Raitzya, however, remained adamant. My urgent pleas to her to travel with us were in vain. She was joined in this refusal by the majority of the personnel, who elected to stay behind. I was left practically without my teachers. Only after arriving at the station, where two freight cars, called *tyeplushki* by the Russians, were set aside for us on a long train of open flatcars, was I able to complete some semblance of a pedagogic technical staff. Fortunately I had found a group of teachers and acquaintances at the station, among them the well-known Yiddish writer, Leib Olitzki (literature teacher in the Kovel *Mittleshul*), who helped me.

We left Kovel at dawn of the 26th of June and on the 30th were already in Stalingrad. The trip was not an easy one. However, that is another story. All of the children survived. And among them, Esther Gallon, now the wife of the renowned Yiddish plastic artist and architect, Isaak Reisman, who now live in Paris.

As we can see, the evacuation of Kovel included most of the Jews; but that was the general characteristic feature in the Western Ukraine and Western Byelorussia, where Polish Jews had settled. Still, if one drew the conclusion that the Soviet government had the special tendency to evacuate Jews deep into the Soviet Union, this would be false. The evacuation was a *general* evacuation. Both in principle and in practice, this was applied to all citizens, without regard for their ethnic identity. This help was extended to all those who did not wish to remain under the Hitler-German occupation.

Concerning the statement attributed to Moshe Kaganovich in his book, *The Jewish Participation in the Partisan Movement of Soviet Russia,* (Rome, 1948, in YIddish, p. 188), that Soviet Pres, Mikhail Kalinin issued an order to evacuate *Jews as a first priority,* I must regretfully state that *such an order was never issued.* The statement aroused doubts from the fact alone that the alleged order of Kalinin does not have a date or number. Incidentally, this has been affirmed by the author himself. In a letter to me from Tel Aviv, Oct. 14, 1979, responding to my inquiry, Moishe Kaganovich writes, among other things: "No, it appears it was not an order from Mikhail Kalinin 'to evacuate Jews first of all.' In a later book, which I published in Israel in 1954, I wrote precisely that there had not been such an order at all from Kalinin. The title of the book in Hebrew is *Milkhome Hapartizanim Hayudim Mimizrach-Eiropa.* Kaganovich adds that a Yiddish translation of the Hebrew text appeared in Buenos Aires in 1956, published by the Central Farband of Polish Jews in Argentina.

What was the attitude of the Soviet population towards the evacuation, called *byezhentzi*? I can attest only to what I personally experienced.

The train upon which we rode travelled four days. We were practically the first refugees of the Soviet-German War that arrived deep in the Soviet Union. En route, at the railroad station, the railroad officials as well as the civilian population received us with pity and sympathy. They treated us to bread, milk and fruit, although we were not lacking in our own provisions. At the time they couldn't foresee that in the near future they, too, would find themselves in a similar situation.

Over Stalingrad there reigned a serenely peaceful atmosphere. The children were very warmly received by the Regional Government. Very soon they were taken to the city of Komishin, 160 kilometers north of Stalingrad, along the Volga.

All told, about 300,000 Polish Jews, and millions of Soviet Jews, remained alive, not as a result of a definite, *special* action on the part of the Soviet government to save them, but rather as a consequence of the general policy of evacuating the populance from those Soviet territories that were threatened by the Germans. It must be stressed that the evacuation was carried out in an organized fashion. Not only were people evacuated, but entire industrial complexes as well, which were dismantled and then brought to the Urals, Siberia and Middle Asia together with the native working personnel and supervisors.

But parallel with it, I must mention the following two points. A few of my colleagues and I were appointed teachers in the Regional Central, Bikovo, 120 kilometers north of Stalingrad, along the Volga. This decision was not to my liking. I felt that I should join the army. A soon as I arrived in Bikovo, I reported to the military commissariat *(Voyencomat)* and asked to be inducted into the Red Army. However, I was met with a refusal, although in a very polite form. "You are needed as the principal of a school. When we will need you, we will call you."

I was very disappointed and felt it was an expression of distrust of me personally. But I soon learned that I fell into the category of those inhabitants, called *"zapadniki"* — of western peoples, i.e. all those evacuees who stemmed not only from ethnic Poland, such as Warsaw, Lodz and Lublin, but also from the Western Ukraine and western Byelorussia, which areas had been incorporated in the fall of 1939 into the Soviet Union as integral parts of the Soviet Ukraine and Soviet Byelorussia. Those *born* in these areas received normal Soviet passports — all the *evacuees* were discriminated against and refused admission into the ranks of the Red Army because of lack of confidence in them. Even those military personnel who were drawn into the Red Army during the first weeks of the war were separated from the Army in accordance with a special order from the highest military command, and were transferred to the so-called "Trud-Front" or work-front in the hinterland. It is self-evident that this order affected all the Jews of those regions; but even so, this was not a special discriminatory act against Jews. It applied to all — Ukrainians, White Russians, Moldavians, etc. from those areas occupied by the Red Army in Bessarabia in the fall of 1939. There were a few exceptions, but very minute ones.

In conclusion, another matter which pertains *only* to Jews. I refer here to the matter of complete *silence,* the suppression of facts regarding the destruction of thousands, millions of Soviet Jews by the Hitlerite occupying forces.

It is well-known that the German forces did not establish any ghettos in the great stretches of the Soviet Union that they occupied. One exception, however, was the city of Minsk in Byelorussia. In the above mentioned occupied territory, the Hitlerite butchers led tens and hundreds of thousands of Jews out immediately upon occupation and executed them on the spot. The Jewish population of each and every city and town had its own Babi Yar. Without ghettos. Not like in Poland.

How then did the Communist Party of the Soviet Union react to this, or the Soviet government with Stalin at its head? Did they alert the world and the peoples of the Soviet Union that Hitlerism had begun to realize its politics of extermination of the Jewish population of the Soviet Union? This occurred even before the erection of the death-camps in Auschwitz and Treblinka, in which there were no Soviet Jews...

No! The Soviet Government did not act that way. Quite the contrary. It began to *hide* such facts both from the world and from its own population in the hinterland. In the Soviet press and on its radio they publicized the fact that the German-Hitlerite hordes were shooting 20,000, 30,000, 50,000 *Soviet citizens.* Formally, this was the truth. The Jews *were* Soviet citizens. Of course the German-Hitlerite occupation forces were brutal to all the peoples of the Soviet Union. The Nazi invaders robbed the Soviet population of their possessions; sent hundreds of thousands off to Germany to serve in forced labor battalions. Hunted down and destroyed hundreds of thousands of partisans, captured activists and conspirators, raped and abused women, and so forth.

True, this touched significant sections of these peoples. But the politics of *total annihilation,* of shooting the entire population, from infants to the aged — such policies *were used only against the Jewish population* in the occupied Soviet territories. It was news of such anti-Semitic racist politics, the politics of genocide, that the Soviet Government, with Stalin at its head, *not only kept to itself, but made every effort to hush up and hide* from public opinion in the world at large and especially within the country itself.

During the years 1941 and 1942, I, being at the time in the hinterland, reading the Soviet press daily, and listening to the Soviet radio, *did not have the slightest inkling* that the hundreds of thousands of murdered "Soviet citizens" were Jews. All information media were centralized and controlled by the government. Private radio-transmitters were confiscated right after the outbreak of the war. Nor did I have any *inkling* of the Uprising of the Warsaw Ghetto. It was not till 1944, when I met some of my comrades from Poland in Moscow, that I learned of that event. Even in 1952 there appeared *only two* sentences in the Soviet Encyclopedia describing the Warsaw Ghetto Uprising (*Bolshaya Sovietskaya Encyclopedia,* Moscow, Vol. 11, p. 190).

What were the reasons for such Soviet policies? There are many. But this is a separate and very serious topic, which cannot be discussed in an answer to several questions that were raised.

I should like to recapitulate: There was no special policy to rescue Polish Jews in the Soviet Union. The Soviet Government maintained silence and deliberately hid the fact that the Soviet *Jewish* population was being annihilated by Hitler and his forces.

July-August, 1980

234

The Ordeal of Hebrew and Yiddish Soviet Writers

By NORA LEVIN

AS we approach Aug. 12th, 32 years after the murder of the greatest Soviet Yiddish writers, I think of the late Haim Grade's "Elegy for the Soviet Yiddish Writers." You may remember his words:

> I weep for you with all the letters of the alphabet
> that made your hopeful songs. I saw how reason spent
> itself in vain for hope, how you strove against regret
> and all the while your hearts were rent
> to bits, like ragged prayer books...

It is a slashing, bitter poem, decrying the compromises the writers made, the shame and agony they had to live with, the "crooked mirror for the world of truth." But the poem is also filled with great pathos and heartache for the treachery they endured and finally faced. Grade knew and, with a poet's power, could penetrate the shifting, blinding sands of their life. But try as we will, we cannot penetrate that life, and our mourning is compounded by this failure.

In a very profound way, we never really knew them. We never really could know them. They lived behind veils, behind masks, in secret places they never could share, speaking with a forked tongue, writing with a forked pen, wary, frightened, learning the balancing act of survival from day to day. They could never be, as we might say, themselves, their true selves and as we mourn their loss, we also grieve over the immense emotional and intellectual toll their survival must have exacted throughout most of their lives in the Soviet Union up to Aug. 12, 1952.

Already as early as 1926, feeling a premonition of doom, Izi Kharik wrote:

> Ikh hob epes haynt derfilt dem toyt,
> Un heyb zikh on far zikh aleyn tsu shemen...

(In a way today I perceived the end, And I begin to be ashamed of myself for myself...)

235

The date, Aug. 12, 1952, of course, has special poignance — because the execution of 24 leading Soviet Yiddish writers and cultural figures was an act of official murder, not only of this intellectual elite, but of Jewish culture. The executions were intended deliberately, officially to destroy Jewish culture, root and branch, to leave it without children, inheritors or transmitters.

But the murders of Aug. 12, 1952 were not an isolated act, or an aberration, not even just a bloody part of the bloody Black Years, but rather the climax of an immense but losing struggle Jews had been waging for many years to develop and sustain an identifiable Jewish culture. If we face the facts of history since 1929, without illusions, we must see that the vicissitudes of this struggle have been entangled in shifting, often contradictory, Soviet doctrines of Jewish nationality, improvisations, political and economic expediency, internal power struggles and foreign policy needs.

It is true, there have been periods of rich creative experience — the '20's and early '30's, for example — when there was still a large measure of literary freedom and experimentation and impressive Jewish scholarship. In the late '20's there was also an ambitious land resettlement plan for Jews in the Ukraine and Crimea that looked toward national autonomy and a Soviet Jewish culture in Yiddish.

But, simultaneously, the government and the *Evsektsiya* the Jewish Sections of the Communist Party, were persecuting Zionists, the impoverished artisans and petty traders in the *shtetlach,* and making Hebrew an illegal language. We tend to forget that the great flowering of *Hebrew* culture in Russia after the March, 1917 revolution was also killed in the Soviet Union. The Hebrew presses were confiscated and Tarbut, the great Hebrew secular movement was closed down. Bergelson, Markish and Hofshteyn, who had earlier written in Hebrew, did so no longer. Hebrew teachers and writers, including Bialik and Tschernichovsky, could no longer earn a living and were forced to emigrate. Thousands of Jews linked to Hebrew and Zionism were sent to prisons and exile. Many died.

As we mourn today, we also call to mind these great losses, including another group of writers who, in the early 1920's believed that Hebrew, like other languages, must have a secure place in the new communist order. They attacked the official disapproval and suppression of Hebrew as illogical and senseless. How could one be illogical and senseless. How could one be hostile toward a language in which the principles of social justice and other revolutionary ideas had been expressed in ancient times? They argued: "we are Soviet writers writing in Hebrew, and we are strangled. For 200 languages there is room and accomodation. Why should only Hebrew be disqualified?"

236

Their work, they said, came out of genuine revolutionary springs. They identified fully with the new communist order and wanted to create in a new revolutionary spirit. But their fragile anthologies and journals were suppressed and destroyed. Many of these passionate lovers of Hebrew languished in prison and exile, desperately reaching out for a crumb of their beloved language. To the many names of Jews who struggled and suffered for the cause of Jewish culture, we should add Haim Lensky, Elisha Rodin, Avraham Friman, Zvi Preigerson, Moshe Hyog and Bat Miriam. The list could go on and on.

During the early and middle '30's, long after these writers were silenced, Jewish writers who wrote in Yiddish were drawn into acrimonious debates and nasty polemics. There was intense hostilty between co-called proletarian writers and censors and those who wanted more artistic autonomy. There were ominous warnings, denunciations and attacks. Quite soon, writers of "petty bourgeois" and "nationalist" deviations and the sin of "individualism" were put into a literary strait-jacket and forced to write according to rigid formulas of proletarian art and "socialist realism." In anticipating criticism or condemnation, they began to slide into demeaning confessions and self-censorship. They began to feel great anxiety about their personal safety and economic security and tried to avoid the slippery slope of "heresies," as we can gather from the guarded letters they wrote to Leivik, Charney and Opatoshu in America. Many took refuge in translating foreign works into Russian and what Der Nister called "reportage."

Meanwhile, the Jewish land resettlement program was swallowed up in the collectivization program and the first Five Year Plan and in the so-called autonomous region of Birobidzhan in 1934. The hopes and expectations for Birobidzhan, however, came crashing down during the purges of 1936-38, when most of the old Bolsheviks and Jewish political and cultural leaders at the time were eliminated.

Among the thousands who perished were not only the leading Jewish writers, Isaac Babel, (1894-1939) Izi Kharik (1898-1937) and Moyshe Kulbak (1886-1940), but loyal Jewish communists: Moyshe Litvakov (1875-1937), editor of *Emes, Evsektsiya* activists: Samuel Agursky, Simon Dimanshtain, Esther Frumkin, Rachmiel Veinshtain; the literary scholar Max Erik (1898-1937) and Joseph Liberberg, chairman of the Birobidzhan Soviet and former head of the Jewish Scientific Institute of Kiev, who made Kiev the center of Jewish linguistics.

With the German invasion of the Soviet Union in June, 1941, there was another switch in official policy. The Soviet Government reached out to world Jewry for support of its war effort by an open apeal to world Jewish solidarity.

In April, 1942, a Jewish Anti-Fascist Committee was formed, emphasizing the need for Jewish unity in the struggle against fascism.

Yiddish writers began making contacts with the Jewish press and organizations abroad. Broadcasts in Yiddish were heard and a newspaper, *Aynikayt*, was published.

Thirty-five members of the committee were literary figures, including the leading writers of the time: Markish, Bergelson, Der Nister, Feffer, Ehrenburg, Hofshteyn. The great actor and director, Shlomo Mikhoels, became chairman of the committee and was to become a central figure in the slowly gathering network of activities in behalf of Soviet Jews, who were now accorded an organizational framework for the first time since the *Evsektsiya* were dissolved in 1930.

A signal contribution of the committee was the revitalization of Yiddish literature and publishing. A strong core within the committee wanted to strengthen and direct Jewish cultural and communal life after the war, to provide aid to refugees and survivors of the Nazi onslaught, and rehabilitate Jewish farms in the Crimea. There was even hope for a Jewish republic there, as you know. Mikhoels and Feffer also made a historic trip to the United States and England in the summer of 1943. The two men were swept up by waves of overjoyed American Jews who saw them as miraculous emissaries of a Jewry long separated. Both men themselves were deeply stirred and expressed the hope that, although there had been estrangement in the past, living contacts and exchanges of books would be possible in the future. Ambitious plans for Jewish projects were made and Jews in both countries believed that a new era loomed ahead.

In Palestine, too, there was a strong feeling that a historic reconciliation between Zionism and Soviet Russia was at hand. Often forgotten, or perhaps not sufficiently well known, were the activities of the V League, the meetings between Ivan Maisky, Soviet Minister to Great Britain, and other Soviet representatives, and Zionist leaders and his visits to several kibbutzim. Illusions again rose only to fall once more in the post-war campaign against so-called "rootless cosmopolitans" and attacks on Jews as American spies. The Cold War and spreading anti-Semitism claimed many Jewish victims. Maisky himself was arrested during the vehement anti-Jewish and anti-Zionist campaigns of the Black Years.

Soviet support at the United Nations for the recognition of Israel in 1947-8 was crucial to the future existence of the Jewish state, but must not conceal the other, larger aspect of Stalin's anti-Jewish policy inside Russia, which to some scholars was already visible in 1944. All efforts to re-start Yiddish schools and newspapers failed. Mikhoels was murdered. The victimization and resistance of Jews during the Holocaust was conspicuoulsy missing from official publications. The Jewish Anti-Fascist Committee, the great Yiddish theater, Ehrenburg's Black Book and numerous other projects were liquidated. Waves of arrests, including those of the Yiddish writers, followed in 1949, and the subsequent Black Years of Soviet Jewry struck terror and fear in the hearts of all Jews. The grotesque

Doctors' Plot erupted in 1953, and there is good evidence that Stalin planned deportations of Jews "to the East" — an ominous phrase.

The hopes for a thaw after Stalin died rose once more, but were short-lived, and in recent years the process of extinguishing virtually every trace of Jewish culture continues. The Soviet Union has now become a prime center for the production and dissemination of anti-Semitic literature. Jewish dissidents have become hostage in Soviet-American global competition and Middle East tensions. I personally see no hope at all for a vigorous, viable Jewish culture in the Soviet Union, even if U.S. Soviet relations improve.

What, then can progressive American Jews do in this tragic impasse? We must work for better relations, of course. We must also continue to protest the present destruction of Jewish culture, but without illusions. Our best and most realistic path, I believe, is to act to preserve the works of Soviet Yiddish and Hebrew writers, to make sure they do not disappear, and to make the original works available in translation — in English here, and in Russian, in the Soviet Union, something which the Soviet Union seems willing to do. These acts of salvage, preservation and translation should become a moral obligation for us, a high duty, so that younger Soviet Jews and Jews here will at least have access to the significant works of Bergelson, Der Nister, Markish, Hofshteyn, Kvitko, among others. They should form an imperishable part of our past. Thus, we will not allow Grade's melancholy lines — "The young have forgotten you and me and the hour of our grief" — we must not allow those lines to come to pass.

July-August, 1985

Babi Yar

By SHIKE DRIZ

*Translated from the Yiddish
by Martin Birnbaum*

IF only I had a ceiling-beam,
I'd hang the cradle with joy
And swing and cradle my tiny boy.
But flames have swept my house away
Where is the cradle to hang now and sway?

Pathways are covered with thorns,
like stubble,
Thistles and thorns
And smoke-blackened rubble!

I would hang the cradle
On a tree somewhere
And swing my other child
High up in the air,
But there is nothing,
Nothing I can do.
Not a thing is left me,
Not the lace of a shoe!

Not a leaf, not a twig
Has been left of our oak—
Only a little mound
With ashes as a cloak.

I would cut off my two long braids
To hang the cradle on,
But I do not know
Where my little ones' bones are gone!

Wail with me, mothers, our ancient wail,
Mothers near and far,
Help me, mothers, help me
To cradle the Babi Yar!

April, 1978

240

Task for Redemption (story)

"**S**TOP shivering, man! And stop crying."

In the fading sunset Rabbi Isaac stared at the face of the Nazi prisoner before him. He had been listening to the man's rasping voice for a little while now without detecting a hint of fear in it. It was this, rather than the crying, that arrested his attention. Other prisoners had cried, but that had not kept him from issuing the verdict: Death. But as he looked from his tall, blond prisoner to the taut faces of the scouts who had brought him in, he decided that there was something about the German that called for deliberation. And because he could not say what it was, the sobbing annoyed him.

The four men made a strange group; the strangest was the rabbi himself. Short and powerfully built, Rabbi Isaac wore the same long black capote he had worn in his *shul* in Sandomir. His graying earlocks and dense beard were as carefully looked after when he was leading his partisans in the field as when his life had been a glorifying of the one God. The broad yellow belt he wore sagged toward his right side because of the revolver in its holster.

The prisoner was of the company that had burned the village of Shernovo and killed every woman and child in it. He had denied taking part in the atrocity. However, his repeated *"Nein, nein"* had not been merely a denial; his voice seemed to be saying something more. This the scouts showed no sign of hearing.

Weighing this overtone, Rabbi Isaac suddenly noticed that his aide, Reb Avreimel, seemed to be observing the group from a distance. But Avreimel abruptly descended into the dugout near which he had been standing, and Isaac re-looked again at the prisoner's face. Then he spoke to the older of the two scouts.

"What do you say, Solokoff?"

"It's true," Solokoff grumbled, scowling at the necessity of corroborating the Nazi's words. "He did come and give himself up even before we leveled a gun at him. But all the same I say shoot him, that's what I say."

"Bitte, bitte," the prisoner broke in, relieved at hearing his captors bear out his assertions. "I came to you myself. You must believe me! I had to run away from them. Two days and nights in the woods and swamps. It is the truth."

241

"And you. Vassilenko?" Rabbi Isaac addressed the ex-teacher, whose jaws were champing a straw.

"Shoot him. His tears can't wash away the blood the murders have shed." Vassilenko's tone left no room for discussion.

"But you brought him to me," said Rabbi Isaac significantly, "and for that I thank you." He opened the brown wallet that had been taken from the prisoner. There was a certificate of identification: Kurt Laubenheim, Schmilka an der Elbe. He pulled out a few letters, fingered them, put them back and thrust the wallet into the back pocket of his capote.

"Laubenheim, you want me to believe that you came to give yourself up. Yet you took part in murdering the women and children of Shernovo — didn't you?" Rabbi Isaac spoke almost vaguely, as if addressing some purpose not yet clear even to himself.

"That I did not do!" The prisoner's words broke out with unexpected vehemence. "Because I could not do it, because I would not kill any more, I had to run away. They wanted to shoot me right after that attack."

Solokoff, without understanding the explosion of words, spat in disgust. Vassilenko gripped his gun tighter and stared coldly into the Nazi's face.

Rabbi Isaac invited: "Tell us about it."

A fit of trembling seemed to shake the disjointed phrases out of the prisoner's mouth. The German commander, enraged by partisan attacks, had ordered the destruction of the village which had been known to shelter wounded guerillas. He, Kurt Laubenheim, was a member of the outfit detailed to destroy the village.

"I was in the squad." Suddenly he seemed overtaken by the need to make himself clear in as short a time as possible. "Yes, yes, I admit I had done the same thing before in other places. I had my bayonet on my gun. When we broke into the school, there was the teacher. She stood in the doorway of the room. And she looked into my face without anger. She did not speak. I couldn't raise my gun. Her face was like the woman's who kept the sweet shop by the river in Schmilka. She stood in the door to hide the children.

I pushed her into the room and shut the door. I couldn't," the prisoner pleaded to the bearded man. "I couldn't do it. I walked out of the building. The corporal beat me because I had not carried out orders. He had watched me through the window and was going to bring me to the captain. It was then I broke away."

Isaac translated the prisoner's words for his companions. Once again he asked them, "What shall we do?"

"Shoot him." The two spoke with one voice.

Rabbi Isaac said firmly, "We will know what to do later. Take him away. We can finish with him after we talk it over again."

He looked after the scouts as they hurried the prisoner off to the small stockade, then walked to the dugout. Reb Avreimel was inside, seated against a wall near the entrance. But Rabbi Isaac was in no mood for talk. Talk was useful after a problem had been mulled over in solitude. Besides, he suspected from long association with his aide that the latter already had a good idea of the problem raised by the prisoner who had given himself up. Avreimel had not let life with the partisans change his habit of listening, without appearing to listen, to everything touching on his, Isaac's, affairs.

The rabbi sat down on one of the steps.

"And if he confesses, as our sages say, does he not set for himself a portion in the world to come?" Rabbi Isaac asked himself in a humming undertone. "And this one had confessed, Father in Heaven, and in doing so has won for himself that portion. But we are dealing here with an enemy whose wickedness is a visitation upon all of us at this very moment. Ai, yes, y-e-s." A reflective hand tugged at his earlock. "But death for him will not assist us against the enemy; death will not weaken the foe who is already weakened by his desertion. What to do? What does one do?"

Isaac got up. went over to his pile of bedding, reached among the blankets for his fine-print Talmud, and returned to the steps. He turned the pages, looked for a certain passage and twisted the long curl of his locks meditatively as he read. But though he considered the rules for the punishment of murderers, noting the exceptions of Rabbi Simon, he was no nearer to the solution of his present problem.

From the stockade the captive Nazi was pleading in a tremulous voice. *"Bitte, bitte, horen sie doch vas ich sage,"* he called again and again. "It is the truth — the murders I have done press on my soul. Please hear what I say to you. Do with me what you like, but believe what I am saying. It is the truth, the truth, I swear it."

The prisoner's voice rose until it penetrated Rabbi Isaac's concentration. The rabbi glanced up, his unseeing gaze resting for a moment on Reb Avreimel, who was poring over a booklet.

"What does one do?" Isaac asked himself again. "Shoot him? An easy way out, but what is the gain? And what may be the loss instead? here he comes crying to us, leaving the murderers. Has something remained, something of what was there before they turned him into a beast? And my answer is 'Shoot him'? But if he is truly repentant, what then? Is this justice?"

Suddenly Rabbi Isaac straightened up. "Avreimel," he called, "you sit there and say nothing. You let me shake the questions around in my head like the seeds in a dry melon. Avreimel, I need help. What nonsensical pages are you wasting your eyes on?"

"Rabbi," answered Avreimel in a conciliatory tone, "there were days when you yourself read to us this story of the Three Gifts of Peretz and bade us take its profound message to heart."

"Peretz he tells me! Oh — Isaac Leib Peretz? And what does he say to you in your gropings through this darkness of Egypt, Avreimel?"

"What does he say? A fine question you ask only because you seem to have forgotten." Avreimel put a hand against the wall to steady himself, jerked himself up, and came over to the foot of the steps where his rabbi was sitting. "A soul in judgment, you might say," he said, parting his beard to right and left. 'The scales stand in perfect balance, the evil not weighing a feather's weight more than the good, the good not a breath more than the evil. Talk about a predicamenat! Do you admit the soul to Paradise? Do you send it to Gehenna?"

"Come, Avareimel," demanded Rabbi Isaac. "If you have the energy to mumble the problem, spare me my agony and give me the solution."

"It's not mine," Avreimel demurred. "It's Peretz', and he, you know, indulged in these soul-weighings and imaginings. The All-Merciful Judge sets the soul a task — to bring to Heaven's Court three gifts which by their worthiness will win the soul redemption and admission."

"I remember — stop! I remember," Isaac exclaimed and his earlocks swayed. "He says he is penitent, that German — we don't know. Go look into the human soul! A chicken — it's opened, you look at the heart, the gall, the gizzard — there's something to go by. But a man's soul?"

"Ich schwoere bei der seele meines bruders," The prisoner shouted hoarsely, his voice slashing through Rabbi Isaac's deliberations. "By my brother's soul I swear I am telling the truth. Hear me and judge."

Isaac's eyes kindled. A Nazi resting his plea on a soul? The thought reminded Isaac of the letters in the wallet. Why had he not gone over them before? Without further word to Avreimel he pulled out the letters and began to read them, intoning the words as if hearing them gave him clearer understanding.

"Tzum tot urteilen veil zie den Prister geshutzt hatte." Death because she sheltered a — no, no, not *a* but *the* priest. But who was the priest? Why had Laubenheim's mother felt she had to let her son know about this particular priest? Why had (he looked more closely at the German script) Frau Volger risked death to shelter this man? And who was Frau Volger?

"Go, Avreimel," Isaac said. "That crying must stop. Ask Professor Gorin to come and also ask Sergeant Ordenko and Militaman Goruskin to join him. Tell Solokoff and Vassilenko to bring the prisoner here. I want the court to hear his plea."

The German would get a chance to reveal himself, Rabbi Isaac thought as he waited. He would urge it if the proposal needed urging. Only his insistence that they wait had held the two scouts from their intention to shoot him. Avreimel, of course, could be expected to understand the delay, but that was because he had had the task of winning over Professor Gordin when Gordin was still wavering between going underground and taking his place openly against the Nazis. Gordin, too, he hoped, would glimpse something of his thought.

What a business this was, Isaac reflected, countering Nazi might with the strength of reason! Man, what art thou? Capable of riding the lightning and yet unready to live as every humane prompting suggested he was designed to. Isaac turned from these thoughts as Gordin came toward him.

He could see that Gordin's experience with the partisans had changed his appearance. His face had tanned and toughened during the months in which he had served as technician to the guerrillas. Out of scraps of metal, stray pieces of wire and his own will power he had devised ways of impeding the enemy's machine. And he had become more fleshy! Isaac felt he hed done well in bringing the professor to the guerrilla outfit.

"Rabbi Isaac," Gordin said, "Reb Avreimel tells me you want to give the prisoner a hearing."

"True," Isaac answered.

"I think I know what you want to do," Gordin said.

"Say it, if you know."

"You want him to prove that he is really a changed man." Gordin stopped as if wondering whether to go on.

"Well?"

"That's why you held off the scouts' decision to kill him," continued Gordin with more certainty. "What's the sense of killing him if he has saved himself from being a beast?"

Isaac smiled in his beard. "So you have taken to reading my mind, Wladislaw?"

"I'll tell you why," Gordin answered quickly. "I need fuses, chemicals, explosives — all we can lay our hands on. He can tell us where we can get them. And — if your decision allows it — maybe he can even join us."

"What do you think? Shall we trust him?" Rabbi Isaac asked.

"There's no judgment I'd sooner rely on than yours." Gordin's hand rested for a moment on the older man's arm in token of the affectionate respect he had never voiced.

"We will see. Come, here are the others."

Together they walked down into Isaac's quarters. The dugout had originally been the root cellar of a small farmhouse. It was roofed with thick beams, which now bore a huge mound of earth to conceal its existence from enemy fliers. Inside it was dry and sweet-smelling, filling at times with the unpredictable emanations of carrots and apples that had vanished long ago. The table on which maps and battle plans were drawn up was Avreimel's work, built out of planks and odd pieces of wood. There were a few stools, a box or two. At the deeper end, on a low platform, were the two blankets that served as Isaac's bedding.

Now Isaac set on the table two tin cans converted into lamps by means of wicks floating in oil. He lighted the wicks, pointed to a box and asked Gordin to sit. He placed a stool on either side of his own seat behind the table. After these preparations he walked forward to greet Sergeant Ordenko and Militia man Goruskin.

Unlike in appearance — the sergeant was a short, ruddy-faced Ukrainian and the militiaman a lean, mountaineer from the Crimea — they were alike in their toughness and burning hatred of the enemy.

These two were the only trained soldiers with the guerrilla unit. Both had been wounded in battle; both had been nursed by villagers after their armies retreated; both, on recovering, insisted on fighting behind enemy lines. They had brought a quality of military discipline to the activities of the partisans.

"You know why I asked you to come, I suppose," Isaac said. They nodded. "Good. I want us to hear this prisoner out. Here he is."

His hands fastened behind, the German shuffled awkwardly down the steps. He was followed by the scouts, their guns in their hands. Avreimel, behind them, paused to draw a curtain of blankets that hid the light coming from within the dugout. Then he descended quietly and took his place behind the group.

The judges seated themselved behind the table amid a thickening silence. The wicks flickered, spattering the judges, scouts and prisoner with an uneven red-yellow light and casting their distorted shadows on the walls. The prisoner tried to control the trembling in his limbs and shoulders.

"You may untie him, Avreimel," Isaac directed. The scouts moved back and Avreimel removed the rope.

"Now, Laubenheim, speak slowly. And you, Professor Gordin, will be good enough to translate if there is anything we don't understand."

"Do with me what you wish, only believe what I tell you now," the prisoner said once more. He rubbed his wrists where the rope had split the skin. "I had burned and killed like all the others. But when we were sent to Shernovo, I was already trying to get away."

He paused, his eyes seeking those of the rabbi. "So much you can do until you start thinking, but after that no more. For me the time had come. There was a letter from my mother. I had it with me when I stole out of the barracks. Yes, yes, there were other times when I felt I could not go on any more. I was drowning in a sea of human blood. I was helping to spill it myself — but we were watched at every step. They were as ready to shoot us down as those they called the enemy. But that is hard to believe — that they would kill their own — until it comes right into your own life. You know they shot a few men from the next squad but you want to believe it was because of cowardice in action, as they told you. Then my mother's letter came from home. In Schmilka, that's where I was born, they shot a woman because she sheltered a priest — my brother."

Rabbi Isaac's lips twitched with the unspoken words: his mother's message. Then he looked away so as to listen more carefully to Gordin's rapid translation. When he had finished, Rabbi Isaac asked quietly: "Who is Frau Volger?"

The prisoner's face contorted with pain and his eyes blazed. "The teacher in Shernovo looked just like her; she was defending the children just like Frau Volger, who died for protecting my brother. They killed my brother, the murderers."

Rabbi Isaac glanced at Gordin and then at Ordenko and Goruskin. Had they noticed that the prisoner, in answering the question, spoke first of the teacher rather than of Frau Vogler? In a Russian face he had found features he had cherished in a German woman. A Russian face, at last, had turned him away from murdering.

Controlling himself once more, the prisoner went on more calmly. "I could not get away before. In the schoolhouse I looked at the teacher and saw Frau Vogler. I could not raise my gun against her. I would be doing the very thing the murderers of my brother had done. My mother could not tell me everything that had happened but it was enough to tell me what Frau Vogler had done. From that moment I could not go on."

He stopped for a moment; the only sound was the rubbing of his hands against his chafed wrists. "Now do what you must do." He said this almost as an afterthought, as if telling his story had eased him of a burden he need no longer worry about.

Sergeant Ordenko said impassively, "He admits the murders. But is he to be trusted now?"

Goruskin asked, "What do the letters he spoke about say?"

Gordin translated them into the quiet. The eyes of the men behind the table never left the haggard, dirty face of the prisoner standing before them. Now that he had unburdened himself he was ready for whatever verdict they would come to. The scouts regarded him with a curiosity that had gradually softened the rigidity of their faces and eased the tautness of their bodies. They were puzzled to find that the man they had condemned to death in their thoughts was capable of words and thoughts stamped with human feeling.

Gordin had finished reporting the contents of the letter. "Your mother does not say that it was your brother who was sheltered by Frau Vogler," he remarked to the prisoner.

"That she could not do because her letter would be read by the military post office," the German answered. "It was enough for her to mention the priest. That told me everything."

"Never mind the letters," said Goruskin, obviously dissatisfied that they were so unlike what he had expected. "Here's a paper. Map out for us the way your camp is laid out." He drew a sheet of paper from his pocket and laid a stub of pencil beside it.

The prisoner leaned forward, picked up the pencil and began to draw. Gordin stood up to observe.

Sergeant Ordenko saw what Goruskin was doing. Among his own papers was a map of the Nazi camp, made by the guerrilla spy who had helped build the house for the Nazi commander. He opened his portfolio and drew out the map. When the prisoner finished, Ordenko put his own down beside the new drawing. Together the solders compared the two diagrams point by point.

"Here's the comander's house; *tak*. That's the commissary, and there's the storehouse for munitions and the garages for the motorcycles; *tak*. Those are the strong points at the entrances to the villages and these the barracks of the different units."

"What was your unit?" Ordenko demanded.

"Unit 103," replied the prisoner and unhesitatingly pointed out the barracks.

The sergeant studied his own map. "*Tak*, he said. "It is correct," he announced and stood up. "And now, for the death he has caused and confessed..."

As if suddenly remembering something, the prisoner reached for the pencil. "I forgot that at the western part of the camp," he said, adding new marks to the paper, "they have been building new strongpoints because they expect an attack there. I would strike lightly where they expect it, but in force at the eastern points."

Solokoff grinned as Gordin translated. He himself had reported the new construction to Rabbi Isaac. It was on that very reconnaissance that he and Vassilenko had picked up the prisoner. The Nazi was telling the truth, all right.

Ordenko had stopped as if surprised by the prisoner's added information. Coldly he said, "Good tactics, very good tactics." Then he returned to his original theme. "And now, for the deaths he has caused and confessed, we can have the prisoner shot. One less murderer to account for in the final reckoning."

Rabbi Isaac rose to his feet and was about to speak. He caught Gordin's eye and waited.

"That's not what we will do," Gordin announced with quiet determination. "This man can help us. He will tell me, I am sure, where we can get the supplies we need. That's one. Second, what he says has proven correct. Your own test shows he has told the truth. We can keep him here while we attack, so his life is still in our hands. What do you say, Goruskin?"

"I will wait for Rabbi Isaac," the militiaman answered.

Rabbi Isaac chose his words with deliberation. "I say he has won the right to live. We have listened to prisoners before. All insisted they had been ordered to torture and kill. This one takes upon himself the killing he has done." He paused. "Because he learned the horrible truth of what he was doing. What would we not give if more of them could learn? And he confesses his own responsibility. He does not even plead for his life. And we see he had turned away from what the beasts trained him to do. To turn against those who have dragged you into the pit, into murder and bestiality — is that something to overlook? When we shot the others we got rid of enemies. If we shoot him we kill someone who has learned what we are. The others we captured. But this man came to us himself. Is that so? Solokoff? Vassilenko?"

"It is so," the scouts answered, as they unconsciously shifted their weight so as to release their grip on their guns.

"*Tak*," said Goruskin. "I too think he has won his life."

The prisoner gazed at Rabbi Isaac. "Only let me go with you when you attack," he whispered. "This time my life will avenge death — my brother's and many more."

June, 1978

IV: Holocaust Memoirs

Flight from Hitler, 1939

Two Letters

By ROSA and OSCAR BERGOFFEN

*These two letters were sent to their 16-year-old daughter, Hedy, then
already in London. Almost a year after the family was reunited in London,
the Bergoffens emigrated to the USA, arriving in New York Jan. 1, 1940.
Hedy is now Hedy Shneyer. Her parents are both dead, Oscar in 1955,
Rosa in 1965. Hedy's anti-fascism is deeply rooted. — Ed.*

Antwerp, Jan. 14, 1939

My Dear:

You might be surprised to receive this letter from the land of golden
liberty. It is eight days since we are out of touch with Vienna. In any case let
me describe our recent adventures, how we made such a fast and drastic
decision which we had been agonizing over in weeks gone by.

A week ago, while Oscar went for his daily check-in with the police, a
security officer called at our apartment asking for his passport. I explained
that he carried the document with him (a lie). The officer ordered his
appearance next day at the security office. This prompted my decision.

I was to meet Oscar in two hours at a small Jewish restaurant in the
center of town. I had to act fast. I went to the expediters to send our large
pieces of luggage to the U.S., got some spare money from my brother, back
to the apartment to pack four valises and take a taxi to meet Oscar, who
suspected nothing. He was shocked by my actions and felt that the security
police would only ask him questions. But my decision (and fear) prevailed.

We set out for the railway depot. Oscar was fearful that we had too
much luggage, but it represented all my remaining earthly possessions. A
part of our belongings were already in Belgium, but I did not want to leave
the rest behind.

The trip went off without a hitch. We arrived in Cologne with a belly full
of worries (but no food in it). We had a number of leads from Vienna of
places that might provide illegal transport across the border. But no one
wanted to take us in. We were told the borders were heavily guarded at the
moment and the snow was piled too high to get across. Finally a small

250

pension took us in and promised to transport us the following day.

We mailed the suitcases to Antwerp, then headed for a Jewish coffee-house. There are many Jews here from Germany and they are not molested. Swastikas are not much in evidence, so we do not know whom we encounter in the streets. On our return the landlady told us the snow was too high for a departure today. But we could settle finances and so we started to bargain.

She wanted 360 Reichsmark per person and we settled for 320. But that was more cash than we possessed and so we settled on a total of 400 Reichsmark [=RM] plus 45 grams of gold (some of my jewelry plus my diamond ring). That left us with RM 20 in cash and a promise that we would start out in the morning. Conditions: transport by car from Cologne to Brussels.

We were appalled at the expense, but since it promised fast action, we had no recourse. We were not officially registered at the *pension,* and there might be a search warrant out for Oscar.

For supper we went to the same coffee-house. We met an acquaintance from Vienna and found out that everyone present in that room was waiting for transport across the border. But the Germans let no one out at the moment and the Belgians did not let them in. Besides, all mountain passes were closed by snow. A crosscountry sprint was not possible and those that have tried had to return. We further learned that payments have been taken from Jews and they were simply left stranded. Our acquaintance had paid RM 120 a week ago, and was not able to move or get his money back. He predicted point blank that we were being bilked.

You can imagine how we felt. Oscar became feverish looking at our predicament: we were flat broke, stranded, wanted by security police, and there were no assets to return to in Vienna. We regretted our trust in handing over money in advance of our departure. it was a terrible night without sleep for both of us.

At breakfast madame told us a "Feehn" (warm wind) had melted the snow considerably. Movement was possible.We sent additional luggage to Antwerp so as to have a minimum of bags to carry with us. At lunch we met our doomsday-forecaster, who again assured us that all was lost (but just in case, he noted our address and the name of the person who was to expedite our departure). That afternoon Madame told us two cars were leaving and we were to take the place of two persons who had the flu.

I fell on Madame's neck and kissed her with tears of gratitude. We met three other people who were to be in our party. The chauffeur turned up and told us the car needed repairs and we could not leave tonight. We resumed our wait with many misgivings. There was a lengthy debate over the phone about getting another car or driver, but suddenly things cleared up. We left. I think they were just waiting for news that a car that left earlier had gotten through.

We traveled in a gorgeous limousine at 80 kilometers through the snowy scenery. it was getting dark. The driver informed us the border was near; when he stops, we are to get out quickly without banging the door (it might be heard at the border guardhouse). We were to get into the ditch behind some bushes and wait there for the guide to come and get us. The car stops, we get out and fall into the snowy ditch. Our hearts are pounding. The car is gone. The night is pitch dark. After 25 minutes, a shadow comes across the field and whispers to follow, avoiding coughs, speech or any sound.

We clump through the deep snow, from one snowdrift to the next, fall into puddles, slip on icy spots, but we keep moving on. Our shoes are sop-wet, our clothes filthy. After an hour's march, one man fell sick. After a short rest he recovered. We continue on to a small wood. There we met the six people who had left in the earlier car. A five year old boy is with them. In the dark we can barely make out their silhouettes.

After a short rest we continue. We are already on Belgian soil, and we move cautiously. The guide tells us we are approaching the Belgian border guardhouse. We can now see a house with lights in the windows and are told that this is our destination. We leave the field and enter the road, one behind the other. Our guide leaves us. We slip and slide on the road the 100 steps to the house and to safety.

Rosa

Inside there was a huge stove with a warm fire, where we dried our shoes and stockings. We are given hot coffee, home baked bread and butter. We look over our travel companions, but they are all strangers to me. Not to Rosa, however; if she gets to the moon, she will at least meet some friends of friends.

Beds are not available, but we bed down on benches and on the floor. The fire will be kept going all night. We don't get much sleep. The windows are covered with cloth so no light can be seen from without. We are close to the border and the road is patrolled. We are to spend the next day here and tomorrow evening, after another hour's walk, another car will meet us.

We spend a cautious day at the house. Our needs have to be attended to in the stable, since we would not go outside. Eleven people and one child waited for the day to pass. At nightfall the guide shows up. He cautions us to leave the house in single file and in absolute silence. The light is extinguished and we await the sign to move out. Just as we begin to move floodlights come on, and we hear the command "Halt or we shoot." Dazed, we look about. There are six of us and, thank God, Rosa is with me. Two gendarmes with drawn revolvers confront us. The floodlights circle the night, but the rest of our party has disappeared.

They took us back to the house and questioned us closely: Why we came, if we knew each other, etc. Then they collected our passports. I began to plead with them not to send us back to the Germans and certain death. Two in our party spoke French and they pleaded with the gendarmes too. I show my papers and decorations from World War I. The gendarmes soften somewhat. The older of the two assures us they will not return us, but they have to take us to the Commander.

We all marched leisurely down the middle of the road to the command post. The Commander, a fine gentelman, again questioned us. In French we try to convey some of the awful things we all recently lived through and that returning us to Germany would cast them in the role of murderers.

He explained to us he had to obey orders, since he had a family to protect and he could not risk his position. He would have to escort us back to the border and leave us there (not necessarily with the Germans). Our passports were stamped "returned," we exchanged cigarettes and with best wishes we started down the road towards the border.

We had struggled a whole night to cover this distance over the fields the night before, all to no avail. The gendarmes tell us that straight ahead is the border, but to the left stands a cottage in which some decent people reside. The women kissed the gendarmes, and they disappeared into the night.

We knocked at the cottage door and they let us in. The owner, a farmer, was of Polish descent, and one of our group was able to talk to him in Polish. We were fed and spent the night sleeping on the floor. In the morning the farmer went to contact our guide, who promised to pick us up at night. In the middle of the day the Commander of the previous night walked in on us. He was surprised to find us there and urged us to quickly move on. At nightfall our guide led us out into the dark. We are sop-wet, going crosscountry.

After one hour we come to a brook, now swelled to a fast-moving stream, which we had to cross. There is no bridge, just two logs and a handrail about 600 feet long across the stream. The logs were icy, we had to pull ourselves across hand over hand. It was a blessing that we could not see the distance to the bottom of the ravine where the brook ran, but we could hear the fearsome rush of water below us. The logs swayed with the burden of seven people. Finally the crossing was accomplished. The worst danger was passed. Border-patrols do not cross the brooks.

We form a human chain and in this fashion grope our way painfully up a steep mountainside in the deep woods. We are drenched with perspiration, our shoes are water-logged. We take a short rest. Flashlights may be used now. After another hour's march we reach a hamlet. The guide takes us to a house where 16 other Jews awaited our arrival. We meet our earlier companions. After coffee and a short rest we all set out again. The worst danger is behind us.

Woods and wind swallow any noise we make. After two hours we reach a village. At a drafty woodshed we are told to wait. The wind blows hard.

Our wet feet freeze. After 30 minutes we hear a car approaching. A regular battle ensued for seats in the car. Rosa and I were separated. We each landed in a different car. After a 20 minute drive our car stopped. The driver feared two people were missing. We all had to get out while he turned back to pick up two more.

Now he tells us he has to drive the guide back to get some sleep. Our complaints did not change their schedule. They walked us to another cottage in the woods where we were told to wait. We ate and warmed ourselves and cleaned up a bit. I was very upset over my separation from Rosa. I knew she would cut up badly if she reached Brussels without me. And so she did. She created a big fuss and the driver just got her out of the car as soon as they reached the outskirts of Brussels.

She did not realize how conspicuous she was, dirty and messy, easy to spot by any police officer making the rounds. She made her way to relatives and from there tried to get news of me by calling Cologne.

I spent a whole day waiting at the cottage. A man in our party suffered a breakdown. I too was most agitated, imagining a car accident or that our drivers had been apprehended. But that night two cars came with drivers so tired, that we soon wound up in a ditch. The driver took a short nap at the side of the road before we continued. In a few hours we reached Brussels and Rosa and I were happily reunited at her cousin's house.

Jan. 16, 1939

I contacted the refugee committee at once. They gave us meal tickets and 70 francs for the week. We will room in the same rooming house as my sister-in-law. All we need is a bed. Rosa found an acquaintance who is a bigshot at the committee who gave us 50 Fr.

Walter, who speaks French, took me to an auction hall, where we purchased a second hand bed. Now at least we will sleep like humans. Bed clothes were given us by various people. The food at the kitchen is quite good, especially for small eaters like us: soup, meat and vegetables, with lots of bread. Now there is no one to send us food packages from Vienna, and without them it will be difficult, since the allowance from the committee provides no extras. Please send stamps so we can keep in touch.

I hope my sister in Vienna does not feel I ran out on her. But 30 minutes before our departure I did not know we were leaving. Tell other friends to send any money they may owe me. I need it badly. Greetings from a free land — Long live Belgium!

Oscar

April, 1977

254

White *(story)*

By JUDAH LEVINSON

EVERYWHERE white, as though the whole world is covered with a white blanket. I am so wretched. The frost bites my face and the wind lashes my body. I gasp for breath, and as I stand here I feel myself stiffen in the bitter cold. My bones are breaking, my head is going round, my legs and feet feel like lead, my hands are swollen from the frost. Every so often I must jump for a minute or so in order to feel the circulation. I do not want to freeze to death.

More than anything, the thought of where to hide myself obsesses me. My temples are hammering, what can I do? Tonight is going to be a most horrible time in the Ghetto, and no one will be allowed outside the fences. There is going to be one of the "actions," when people are brutally caught and taken away somewhere to be shot, or sent in trucks to concentration camps, and the rest will still remain for some time in the Ghetto. No one knows for how long.

Today I am working for the Germans outside, and in order to avoid the "Action" I must remain for the night in the main town. I must steal away from the working party and find a hiding place in order to save my miserable life. This thought will not leave me. The time is running out. I don't know the time; I am all mixed up because I have no place to go to for the night. But I must remain in the city, this strange city, filled with hate towards me; a city of danger, a city where I fear the slightest movement. Yet in this same city, a year ago, I had pleasant walks, here I found pleasure and happiness. Now it has become my enemy. It has become a place of terror, a city of slavery — yet I must remain here to avoid the "action."

The frost becomes increasingly severe. the day is drawing to its end and the workmen are getting ready to go back to the Ghetto. I must be resolute. I must decide what to do. I have eaten nothing since last night and I am very hungry, but I must not even think of food now. I move away to a corner of the works area and remove the signs of the Ghetto from my clothes. I climb quickly over the fence, and now I am outside in the street.

I must be very cautious; no one must notice me. I move away to the side of the street where I must linger on for some time until the darkness covers me. I lie down by a large heap of timber, but I must not lie here for long because I will get frozen. Now it is getting late: I must go and seek a place for the night. Perhaps someone will have pity on me and help me to save myself from death. Although my life is meaningless, I want to live through this world catastrophe, after which there may arise a normal world with rights for everyone.

I walk about the streets, and any silhouette or shadow throws me into a panic. I look cautiously in all directions, and think that everyone recognises

255

me; that all are pursuing me and that my thoughts on wanting to hide myself are known. I approach a house. My heart is beating fast. I peer on all sides. I want to knock on the door, but I think again; perhaps not here; I must not take too much risk. I shall go further, in another street, further away. I move away from this house and walk rapidly on, but it is late and I do not see any people in the street. The cold is unbearable and the snow crackles under my feet. It seems to me that everyone can hear me, and I keep walking. Even my own shadow terrifies me. I am now afraid that everyone knows me, that everyone had already seen me and knows what I want to do. I feel impatient, but I must not make anyone suspicious.

I am very tired, almost out of the city. It is now very dark. In the distance I see the glimmer of an electirc lamp. There is still light for some one, but for me it is dark, dark, dark. There is such a long, cold, dark night in front of me. Where will I put myself? I now begin to regret my move. Was it worth taking this risk? Yet the will to live is very strong in me. I am now climbing slowly up a steep street where I can see cottages. The district is poor; the cottages are very small, only a feeble light can be seen from the windows. Perhaps these people will help. They will not report me to the police. They will surely allow me to warm myself a little!

I knock on a door; it takes some time before a woman's voice calls from another room. I can scarcely hear what she says. She asks, "Who is there?" I am afraid to answer. I wait until she opens the door. She is elderly. "What do you want here?" she says, and does not let me over her threshold. I say to her, "I want to get warm" but she starts to shout, "Go quick, quick away from here! Don't ruin me. The neighbors will get to know that Jews come to me and they will report me. I am ruined as it is! Go away! Don't stand there!" And she shuts the door in my face.

Now my spirit sinks even lower than it was. I think to myself that if such an old, lonely wonan had no pity after I appealed to her and begged so hard, who then will help me? What am I to do now? It is so dark, only the snow gives me a little light. I am very frightened. People don't come out on such a night; the frost is too severe. I stand in my thin rags and decide I have nothing to lose come what may. Soon it will be too late to knock on doors. Although I am terrified to death, I must try to get in somewhere; perhaps I can find a stable where I can conceal myself.

I am near a house and I walk to the front door, but I hesitate. I creep round to the back door because I have to be very careful in case there are visitors. I knock on the back door and a woman opens it. I ask her if she would permit me to warm myself because I am frozen. The woman speaks in a low voice and urgently tells me to run away quickly to save myself from her husband. In the instant, he is standing there and shouts to his wife, "Don't let him go! I am going to ring the police. These dogs of Jews, you can't get rid of them, the cursed devils!" And he starts to shout at the top of his voice. The wife pleads with him to let me go and not to bother with me.

256

I don't stay to hear the end of the argument but gather my last remaining strength and run until my breath gives out, too frightened to look behind me, feeling hot then icy cold, and my heart banging against my breast. I don't know how far I have run, but I find myself close by a church. I stop for a moment and look round. It is dark inside. I do not know how late it is; there is no one inside the church. I lean on the wall to get my breath and to collect my thoughts on what I should do next. I stand there for several minutes and feel the cold coming through me again. I see an object in the distance, moving, but cannot discern what it is. I think it is safer to disappear, so I move away in the opposite direction and look for another quiet, poor street. I think I shall try once more, and if I cannot find a place this time, I shall give up the search. I have no more strength left, after a whole day and night without food or drink and so much walking and running, always in terror.

I am looking for a house. Two people pass by me and my nerves are in rags. I talk to myself, "People, have pity! Let me find shelter for the night, in a stable, a cellar or a loft; anywhere so that I should not have to walk and walk all through this freezing, fearsome night."

I stop at a house and look around. There is no one in sight, only a faint light which I can see from a chink between the thick curtains. I look for the door, but decide it would be better to try the back door and hope there is no dog to bark and so arouse the suspicions of the neighbors. I hold my breath and pray this time I shall have good luck, and knock at the door, but there is no answer. I knock a little louder and a woman's voice calls "Who is knocking?" I ask her to please open the door. A silence follows which seems interminable. Perhaps she doesn't understand what I said, but she comes to the door at last and opens it. "What do you want here?" she asks, and I beg her to let me in to warm myself for a while, for I am frozen, the cold is terrible outside. She understands that I am a Jew although I have no Ghetto signs on me. The woman says, "I am afraid of my neighbors. People have lately become very wicked, one would swallow the other, one has to be very careful."

I plead desperately. "No one saw me. I will certainly not tell anyone. I will go very early in the morning before people are about." I begin to tell her my bitter situation, that I committed no crime, that I know people are very wicked these days, and that if she understands this and has suffered also, then she must help me. This talk goes on in the kitchen in the dark. In the next room is only a small lamp and all the windows blacked out.

I begin to feel the warmth penetrating my limbs and I would like to stay there as long as possible. I try to explain to her my position, and implore her to let me stay. But she keeps saying, "Don't you know that no one can be trusted these days, these are bad times, everyone is an enemy?" I try to appeal to her conscience and praise her up to the skies, and tell her how she understands everything, what a good soul she is, and surely she would not

257

drive me out of the house on such a night and so late! She must not do it; she *must* help me.

After much talk, she eventually agrees to let me stay the night in the woodshed which is open, and very early in the morning before anyone can see me, I must disappear. I can not thank her sufficiently for this offer. I go to the woodshed and stop for a few minutes by the door in order to get used to the darkness. I feel happy with my lodging place. When I am able to discern things in the dark, I see that the place is empty but for several thick trunks of wood. There are big gaps in the walls and in the roof through which the wind blows and the terrible frost penetrates.

For some time I stand in one place without moving, and this terrible cold begins to torture me again. I look around and see a big box in a corner, but I am afraid to move about in the dark, lest I knock against an object and make a noise which may draw someone's attention. So I remain where I am, wondering what the time is and how long I will have to endure standing here in this bitter cold. Certain moments in my life come to me, and I ask myself why I have to suffer so much and how long it will go on. Will there be an end to all the trouble and sorrow, and if so, will I live to see it? How long can I exist under these conditions without proper food and drink, little sleep and scarcely any protection against the bitter weather –– and only work, endless work.

There is so much time on my hands and it drags so slowly. Suddenly I hear a church clock striking and I count up to 10. Only 10 o'clock! I shudder to think I shall have to stay in this icy desolation for so many hours. My thoughts torment me. What sin is it that I want to live? And because I want to live, I must stay in this freezing shed. Now my speculations carry me to the Ghetto. Who knows what is going on there at this moment? People being caught and dragged to their death. The poor creatures want to live as much as I do.

Needless to say, I did not sleep that night, but perhaps it was better so, for I might have died of the frost while asleep. As the dawn broke, I crept out of the woodshed and sneaked away to the working place. The slave labor parties had not yet arrived, so I lay under a heap of snow-covered timber to await them. Everywhere white. At the last the workers arrived and I emerged and mingled with them. No-one knew whether I came from the Ghetto or anywhere else.

March, 1982

258

Anne Frank

By MILTON A. SHAHAM

SHE would have hankered after clothes too,
And the other spoils of life.
In a debarring coop in Holland,
She repudiated horror
With a multiplicity of zests;
Nothing in the hovel of hiding
Excised the incitement of youth:
The new knowledge of body,
The fresh mind's extruding range.
She gathered in the life she had,
And for the regions she was never to know,
Felt with an avid, joyful hunger.

April, 1976

The Uprising in Sobibor

By a participant, THOMAS BLATT

ONE April day [1943], I together with the last Jew of the little town of Izbica, Poland, entered the gate marked "Sondercommando — Sobibor." It seemed to me I was entering a beautiful settlement. This was a death camp? Little paved streets, flowers alongside. On the right, a side rail resembling a railway station — a platform nearby. Little tidy houses in Tyrolian style. At the cross-streets wood carved signs giving directions to the baths, canteen, theatre, etc., as for example, a waiter with a tray to point the way to the mess hall. I noticed, too, that the villas ironically had names like: *Gottes Heimat* (God's House), *Schwalbennest* (Swallow's Nest), and others no less idyllic. Surely it was not possible for such a spot to be an extermination camp!

Our group was halted on the way to the gas chambers, and a fat SS man selected a few of us, including myself, a youth of 15, as replacement for workers, who had just been gassed. The remainder, including my mother, father, and brother, went the way of NO RETURN...

Under the direction of Sasha Pechersky, Leon Feldhandler and a few others, a secret group was formed to organize an uprising and destroy the camp. From a few plans they chose the following:

On a specific day, between 4 and 5 P.M., certain prisoners would lure the Germans and Ukrainians under some pretext to an unsuspected place and silently kill them. Meanwhile, those prisoners who had access to the Ukrainian guard's rooms as *"Putzers"* (shoeshiners), and others, would steal available guns and bring them to the carpenter shop.

About 5 P.M., when the bugler as usual sounded the end of work, all would return to the barracks for roll call. Now the last act would be played — the open revolt. All of us would throw ourselves on the gates and barberd wire. A special group would take the weapon storeroom and cover the escape...

The hands of the clock moved lazily to the fateful hour. It was Oct. 14th, 1943. The sun was inclining slowly in the west. It was a beautiful day... Would I live to see tomorrow?

It was close to 4 o'clock. All was quiet. Everything appeared normal. The tension was unbearable. I watched through the open door for the arrival of the conspirators.

The hands passed four. Not again postponed!

260

"They're coming," whispered my friend Wycen. I looked out and saw "Kali Mali" coming through the gate with a basket... His real name was Szuajero, and he was a Russian Jew, an engineer, about 25 years old. He was led by Benia, a Kapo, also in the conspiracy, giving it a natural look. (With a Kapo they had authority to move freely between sections.) They hid in the clothing of the storeroom.

A young boy named Fibbs went up to a German standing nearby, and asked, would he be so kind as to go to the storeroom to try on a new leather coat, especially set aside for him? (Better clothing was saved and sent to German families.) Unsuspecting, he entered.

So It had begun. I left my regular place of work and went to the sorting area next to gate one. As usual, a certain Dutch Jew was standing guard to prevent movement between sections. Because he was so close to the storeroom, my job was to see if he realized what was taking place (he was not in on the plot), and to prevent him, or anyone else for that matter, from leaving or going in.

Tension mounting, I watched the storeroom door.

Meanwhile, in one of the many areas of the storeroom, a few "subdued" prisoners were sorting clothing: children's to children's, men's to men's, women's to women's. Off to one side, lay the bait — shiny and smooth — a long leather coat.

The SS man entered. The workers bent to their tasks. An order from the Kapo, and two inmates fetched the coat and helped the German into it. In a split second, like in a film, the picture changed. The imprisoned arms could not move from the sleeves. The flash of an axe in the hands of Kali Mali, and the Nazi fell with a split head. The workers finished him off with their knives and in a moment the body was covered with piles of clothing, and the blood was covered with sand. The trap was waiting for the next victim.

Fibbs came out of the storeroom and called the next German. I was no longer tense. I became relaxed and calm. I knew there was no turning back now. "The die was cast."

At Fibbs's beckoning, the SS man Beckman started for the storeroom. He got to the door, hesitated for a moment as if sensing something, then headed for the valuables storeroom, where gold and diamonds of the dead were kept. Here, despite unfavorable conditions, he also was liquidated. The next victim was SS Stoybel.

Then a 10-year-old boy named Drescher, sent as a courier form the first section, arrived and told us that the vice-commandant of the camp, Untersturmfuerer Neumann, had been killed there, as well as Grenzschutz, Getzinger and the Ukrainian guard Klatke. He gave us a blow-by-blow account:

Neumann, on horseback, was approached by a tailor who asked him to try on his uniform which was ready (the shops in the camps worked exclusively for the Germans). The tall handsome officer tied the reins and went in. He took off his holster with revolver, then his jacket. Pretending to measure him, the tailor positioned him with his back to the Jewish accomplice. Once, twice, with the hatchet, and the German went to the other world. Only the loud neighing of his horse broke the stillness...

Grenzschutz was killed in the shoemaker's shop. When he put on his shoes for a fitting, Arkady Wycen, standing behind him, carefully took aim, and with one blow of the axe, finished him. They had barely time to hide his body and cover the blood with sand, when in came Klatke, the Ukrainian, calling his chief to the telephone. He never left. In similar fashion Getzinger was liquidated.

All was well so far. I stood and waited impatiently by the gate. The older Jews, realizing by now what was going on, began to complain — that it was all unnecessary — we would have been able to live a while longer in peace — and now what will happen?

"My Dutchman," now suspecting something, asked why SS Wolf was still in the storeroom. Nervously I explained we were making a revolt, and Wolf was finished. He wanted to warn a friend in another section, but I explained he couldn't leave. However, realizing I wouldn't be able to keep him, and he could unwittingly betray our action, I called a tall Jew named Sender, who forcibly took him into the labyrinth of suitcases, and under threat of death ordered him to be quiet.

A bugle resounded from the tower — the end of work. The Kapos led the inmates to the dormitory barracks. Everything appeared as usual. Only then did I notice how many people still did not know what was going on. Whoever was aware was not thinking of bread — he was getting ready. The line for rations, at first almost as long as usual, quickly melted down...

The decisive moment was drawing near. Procrastination could be dangerous; the absence of the Germans could be noticed. I was in the locksmith's shop in the first section, run by 20-year-old Stanislaw Sjmyzner. He was examining a rifle that the 10-year-old "bootblack" Drescher had stolen from the Ukrainian guards and smuggled in with a sack of brooms.

Suddenly, unexpectedly, the SS supervisor of barracks construction appeared. He was asked to go to the barracks concerning a "broken" bunk. There he, too, was killed with an axe.

In the roll call square there was now intensified movement. Some were bidding each other farewell, realizing they might never see each other again; others prayed; those more practical searched feverishly for money and valuables, which not so long ago had absolutely no worth, and now in case of a successful escape would be indispensable.

The guards, stationed on towers and among the barbed wire fences, for the time being suspected nothing. They probably thought this was usual for

262

this time of day in preparation for the roll call. Nervously we waited. The tension mounted.

The Escape

Bulges in jackets and coats betrayed the presence of axes and knives behind belts. One more minute, and the revolt, inspired by the fury of revenge and hope, would burst forth. I saw Sasha Pechersky, the organizer of the rebellion, standing on a table, addressing the crowd: "Brothers," he said, "our moment of destiny has arrived. Our organized group has killed most of the Germans. Now all of us will rise up against our oppressors. We don't expect to survive. Our real objective is to destroy this death factory, to render it useless and, in fighting, at least to die with honor. However, whoever should by chance survive, he should remember his duty is to be a witness — to tell the world what happened here."

Somebody shouted "Hurrah, hurrah!" Suddenly there was pandemonium. The crowd rushed toward the main gate. A Ukrainian guard, riding through just then, was toppled from his motorcycle, and gun taken, before being trampled to death by the onrushing prisoners. The guards were completely taken by surprise. Their superiors already killed, they awaited their orders in vain. Some 15 feet from me I saw a guard, stunned, rifle in one hand, turning around on one spot.

I found myself among a group running towards the main gate. Already behind us was the gate of the rally square; we kept on running.

Suddenly shots. It was the German cook. Protected by the canteen wall, he was shooting from behind the corner. The remainder of the Nazi crew began to rally from their stupor and opened disorderly fire. I was at the forefront, under fire. We retreated a few yards. The masses, however, pushed us forward, till I found myself with a few others in the guards' corridor between barbed wire fences. Possibly, in the confusion, we had run into the entrance. In this way, we did not have to pass two barbed wire fences, and a wide deep and steep moat filled with water — they were already behind us. Ahead of us, only one more barbed wire fence (we had already shut off the electricity), and 15 yards of mine fields.

We stopped. Someone was trying to cut a hole in the wire fence with a shovel. Beside him stood Stanislaw, rifle to shoulder, calmly aiming and shooting in the direction of the machine guns. I marvelled at his composure.

Our group was crawling through. Behind us new escapees pressed on, and not waiting to crawl through, tried to climb over the fence. While I was only half-way through, the fence, under the combined weight of so many, fell on top of me. Possibly this saved my life, for lying under the wires, trampled by the stampeding crowd, I saw mines exploding every few

263

seconds. Although we had planned to touch them off with bricks and wood, no one did. They couldn't wait, they preferred sudden death to a moment more in that hell. And I realized, had I gotten through, I would have been killed with them.

The combined noises of rifles, exploding mines, grenades and chatter of machine guns assaulted my ears. Corpses were everywhere. The Nazis kept a distance, shooting, and in our hands were only primitive knives and hatchets.

The first wave of escapees had passed over me. I had to think fast. I tried to extricate myself. It was relatively easy. I simply slid out from under my leather coat (stolen in preparation) and left it tangled there.

I ran through the mine fields, jumped over the wire fence holding the sign "caution — mines," and I was outside the camp. Now to make it to the woods ahead of me. It was so close...

Ahead of me — stooped figres, running cautiously. We were the last of the fugitvies. Down I went a few times, each time thinking I was hit. Each time I got up and ran further.... 100 yards... 50 more yards... 20 yards... and at last — the forest...

Behind us — blood and ashes.

Postscript

Watching the *Holocaust* [on TV], I was taken by surprise by the dramatization of the actual revolt in the death camp Sobibor, of which I was a part.

It was realistically done. However, it gave the impression that *only* Russian prisoners-of-war organized the revolt. I would like to set the record straight. The prisoners-of-war, like all the rest of us in that camp, were *Jews.* The organizers were mixed — civilians from ghettos, with a few Jewish prisoners-of-war. What is worth noting is that the Germans themselves, referring to Sobibor, used the words "Jewish uprising," in their official documents (AMSW — the files of the German gendarmerie #107-K2). Only twice was the word "uprising" used by the Nazis: once, referring to the Warsaw Ghetto, and again regarding Sobibor.

The Sobibor uprising was the most efficient and successful revolt in any German camp during World War II. Ninety percent of SS leaders were killed, and over 300 prisoners escaped. Of these, unfortunately, only 30 survived the war and 14 are alive to-day.

December, 1978

(Translation)

Jewish Historical Institute   Warsaw 10. V. 1957
  WARSAW
General Swiarczewski Blvd. 79
             L.Dz. 789/57 S.G.

CERTIFICATE

This is to certify that Tomasz Blatt, son of Leon and Felicija, born on April 15, 1927 in Izbica, stayed during Hitler's regime in the ghetto of Izbica (District of Lublin). In October 1942 he ran away from the ghetto but having been recognized as a Jew, he was put in prison in Stryj (District of Lwow) from which he succeeded in escaping at the end of January 1943. On returning to Izbica he was taken with his parents and his brother in April 1943 to the extermination camp at Sobibor. Tomasz's family was gassed immediately on their arrival in the camp. On October 14, 1943, during and uprising in the camp, together with other prisoners, he regained freedom. Following this he was hiding out in various hideouts until the liberation of July 22, 1944.

The above statements were certified on the basis of materials from the archives in the Jewish Historical Institute.

Chief of Archives   Director of JHI
                           Stamp
(signed) T. Berenstein   Prof. B. Mark

Sofievke

By *A.H. WHITE*

*Translated from the Yiddish
by Rebecca Soyer*

I WENT to live in Sofievke at the end of 1939. I had visited many cities before, but it seems to me that Sofievke was different from anything I have seen or read about. Real Jewish peasants lived there. The inhabitants of Sofievke served as a refutation of the slander that a Jew does not want to work, that a Jew has no attachment to the plough nor to the animal that nourishes him. Sofievke disproved these calumnies once and for all.

Sofievke no longer exists and so I want to record for future generations that place and its people, who perished among six million Jews during the Nazi period.

Most of the material comes from my own experience. As an officer of the Polish army I visited Sofievke at the beginning of 1944. It was after the Germans were routed from Lutzk.

Some episodes were related to me by the partisan Haim Zagatovchick when we set fire to the haystacks in Sofievke. Both of us looked and searched. Perhaps we would be able, by the bright light of the flames, to spot at least one Jew. But they had all perished.

Sofievke, a peculiarly Jewish place, is situated in Western Ukraine, 38 km. north of Lutzk, a major regional city. The village is surrounded by magnificent forests, giving the impression of an island in a sea of trees. The soil is swampy, not fertile. In summer one has to gasp for breath after walking a short distance in deep silt, and during the autumn rains everyone is prepared to lose one boot or both in the mud.

The village consists of one street, the length of which could not be shamed in the biggest modern city. It is unpaved. On both sides are white wooden houses covered with gray shingles upon which green moss has permanently settled.

Only Jews really live in Sofievke, except for a Ukrainian *feldsher* (paramedic) and a Polish postmistress with her nine-year-old son, who speaks a better Yiddish than Polish and also studies Hebrew with a rabbi; and the only Polish worker in a Jewish tannery whose children know only one language, Yiddish. The Sofievke Jew is a simple Jew, a simple peasant, a simple person, possessed of all the traits and faults of a Jew, all the good points and bad points of a non-Jewish peasant.

266

His piece of land is seldom more than one acre. Along the length of every house there stretches a long strip of garden. tall, thin, poles support delicate pea-vines; large, wide watermelon leaves push themselves up among the beet plants, carrots, parsley and onions. The biggest and most important place is allotted to potatoes, for that is the main food staple both for people and cattle. Some grass is left for the cow and goat, for these animals bring the Sofievke peasant his greatest income.

All week the Sofievke peasants toil, working on the land. Isaac Kleiner borrows a horse from Leib Shuster to work with his own and, with a merry Sabbath tune, follows the team pulling the iron plough. With a warm *"Gotthilf"* he greets his neighbor, Leah Burak, who, bent over, is industriously pulling carrots. Her 12-year-old daughter cradles the little Moishele in her arms and when he falls asleep, lays him on the grass and helps her mother.

Jewish melodies are heard at every step: at home, at the cooking stove or in the workshop, on the street or in the field. Isaac clicks his tongue at the horse, whips his neighbor's horse, and continues his work, singing a liturgical song.

Friday afternoon one can smell from the washed young heads the odor of kerosene. Everyone, young and old, dresses up — the boys in Sabbath jackets, the girls in new skirts, not longer than in the distant, modern world. On the stoop of neighbors, men and women. The talk is of general news, and the important role is played by Fishele Shterbotti, a modern Jew, a private teacher: "Hitler can swallow up Poland in a few days. England is not prepared, and would not be very angry should that Haman march into Paris. If I had a foodstore and my neighbor had one, I would not be very sorry if he, my competitor, lost his business. We Jews more than anyone else are in danger."

The listeners fold their arms over their chests, shake their freshly-scrubbed heads in despair, until old Shmuel-Leibles comforts them with "We Jews have a great God; we must hope that he will not abandon us in a time of trouble."

Almost all the Jews in Sofievke are fanatically religious. They have seven houses of prayer for 2,000 Jews. The only brick building with an upper floor is the synagogue, the eighth holy place, with the only roof of tin in the town that reflects the sun's rays and dares to shine brighter than the One above.

On the Sabbath Sofievke looks new. From the red brick building stream old and young, transformed by Sabbath clothes into Jews like any other Jews of any other small town. Together with the men saunter the cows and the little goats, who apparently know that it is the holy Sabbath. They walk along slowly, with dignity, their heads with the bent horns held high. When one of the cows recognizes her master, proudly walking with his prayer shawl under his arm, returning from the synagogue, she leaves her "friends" and runs over to her provider, greeting him with a warm Moo, and walks home with him. The Sofievke peasant isn't embarrassed and not angry. With one hand he holds the prayer shawl and prayer book and with the other he pats his "Lisa" and marches home with her.

Sabbath, June 21, 1941. After the Sabbath meal the Sofievke Jews take their nap. The maidens and young men walk in the street, then, singing merrily, they go into the Radziwill forest. Women sit on stoops and chat. A beautiful summer came early this year, so the people in Sofievke take advantage of the warm weather and go walking until late at night.

Old David Shuster, though it is after 2AM, is still sitting at the radio that his son bought him just a few weeks before. Important news is being broadcast by speakers all over the world. Moscow plays beautiful music, and finishes its program at the usual time. It is already broad daylight when the old man wakes his son!

"Yankel, get up. It seems to me that it had already started. Moscow doesn't say anything, but I..."

"Father," says sleepy Yankel, "Go to sleep, it's nothing. If Moscow says it is nothing, it is nothing."

The old man walks out into the garden, as far as the woods and back, again and again. The Jews have already gone out with their cows and horses to the fields. Suddenly everything stops, and, as if by command, all look up at the sky. The birds tear themselves away from the trees and hover around in the air, refusing to get settled.

The earth trembles.

Soon the same thing is repeated. Everyone looks up at the sky. Men. women and children leave their houses with faces full of fear and despair. At twilight one can hear explosions of mines and artillery nearby, becoming more frequent and clearer. And trucks with dead bodies, some covered and some uncovered, some with faces that no longer look human, going east. Cries of the wounded, despairing calls, all this indicates that one must take with a grain of salt Yankel's information about the great victories of the Red Army.

All over mothers are now bewailing their children, wives their husbands. In Lutzk the Germans, soon after their entry into the city, hurriedly round up 2,000 young Jewish men and "send them away." In Tsuman they killed 24 men on the spot because there were no more there. Every day brings fresh news, and every bit of news is worse and more horrible than that of the day before.

In Sofievke there are still no Germans, but there is no lack of Ukrainian nationalists. Kolki, and the nearby villages, are their center. From there scores of Ukrainian thugs, armed from head to foot with weapons that the

268

Reds have left in the woods, invade Sofievke. They run in two rows, on both sides of the road, shooting in the air and beating every Jewish man, woman and child they encounter. And so the establishing of "Independent Ukraine" starts with robbery and violence, as they leave Sofievke singing a song about a "great hero and freedom fighter, Bohdan Hmelnitzky."

Finally, the "lords" themselves, the Germans, begin to appear, in grey-blue or brown uniforms.

It is a dreary day. Rain soaks the road leading to Sofievke. On such days the people do their work calmly in the fields, for everyone feels certain that no Ukrainians will drag themselves to Sofievke. Still, at about 10 in the morning an auto, the looks of which indicate that a high-ranking Nazi will emerge, drives up to the home of the *feldsher*. Nobody sees the Nazi, for all the Jews have run off, some to the Radziwill woods, others among the tall peas or chestnuts, a few in places where a person satisfies physiological needs.

The visit lasts a half hour. Everyone comes out from the holes and hiding places. The *feldsher* summons a few householders: "As you see, the messenger from the district commissioner came here to appoint me chief in Sofievke. You must carry out all my orders, so that I will not have to employ the measures which the Commissioner authorized me to use."

He was smiling shrewdly. The Jewish leaders understood that he needed two or three pair of boots and another bribe.

"Your first task is simple: tomorow morning all cows and horses belonging to Jews in Sofievke will be sent to the district of Tsuman. If after the deadline an animal is found in a Jew's possession — punishment by death."

Whoever did not know the Sofievke Jews and their attachment to their animals, whoever did not see how a Sofievke woman cries when her cow gets sick, could not understand the pain caused by this edict. It is not only the material loss that hurts, but the thought that "Lisa," who was raised in the Sofievke barn, whose great-grandmother lived in the home of a Jewish peasant in Sofievke, must now go off to strangers.

Some cows that belong to bolder householders walk over that night to Vassily, to Ivan, to Yashik, who promise to give a quart of milk every day. But the "best" of them later drive off with a cane, or set their angry dogs upon, the Jewish children who come to see their "Lisa" or drink a drop of milk.

A herd of 600 cows and horses leave Sofievke the following morning amid heart-rending wailing and weeping. For several kilometers the women accompany their four-footed friends, then bid them farewell and return home with swollen eyes and broken hearts.

It is Tuesday, July 14, 1942, when several Jews gather in David Shuster's house. Reb David announces there is nothing to conceal — the situation is clear. "I don't understand at all," he adds, "why the world is silent. One can't seek justice from a scoundrel, but the world does have a conscience. Where are their counter-attacks, why are they silent?"

Those present just shake their heads. they sit there and chatter, seeking a way out, a way to save themselves and others, racking their brains in vain.

Meanwhile it gets dark. Reb David does not want to light a candle, for even the weak rays of a candle would be too light for the grim mood that prevails. The door opens slowly, and a young man, looking more dead than alive, drags himself into the room on all fours. Bowed and broken down, miserable and pale, with swollen eyes and dry lips, he asks for water. Everyone waits impatiently for the visitor to revive in a few words he relates everything:

"All night long they murdered. There are no more Jews in Rovne. A year ago we still had 600 Jewish workers, and yesterday came the end. I saved myself, thank God, in a chimney, and at night I left the city..."

The catastrophe was not long in coming. With the aid of the *Judenrat* and the police, it is made known that at 11:00 A.M. all the Jews must assemble in the street and form two lines. There are still a couple of hours left, and that is time enough for almost half the Sofievke Jews to leave the village and go deep into the woods. Mostly workers and their families come to line up, for they feel a bit more secure.

The *Judenrat* place themselves at the head of the lines. The Ukrainian militia keep order, beating people with guns and sticks.

The Sofievke population is divided into three categories. The first and best group consists of nine pre-War tannery owners. They all remain with their families in their homes, because they have to take care of the hides in their tanneries which had been ordered for the German Wehrmacht. The second group consists of 40 tannery workers and eight comb-makers with their wives and children.

For a few rubles, the tannery workers had found out from the policemen that the third group would probably be liquidated.

Isaac Kleiner and Hanina Aronsky get an idea. They are single men, but they'll get young girls to come as their supposed wives and thus save them. Ukrainian police are in control, and Isaac knows what to do — he tells a girl to hand the blackguard a sheet of paper with some writing on it, knowing that the police rarely know how to read. It works; another Jewish girl is saved.

"Men are to come out into the street and line up!" The announcement comes, in Ukrainian, the next day. Women begin to beg for their husbands and sons. They offer all sorts of possessions, but it is no use. The police take the things, but continue shouting that the women must remain indoors. All the men are needed for a very important task.

Not quite two kilometers from Sofievke, there is a small forest. It is here that the the important task is to be done. About 80 Jewish men, young and old, are standing with spades, listening to the instructions of a Hitlerite in a beautiful uniform: "I will mark out in this glade two rectangles which you must dig up by 5:00 this afternoon, deep enough until you almost reach ground water. The work must be nice and clean, or you will not come out of these holes. Understand?"

With two policemen he measures off two spots, 30 meters long and 8 wide, than sticks his spade in the grass and shouts: "Start!"

They work, wipe their sweat, continue to work. The police and militiamen are more polite than before. They do not beat anyone, but explain that "here you must level off a bit, there smooth the wall from which some soil is slipping off." The engineer himself inspects and measures with a special rod. "No! It's too deep here. I told you only one meter 80 deep and you already have one meter 98. Here again it's too deep, water is beginning to show. That must not be."

Here, they say, there will be anti-aircraft artillery, a defensive position against the Bolshevik planes.

The tra-ta-ta of machine guns silence everyone. The execution of nearly 6,000 people, Jews from Sofievke and surrounding villages, begins...

April, 1979

One Survivor's V.E. Day

By ISAK ARBUS

FORTY years ago, on May 8, 1945, there was dancing in the streets of Europe. It was the day the Third Reich finally capitulated to the victiorious Allies.

I ask myself, can a Holocaust survivor like me celebrate that day as a Victory Day? I shall try to answer in the good Jewish tradition, by telling a story. A story of World War II as I experienced it. I shall try to be brief and omit the gory details. The full story needs a full book-length treatment, on which I am working now.

In the spring of 1939 I was drafted into the Polish Army. On Sept. 1, the Germans invaded my country. After two weeks of fruitless marches, where the Germans were always ahead of us, we were ordered to proceed toward Warsaw. On the way three of us were captured by a Waffen SS tank. I took a dangerous ride on top of the tank, while Polish soldiers shot it up. Fortunately, I was not hit. That night I spent in a fire house, from where I could see German big guns bombarding my home town, Warsaw. A young soldier guarding us tried to console me: "It is not your fault, this war, blame the Jews and the English."

After three Stalags (POW Camps), where we lived in huge tents, 500 Jewish prisoners were sent to work in a huge sugar mill at Genthin, near Berlin. In March, 1940 the production at the mill was halted, and we were removed to another Stalag, Altengrabow. After a week of starvation, the Germans formed a transport of about 6,000 POW's, all Jewish, and sent us back to Warsaw. Thus, the Geneva Convention did not apply to us anymore.

The Warsaw Ghetto was then still in the planning stages, and open. My family was still intact. My older brother, David, was recovering from a wound sustained during the defense of Warsaw. My two other brothers escaped to the Soviet zone. My parents and two married sisters with children were all in Warsaw.

A few weeks after my return I held in my hand a curious document delivered to my mother by a Polish gentile, from the Polish Red Cross. The document proclaimed that I, Isak Arbus, rifleman of the 32nd Infantry Regiment, stationed at the Fortress Modiln, did not exist anymore, having been killed in action at Kutono, in Sept. 1939.

Friends and relatives took this as a sign that I will survive the war. How

272

prescient of them! Unfortunately, almost none of my well-wishers lived to see their prophecy fulfilled.

The scene shifts now to Konskowola, a *shtetl* in the Lublin area. I am a medic in a forced labor camp under supervision of Jewish police from Warsaw. It is now 1941. Our inmates had just finished building a road going East. Suddenly we begin to see thousands of German troops on trucks, motorcycles, jeeps, bikes. Huge truckloads of bombs and other munitions. Tanks. All marching towards the Soviet border. Where was Soviet Intelligence? They must have been blind not to see the massing of German troops.

A group of Jewish POW's from the Soviet Zone, that, unlike our group, had not been sent home but kept in a camp at Lublin, arrives at Konskowola. We have now civilians and POW's at our camp. I then made a decision which helped to save my life later. I simply rejoined the POW's by getting hold of a Polish uniform and army boots.

One day the whole Jewish population of Konskowola is assembled in the main synagogue, where I run an infirmary, and see Nazis trampling on a Torah scroll, which is unrolled and stretched across the square.

A few hours later the town is emptied of Jews. Our camp still stays. Soon a transport of Slovak Jews arrives in town, and I watch how quickly they deteriorate under the squalid conditions of the place. One day they too are removed from the town, this time along with the civilian Warsovians. We, the POW's, are taken to another camp at Budzyn, a division of Maidanek. The conditions here are very bad. The commandant of the camp, Oberscharfuehrer Feix, is a sadist and killer.

Again I am working as a medic. But here things can be dangerous. One day Feix leads me to the execution area, near the garbage dump, but I am reprieved at the last munute by the courageous intervention of my supervisor, a Viennese doctor, who, himself a prisoner, has the guts to plead for me. I get away with 75 lashes. I soon recover.

In the summer of 1943 a large group of Jews is brought from Warsaw via Maidanek and we are told for the first time of the uprising in the Warsaw Ghetto. Among the new prisoners are prominent professionals, including several well known Jewish physicians. The Ukrainian SS, all former Red Army POW's, are particularly vicious in manhandling the newcomers, calling them "bandits." (The term "terrorist" was not in vogue then.) When these Ukrainians marched, they often sang popular Soviet patriotic songs, except that Stalin's name was replaced by "Gitler," the Ukranian version of Hitler.

After a couple of other camps, I arrive in Aug., 1944 at Flossenburg, where, for the first time, we are incarcerated with other nationalities. We are in Germany now. (What follows should interest particularly psychologists among our readers.) At Flossenburg things start differently. There is a pile of clothing 10 feet high in one corner, while about 5,000 of us walk around naked for a full seven days and seven nights. By some trick of fate my saviour, Dr. Foerster, and I, remain fully dressed for two days. When we arrived, some kapos took us into an office to examine our medical supplies; thus we did not get the order to undress. On the third day an SS Officer notices us two. He is shocked. He barks an order: *"Sofort ausziehen!"* (Undress immediately!) We obey and feel strangely relieved. We are not so visible any more.

One day, still naked, we are assembled in the roll-call area. Barbers cut all our hair and each of us faces a short senile-looking SS physician, while we stand on a chair. He looks at us for a moment, we climb down from the chair, and the little monster paints a number on our foreheads. I get #1, my friend, Dr. Foerster gets #3. (He is about 70 years old but still athletic looking). We are aware that the numbers we just got might decide our future, but the scene is so surrealistic that we find the whole affair almost humorous.

A few camps later, I arrive at Dachau. Here we encounter old prisoners who are incarcerated for political "crimes." They are here since 1933, and it shows. They are tough characters, some quite decent.

One night there is a raid. The camp is fully lit. The SS guards, hiding their rifles, mingle with the prisoners. What an experience! Next morning we are taken to a bath; at least that is what we are hoping it is. While we are lined up outside, a group of new prisoners arrives. They appear to be Germans, some well dressed, in fur coats, carrying elegant suitcases. Some appear to be working-class. They enter and emerge from the building a half hour later. What a metamorphosis! All are shaven, hair cut short, in striped clothing, wooden clogs on their feet. Where before we saw individuals, they now look all alike, dehumanized.

We must stay out of the barracks all day. Each block is like a separate camp, with its own gate. The adjoining block is full of Catholic priests, mostly Polish. The day is chilly and wet. A thousand of us link arms and sway in unison, softly humming international songs. It is warmer and a little more cheerful that way. An unforgettable scene. In the ranks are many nationalities, including Italians, arrested by the Germans after Mussolini's ouster.

My next camp is Augsburg, where we are housed in the huge Luftwaffe garages. The place contains remains of a Messerschmidt airplane factory and is raided daily. We have here a special satisfaction to be ordered to run for safety along with German fliers. Each time they drag heavy suitcases, full of loot, no doubt, and curse the war and sometimes even the "Fuehrer," but never leave their suitcases in the barracks. One time I found myself on a hilly spot, where I saw the bombs raining down on targets and a piece of hot metal, a part of the bomb propeller, fell near me.

The scene shifts to Leonberg, near Stuttgart. Our people toil in a tunnel, formerly part of a superhighway. Above, on a hilly landscape, are vineyards. The Allies are closing in. We hear artillery booming in the distance. Often raiders bomb the entrances to the tunnel, and lights go out. One day we get orders to get ready for evacuation. it is now April 4, 1945. They march us, five to six thousand mostly emaciated prisoners, into the tunnel. Boxes of dynamite are piled on both sides of the entrance, wired and guarded by soldiers.

The tunnel is long and we begin to wonder if we will ever see the other end. Finally we are out, and there is dynamite at this end also. Everybody is relieved. We march through the streets of Stuttgart amid indescribable destruction. Streetcars stand abandoned on the streets, empty. A column of trucks full of German soldiers passes us and, incredibly, they toss candy and chocolate into our ranks. It is obvious that the end is fast approaching.

A few days later we are in eastern Bavaria. A place called Ganacker. Again air raids; a few of our people are hit by machine gun fire. I am the only medic, not a doctor in sight. I improvise with paper bandages, gauze and iodine. My dispensary is a primitive hut made of thin plywood. Once I am forced to cut a piece of it to make a splint for a prisoner who was hit in both shoulder blades by an Allied raider, who, of course did not know who we were.

It is the middle of April now. Camouflaged Luftwaffe planes are hit and burst into flames. Also a fuel dump is hit and we have the satisfaction of watching barrels explode in the air all day long.

A few enterprising inmates cook some potatoes, using parts of the burning planes as fuel. The German pilots find it very amusing, maybe because they feel relieved they won't fly these planes anymore.

Finally, on April 25, the SS become panicky. The Red Army is closing in. The main camp, Flossenburg, is already in their hands. We are hastily assembled for evacuation. Unfortunately, we must leave the very ill behind, to an unknown fate. The SS is dividing us into groups of 50 and we march off, heavily guarded by SS and dogs. We feel it is our *"letzten veg."* Later we discover that Himmler had ordered all surviving prisoners to be taken to the Tyrolean Mountains for final disposal. The SS is jittery and shoot at the slightest pretext. We are in great danger, just as liberation is so near!

On the morning of April 27, our guards are hungry. We, of course, don't count. They stop at a nearby farmhouse and lock us up in the barn. They go to the house to eat. They are careless and forget about the other door, leading from the barn into the fields. Five of us decide to take off. We quickly open the other door and run for our lives.

For two days we stay on a farm owned by a Nazi party member. But he is a shrewd Bavarian and is willing to help us. It might help him later. A daughter smashes the phonorecord of the infamous "Horst Wessel Lied," the one that sings about Jewish blood dripping from the Nazi knife.

Luckily for us, a nearby Wehrmacht warehouse was looted by Germans a day before and we don Wehrmacht summer uniforms and go with the farmer to his fields to help gather hay. It is still dangerous to be Jewish; the fanatical SS and mobilized youth hunt in the vicinty for escapees.

On April 29, we notice, to our joy, white sheets hanging from many farmhouses. We run to the country road. In the distance we see some soldiers in unfamiliar uniforms marching in our direction.

A platoon of unshaven, dust-covered men is steel helmets march by, while we wave. We try to communicate with these friendly Americans in Yiddish, Polish, German. A few respond. This then is our great moment. We are liberated. But where is our joy? We try to show it, but it comes hard.

On May First we are invited to a big party by the liberated French POW's from the vicinity. We drink wine, eat rice, chocolate, foods we had not seen for years. The French then pack up and joyfully start on their way home to their families, wives, sweethearts, friends. There, no doubt, they will again celebrate. Other nationals also get ready to go home. Soon we see truckfuls of Russians, red flags flying, singing familiar Russian songs, pass on the highway.

But what about us? We are left in limbo. Slowly the news of the fate of other Jews begins to trickle in to us. V.E. Day comes and goes. Of course there was joy on the streets of liberated Europe. But where are *our* streets?

We move to a larger town, Eggenfelden, where several hundred of us form a D.P. Camp. Meanwhile, at Bergen-Belsen, Dachau and other liberated camps people are still dying. Disease and extreme exhaustion take their toll. The bitter truth is that the Allies, flushed with victory, were not prepared to deal with the half-dead liberated inmates. Often the well meaning soldiers distributed canned beans, spam and other military rations, totally unsuitable for the shrunken stomachs of survivors. When organized help finally arrived, for many, alas! it was too late.

Other survivors quickly fill the new D.P. Camps. Credit must be given to the U.S. Army personnel, to Jewish chaplains, to U.N.R.R.A. and the American Jewish Joint Distribution Committee, for organizing these camps.

A few months later I go to Poland to search for my family and friends. A group of us spent the first night in Poland at Katowitz, on the wooden floor of a synagogue, because the Polish Red Cross declined to help us. "You men are Mosaic, you must go to the Kehilla for help," the official coldly announces. This is now People's Poland, and we swallow our tears. In Warsaw, at the Jewish Committee, I check the lists of survivors. I find only a couple of friends. That night, in my home town, I sleep on the wooden top of an old fashioned tub, in an apartment where two women are taking care of Jewish children, retrieved from Polish families, where they managed to survive, and whose parents' fate is unknown.

I travel by train to Lublin and other towns, where my family came from originally, searching. I take a grave risk, because Polish fascist bands often attack those trains and mercilessly kill all Jews and uniformed personnel. I find my friends, a mother and daughter, in Lodz. They tell me a tragic tale. When Warsaw was liberated in the winter of 1944, they rushed to the former Ghetto, and, without tools, began to tear at the accumulated snow and ice, to get through to a bunker which, they knew, sheltered their daughter, my brother David, and another couple. They find only four skeletons...

A few months later I am back in West Germany, having found Poland a cemetery of my people. My liberation is complete.

July-August, 1985

After Yad Vashem

By MICHAEL ENGEL

"Forgetfulness leads to exile, while remembrance is the secret of redemption."
                                                  The Baal Shem Tov

Transmigration of souls of
    martyrs of victims
into this single soul or
I who am memory
And them
contain within myself history
nothing emanates from me
without them

April, 1982

V: Portraits and Self-Portraits

The Incomparable Rahel

By FREDERIC EWEN

H ANNAH Arendt's *Rahel Varnhagen** has its own ironic history. Originally completed in Germany in 1933, it was published in England in 1957, in Germany in 1959, and reappears now in an American edition, slightly revised. Between these years a great deal of the original material that might have served for a definitive study of a very remarkable woman has been dispersed, or has disappeared, so that this book remains something of a fragment. It is unfortunate too that unlike the German edition, the present one, possibly for reasons of economy, does not contain a selection from Rahel's letters that might have served to deepen our understanding of her character and struggles at a critical time in the history of Germans and Jews. In Germany, there is now a renewed interest in her life, and a new edition of her numerous letters is in process of publication. It is to be hoped that in time the lost archives will be recovered, and English-speaking readers will be offered a full-sized portrait, set within a proper historic frame.

She was born Rahel Levin, later changed her name to "Friederike Robert," and ended as the baptized wife of a minor diplomat and man of letters, Varnhagen von Ense. In these names and their mutations is contained an enlightening history not only of one woman, but of three generations of German-Jewish life in Prussia. Rahel Levin was born in Berlin in 1771, the daughter of a well-to-do Jewish merchant, and died in 1833. Her generation was therefore the witness of the French Revolution of 1789, of Napoleon's rise and fall, of the Restoration and reaction following 1815, and finally of the outbreak of a new revolution in France in 1830. In her lifetime, though not herself a prisoner there, she saw the Ghetto gates opened wide when Napoleon crossed the Rhine; she saw them close again upon the Jews some years later. She was a child of the 18th century Enlightenment, when under Frederick the Great, Moses

Rahel Varnhagen: The Life of a Jewish Woman, by Hannah Arendt. rev. ed. Tr. by Richard and Clara Winston. Harcourt Brace Jovanovich, N.Y., 1974, 236 pages, $7.95.

Mendelssohn, a Jew, was extolled as "Nathan the Wise" by the Protestant philosopher and playwright, Lessing. It was a time also, when it seemed that for rich Jews the path to success was wide open, while their less fortunate co-religionists still languished in their Ghetto. She lived long enough to see a tragic turn of events when Prussia lent herself to anti-Semitic pogroms, and Jews would be calumniated as poisoners of Christian wells.

At first it was a heady time. Of course, the great new "liberator" of the German Jews, Moses Mendelssohn (celebrated as the third Moses after the Moses Maimonides!), could never have imagined that the new "emancipation" of the Jews from the Ghetto, his proclamation of the equality of all religions, and his insistence that the Jew must be made a partner in a general European culture would lead to a kind of "assimilation" he never dreamt of — an "assimilation" that would soon see Christian baptismal fonts crowded with Jewish men and women seeking regeneration. In his own household, his daughter Dorothea would follow the trend; as would his musical grandchildren! And many, many others, people of substance, did likewise; aspiring students and writers too — witness the unforgettable example of Heinrich Heine. The baptismal centificate was the passport to European culture, as the latter remarked bitterly; and, one might add, to practical advancement. Others, with deep and tragic sincerity believed this to be the only way to solve the Jewish problem.

Rahel Levin too basked in that dream. Although she herself was not to be converted until she was in her forties, she took the idea for granted. As a woman of a brilliant intelligence and great potentialities, and as a Jew, she rebelled against the constrictions that she had fallen heir to. She had numerous companions in her resentments. For this was an era when there were many women, Jewish and non-Jewish, who felt the need for a wider scope for their talents. The field of political and social action was closed to them by an unspoken traditional consensus. Prussia, the most powerful of the many German states, aside from Austria, was still steeped in an absolutist feudalism, economically and politically far behind such countries as France, not to mention England. By comparison with Paris or London, Berlin was a minor provincial town. Yet it was intellectually active, and could exhibit in its "salons" as rare a collection of talent, even genius, as any other cultural center in Europe.

These "salons" were presided over by women. Of course they could not compete in splendor with those of Paris. Rahel called hers the "garret-salon." But they offered a sphere of sharp intellectual activity. Another Berlin salon was presided over by Rahel's co-religionist, the celebrated Henriette Herz (1764-1847), soon also a candidate for conversion.

Rahel's "garret" became famous. For those salons were actually spiritual enclaves, refuges from the aridity of the outside world. Political and social questions were, of course, taboo. So much more room then for fiery discussions of philosophy, religion, morality, books, art, science. Here persons conscious of rank and status would not hesitate to rub shoulders with actors and actresses, writers, students, Jews. Here the inhibitions to action were compensated for by uninhibited speculation and emotional profusion. This was the hey-day of German romanticism, and its high priests were present in these rooms. Here the heaven of the imagination prevailed, and philosophy was transcendental and ethereal and the objective world disappeared before this empyrean scrutiny. Here the Ego could rule triumphant, creating worlds and fantasies more beautiful than any Nature could offer.

That which could not happen on earth, as Schiller once put it, could be realized in the realm of the Beautiful in Art. Self-cultivation, which the great master Goethe had preached, became the road to personal salvation. The atmosphere was thick with cloud-borne flights into what was believed to be Freedom — which came to mean freedom to express everything within you, freedom to feel deeply, sometimes too deeply, freedom to love — every freedom but that to think about the state, the King, politics, society; every freedom but that of doing, acting.

Everyone who came in contact with her attested to Rahel's extraordinary magnetism. Physically she was not attractive (as she knew only too well); yet she drew people toward her and knew how to drew them out, elicit the best within them without pretense or ostentation. She was candor itself. She knew how to be "with" them, a talent only too rare at any time. She was totally self-educated, yet she could stand her ground with any of her guests. Even her letters cannot fully convey her personality, rich as they are in introspective, self-analytical, unconstrained insights.

Turmoil, rebellion, self-search, restlessness, as well as self-appreciation as a personality were the earmarks of her being. As a daughter, she had rebelled against the brutality of a father who had sought to crush her individuality. As a woman she felt herself deprived of rights, utterly dependent as she was on the good-will of the male members of her family. Like her co-sisters of the time, she rebelled against the compulsions of a forced marriage as an escape from domestic servitude; she rebelled against emotional constraints.

Had not Dorothea Mendelssohn, married off at the age of 15, broken her marriage ties to become the lover, later the wife, of Romanticism's arch-priest Friedrich Schlegel? He was one of the great stars of Rahel's salon, as were the scientists, the Humboldt brothers, the theologian Friedrich Schleiermacher, the many poets, novelists, historians, philologists, even important political figures like Friedrich Gentz, destined to become, like Schlegel, one of the pillars of the political reaction in the service of Prince Metternich.

Exhilarating as were the evenings in her "garret-salon," she could not help asking herself the question: What now? There was a life outside — tempting, glamorous, if only she could reach out and take hold of it. But how? Marriage was a way out, and even up. She was a passionate nature, and could love deeply. She did fall in love with a member of the nobility, and they became engaged. But alas! when it came to marrying the Jewish woman, brilliant and overpowering as she might be, the chains of rank and station triumphed over love! So it happened not once, but twice. It was one thing to love such a woman; it was another to have her join an ancestral line till then "uncontaminated." She discovered that the Ghetto she thought she had exorcised still existed; and what was worse, it existed within her. The yellow badge had been there all the time!

She was a woman, a Jew, and a German. How to reconcile those three? As a woman she could and would proclaim the rights of free love, even practice them. But there was the middle term that always obtruded itself. Liberation must lie in its elimination, she believed. An ancestral curse hung over her.

"I imagine," she wrote, "that just as I was being thrust into this world a supernatural being plunged a dagger into my heart, with these words: Yes; have feelings, see the world as only few see it, be great and noble; nor can I deprive you of a restless, incessant need to think. But with one reservation: Be a Jew! And now my whole life is one long blood-letting. How loathsomely degrading, offensive, insane, and low are my sorroundings, which I can not avoid. One single defilement, a mere contact sullies me and disturbs my nobility. And this struggle goes on for ever!..."

How to remove that cancer within her that was destroying her? "The Jew," she wrote again, "must be extirpated from us; that is the sacred truth, and it must be done even if life were uprooted in the process..."

Assimilation — baptism — a universal elimination of all that savored of the Jew and his "dark past" — that was the answer, she concluded. All around her friends had become Christian. What had she to do with religion? What did it matter whether she was Christian or Jew? She was a pantheist, like Goethe. And had not one of her distinguished co-religionists, David Friedlaender (1750-1834), advocated a universal baptism for all the Jews of Prussia — a kind of mass conversion? But the Christians did not take kindly to that idea.

As for Rahel, she was still living in the 18th century — outside of history. And now history took hold of her and thrust her into the 19th. Her painful reeducation began with the year 1806 — what Karl Marx was to call the "reform of consciousness." This was the year in which the Napoleonic armies crushed Prussia and invaded the German states. The French were in Berlin. With that year began that mobilization on the part of the German rulers of their subjects for what was to be called a War of Liberation — when Kings and Dukes sprinkled their adjurations with all sorts of liberal

282

promises and future concessions, extending them even to the Jews. (All of these to be repudiated after 1815!)

Chauvinism, Patriotism, Nationalism now took over. Romanticism became Christian, even Catholic. With the catastrophic defeats of Napoleon in Russia and at Waterloo, came the Congress of Vienna in 1815 and the so-called Restoration: that is, the attempt to restore Europe to what it had been before the French Revolution. Promises of constitutional reforms were forgotten, all liberal ideas were subjected to persecution, the Old Order and the Holy Alliance now reigned over the Continent.

Patriotism brought with it the cult of Medievalism — a return to the Middle Ages. Friedrich Schlegel and Gentz joined Metternich, the eagle-eyed policeman of Europe. The well-to-do Jewish bourgeoisie, now increased in numbers and power, found itself confronted by an unmitigated hatred of its Christian competitors, and anti-Semitism became virulent. The notorious war-whoop of anti-Semitic students, the frightening "Hep-hep!" was heard more frequently, and in 1819 there were pogroms in Prussia; soon worse libels and persecutions were to follow.

Rahel too was tossed on these waves produced by great historic changes. In the patriotic war, she became a patriot, and tended wounded soldiers in Prague, thus for the first time coming in contact with war and its victims. That "other" world — of the poor and the stricken — had been closed to her. It was not easy for her to adjust to what had happened. To achieve a more settled life she had joined her fate to that of a minor but ambitious Prussian public official, Varnhagen von Ense, whom she later married after being baptized. Though no outstanding intellect, Varnhagen, younger than she, adored her in terms too hyperbolic for even that hyperbolic time. He considered her "the third glory of the Jewish nation," along with Christ and Spinoza. But he also made himself posterity's eternal creditor by collecting Rahel's innumerable letters and diaries, though he was not above now and then correcting them to suit his own purposes.

She reestablished another salon in Berlin, again resplendent with not-abilities — such as Hegel, and the historian Ranke. but she was now much more open to influences from abroad, especially from France. As the political life of Prussia became more and more constricted, her own range widened. Eduard Gans, the keen philosopher of law, also a converted Jew, acquainted her with the newer philsophical currents of the times, particularly those having a profound social bearing. She began reading the *Globe* — which became, as she put it, "her daily bread." This was the Paris organ of the Saint-Simonian utopian socialists, and she responded to their "doctrines" concerning the emancipation of women, the "amelioration of the poorest class" through a reorganization of social wealth, its redistribution through the abolition of the right of inheritance, and to their proclamation of the possibilities for the good of mankind inherent in the new science and in the industrial advances.

It is likely that it was in Rahel's salon that the young Heinrich Heine, then a student in Berlin, and already a poet in the making, came in contact with these ideas. She could not have foreknown that of all the companions in her salons, he was destined to be the one to carry her inchoate hopes to unimaginable rich fruition.

It is unfortunate that Dr. Arendt ended her book without enlarging on this last period of Rahel's life, and the remarkable changes in her outlook. It was during this time that Rahel exercised a powerful influence on the more advanced and dissident poets of Germany, the "Young Germany" school, with which Heine was associated. It may be useful therefore to supplement this book with a few pointed quotations from other sources, including the long out-of-date biography by Ellen Ken [1849-1926], the Swedish feminist. Rahel was deeply responsive to the problems of women. Along with her generation, she frequently became vehement on the subject of women's oppression. She joined slavery, war and marriage together as special objects of execration.

Concerning marriage she exclaimed: "Away with the walls! Away with the ruins of them! Let this pernicious custom be levelled to the ground, and then shall flourish everything that had life in it — a whole new growth!"

She had novel ideas on the subject of women and children: "Children," she wrote, "ought to have mothers and bear their name, and the mother ought to be in possession of the authority and power in the family; so nature ordains it. We have only to make nature more moral... Nature is terrible in this respect, that a woman can be misused and can bear children against her inclination and her will. This injustice must be redressed through human intervention and dispositions, but it shows to what great extent the child belongs to the woman. Jesus had only a mother. For every child an ideal father is to be appointed, and every mother ought to be considered innocent and held in as high honor as Mary."

Her social thought, too, had wider dimensions than are suggested in Dr. Arendt's book: "I... considered," she wrote, "the whole mass of human culture, and whether its quintessence, the highest delight of noble, richly-gifted persons in each other, and every other bright and lofty element in life is worth all the suffering and misery of those who who are required for centuries as its manure. Working cartmen and myself suggested this thought to me."

She saw in Saint-Simonian socialism, "the new, grandly discovered instrument, which at last touches the great ancient wound, the history of mankind upon earth... It has already brought to light irrefragable truths, arranged the real questions of the day in order, and answered many important ones... I am the most profoundly convinced Saint Simonist. For my whole faith consists in the conviction of progress and perfectibility of the universe, its development to ever greater understanding and welfare in the highest sense: happiness and making happy."

284

At the outbreak of the Paris Revolution of 1830, she exclaimed: "Yes, it is a pleasure to live now, since the world is really, actually moving, since ideas, happy dreams enter into life, and since mechanics, industry, inventions and associations are realizing these dreams... One thing is certain. Europe no longer desires to conquer pieces of ground, but something more serious: equality... The talk is of rights and no longer of origins."

These were words that Heine a few years later would turn to ringing battle-cries. He was, after all, the finest heirloom she devised to posterity, and he in turn never forgot what he owed to the remarkable Rahel.

On her death-bed she reaffirmed her kinship with her fellow-Jews: "What a history!" she wrote. "A fugitive from Egypt and Palestine, here I am and find help, love and care in you people. In solemn transport I think of this origin of mine, and of the whole interconnection of destinies through which the oldest memories of the human race are associated with the present state of things, and thus the forms the most widely separate in time and space become connected with each other. That which for so long a period of my life appeared to me the greatest ignominy — the bitterest suffering and misfortune, namely being born a Jew, I would not now renounce at any price."

January, 1977

285

Franz Boas: Founding
Father of Anthropology

By PHILIP ROSEN

THE Bicentennial should be seen as a celebration of the whole 200 years of American life, and Founding Fathers should not be limited to one time period nor one area of endeavor. Because of their small numbers, religious restrictions and historical situation, Jewish contributions in the early period were meager. Not until the latter half of 19th century, when large numbers of Jews immigrated here, was their impact felt. Jews were Founding Fathers in a number of fields — unionization, labor law, preventive medicine, mass retail selling, atomic research and anthropology.

The Founding Father of American anthropology was Franz Boas. He was the first teacher of this social science, graduating and guiding the greatest names in the discipline — Ruth Benedict (1887-1948), Melville J. Herskovitz (1895-1963), Robert Lowie (1883-1957), Clyde Kluckhohn and Margaret Mead.

Boas was the foremost fighter against racism of his time. The precise professor fought the "survival of the fittest" Social Darwinists. He fought the long-lived American traditions that relegated Indians and Blacks to inferior positions. He fought against the prevailing view of academicians that immigrants from eastern and southern Europe were genetically inferior to earlier immigrants from Nordic lands, "the Nordic Myth." He fought against the claims of psychologists that intelligence tests measure innate intelligence and that the tests prove the superiority and inferiority of racial groups. He fought against the charge that non-Nordic groups were unassimilable into American society. This Jewish immigrant from Germany stamped the legacy of environmentalism on American social science. His tenet that great mental and body-form modification is possible without any change in the germ plasm was not seriously challenged in this country until the past few years.

America's foremost environmentalist was born in Minden, Germany, in 1858, the son of the only Jewish family there that had not converted. He attended the Universities of Bonn, Heidelberg and Kiel, graduating as a Doctor of Philosophy in Physics with a minor in Ethnographic Geography. In 1883, at age 25, Franz went to Baffinland, North America, a journey

286

which was to launch him into a career in anthropology. He was assigned by a German journal to a meteorological station to make geographical and ethnological observations to publicize Germany's contribution to the International Polar Exploration. Fascinated by the Indian customs, Boas left the party and chose to live among the Eskimos, "an Eskimo among the Eskimos."

Ruth Benedict, distinguished colleague of Boas, stated that when her teacher went to live with the Eskimos, he thought their culture could be explained as a natural reaction to their environment, but he came to realize that such an explanation was inadequate. Said Benedict in the *American Anthropologist,* Sept., 1943:

"He learned that the facts of experience could not be explained merely by reference to laws of physical or material substance; they depended even more largely upon man-made conventions, products of the human mind. These cultural inventions could fly in the face of objective reality; they could be rational or irrational. They had their own rationality, however, and he [Boas] believed this could be discovered only by tracing them in detail in specific cultures, following them into the grammatical categories of the language, tracing their diffusion from tribe to tribe and from continents, and identifying the same convention as it was expressed, for instance in religion and social organization."

For Boas, it was essential to study a culture *in the field,* employing a thorough investigation of the language, beliefs and customs of the subjects. Boas believed that an adequate command of the language of the tribe an anthropologist wished to study was essential because "much information can be gained by listening to conversations of the natives and by taking part in their daily life, which to the observer who has no command of the language remain entirely inaccessible."

Later, Boas was to insist on field work as a prerequisite for a degree in anthropology. His students were to approach a culture with a minimum of ethnocentric preconceptions, with no value judgments founded on the values of our own culture. Boas had great influence in making the attitude of "cultural relativism" a commonplace in anthropology.

In 1887, feeling restricted as a professor in Germany, "attracted to the ideal of democracy," he shed German citizenship and stayed in the United States, serving as the associate editor of *Science,* a learned journal. In the same year he married Marie Krackowitzer, then headed off to study Indian tribes in British Columbia.

From 1888 until 1892 he taught at Clark University in Worcester, mentoring the first American graduate students in anthropology. From 1892 to 1896 he held various jobs as curator until he accepted a joint position as curator of ethnology at the American Musum of Natural

History in New York and professor at Columbia University. At the latter job he advanced to head the Department of Anthropology, a post he held for 50 years, influencing the field until his death in 1942.

Boas was an unbelievably active man, a many-sided virtuoso. He founded the *Journal of American Lingustics* (1917), edited the American Ethnographical Society's publications, founded the international School of American Archaeology and Ethnology in Mexico (1910), was president of the New York Academy of Sciences (1910) and president of the exclusive 300-member American Association for the Advancement of Science (1931).

In the time between his academic responsibilities, Boas campaigned against the vicious attacks on the "new immigration" from eastern and southern Europe, and supported the drive for social justice for the American Negro. His activities brought him before the infamous Dies Committee. Accused of being a communist, he would not slacken in his efforts against the race supremacists. He opposed the communists for their dogmatism and worship of authoritarianism, but he would cooperate with them on specific activities to promote racial harmony.

Boas recorded most of his massive research and study in over 600 articles in professional journals. He wrote only four books: a three-volume *Handbook of American Indians,* which contains the grammars of 19 Indian tongues, the *Mind of Primitive Man* (1911), *Primitive Art* (1927) and *Anthropology and Modern Life* (1928).

The book that summed up his thoughts on race and the interrelationships between body constitution, hereditary endowment and culture was the *Mind of Primitive Man.* This work has become the bible for progressive social scientists and its conclusions are axiomatic for them. The book demonstrated that there is no fixed relation between function and anatomy, between mind and brain, for example, such as to warrant the view that any race is incapable of participating in any culture or even creating it. Boas reported that 35 eminent men were examined and their brains were found to have weighed less than the average, whereas, the brains of 45 murderers were measured and the weight of each was more than the average.

Another major axiom expounded was that no racial group can lay substantial claim to hereditary purity: "The people of Great Britain, as well as those of Germany, France, Central Europe, and even Italy, are all greatly mixed up and built up of much of the same racial elements." Boas was a great leveler, a believer in the essential similarity among peoples. The average difference he found in physical characteristics among races was small in contrast to the great overlapping of range and duplication of types among them: "I think the essential point to stress is that there are many

288

inferior strains in every race, including the 'Nordic,' and that there are many superior strains also in other races, no matter what they may be."

Boas believed that differences among racial groups (a term used at that time to include ethnic groups) were not great genetically; what physical, mental and behaviorial difference appeared was primarily caused by environment. Thus he wrote at the conclusion of the *Mind of Primitive Man:*

"The traits of the American negro (sic) are adequately explained on the basis of his history and social status. The tearing away from the African soil and the consequent complete loss of the old standards of life, which were replaced by the dependency of slavery and by all it entailed, followed by a period of disorganization and by severe economic struggle against heavy odds, are sufficient to explain the inferiority of the status of the race, without falling back upon the theory of hereditary inferiority."

To those who viciously attacked the new immigrants on the basis that they could not be assimilated, and that they constituted a racial type too alien for the Old American Stock, Boas offered remarkable evidence to counter the immigration restrictionists and to support the theory of America as the "Melting Pot."

In 1908, the United States Immigration and Naturalization Service asked Boas to study the question of whether significant physical changes occur in the descendants of immigrants in America. Over a period of 27 years the anthropologist amassed evidence that such changes *did occur.* In his first study, he concerned himself largely with Jews and Sicilians, groups that were generally considered most hopelessly "non-Anglo-Saxon."

Under his precise instruments came the cephalic index (the measurement of the contour of the head), a physical characteristc assumed by the race theorists to be very stable. This was a truism in Europe; indeed, when Boas investigated in their native lands, the children of Russian Jewish and Italian parents had head shapes like their parents. But for the American-born children of immigrants it was another story. In the *Reports of the Immigration Commission* (June 8, 1911, 61st Congress) Boas wrote:

"The results of our inquiry have led to the unexpected result that the American-born descendants of these types differ from their parents, and that these differences develop in early childhood and persist throughout life. It is furthermore remarkable that each type changes in a peculiar way. The head of the American-born Sicilian becomes rounder than that of the foreign-born; this due to loss in length and an increase in width. The face becomes narrower, the stature and weight decrease.

"The American-born Hebrew has a longer and narrower head than the European born; the head is therefore considerably elongated. His face is narrower; stature and weight are increased."

Boas found not only that cephalic indices changed, but changed toward a more "American type." The great environmentalist was very optimistic about the future Americanization of the new immigrants: "We are compelled to conclude that when these features of the body change, the whole bodily and mental make-up of the immigrants may change... All the evidence is now in the favor of the great plasticity of human types."

Much of what Boas found in his study of children reads like current literature on child growth and development. He postulated that constitutional changes in the body of the mother could bring about modifications in prenatal growth which to the superficial observer might give the impression of hereditary change (*Journal of American Statistical Association*, June, 1922).

His belief in the importance of a healthy infant environment was evident in his study of orphaned children ("Studies in Growth," *Human Biology*, 1932, quoted in Boas, *Race, Language, and Culture*, 1940): "This investigation was made in the Hebrew Orphan Asylum in New York City in 1918, and repeated in 1928 on children entering after 1918. The former investigation had shown that life in the Orphan Asylum affected growth during the first few years unfavorably, and that it took a long time before the loss could be made up. In 1918 the general policy of the administration changed. *There was a change in diet, less regimentation, more outdoor exercise and an effort to meet the needs of individual children* (italics mine).

"The results of the measurement of children at entrance are given in figure 18. It will be seen that the children placed in charge of the Hebrew Orphan Asylum before 1918 were, at the time of admission, *shorter* (italics mine) than those admitted after 1918."

During World War I, intelligence tests were given to American soldiers and the results classified according to ethnic group. Psychologists Carl Brigham and Robert Yerkes administered the tests and interpreted the results. They were convinced that the statistics proved the superiority of Nordic immigrants over those from southern and eastern Europe, and that the Negro was hopelessly inferior to all groups.

Boas attacked the conclusions of the psychologists, using Yerkes and Brigham's own data. Typical was his article in the *American Mercury* (Oct., 1924), in which he noted the superior scores of Northern Negroes over Southern whites. He interpreted the higher scores as meaning that Negroes experienced better social conditions in the North. Chiding anyone who claimed he could measure innate mental characteristics, the anthropologist used an argument that is today called the "culture bound fallacy":

"We may well ask whether the tests do not show the upbringing of children fits some of the groups better for the kind of reaction demanded in the test than others... I am convinced that a test, for instance, based on Negro music would show a complete lack of rhythmic ability among us."

290

In regard to the differential scores among Europeans, Boas saw the environmental factor of length of stay in the United States as crucial:

"Before accepting the results of the tests as criteria of hereditary intelligence, we ought to insist that each individual be given an opportunity for adjustment... When he finds that immigrants who came here 20, 15, 10 and five years ago do not respond equally well to his tests, the most recent arrivals showing the lowest records, we have to consider that they are not equally adjusted."

The Founding Father of American anthropologists challenged the view held by race supremicists and eugenicists that when certain populations are mixed, disharmonies — long arms on short trunks, huge teeth in a small mouth, etc. — and other inferior physical characteristics emerge. Boas' studies of mixed breeds of Indians in North America and studies of South African Negroes convinced him that mixed populations preserve their full vigor. As early as 1894, writing about the "half-breed" Indian in *Popular Science Monthly,* Boas found that mixed Indian populations had taller children, and when these children grew up they were more fertile.

In a *Yale Review* article entitled "The Problem of The American Negro" (1921), the anthropologist's leveling tenets are manifest. He cannot agree with the very concept of disharmony, "since the anatomical differences between the races of man are very slight... There is a generous margin of safety which permits the adaptation of the organs of the body to the varying conditions under which they have to perform their functions." He cites favorable results of race mixing, using both a geographical and historical approach:

"No evil results of race mixing are found in the mixed populations of Africa in the northern borderland of negro (sic) countries where Mediteranian races and negroes (sic) have intermarried. Under favorable conditions the mulatto is healthy and may attain to great eminence as in the cases of Dumas and Pushkin."

By 1936, Boas decided to retire from his active schedule at Columbia University and devote himself full-time to the political area, attacking Nazi race theories and encroachments, here, on intellectual freedom. Boas, the cosmopolitan scientist, had the honor of having his books burned as "Jewish poison" along with Freud's and Einstein's. What he had feared in Germany, the race and folk beliefs which he had left behind in becoming an American citizen, were now infecting the world. Boas initiated the Manifesto on Freedom of Science signed by 1,200 U.S. scientists and issued Dec. 11, 1938, declaring that true science could develop only in a democracy. From this project grew in 1939 the American Committee for Democracy and Intellectual Freedom, with Boas as chairman. He died Dec. 21, 1942 debunking the "blond superman" theory.

Psychologists Arthur Jensen and Richard Herrnstein have raised the issues of racial and class intelligence again. These new hereditarians use terms reminiscent of the early decades of the 20th century such as "permanence of the germ plasm," and "dysgenic and eugenic populations." Their detractors counter (without a credit line to Boas) by citing cultural factors of tests and nutritional and early childhood factors inhibiting mental growth. The implications these hereditarians make for public policy would be fatal to our democracy. We must heed the advice of the Founding Father of American anthropology as stated in the concluding paragraphs of *The Mind of Primitive Man:*

"Our tendency to evaluate an individual according to the picture that we form of the class to which we assign him, although he may not feel any inner connection with that class, is a survival of primitive forms of thought. The characteristics of the members of the class are highly variable and the type that we construct from the most frequent characteristics supposed to belong to the class is never more than an abstraction hardly ever realized in a single individual, often not even the result of observation, but an often heard tradition that determines our judgment.

"Freedom of judgment can be attained only when we learn to estimate an individual according to his own ability and character. Then we shall find, if we were to select the best of mankind, that all races and all nationalities would be represented. Then we shall treasure and cultivate a variety of forms that human thought and activity has taken, and abhor, as leading to complete stagnation, all attempts to impress one pattern of thought upon whole nations or even the whole world."

June, 1977

First Job, First Date, First Strike, 1917

By ANNE SAFRAN

ON Monday morning Uncle Benny took me downtown to the shop where our cousin, Mr. Wapnick, was foreman. "The millinery trade needs to be organized," Benny said. "I'm taking you to a non-union shop, which means piece-work, longer hours and less pay. But at least you'll have a chance to learn the way the work is done here. The working system is different and more productive than in Europe."

We stood in the subway, pressed together like sardines. "Is it always so crowded?" I asked.

He nodded. "It is always crowded in the rush hours, that is, when one goes to and from work."

I was hot and perspiring by the time we reached the Astor Place station. It was good to be out in the open air even for the short walk to Broadway, where the shop was located.

Benny took me up in the grimy elevator to the third floor, left me there with Mr. Wapnick, and rushed to his own job. He'd come back for me at six o'clock.

Mr. Wapnick took me to a window, where a woman jotted down my name and gave me a bunch of hats together with cut-up ribbons and linings. "Here is a sample," she said in a broken Yiddish. "Make it just like that. You can sit at the end of the table on your left. The dressing room is on the right."

"I have to leave you," said Mr. Wapnick, "I work with the operators and blockers over there." He pointed to the rear of the room, where the whir of sewing machines was heard. "I'll look in on you at lunchtime. Meanwhile, if there is anything you don't understand, you can ask the girl next to you."

I thanked him and turned around curiously. "So this is an American shop and I am going to work here," I said to myself.

No one paid any attention to me, so I stood for a few moments observing the sooty walls and the closed, dirty windows. About 30 girls sat bent over their sewing at two long tables over which hung lamps with green metal shades. In front of each girl was a stock of untrimmed hats. Nearby stood a rack on which the trimmed hats had been hung.

Except for the noise of the operating machines in the rear, it was quiet, no one talking or singing as I had imagined girls would do while at work.

293

I finally went to my place on the left and settled down to work. Aunt Rebecca had provided me with a needle, thimble and scissors and there were plenty of spools of colored thread on the table. I turned to the girl sitting next to me. "My name is Anna" I said, "what is yours?"

She looked up for a second. "Bertha," she said, "Are you a *greeneh*?"

I grinned. "Yes. This is my first day at work."

"You better not talk," she said. "Our forelady doesn't like it when you talk at work."

I copied the trimming on the sample easily. Nothing to it. I was pleased with my work — neat and accurate. It took me about a half hour to trim one hat.

"What do they pay for trimming a hat?" I asked Bertha.

"Thirty cents a dozen."

"A dozen?! That's all?"

"Stop asking so many question," she said impatiently. "A real *greeneh hayeh!* You better hurry up or you'll go home without pay!"

I felt as though someone had suddenly slapped my face. I swallowed my tears and began working feverishly. But no matter how I tried I could not work as fast as Bertha.

By the time the whistle blew for lunch I was exhausted — and I had managed to trim only 10 hats!

Before we left that morning, Aunt Rebecca had handed me a paper bag with a cheese sandwich and an apple. She also slipped a quarter into my palm. "Buy yourself a drink," she said, "there's usually a peddler around selling things." But I didn't feel much like eating or drinking this noon.

Mr. Wapnick tried to cheer me up. "It's your first morning — what did you expect? You'll do much better after you get the knack of it."

I did feel better after my talk with him. After I finished the first dozen hats, I went to the window for another dozen and by the end of the day I had trimmed two-and-a-half dozen hats.

"How was it?" Benny asked me on the way home.

"I made very little today. I'm afraid I'll never be as fast as the other girls."

"Piece-work," Benny said, "it's real slavery. They rush the life out of you. But you need not be discouraged. You'll learn after a while how to save a stitch here and there and it'll go faster."

"To save a stitch," that was the idea. I noticed that Bertha made one big stitch where I made three. She also used a very long needle.

"Where do you buy these needles?" I asked here.

"In a store," she replied.

"Could you be so kind and buy one for me?"

She looked at me angrily, then she softened. "All right. I'll buy one for you. It's 10 cents."

I wasn't used to sewing with such a long needle. I kept sticking it into my fingers. At the end of the week two of my fingers were infected.

I soaked and bandaged them at night, but I was ashamed to come to work with bandaged fingers, so I took off the bandages in the morning. They hurt real bad.

On Monday I received a small envelope with my pay. My first earnings. Slowly I tore the envelope — five dollars and 40 cents!

By this time I knew how to go home by myself. I caught up with a girl from my shop who walked my way to the subway. She was younger than Bertha and prettier.

"You got your pay?" she asked.

"Yes, I'm afraid it's very little."

"You made $15?"

"I'm ashamed to tell you — only five."

"How do you come to work as a trimmer?"

I told her that I had learned the trade in Europe. Over there I did not only trim, but I made the entire hat by hand. I even made the wire or buckram frames for it.

"Really? So why do you work in our place? You are not just a trimmer, you are a copyist — that pays much better."

"A copyist? Are there factories for handmade hats?"

The next day I asked Mr. Wapnick whether he knew of a shop where they employed copyists.

Our cousin Grace told us that her husband and she had bought a house in Bath Beach and would move out there soon.

"What about Josephine?" I asked.

"Josephine is coming to live with us," she replied. "We've become so attatched to her, we couldn't think of having her move to strangers."

Beatrice and I had met Josephine during our first visit with Grace. She was a beautiful, vivacious blonde of about 20, full of fun and infectious laughter. A native of Antwerp, Belgium, she had left her widowed mother and brother to find a new life in America. Some friends of Sigmund in Antwerp had written to him about this girl and as soon as she had landed in New York, she came to live with the Charlaps. Like all immigrants she paid for her room and board from her meager wages as a sewing machine operator in a petticoat shop. However, her strained circumstances never dampened her spirit.

"Our house is one block from the Bay," Grace told us. "It's cool there in the summer and there is a beach where we can go swimming. As soon as we settle down, I want you to visit us."

We went there at the end of June. We liked the small private homes, the smell of sea air, and the park some blocks away, facing the Bay.

"Why don't you come here for the summer?" said Josephine. "You could share my room. It'll be fun living together."

I looked at Beatrice. She seemed to like the idea. "It isn't just sleeping," I said, "where would we eat?"

"I cook big meals," said Grace, "So there will be two more at the table."

That first summer in Bath Beach was of great consequence to us in the years that followed. Beatrice slept with Josephine and Grace put a narrow cot for me next to their bed. We were very crowded in that small room, but enjoyed every minute of it. Of course, we paid our share of room and board, but for the first time since we landed in the United States, we had a close friend, a gay, lighthearted person who was a lot of fun.

Josephine made friends easily and soon her friends became our friends. After a hard day's work, we looked foreward to an evening of relaxation. The West End subway was not as crowded and stifling as on the Lexington Ave. train — and then into a swimsuit and toward the Bay! One of our friends taught me to swim and after a while I actually swam by myself...

All the women and men we met at the beach were older than we and spoke better English than we, since they had arrived in New York some years before the outbreak of war. They all worked in the needle trades except for Freddie, who worked as a typesetter for a big English newspaper.

Freddie lived in Harlem. Like us he boarded with relatives in Bath Beach for the summer. He was in his early twenties, short, small-boned and wore thick glasses over his nearsighted gray eyes. He spoke in French to Josephine and somehow attached himself to me.

I was not at all boy-crazy like other teenagers. To me they were people, interesting or not. Freddie seemed to be more knowledgeable, more educated than the others and, because of his short stature, in need of friendship.

In the evenings, Josephine, Beatrice and I would walk to the Gravesend Bay Park, where we'd meet with our friends. We'd sit in a circle on the grass and sing Yiddish and Russian songs. Once in a while Beatrice and I would recite poems by Bialik, Frug, Edelstadt, Rosenfeld and Reisen, which always brought requests for more. Sometimes we'd go down the beach, make a bonfire to keep the mosquitoes away and sit around it, talking and singing. Two fellows, Sol and Nat, accompanied the chorus on a guitar and mandolin. A crowd would gather to listen, clap hands and applaud. The evenings were sweet and cool with mild breezes blowing from the sea. And Freddie always sat quietly beside me.

The summer passed quickly. Beatrice and I returned to the Bronx and our aunt Mirl told us that her boarder, Manya, had married and moved out. We could have her room if we wished. We were certainly glad to pay the rent and have a room for ourselves.

Several weeks later I received a letter form Freddie. "Would Miss Kahan care to go to a Philharmonic Symphony Concert with me? She may reply in any of the six languages she knows."

I replied in Yiddish that I'd very much like to go to a concert with him and I thanked him for the invitation.

There was no telephone at my uncle's house. A pay telephone was installed in the basement and the incoming calls were answered by the janitor who'd ring a bell and shout up the dumbwaiter. One evening I was startled hearing her call: "Telephone for Miss Kahan."

I ran down the five flights and picked up the receiver breathlessly. It was Freddie. Could I meet him Thursday evening inside the 96th Street station? He'd be waiting on the platform near the front car.

My first date in the United States. I looked forward to the concert, but I was not at all excited about meeting Freddie.

He was there, waiting, his usual small, neat self. He walked right into the car where I stood smiling. The doors closed and we shook hands.

He told me that a friend and he shared two season tickets for the Philharmonic Symphony Concerts at Carnegie Hall. His friend took out his girl one time and he could take a friend the next time.

I enjoyed the concert immensely. We seemed to have the same reaction to certain passages, because Freddie looked at me, and sometimes even pressed my hand.

On the way home I told him that he need not go as far as the Bronx, since tomorrow was a working day for him as well as for me, and I was not at all afraid to go home by myself. Gentleman that he was, he wouldn't think of it. We talked and joked all the way to the door of my building where we shook hands and he remained waiting until I ran up the four flights of stairs.

Freddie took me to many concerts during this and the next winter. He was a delightful companion, but there was never any talk or demonstration of love between us. He needed encouragement, which I did not care to give.

I had a difficult time the next summer at my place of work. The new line of winter hats was complicated and didn't pay well. Each new sample had to be studied and often we found the cut-up material in our bundle too short to cover the buckram frame. And we never knew how much we'd get paid for our new work until the following Monday when we received the little book in which each sample was marked by its number together with the amount paid for it.

We were particularly shocked and indignant when we found that the black-and-white velour picture hat with handmade flowers paid only $3 a dozen. It took two days to make a dozen such hats!

"Are we going to keep quiet about it?" I asked.

"What can we do?" Mollie began to cry.

"We won't work on this number until they double the price," said Mildred, the girl sitting across form me.

I looked at my cousin. I had spoken to her rarely since I found out that the week she had met me in the subway and convinced me to work for the Elmer Hat Co., the forelady, Miss Wolfson, had promised $10 and a box of candy to anyone who'd bring in a new girl.

"What about you? What do you propose to do?" I asked her.

"I think that we should not accept any work at all until all the prices are raised." she said.

There was a sudden silence and then a chorus of vioices: "Let's stop working."

Three of the fastest workers kept sewing through this. They had no complaints since they always received the best hats, hats that could be done in half the time of others.

"Why don't you speak up?" said Mildred to Rose, the oldest of them. "Are you with us, or not?"

Rose raised her head and looked at the strained faces of the girls around the table. "Let's finish the work," she said, "then we stop."

"That's reasonable," I said.

In a few hours we finished our work. No one went for another bundle. We ate our lunch and remained sitting idly at the table. I picked up my book of stories by O'Henry and read.

The cutter and shipping clerk rushed to Miss Wolfson as she came up from lunch. They whispered for a while to each other, then she approached us with a big smile.

"What the hell is the matter? Taking a holiday?"

"We won't work until the prices are fixed," I said, looking straight into her eyes.

She lost her benevolent smile. "You *greeneh* snot-nose," she said angrily, "you speak for all of them?"

My cheeks were aflame and my heart raced. "Ask them," I said.

"That's right, Lydia," said Rose. "We won't do a stitch until you meet our demands."

Miss Wolfson was flabbergasted. She had had some arguments before about prices, but they were minor and a raise of 20 to 50 cents on a dozen would settle the dispute. This was different.

"You can sit here all day," she said, "you won't get any raises this way!" And she went to see Mr. Elmer in the office.

Several hours passed. Every once in a while the shipping clerk came around asking whether anyone wanted a bundle. Some girls began to falter, but my weak, crying Mollie was not among them.

"Speak to them," she said to me. "They have respect for you, they'll listen."

I stood up. I was the youngest, but I felt sure of our purpose. "May I speak to you?" I said calmly, looking around the table at my co-workers. "Yes," they said. "You started it, what do you have to say now?"

"The hours are passing and we are all getting impatient," I said, "we need the money we are losing now. I think that I need it more than anyone here, some of you may know the reason why. Yet, I would sit here today and tomorrow and after tomorrow until we win. But I'm sure it won't take that long. It's the height of the season and they have many orders to fill. They can't afford to be idle now. We are united and that makes us strong. Let's not give in, let's hold out a little longer!"

I was surprised at the applause that followed. After a while Miss Wolfson walked in, the usual smile on her lips.

"What the hell," she said. "Mr. Elmer is willing to raise some of the prices. So you better get back to work."

"We are not going to wait until next Monday to find out how much you raised," said Mildred. "We want to know right now!"

"You, too?" said Miss Wolfson.

"Don't point at anyone," said Rose, "we are all in it."

"Miss Wolfson went back to the office many times before a compromise was reached: a raise of $2 a dozen on the picture hat, raises from 50 cents to a dollar on each dozen of other hats.

I think this was one of the first, if not the first, sit-down strikes in the United States.

September, 1982

In Memoriam: Clara Lemlich Shavelson (March 28, 1886 — July 25, 1982)

Remembering the Waistmakers General Strike, 1909

By CLARA LEMLICH SHAVELSON
Ed. by Morris U. Schappes

[When Clara Lemlich Shavelson died in a Los Angeles nursing home July 25, the death notice of the family in the N.Y. Times *July 30 and Aug. 1 identified her as the "loving Mother and Grandmother who sparked 1909 Shirtwaist Makers' Strike." That action of hers has assured her a place in the history of the American labor movement, of the socialist movement and of American Jewish life. Thus the article about her by Paula Scheier that we published in Nov., 1954 has been reprinted in full in* The American Jewish Woman: A Documentary History, *compiled by Jacob Rader Marcus (see our review, May, 1982). The strike and Clara Lemlich's role in it are described in Philip S. Foner's* Women and the American Labor Movement from Colonial Times to the End of World War I *(Free Press, N.Y., 1979, 634 pages, indexed, $15.95, Ch. 18, "The Waistmarkers' Revolt," pages 324-345); in the Marxist feminist Meredith Tax's* The Rising of the Women: Feminist Solidarity and Class Conflict, 1880-1917 *(Monthly Review Press, N.Y., 1980, 332 pages, indexed, $17.50, Ch. 8, "The Uprising of the 30,000," pages 205-240); in Mari Jo Buhle's* Women and American Socialism, 1870-1920 *(University of Illinois Press, 1981, 364 pages, indexed, $21.95, pages 190-194); and in Carol Hymowitz and Michaele Weissmann's* A History of Women in America *(Bantam, N.Y., 1978, 412 pages, indexed, paperback $3.50, pages 249-252). The ILGWU monthly organ,* Justice, *contained a full tabloid page obituary, "Clara Lemlich Dead at 96; Heroine of Cooper Union," in its Sept. issue.*

Yet, while the article we present below contains her own unpublished recollection of that Cooper Union meeting, we wish also to record that while her shining historic moment was in that desperate 13 week strike in 1909-1910, Clara Lemlich continued her activity in the labor, suffragist, socialist and Jewish movements for another half century until physical incapacity took her to the sidelines. Right after the strike she was appointed a Factory Inspector by the ILGWU, she was on the Executive Board of the Women's Trade Union League of New York (which played a strong supportive role in

300

the strike), and continued her socialist activity. After marrying the printing worker Joseph Shavelson in 1912 and beginning to raise three children, Irving, Martha and Rita, she became a member of the Communist Party in 1926 and in 1933 and 1938 was its candidate for local office.

In the 1920's, she was an organizer for the United Council of Working Class Women; when the Depression began, she helped organize the first Unemployed Council in Brighton Beach, Brooklyn, and in 1930 and 1932 she went on the historic Hunger Marches to Washington to fight for home relief and unemployment insurance. Active also in the anti-fascist movement, she was a delegate in 1934 to the first International Women's Congress against War and Fascism in Paris (and while overseas visited the USSR). In 1935 she was active in the Progressive Women's Council in Brighton Beach; in 1941 she was the N.Y.C. secretary of the Women's Division of the International Workers Order. In 1951 she was on a trade union delegation to France, Italy, Czechoslovakia and the USSR — and also became a charter member of the Emma Lazarus Federation of Jewish Women's Clubs. The last time I saw her in action was on a picket line to save the Rosenbergs. In 1954, with the aid of the late David Dubinsky, she was granted a pension by the ILGWU. Both Clara Lemlich and Clara Lemlich Shavelson deserve our respect, admiration and honor.

The article by her that we publish now originated in the following circumstances: Having supplied Herbert Aptheker, head of the American Institue for Marxist Studies, with bibliographical material on the 1909 strike, I received a letter from him dated Feb. 5, 1965 asking me to try to get from Mrs. Shavelson written answers to questions posed by a graduate student in a West Coast university who was working on a thesis on that strike. Mrs. Shavelson's answers were postmarked March 15 from Long Beach, Calif. and I forwarded them promptly to Aptheker to give to the student. (The bibliography was published in the AIMS Newsletter, *Vol. 2, No. 2, March-April, 1965.) — M.U.S.]*

I PERSONALLY came to this [country] in 1903.[1] I knew very little about socialism. I went to work 2 weeks after landing in this country. We worked from sunrise to sunset 7 days a week. Saturday till 4:30 o'clock. The shops were located in old delapidated buildings, in the back of stores. Those who worked on machines had to bring their machines, particularly the men. They had to carry the machines on their back both to and from work.

Most of the shops had both a foreman and forelady. The shop we worked had no central heating, no electric power. The shop was heated by [a] coal stove which was in the center of the shop. The ashes were emptied every morning but ashes were taken away once a week. The hissing of the machines, the yelling of the Foreman, made life unbearble. The girls, whether socialist or not (had) many stoppages, and strikes broke out in many shops. However every strike we called was broken by the police and gangsters hired by the bosses. In 1906[2] some of us girls who were more class conscious called a meeting at 206 East Broadway, where we organized the 1st local of the waist markers. We elected S. Shindler[3] as our first secretary. We named the local Local 25 of the Waist Makers Union.

But since every strike we called was smashed by the bosses, the union decided to call a mass meeting at Cooper Union.[4] The hall was packed. On the platform was Samuel Gompers[5] of the American Federation of Labor, Leonora O'Reilly[6] of the Women's Trade Union League, B. Feigenbaum[7] of the *Jewish Daily Forward.* Each one talked about the terrible conditions of the workers in the shops. But no [one] gave or made any practical or valid solution. Suddenly a young girl[8] in the audience asked for the floor. When she was given the floor she said, "I make a motion that we go out in a general strike." The entire audience rose to its feet. Men threw their hats in the air, women waved their handkerchiefs.

The girl who made the motion was called to the platform. Mr. B. Feigenbaum of the *Jewish Daily Forward,* who was chairman of the meeting, raised the right hand to the girl and made her repeat the famous Jewish oath: "May my right [hand] wither from [my] arm if I betray the cause I now pledge." The following day 20 thousand waistmakers, both men and women, came out on strike.

That's why this strike is known in the labor movement [as] the strike of the 20 thousand.[9]

Now as to the question whether the girls were socialist, is hard to tell. All I can tell you [is] that many of us marched in the streets of downtown N.Y. with [Alexander] Trach[t]e[n]berg[10] as our leader. Rose Pastor Stokes[11] marched with us. Many of the girls became leaders in the Women's Trade Union League. Some of them joined a political party.

I[n so] far as I am concerned, I am still at it.

/s/Clara Lemlich Shavelson
145 Lincoln Rd., Brooklyn, N.Y.

NOTES

1. The Lemlich family left Tsarist Ukraine after the Kishinev pogrom of Easter, 1903. In three days, 47 Jews were killed, 437 injured and 1,500 homes and stores pillaged. After a few months in England, the Lemlichs came to New York.

2. Louis Levine, *The Women's Garment Workers,* N.Y. 1924, p. 149, says that Local 25 was chartered in 1905. At the 1906 ILGWU convention, the local reported its "weekly [dues] taking were not more than $4 or $5." At the 1908 convention, the local was reported in a "precarious condition owing to loss of strikes and general crisis" (1907 Panic) and asked to "be financed until such time as it will be able to pay its way."

3. S. Shindler was a wrapper-maker; in 1909 he was also recording secretary of the United Hebrew Trades, which played a big role in the shirtwaist strike (B. Weinstein, *40 Yorn in der Idisher Arbeiter Bavegung* — 40 Years in the Jewish Labor Movement —

N.Y., 1924, pages 237-244). By 1924, Shindler had left the labor movement and was owning a summer hotel.

4. The meeting at Cooper Union Nov. 21, 1909 was the largest of many simultaneous meetings held that evening organized by a General Stirke Committee elected at a conference called by the United Hebrew Trades to extend strikes already under way at the Triangle Waist Co. and at Leiserson's, where Clara Lemlich was working. At that Conference, she was elected to the strike committee for she was a well-known militant, having been arrested 17 times while picketing Leiserson's and having been beaten so badly she was hospitalized with six broken ribs.

5. Samuel Gompers (1850-1924) had been president of the American Federation of Labor since 1886 (except for 1895).

6. Leonora O'Reilly (1870-1927) was a worker at 11 and a union member at 16 in the Knights of Labor. After becoming a sewing teacher at the Manhattan School of Girls, she was active in the Women's Trade Union League, and was a powerful agitational orator. She was not, however, a speaker at the Cooper Union meeting; Mary Dreier spoke for the WTUL. Mrs. Shavelson was perhaps confusing the Cooper Union meeting with the Dec. 5 rally of 7,000 at the Hippodrome, at which both Leonora O'Reilly and Rose Pastor Stokes were speakers. After the strike, when the Wage Earners' Suffrage League was formed by a group that seceded from the National American Women's Suffrage Association, which paid little attention to working women, Clara Lemlich was vice-president, with O'Reilly as president.

7. Benjamin Feigenbaum (1860-1923) had been a primitive anarchist anti-religious agitator in London from 1887 to 1891, when he left for the USA. Here, while continuing to be an anti-religious satirist, he began to use his knowledge of the Bible and of Jewish tradition to promote socialist ideas. It is significant that is was he who called for the taking of the ancient Jewish oath. Among his many works are his 1911 translation into Yiddish of August Bebel's *Women and Socialism* and in 1914 his *Yiddishkeit und Sozialismus* (Jewishness and Socialism).

8. Of course this was Clara herself, then 23 years old but so slight she looked like a teener.

9, Foner, work cited, pages 328n-329n, says estimates vary from 15,000 to 30,000. B. Weinstein said the UHT signed up 18,000 strikers in three days. WTUL records studied by Helen Marot in 1910 showed 30,000, which she breaks down to: "20,000 to 21,000 Russian-Jewish women, 6,000 Russian-Jewish men (cutters and pressers), 2,000 Italian women and approximately 1,000 native-born American women."

10. Alexander Trachtenberg (1884-1966)was a socialist economist and educator. She may have studied with him at the Rand School in 1915 and thereafter. Like Mrs. Shavelson, he was a charter member of the Communist Party and later established International Publishers as a Marxist publishing house.

11. Rose Pastor Stokes (1870-1933) created a sensation on the Lower East Side when she married James Graham Phelps Stokes (1872-1960), a wealthy socialist, in 1905 (they were divorced in 1925). At the time of this strike, she was a socialist and lectured for the Intercollegiate Socialist Society, which her husband then headed. She was a popular and effective speaker. In 1919 she also became a charter member of the Communist Party.

November, 1982

Leo Frank's Letter
From Prison, 1914

Edited By MORRIS U. SCHAPPES

[Shortly after the Nashville Tennesseean *March 7, 1982 broke its story corroborating the innocence of Leo Frank, who was lynched Aug. 17, 1915 in Marietta, Ga. (see our May issue, p. 24), we received a letter from a long-time subscriber in Ojai, Calif., Mrs. Orilla Winfield. Enclosing a clipping about the story from the Quincy, Ill.,* Herald-Whig *of March 8, she wrote to us March 24: ".... I come from a Protestant, mid-Western farming family. Our uncle went to Cornell with Leo Frank and we have in our possession a letter written to our uncle while Frank was either awaiting trial or in jail. And as children we were raised on the injustice and horrors of this event. I never heard the word anti-Semitism until I went away to College. Considering the rise of anti-Semitism in this country, I think the story should be told again."*

It is with Mrs. Winfield's kind permission that we publish the letter sent from prison in Atlanta on Oct. 29, 1914 to John Gould (1879-1929), an Illinois farm boy educated in local schools until he went to Cornell, majoring in engineering. There he met Leo Frank, who got his degree of Mechanical Engineering in 1906. Frank was now incarcerated in the Fulton Tower, Cell 2 of the South Corridor, where he read in the evenings by candlelight plus the light from the single electric bulb in the outside corridor. He was allowed visitors daily (and evenings) and sometimes played chess with them. One such visitor was Anne Carroll Moore, a librarian at Pratt Institute in Brooklyn that Frank had frequented as a high school boy. She saw him every day for eight days in June, 1915, found him "always cheerful, serene and hopeful, as ready to listen to others as to talk himself but with a fund of conversation as rich and inexhaustible as it was varied and interesting" (Frances Clark Sayers, Anne Carrole Moore, A Biography, *N.Y., 1972, p. 164).*

When the letter to Gould was written Oct. 29, 1914, Frank had already endured a terrible ordeal. Arrested April 29, 1913, Frank, the superintendent of the pencil factory in which he was alleged to have murdered 13-year-old Mary Phagan, a worker in the factory, was tried July 26 to Aug. 25 in a lynch atmosphere both inside and outside the courtroom. He had been found guilty and sentenced to death by hanging — by a judge who did not himself believe Frank was guilty! On Oct. 31 the same judge

304

had denied a retrial and Feb. 17, 1914 the Georgia Supreme Court had affirmed the lower court decision. Frank's case was again on appeal to the Georgia Supreme Court. Frank was permitted to receive and send letters freely, and to use his own office stationery. — M.U.S.]

October 29, 1914

MY dear Gould:
Your letter was to me like a "voice from the long ago," just to think that it is now over eight years since I have heard from or seen you. I certainly appreciated your words of cheer and confidence.

Since graduation, the years have been good to me. In Atlanta, since August 1908, I have held a nice position with the above firm, a position of trust and responsibility. In Nov. 1910 I married a lovely, beautiful girl, with whom I was very happy.[1] It was while I was in pursuit of my happy life and along its even tenor, that in April 1913, this most unjust and outrageous trouble overtook me like a bolt from the blue. The charge was so preposterous, that at first, I treated the matter disdainfully, it was all so foreign and far removed from my most fantastic conception or thought. Still the public, so easily aroused here in the South,[2] conceived a vicious animosity and vindictive hatred toward me, aided and abetted by racial prejudice & getting the man higher up. Discretion and intelligence was thrown to the winds and unreasoning mob rule took its place. A dwarfed and cowardly judiciary,[3] in spite of the truth & the facts, lent its ear to the popular outcry; hence my present predicament.

In spite of it all, however, I am still fighting & must win in the end. Of the ultimate happy outcome, I have never been in doubt. We are still before the state courts, and will fight to Washington if we have to do it.[4] The best of brain and heart has been enlisted in my defense.

Doubtless, you have read various accounts of my trial in August 1913, the conditions surrounding it, and subsequent developments. One of the most startling recent developments was the declaration of attorney Wm. M. Smith, counsel for Jim Conley,[5] the star negro witness against me, & the *only* incriminating witness introduced, (a prejurer and jail-bird).[6] Mr. Smith states that *Conley is guilty,* and that I am innocent and that he will *prove it!* Smith's declaration aroused a storm of disapproval, and lynching threats. However Smith appears to have backbone and is not to be scared off. I will send you his statement as it appeared in the local newspaper, in a day or two.

I am enclosing you some of my leaflets (1,2,4,6 & 7)[7] covering vital points of the trial, that have not appeared in the public prints & upon which the public does not seem to be intelligently enlightened.

I will be glad to hear from you at any time and will give you any information you may desire.

With best wishes and warm personal regards, I am,

Cordially yours,
Mr. J.H. Gould
    Detroit, Michigan

Georgia State Senate Res. 423 on Leo Frank Case

Whereas, Leo Frank was tried in the Superior Court of Fulton County in 1913 for the murder of Mary Phagan; and

Whereas, he was convicted in an atmosphere charged with prejudice and hysteria; and

Whereas, he was sentenced to death but his sentence was commuted by Governor John Marshall Slaton; and

Whereas, in August of 1915, he was taken by a mob from the state institution in Milledgeville and carried to Cobb County where he was lynched; and

Whereas, Alonzo Mann, a 14-year-old witness at the Frank trial, was threatened with death and was not asked specific questions which could have cleared Frank; and

Whereas, Mr. Mann has come forward to clear his conscience before his death and claims that Leo Frank was not guilty of such crime, it is only fitting and proper that his name be cleared, even after his death.

Now, therefore, be it resolved by the Senate that this body strongly requests that the State Board of Pardons and Paroles conduct an investigation into the Leo Frank case; and, if the evidence indicates that Leo Frank was not guilty, the board should give serious consideration to granting a pardon to Leo Frank posthumously.

Be it further resolved that the Secretary of the Senate is authorized and directed to transmit an appropriate copy of this resolution to the State Board of Pardons and Paroles.

(Authored by Senators Robert Bell, Pierre Howard and Floyd Hudgins, this resolution passed without a dissenting vote.)

Justice for Leo Frank?

THE Georgia State Board of Pardons and Paroles has been petitioned to exonerate Leo Frank. On Sept. 17, 1982, Jewish organ-izations in Atlanta wrote to the Hon. Mobley Howell, chairman of the Georgia State Board: "On behalf of the Atlanta Jewish Federation, the American Jewish Committee and the Anti-Defamation League of B'nai B'rith, the undersigned representatives of these organizations respectfully request that you and the members of the State Board of Pardons and Paroles grant a full and complete pardon exonerating Leo Frank of any guilt for the crime for which he was convicted by the Superior Court of Fulton County, in 1913...

"We submit our application to you with the same motivation that impelled the Georgia Senate to adopt Senate resolution 423 (see text above) in its 1982 session: to finally right an historic injustice by exonerating Leo Frank, thereby demonstrationg that our legal system can indeed be called upon to find the ultimate truth and to proclaim it. This case presents a rare opportunity for us to obliterate a terrible stain which history has ascribed to the Georgia Judicial system because of the injustice done to Leo Frank. We should not let this opportunity pass. We believe, as we know you do, in following the biblical injunction, 'Justice, Justice thou shalt pursue.'" (Reported in *The Jewish Floridian,* Miami weekly, Nov. 26, 1982, in an article by Wiliam A. Gralnick.)

[Leo Frank was given a posthumous pardon, but not exoneration, by the Georgia Board of Pardons on March 11, 1986 — Ed.]

NOTES

1. Leo Frank married Lucille Selig, daughter of a rich Atlanta family.
2. In the South from 1900 to 1914 1,079 Blacks had been lynched; in Georgia from 1889 to 1928 there were more lynchings than in any other state (*The Negro Handbook,* p. 99; Leonard Dinnerstein, *The Leo Frank Case,* N.Y., 1968, p. 148).
3. "In all, Frank would petition the higher courts of Georgia and the United States 13 times and never find redress" (Harry Golden, *A Little Girl Is Dead,* Cleveland and N.Y., 1965, p. 238; paperback, 1967, p. 234).
4. Shortly after his letter was written, the Georgia Supreme Court Nov. 14 again denied a new trial and Nov. 18 refused to review the case. In Washington, the Supreme Court denied Frank's appeal for review Dec. 7; on April 19, 1915 the Supreme Court, by 7-2, affirmed the District Court decision denying a writ of *habeas corpus,* with Charles Evans Hughes and Oliver Wendell Homes dissenting. Holmes wrote: "Mob law does not become due process of law by securing the assent of a terrorized jury. We are not speaking of mere disorder, but of a case where the processes of justice are actually subverted." This dissenting view became the rule of the Court majority from 1923 on, when Holmes, for the Court, reversed the conviction, in *Moore v. Dempsey,* of five Arkansas Blacks convicted by mob law (Dinnerstein, p. 151). Louis Marshall, president of the American Jewish Committee, who argued Frank's appeal before the Supreme Court, later wrote to N.Y. State Court of Appeals Justice Irving Lehman, "What really convicted Frank was the suggestion that he was a Jewish capitalist engaged in abnormal sexual practice."
5. On Oct. 2, 1914 William M. Smith, lawyer for Jim Conley, the Black janitor in the pencil factory who had been the chief witness against Frank, issued a public statement that Frank was innocent, that his client, Conley, was the murderer and his story about Frank was a "cunning fabrication." Dinnerstein writes, "The national press used Smith's statement to reintroduce Leo Frank to their readers. From June, 1914, when a Georgia court had denied

his appeal for a new trial, until Oct., 1914, when Smith announced his belief that Conley had killed Mary Phagan, Frank's name rarely appeared in print. But Smith's remarks gave the newspapers an occasion for reviewing the events in the case and stimulating further interest in Leo Frank" (p. 115).

6. Conley, at 27, had served several jail terms for "petty thievery" and often been fined for disorderly conduct. For allegedly helping Leo Frank remove the body of Mary Phagan, Conley served one year on the chain gang. In 1918, for trying to burglarize a drug store, Conley was sentenced to 20 years in prison. Ordinarily the testimony of such a witness against a white man would have been discounted in Georgia, but the anti-Semitic fever inhibited any such compunctions in the jury and the court.

7. These five (or seven) "leaflets" (which Mrs. Winfield has made aviailable to us) are mimeographed statements written and signed by Leo Frank while he was in jail and dated, respectively, May 22, May 26, May 28, May 29 and June 3, 1914. They are two, four and nine pages long and contain detailed refutations of the testimony given against him. Alonzo Mann, the office boy, whose revelation last year at age 83 that his mother had kept him from telling all he knew at the trial, is mentioned in Leaflets Nos. 2 and 7, but of course Frank did not know what Mann was holding back: that he had seen Conley carrying the limp body of Mary Phagan on the day she was murdered, and that Conley had threatened to kill him if he revealed what he was seeing.

Leo Frank, after his sentence was commuted to life imprisonment by the courageous Gov. John Marshal Slaton, was transferred to the state prison farm in Milledgeville. Aug 16 he was wrested from prison by 25 self-styled (and easily identifiable) Knights of Mary Phagan and lynched next morning in Marietta, Ga. On Nov. 15, 1915, the Kinights of Mary Phagan gave birth to the new Ku Klux Klan, burning a cross at Stone Mountain. (The original KKK had on Aug. 15, 1868 lynched S.A. Bierfield, a young Russian Jew operating a dry-goods store in Franklin, Tenn., and his Black clerk Lawrence Bowman. A second Black clerk, Henry Morton, escaped to testify at a federal inquiry into such lynchings. For details see Morris. U. Schappes, *A Documentary History of the Jews in the Untied States, 1654-1875,* pages 515-517 and 717-718).

The *Southern Israelite* in Atlanta, in a March 12, 1982 editorial, declared, "it is time to clear the official record... " In Massachusetts, Gov. Michael Dukakis, acting on an investigating commission report, cleared the martyred Sacco and Vanzetti by a historic proclamation July 19, 1957, 50 years after the executions. The centennial of Leo Frank's birth April 17, 1984 would be an appropriate occasion for his official exoneration.

February, 1983

Return to Vitebsk

By MARC CHAGALL

Excerpted from Marc Chagall, A Jewish Boy from Vitebsk, *in Yiddish and French, edited by Leon Leneman, published by Comite Pour La Langue et la Culture Yiddish, Paris, 1983.*

Leon Leneman, born in Warsaw in 1909, has lived in Paris since 1947. Since 1967 he has been president of the Association of Yiddish Writers and Journalists in France. For a quarter of a century he has been a friend and colleague of Marc Chagall. Mr. Leneman has been a correspondent of the Tog Morgn-Zhurnal *(N.Y.)* Letste Neies *(Tel Aviv) and* Neier Moment *(Sao Paulo); he has also written for various French publications. His* La Tragedie des Juifs en URSS *was published in Paris in 1959. The present volume contains Chagall's reminiscences of the years 1914-1922, as well as articles by Mr. Leneman on the artist's attitudes toward his work, the Jewish people, his two "homelands" — Russia and France — and the State of Israel. The Yiddish is Mr. Leneman's translation from Chagall's Russian. The French is also by Mr. Leneman. The book contains reproductions of many Chagall sketches and facsimiles of the artist's letters written in Yiddish.*

In the extract translated here by Max Rosenfeld from the Yiddish, Marc Chagall has just returned from a short stay in Paris.

Max Rosenfeld

NOW I am back in Russia, but is it really Russia? I have never actually taken a good look at my Russia. When you come right down to it, what had I ever seen? I didn't know Novgorod, Rostov, Kiev; had seen only Petrograd, Moscow, a surburb of Lyazne, and Vitebsk.

But Vitebsk is a separate country, anyway. A sad, unfortunate city. A city full of girls that I never got around to touching. (For that, I lacked either time or brains.) Scores, hundreds of synagogues, butcher shops, passersby. Is that Russia? No, it's only my city, which I have rediscovered — with strong feelings.

Around this time I painted my Vitebsk cycle of 1914. I painted everything that happened to pass before my eyes. I painted from a window, never going out into the street with the paint-box on my shoulder. Sufficient for me was a fence, a post, a floor, a chair.

But there sits a humble old man, sunk deep into his chair, a samovar on the table in front of him. With my eyes I ask him: "Who are you, friend?"

309

"You don't remember me? You've never heard of the Slutsker *magid* (preacher)?"

"Listen to me, friend, please come with me. I'll make something for you — a — how can I explain it to you?" I'm afraid if I tell him, he'll get up and disappear and I'll never see him again.

Still, he did come. Sat down on a chair and fell fast asleep. Have you seen my painting of a Jew in green? That's him.

Another old man walked past our house. grey hair, a forlorn look in his eyes. A sack over his shoulder. I ask myself: Can he at least open his mouth to ask for a *nedoveh* (hand-out)? He is a silent man, however. Steps across the threshold and waits at the door. Stands there like that for a long while, and if you don't give him anything, turns and goes away, as quietly and silently as he came.

"Listen," I say to him, "sit down and rest a while. Good. You don't mind, correct? Just rest here, and here are 20 *kopeks* for you. But please put on my father's *tallis*. And stay in the chair."

You saw my painting of the Jew in *tallis and t'fillin* (prayer shawl and phylacteries). That's him.

It was wonderful when I could work in peace like this. At times I had a figure before my eyes so old and tragic that it was like an angel from another world.

Have you seen my painting of an old man bent over a Talmud? He was such a figure.

In this way I painted and painted. But one rainy evening I found myself under a wedding canopy, a real *khupa* like the one you see in my pictures. They married me *k'das moshe v'yisroel,* in accordance with the laws of Moses and Israel.

But before that, something interesting happened. The parents and the entire big family of my — yes, my wife — were displeased with the lineage of *my* family. After all (they complained), my father was only an ordinary servant. And as for my grandfather...

Whereas *her* father — my goodness! — he owned as much as three jewelry stores in our town. In his show windows, the cold fire of rings, necklaces and bracelets shines and sparkles brilliantly. Wall-clocks tick and alarm-clocks ring. In their kitchen they bake mammoth apple-cakes and cheese cakes three times a week and serve slices of them for breakfast. In our house, all we had was a still life of scraps.

Their father loved raisins just as much as *mine* loved — onions. And a chicken, which we saw on our table only once a year — for *kapores* (Yom Kippur scapegoat) — they ate every day in the week. Her grandfather, an old man with a long beard, used to walk around the spacious house searching for Russian books, Russian newspapers, and as soon as he found one he threw it into the oven. he couldn't stand the idea of his grandchildren attending the Russian high school.

"Not necessary! Not necessary! Go to *heder* (Jewish one-room school)!"

All day long he sat and "learned." Yom Kippur he wasn't part of this world. But in consideration of his age, the rabbi himself gave him permission to swallow a few drops of milk. My wife serves it to him in a spoon. His tears slide down his long beard into the milk. Witnessing his anguish, my wife also starts crying and her hand trembles so much that the milk spills, leaving barely enough for her grandfather to moisten his lips. I myself can't find the strength to speak. My thoughts are all confused. My bride's mother says to her daughter:

"Listen, my child, people say he smears red paint even on his cheeks. What kind of man can he be, this fellow of yours, with cheeks as rosy as a young girl's? He'll never earn a living!"

But it didn't help. They couldn't convince my bride.

"You'll come to grief, my daughter, right along with him. And for what? Besides, he's an 'artist,' whatever that is. And what will people say?"

In this manner they nagged the life out of my bride, from early morning to late at night. But twice a day she brought to my studio slices of cake from home, broiled fish, warm milk, even pieces of stuff out of which I made drawing-boards.

All I had to do was open the window of my room, and the blue air, the love, the flowers, would come in with her. Dressed all in white, or all in black, she has been floating in and out of my pictures, showing me the way in my art. I never finish a painting or an engraving until I ask for her "yes" or "no." What do I care about the opinion of her parents, her brothers, may the Almighty have mercy on them!

My poor father. "Come, *Tatte,* we're going to my wedding." Like me, he would much rather have gone to sleep. Was it worth it just to become connected with such a highborn family?

Arriving very late at my bride's home, I found their whole sanhedrin already assembled. A pity I am not Veronese, so I could capture that scene on canvas. Around the long table sit the rabbi (a wise old man, he still loves to tell jokes), merchants of the First Guild, a bunch of businessmen and other modest personages. They are waiting impatiently for me and for — the feast. Without me, of course, the kitchen can't start serving. I knew that, and somewhat deliberately teased their appetites.

That this evening was perhaps the most important one in my life, and that — without music, without stars and without a sky, but against the background of a yellow wall — they would soon marry me under a red *khupa* (canopy) — this didn't seem to concern them one bit! But at this most festive hour I felt lost among the crowd of guests — seated and standing, walking back and forth, greeting new arrivals, relatives from near

311

and far, sisters-in-law, servant-girls with ripening breasts. All smiles, they were preparing the confetti with which to shower the bride and groom.

As they waited for me, they gossiped. It was hardly fitting to admit that the bridegroom was an artist, particularly one who "already has a reputation, and people are even paying money for his paintings! Is that really true?"

"Still, it's not a real livelihood," sighs one of the relatives.

"Go on! It's fame and honor!"

"Well, but do you know who his father is?" And no one says another word.

At that moment, if they had laid me in my grave, my facial features would have had more elasticity and been less rigid than the mask which sat down beside the bride. My only regret was that on account of my foolish modesty, I didn't dare touch the mountains of grapes and other fruit and delicacies that lay spread out before me on the table...

June, 1985

William Gropper (1897-1977)

By *MILTON W. BROWN*

WILLIAM Gropper's work remains to testify to his greatness as an artist. No matter that some today cannot read the signs. His works are the eternal witness to his achievement, and I am sure that subsequent generations will recognize the fact. Bill Gropper is a landmark in American art. His line had been indelibly inscribed across the face of America. To have seen his patterns of black-and-white on the newsprint of our day is to have experienced the past half century of history, to have been made more stunningly conscious of being and understanding, to have caught a flash of the truth, to have shared a sentiment, to have tasted compassion as well as hate.

Bill belonged to that small group of involved, committed and passionate artists who are compelled to express themselves pointedly and immediately, in whatever means, about the present, now, today; about the nature of the human condition in its most specific and temporal conditions. Bill's art had to do with life and politics, not with private feelings or esthetic sensibilities. It dealt with war, revolution and genocide; with poverty, exploitation and injustice; with chicanery, venality and corruption.

His picture of our world was not a pleasant one. Why should it have been? He came up the hard way, out of poverty, exploitation and injustice. The images of his youth stayed with him, in his eye, his heart and especially in his gall. He knew whom and how to hate as did Daumier before him. And perhaps, because of this, his compassion for the little tailor, the cigarmaker and the dishwasher went so deep.

Bill's art came from a long and honored tradition in the history of art. Really, from several traditions. From Breughel. Bouwer (c. 1605-1638), Rembrandt and Van Gogh, all of whom expressed an affinity and sympathy with the lower classes. More obviously, it derives from a more recent and more outspoken tradition of social consciousness, out of Goya, Daumier, Gavarni (1804-1866) and Forain (1852-1931). Closer in time and more immediate geographically was the early 20-century American Ashcan tradition which had its roots in journalistic experience.

In his early years, Bill attended the Ferrer School, an anarchistic experiment in education, where he studied with Robert Henri and George Bellows. This was his first-hand connection with the Ashcan tradition, with Henri, Sloan, Luks, Glackens and Shinn, ex-newspaper artists, who a scant generation earlier were upsetting the complacency of the academic art

313

establishment by calling for a return of art to life, to New York City life, to the life of the people in the slums and ghettos of the city. It was also his connection with the *Masses,* where John Sloan as art editor was soliciting drawings and cartoons from his friends and students, including George Bellows, Stuart Davis and Glenn Coleman.

Bill must also have been aware of the political cartooning tradition in American art from the Civil War drawings of Thomas Nast to the contemporary efflorescence of the tradition in the daily and weekly journals of the time — Art Young, Robert Minor, Boardman Robinson and Daniel Fitzpatrick. Bill was a natural — avid, sharp, ghetto-wise, with a mordant wit. He was soon established as a newspaper artist and by the 1920s, had emerged as unquestionably America's leading satirical artist. Only George Grosz could rival him abroad.

Bill combined the traditions of the Ashcan School with those of American political cartooning; he embodied the finest in our native realistic artistic heritage. but he also added some personal and indispensable ingredients. Younger than those we have already mentioned, Bill had, like Stuart Davis, though to a different degree, become aware of modern art after the Armory Show in 1913 in New York. He was also, it seems, pretty well aware of Japanese prints. These influences had a profound effect on his style, and it might be said that he single-handedly transformed American cartooning esthetically, except that he really never had any imitators or spawned any followers.

The daring artistic innovations that carried his political statements were riveting and pertinent. He cut through the esthetic cliches, the stock types, the involved literary accompaniments of the standard political cartoon, as well as the heroicizing, moralizing and didactic patterns of left-wing polemicists, to produce a new, slashing, satirical style, sophisticated, allusive and esthetically exhilarating. More than anything else, he had wit — though I remember his as more truculent than comic — a particuilar kind of American wit that goes back to Mark Twain, and perhaps, partially Jewish, out of Sholem Aleichem.

I might add that it was more visual than literary — a rare kind of wit, indeed. The drawing as well as the point made was witty. One could delight in the process of recognition instead of accepting the illustration of an idea. The brilliant composition of black-and-white, the spirited spattering of india ink, that incredibly sensitive and fluently descriptive line — all were in the service of an idea. The rapidity with which he worked, the amount he produced, the standard of quality remain amazing. His cartoons from the *Freiheit,* the *Daily Worker,* the *New Masses,* if the pulp paper has not crumbled by now, are as worthy of framing as those of Daumier from *La Caricature* and *Charivari.*

Which brings us to the fact that when Bill Gropper made his decision to join the *Freiheit* in 1925 and the *New Masses* in 1926, just over 50 years ago, at the height of his success as a cartoonist, he was being true to himself. Bill was no hired gun. He was his own man. For the rest of his life, in spite of the unpopularity of his politics, in spite of red-baiting, in spite of witch-hunting, in spite of esthetic sniping, he remained true to his basic beliefs, to humanity.

He used his art as a weapon in defense of the unfortunate and disenfranchized, for peace, justice and a better world. He was truly an artist of the people, a proletarian artist, a popular artist. His paintings, his prints and his mural decorations, all of which became more important to him in later years, were but an extension of his fundamental commitment to a social art, an art that dealt with people, with issues and with ideals. Above all Bill Gropper was a man of honesty and courage. It was a privilege to know him.

January, 1978

Martin Buber's Social Vision

By LOUIS HARAP

ONLY 13 years after Martin Buber died in 1965, the centenary of his birth is being celebrated this year. Buber enjoyed a many-faceted achievement and influence. Because his work was so deep and ranged so widely, he means many things to many people. As we look back at his rich, imaginative and earthly labors, what is there in his life and thought which specifically attracts progressive people?

Buber was in no way a remote scholar and religious, aloof from the imminent problems of his time. On the contrary, his work touches on the most pressing problems of his day and ours, of mankind as a whole, as of the Jewish people.

He was not only a profound thinker who gave a religious interpretation to the alienation that afflicts our era, but the kind of Zionist who urged unceasingly the necessity of Arab-Jewish rapprochement. He was a socialist from his early years. As a scholar he made fresh explorations into the Bible and was an important influence in the revivification of Hasidism.

In all the areas of human activity and inquiry in which he engaged, Buber was independent of authority and the establishment. It is paradoxical that, while Buber was probably the most influential Jewish man of religion and philosophy of this century, his influence is generally conceded to have been greater among non-Jews than Jews.

The reason was his dissent from the various Jewish establishments. His rejection of nationalism and his urgent insistence on Arab-Jewish amity did not endear him to the Zionist establishment. His rejection of institutional religion alienated him from the Orthodox. And his often heterodox political ideas, such as his vocal opposition to the death penalty for Adolf Eichmann, often made him *persona non grata* with the political establishment.

Many of his ideas were seized upon by non-Jews who felt no responsibility toward the religious, Zionist or political Jewish establishments. Further, the universal aspect of his teachings, especially of his "I-Thou" philosophy, proved attractive to non-Jews. Where he was influential among Jews, it was very often among non-conformists.

Thus, it should not surprise us, as it would not have surprised him, that the centenary conference on "The Thought of Martin Buber" held in Jerusalem in Jan., 1978, contained no session on his socialism, unless a paper on "Martin Buber and A.D. Gordon" be so interpreted. A letter in the *Jerusalem Post* Jan. 10, 1978 from several members of the Kibbutz

Hazorea complained about the omission from the symposium of Buber's "need for the realization of ideas in the reality of social life."

Similarly, the Israeli magazine *New Outlook*, devoted to realization of Jewish-Arab rapprochement, refrained from participating, despite the fact that "its allegiance and commitment to Buber is very deep. *New Outlook* was founded at Buber's inspiration" (Feb.-March, 1978, p. 55). The symposium, the magazine felt, was an attempt "to use his [Buber's] fame to raise the prestige of the state wihout paying attention to his teaching." And Buber's granddaughter, Dr. Judith Buber-Agasi, "who was brought up in his [Buber's] home, also decided to boycott the conference" (*Ibid.,* p. 61).

Zionism was a central preoccupation throughout Buber's life. In 1898, while still at the university, he became interested in the newly-formed Zionist movement, and was a delegate in 1899 to the Third Zionist Congress at Basel. He was a follower of Ahad Ha'Am's cultural Zionism, which looked to the development of Palestine as the world center of Jewish culture. This position was opposed to Herzl's purely political Zionism, which viewed Palestine as a haven for oppressed Jews and restoration of the national dignity of the Jews as a people.

At the Fifth Zionist Congress in 1901 Buber was active in the anti-Herzl faction, which included Haim Weizmann, and opposed Herzl's autocratic outlook and his diplomatic political schemes to appeal to the Sultan and the Tsar to gain Palestine as a Jewish political entity. Instead, Buber's group argued for settlement and cultural development as the highest priorities of the movement. Already in 1901 Buber's stature was recognized by his designation as the editor fo *Die Welt,* the leading Zionist organ.

After World War I Buber began urging upon the Zionist movement close fraternal relations with the Arabs "in all areas of life" and establishment in Palestine of "a comprehensive fraternal creation."[1] At the 12th Zionist Congress in Karlsbad in 1921 he was the spokesman for the socialist Halutz (pioneer) youth movement. Speaking for both Hashomer Hatzair, socialist Zionists of Palestine, and Zeire Zion, Diaspora socialist Zionist youth movement, he offered a resolution to consider the Arab problem as their own and urged that the movement make friends of the Arabs, instead of enemies.

"Our return to Palestine," said Buber, "through increasing immigration has no interests of harming anyone. In a just alliance with the Arab people in our common land, we desire to create a culturally and economically flourishing community whose rise will assure each of its national components' unhampered autonomous development."[2]

Buber was supported in this position by the Tolstoyan socialist A.D. Gordon (1856-1922) and the brilliant young Haim Arlosoroff (1899-1933), a Buber disciple. When the Congress adopted a much weaker position on the resolution, Buber was deeply disappointed and "withdrew from official Zionism" for a number of years.[3]

In 1925, Buber joined others in founding Brith Shalom (Covenant of Peace) to promote Arab-Jewish cooperation in Palestine. He was among the leaders of every subsequent movement toward this end. When the League for Arab-Jewish Rapprochement and Cooperation was formed in 1939, he was among its founders; and in 1942, together with Judah L. Magnes (1877-1948) he helped to form Ihud (Unity), which advocated binationalism. He clung to this position until the 1947 U.N. decision, when he became reconciled to separate Jewish-and Arab states.

Buber held that the Bible had revealed the Jewish people to be like no other people, but "elected" by God. "The land," Palestine, he believed to be also "elected" by God as the land of this people. From very creation the people and the land came into being for the express reason of fulfilling a divinely ordained purpose."[4] There is, he said, "the most intimate relationship between God, the people and the land."[5]

What raises this concept out of the vulgar notion of national superiority is that this "election" placed the land and the people under obligation to fulful "a mission from above to set up a just way of life through the generations of our people."[6]

Thus, while election is a divine privilege, it also imposes a cosmic obligtion to lead the world to justice. The vocation of the Hebrew prophets is to recall the Hebrew people repeatedly to this obligation and to make justice prevail.

Even if one does not share Buber's theistic assumptions, the politics he derived from them often led him to social insights such as his ardent defense of the national rights of the Arabs. The Jews, he warned before the Anglo-American Commission in 1946, should not "create another national movement of the European type."[7] How profoundly dangerous he regarded the conventional modern European type of nationalism can be judged from the extremity of his language: "... of all of the many kinds of assimilation in the course of our history, this is the most terrifying, the most dangerous, this nationalist assimilation."[8] No wonder Buber was not greatly in favor with the Zionist and religious Jewish establishments.

In light of the depth of Buber's Zionist convictions and his teachings about the sacred character of the land and Jewish election as of the necessity of acting toward realization of his ideas, it is hard to understand why he did not emigrate voluntarily to Palestine.

Especially in the earlier years of the movement, before World War I, Buber exerted great influence among central European Zionist youth. Why, then, did he not join them on aliya to Palestine? Gershom Scholem observes that Buber's failure to act on his own convictions about Palestine "ended in bitter estrangement" from the youth he inspired to aliya.

Apparently Buber himself, says Scholem, "did not draw the consequences they expected from his own message. Buber, a most multifaceted and complicated human being, had summoned these youths to go to the land of Israel and out of a creative impulse to undertake the formation of a new life that was to grow there. They never forgave him for not coming when the chips were down."[9]

Buber finally did settle in Palestine in 1938, not out of free choice, but only because his life in Nazi Germany was no longer tenable. The Nazis had removed him in 1933 from his professorship of the philosophy of Jewish religion and ethics at Frankfurt University, a post he had held since 1924. One can understand why he did not in 1933 leave Germany for Palestine, as he was urged to do. He felt it his duty to remain in Germany to encourage Jewish "spiritual resistance" to the Nazis. After Jews were excluded from all educational institutions in 1933, Buber became director of the Central Office for Jewish Adult Education and was also head of the Juedisches Lehrhaus (Jewish School of Education). Through these institutions he was able to rescue many German Jews from meaningless despair. Finally responding to friendly advice in 1938, he went to Palestine and became professor of sociology of religion at the Hebrew University.

Another aspect of Buber's early career should be noted, if not overemphasized. As a young man he advanced views derived from Nietzsche. He sometimes mixed his Zionist ideas with the notion of *Blut und Boden* (Blood and Land), a view later propagated by the Nazis. As Walter Laqueur notes, his writing in this manner, while "innocent enough when written,... when later torn out of their historical context... make embarrassing reading" today.[10] Buber soon abandoned these ideas, and later indirectly implied their repudiation. An essay of 1942 is at pains to declare that "Nietzsche did not foresee" how these ideas would be applied by "men without restraint,"[11] that is, the Nazis.

Buber's conception of the prophetic injunction to advance social justice received expression in his socialist convictions. During World War I he came under the influence of his close friend Gustav Landauer (1870-1919), a non-Marxist socialist who eschewed the class-struggle approach, but was nevertheless minister of information in the short-lived Bavarian Soviet Republic in 1919. In that year Landauer, like Rosa Luxemburg (1871-1919) and Karl Liebknecht (1871-1919), was murdered by counterrevolutionary soldiers on the streets of Munich. Buber made Landauer's conception of socialism as a "community of communities" his own for the rest of his life. He regarded this as integral to the "religious socialism" he espoused.

Buber found precepts of socialism in the Bible. In a letter to Gandhi in 1939, Buber wrote that "the Bible tells us" that the Jews came to Palestine to fulfil a "mission from above to set up a just way of life." Such a way of life, he continued, "can be realized not by individuals in the sphere of their private existence but only by a nation in the establishment of a society: communal ownership of land (*Lev.,* 25:23), regularly recurrent levelling of distinctions (*Lev.,* 25:13), guarantees of the independence of each individual (*Ex.,* 21:2), mutual help (*Ex.,* 23:4ff), a common Sabbath of serf and beasts as beings of equal claim (*Ex.,* 23:12), a Sabbatical year (*Lev.,* 25:5-7)."[12]

Translated into the needs of Palestine and later Israel, his socialism was close to that of A.D. Gordon who, Buber thought, was "the most remarkable of all the Jewish immigrants."[13] He thought Gordon most nearly realized his own vision of the new Jewish settlement, for Gordon's conception of the commune also was harmonious with his own. The modern Jew, thought Gordon, was leading an abnormal life in which he had lost touch with the land, with nature and with the labor of his hands. Socialism would not be brought about by class struggle, but by changes in the individual through contact with the soil in agricultural labor.

Buber was drawn to Gordon's view that humanity would be renewed through the "demand for a life truly in accordance with Nature."[14] It was the integral continuity of human life with that of Nature and the Cosmos that would redeem man. Gordon not only projected this idea: he lived it. To Buber this seemed a practical application of his own idea of the intimate relation of the Jew with the land of Israel. The land was not something inert to Buber, but somehow an active participant in a common life with the Jewish people. "Gordon had become the mouth of the land," wrote Buber.[15]

There can be no doubt that Buber regarded socialism as an essential, organic part of his outlook. In addition to several essays on ideas related to socialism, Buber in 1945 completed a series of essays that formed the book, *Paths in Utopia,*[16] his fullest statement on his understanding of socialism. "To be a 'Utopian' in our age," he wrote, "means: to be out of step with modern economic development, and what economic development is we learn of course from Marxism."[17]

While he may have accepted Marx's view of economic development, he did not follow Marx in its implications, and he rejected Marxism as a socialist solution because he thought its tendency toward extreme centralization spelled death to the spirit. He accepted much of Kropotkin (1842-1921), though he cannot be said to have been a fullblown anarchist. He rejected the absolute alternatives of centralization or decentralization. Both are needed in relation to actual circumstances, and the degree of each can be determined only "ever anew,... ever changing in accordance with historical circumstances."[18] Buber's socialism envisioned creation of decentralized communities which would federate into a "community of communities."

320

Buber reviewed past histories of attempts to set up communes and cooperatives. These attempts in the past 150 years, he writes, failed either because they "disintegrated," or "took on a Capitalist complexion, thus going over to the enemy camp," or they lived in "isolation."[19] In all history he recognized only one venture that did not fail — the "Jewish Village Commune [*Kvutza*] as formed in Palestine," although he added that this can be called a "signal non-failure" rather than a "signal success."[20]

These communes, growing out of the special demands of the Jews in Palestine, were directed toward creation of that community of justice and peace enjoined upon the Jewish people by the prophets. Finally, he held, the modern world "must designate one of two poles of Socialism between which our choice lies, by the formidable name of 'Moscow.' The other, I would make bold to call 'Jerusalem,'"[21] that is, the idea of *kvutza.*

Buber rejected the Soviet State because its centralization had deprived the human being of spontaneity and mutual concern among individuals, and was pursuing power for its own sake. His "community of communities" should be decentralized so far as possible consistent with the maintenance of living, spontaneous, altogether direct human relationship between individuals, rather than the power relationships that he believed to obtain both in capitalist and existing socialist societies. "All holiness," wrote Buber, "means union between being and thing, between being and being; the highest rung of world-holiness, however, is the unity of the human community in the sight of God."[22]

Buber's socialism is utopian in the Marxist sense that it is not directly based on socioeconomic analysis to ascertain the actual structure and mode of operation of capitalist society in order to discover specifically *what* must be changed, *how* such change can be brought about compatibly with the demands of social justice, and *how* such change can be brought to realization. The assumptions of a non-utopian socialism are radically different from Buber's. Change will not occur unless one knows the points of leverage from which energies must be applied if the ruling powers with an interest in maintaining the status quo are to be overcome. This requires an intimate knowledge of the actual workings of society, and of the interests of the various classes and strata of that society so as to assemble to one's own side a maximum of support for the change desired.

Buber's notion of socialist success in the Jewish Village Commune — the *Kvutza* — argues against the adequacy of his view of socialism. The fact is that this "success" has left out the overwhelming majority of Israel's people — 97%, in fact — who live under an increasingly intrenched capitalist order. A viable socialism must be universal in any given society. The entire population must exist under a socialist way of life. The *kvutza* can be said to be "successful" only in the most drastically limited sense. Even the kibbutz system, under the pressure of an intensifying Israeli capitalism has felt obliged to abandon one of its basic socialist concepts, prohibition against hired labor, thus becoming involved in a capitalist type of labor exploitation. Only by elimination of capitalism itself in the entire society can socialism be said even to have been tried, let alone succeeded. This is not to say that socialism cannot learn from the kibbutz experience. But a federation of kibbutzim embracing a small precentage of the population cannot be said to make a socialist society.

It would be a mistake, however, simply to dismiss Buber's notions of socialism. "Socialism in its truth," wrote Buber in his exposition of religious socialism, "is not a doctrine and tactics but standing in the abyss of the real reciprocal relation with the mystery of man."[23] To one not a religious socialist, this has limited meaning. But some so-called scientific socialists neglect the truths that can be derived from Buber's conception, namely, that socialism is ultimately desirable because it holds the possibility for the creation of a new humanity, a new structure of human relations compatible with the socioeconomic limitations of societal existence. What is needed is a socialism which combines hard-headed social analysis with humanistic goals for mankind. A socialism lacking in one or the other of these is to that extent incomplete. Buber's socialism sheds light on the humanistic aspect of socialism, and to this extent holds value for the scientific socialist. Additionally, as Buber showed in his persistent support for Arab-Jewish cooperation, his approach can reinforce efforts for a socialist policy.

The modernity of Buber is signified not only by his involvement with socialism. For he also delved deeply into what is needed to combat the ravages of captitalist society on the individual. His "I-Thou" philosophy is one more attempt in more than a century past to grapple with the problem of alienation produced by capitalist society. Increasingly modern persons have encountered difficulty in establishing contact with their work, with each other, and with their own inner being. Of the many responses to alienation, that of the existentialism of Kierkegaard (1813-1855) is among the most important, and it influenced Buber's thought along these lines.

One major attempt to deal with this condition was Marx's theory of alienation, which he viewed as arising out of the capitalist structure of society. The capitalist's relation to the worker is that of a person to a thing, for the capitalist deals with the worker as a commodity on the labor market. Deprivation of a person's humanness makes that person a thing. In modern industry, Marx wrote, the worker "is depressed spiritually and physically to the condition of a machine."[24] Indeed, Marx held that the entire form of capitalist production is one of estrangement of man from himself and of man from man.

As a member of capitalist society, wrote Marx, "man acts simply as a *private individual,* treats other men as means, degrades himself to the role of mere means, and becomes a plaything of alien powers."[25] In the *Communist Manifesto,* Marx asserted that capitalism "has left no other

322

nexus between man and man than naked self-interest, than callous cash-payment."[26] So pervasive and penetrating are these conditions that they permeate all human relations, and persons tend to relate to one another as means to their own ends, and not as persons.

Buber's "I-Thou" philosophy, based in religion and his idea of God, is another attempt to confront the same phenomenon as Marx's theory of alienation. In 1923 Buber set forth this idea in his central religio-philosophical work, *I and Thou.* He recognized two basic types of relation into which human beings may enter, "I-Thou" and "I-It." In the I-Thou relation "the whole being" of the I goes out to "meet" the Thou, the other, and the result is a relation which "transcends," is above and beyond Nature, out of time and space. In the I-It relation the person is related to some object or person as an object or thing within the context of time and space — it is an experience with objects in the sense in which we are familiar in ordinary life.

The world of I-Thou is the world of "Spirit." Buber writes that "Spirit is not in the *I,* but between *I* and *Thou.* It is not like the blood that circulates in you, but like the air in which you breathe. Man lives in the spirit if he is able to respond to his Thou. He is able to if he enters into relation with his whole being."[27] While cause-and-effect prevails in the world of I-It, it is totally absent from the world of I-Thou. But more is involved in any given I-Thou relations than I and Thou alone. There is an "eternal Thou," an illimitable Thou in relation to which all finite Thous are somehow embraced.

This "eternal Thou" is God, defined by Buber as "him who — whatever else he may be — enters into a direct relation with us when in creative, revealing and redeeming acts, and thus makes it possible for us to enter into direct relation with him.... The concept of person being is indeed completely incapable of declaring what God's essential being is, but it is both permitted and necessary to say God is a Person."[28]

Buber's total "I-Thou" concept is a difficult and subtle philosophical notion because it relates to a realm beyond common experience and presupposes some sort of non-natural order of things. Buber's philosophical and transcendental thought tended to be obscure. The philosopher Morris R. Cohen (1880-1947), a stickler for precision of meaning, once wrote in the course of an essay on Ludwig Lewisohn that this writer discoursed on Judaism, "like Buber," in a "misty cloud of modern romantic phrases."

This is not the place to set forth and analyze I-Thou relation in detail, but it must be observed that many have tried to reduce it in practical terms to benevolent human relations quite lacking in the transnatural and theistic aspect which is fundamental to Buber's notion. This perhaps unconscious "naturalization" of Buber's view is quite understandably made not only because of the difficulty of comprehending it, but also because people grasp eagerly at his ideas out of desperate need to remedy the pervasive effects of alienation. The I-Thou relation can be understood in social terms, if stripped of its "transcendent" status, as a relation of one person to another as a *person,* not as a thing or instrumentality. Thus the I-Thou relation can be brought down to earth.

Different as Buber's theory is from Marx's, one can perceive the way in which both were attempts to grasp and deal with the same root problem. The scope of Buber's distinctions is nothing short of cosmic, whereas Marx's analysis is limited to social actuality and what is needed for people to live in dignity and happiness on earth, and not on some "transcendent" level. There is no "hallowing of the everyday," no sanctification, no resort to deity in Marx, but only the possible and desirable goals toward a civilized life. Marx and Buber offer alternative answers to the basic human and social problems of modern life, and they differ in intelligibility and potentiality for realization.

Buber was at pains to point out his differences with the Marxist view. For Buber the Marxist solution represented a world in which the I-It relation dominates the entire human sphere because, Buber thought, under it overwhelming power was handed over to the centralized state. In this way, thought Buber, Marxist socialism completes the process of "association," that is, "mechanical association of isolated self-seeking individuals." This contrasts with the "community" toward which Buber was striving, that "organic unity which has grown out of common possessions, work, morals, or belief."[29] Buber concluded this from his understanding of the actualities of both the Marxist movement and the Soviet State.

Considering the theory and practice of socialism that Buber was acquainted with when he wrote thus, his diagnosis has a certain relevancy. But we know today that total and exhaustive identification of these social developments with Marxism is no longer accepted by large numbers of individuals and parties that regard themselves as Marxist. Buber's view of Marxism was also influenced by the anarchist tendencies of his close friend Gustav Landauer and his own reading of Kropotkin. For Buber, as for Landauer, "True socialism is real community between men, direct life relations between I and Thou, just society and fellowhip."[30] This, he thought, differed from Marxism as he understood it.

As a "religious socialist" Buber was especially attracted to Moses Hess (1812-1875). He considered Hess to have been "the first religious socialist in the history of Judaism."[31] Buber also commented, interestingly enough, that while Hess projected Zionism several decades before Leo Pinsker (1821-1891) in the 1880s and Theodor Herzl (1860-1904) in the nineties, Hess was really more advanced than either. The reason was that the first two grounded themselves in liberalism, while Hess founded his Zionism on the later doctrine of socialism.* "Religion and socialism," wrote Buber, "are essentially directed to each other," because, he added, "each of them needs the covenant with the other for the fulfilment of its essence."[34]

The depth of Buber's religious convictions cannot be doubted, yet his approach was independent, unique. He ignored institutional religion. In his thirteenth year he did go through the *Bar Mitzva* ceremony while he was living with his grandfather, the noted Talmudic scholar and man of Haskala, Solomon Buber (1827-1906). But, at 14, he set aside his *tallis* and *tfillin* and had nothing to do with the synagogue from then on. He could not endure the rigidities and fixations of organized religion. Consequently, he has been ignored by the Orthodoxy.

In these early years Buber's Zionism drew him intensely into Jewish studies. From 1904 to 1909 he immersed himself in Hasidic writings, and came to regard the Hasidic life from 1750 to 1825 as the most authentic, when it was an inspired and genuinely people's form of the religion of ordinary life. He wrote a number of books on Hasidism, as well as several volumes setting forth his version of Hasidic tales and legends. According to Gershom Scholem, Buber has made "a decisive contribution" to our knowledge of Hasidism.[35] Buber was drawn to mysticism in his university years by his study of the Christian medieval mystics Meister Eckhart (1260?-1328?) and Jakob Boehme (1575-1624). Buber's Zionism and then Hasidic studies drew him toward Jewish mysticism.

What attracted him powerfully was the traditional optimistic form taken by Jewish mysticism, in contrast to the pessimism of the Christian variety. The Hasidic movement, he wrote, "kindled both its simple and intellectual followers to joy in the world as it is, in life as it is, in every hour in this life, as that hour is."[36] Buber does not thereby endorse Hasidic quietism, which keeps its followers away from the social struggle, but rather the sanctification of ordinary life, "the hallowing of the everyday," as his characteristic description of Hasidism went. The vitality of Hasidism was reinforced in Buber by the influence of Nietzsche's affirmation of life and the philosophy of *Erlebnis* (experience) learned from Buber's teacher Wilhelm Dilthey (1833-1911), which gave centrality to concrete personal experience in living and interpreting the world.

Buber's contribution to our knowledge of Hasidism is universally recognized, but scholars, from Buber's old friend Gershom Scholem, the

---

* Buber is in error when he writes that Hess's essay, "On the Nature of Money," was "written under the influence of Marx's treatise *On the Jewish Question*, which had appeared before."[32] The fact is just the opposite. It is true that Marx's essay appeared in 1844 and Hess's in 1845. But as Auguste Cornu points out, "Hess exerted a profound influence on Marx and Engels by his article 'On the Essence of Money,' which Hess had sent to the *Deutsch-Franzoezische Annalen* edited by Marx but which did not appear until later, in 1845, following suppression of the journal.[33]

primary scholar of Jewish mysticism, to the Buber scholar Malcolm L. Diamond, agree that his "reading of Hasidism is highly selective."[37] Hasidism as Buber understod it may well not have been quite the same as the creed practiced from 1750 to 1825. However we may view his interpretation, it is quite clear that it did not leave him a passive member of society. His involvement with social action grew rather than diminished, once he emerged from his intensive study of Hasidism in the early years of this century.

Buber's involvement in the spread of education about Jewishness grew with the years. Already in 1902 he had helped establish the publishing firm, Juedische Verlag. In 1916 he founded the monthly *Der Jude,* quickly recognized as the most respected journal of Jewish life in Germany and an organ for advancing his cultural approach to Zionism. Until publication of his basic and most original work, *I and Thou,* he was actively expanding his Zionist and his heterodox religious views in lectures and writing on behalf of a "Jewish Renaissance." At about the time he was also gestating his I-Thou philosophy, he became deeply involved in Bible study and scholarship. For Buber the Bible was "a record of dialogical encounter between God and man."[38] Together with his friend Franz Rosenzweig (1886-1929), a leading philosopher of Judaism, he began in 1925 a new German translation of the Old Testament, or "Hebrew Bible," as he preferred to call it. When Rosenzweig died Buber continued alone the herculean task, which he completed in 1961. This translation is considered altogether remarkable and unique in any language because it attempts to reproduce in German the forms, rhythms and exact meanings of the original as if it were a *spoken* communication.

"The theme of the Bible," wrote Buber, "is the encounter between a group of people and the Lord of the World in the course of history, the sequence of events occurring on earth."[39] However, modern man cannot, nor does Buber, believe the Bible to be a literal history. Neither is it allegory nor metaphor, says Buber. It is rather the "revelation" that people derived from the actual events. What happened in the Bible is that the people who lived through these events listened "to that which the voice, sounding forth from the event, wishes to communicate to its witness, to his constitution, to his life."[40]

As I understand Buber here, he regards the Bible as a *revelatory interpretation* given by and conveyed through the succession of actual events in the early history of the Jewish people. While Buber was far from a fundamentalist believer in the Biblical "miracles," his interpretation of the relationship of God and man "revealed" in the Bible was a "transcendent" one, not supernatural in the naive sense. His belief was a sophisticated form of non-naturalism.

Buber's life and career show him to have been independent of any establishment whatever — the anarchist influence is in part evident here — whether capitalist or socialist. He was loyal only to his religious conception of man and nations. In his mature thought he interpreted this to be an "I-Thou" relation, a "dialogical relation," to society and to all being, animate and inanimate. His socialism finally derived from this aspiration to a transcendent relation of all men with each other and all things. But this aspiration toward transcendence did not remove him from worldly affairs — quite the contrary, it commanded him to uncompromising engagement with affairs. .

Buber was a modern man who tried to mediate between the modern scientific mentality and an etherealized interpretation of traditional Judaism and change in the social order. If his vagueness and illusionism were not convincing to every one, his ideas still had many elements of a basic humanistic approach to life and society which can provide vivid inspiration to the non-religious modern progressive secularist and socialist.

NOTES

1. Aharon Cohen, *Israel and the Arab World,* New York, 1970, p. 241.
2. *Ibid.,* p. 242.
3. Nahum M. Glatzer, "Foreward" to Martin Buber, *On Zion: History of an Idea,* New York, 1973, p.x.
4. Martin Buber, *On Zion,* p. xix.
5. *Ibid.,* p. 18
6. Martin Buber, *Pointing the Way,* ed. and tr. by Maurice S. Friedman, New York, 1979, p. 34.
7. Martin Buber,*On Zion,* p. xiii.
8. Malcolm L. Diamond, *Martin Buber: Jewish Existentialist,* New York, 1960, p. 154.
9. Gershom Scholem, "Martin Buber's Conception of Judaism," *On Jews and Judaism in Crisis,* ed. by W. J. Dannhauser, New York, 1976, p. 127.
10. Walter Laqueur, A History of Zionism, New York, 1972, p. 398.
11. Buber, *Pointing the Way p. 160.*
12. *Ibid.,* p. 143.
13. Martin Buber,*On Zion,* p. 154.
14. *Ibid.,* p. 155.
15. *Ibid.,* p. 161.
16. Martin Buber, *Paths in Utopia,* trs. by R.F.C. Hull, Boston, 1958 (first published in England in 1949).
17. *Ibid.,* pp. 5-6.
18. *Ibid.,* p. 134
19. *Ibid.,* pp. 140-41.
20. *Ibid.,* pp. 141, 148.
21. *Ibid.,* p. 149.
22. Maurice S. Friedman, *Martin Buber: The Life of Dialogue,* Chicago, 1955.

23. Buber, *Pointing the Way, p.113.*

24. *Karl Marx, Economic and Philosophic Manuscripts of 1844,* Moscow, n.d., p. 25.

25. Karl Marx, "On the Jewish Question," *Early Writings,* tr. and ed. by T.B. Bottome, New York, 1964, p. 13.

26. Karl Marx, *Selected Works,* 2 vols., New York, n.d., p. 207.

27. Martin Buber, *I and Thou,* 2nd ed., tr. by Ronald Gregor Smith, New York, 1958, p. 39.

28. *Ibid.,* p. 135.

29. Maurice S. Friedman, *Martin Buber, etc.,* p. 45.

30. *Ibid.,* p. 210.

31. Martin Buber,*On Zion,* p. 119.

32. *Ibid.,* p. 115.

33. Auguste Cornu, *Moses Hess et la gauche Hegelienne,* Paris, 1934, pp. 93-94.

34. Buber, *Pointing the Way,* p. 112.

35. Gershom Scholem, "Martin Buber's Interpretation of Hasidism," *The Mesianic Idea in Judaism,* New York, 1971, p. 228.

36. Martin Buber, *Tales of Hasidism: The Early Masters,* New York, 1961. p. 3 (first published in 1947).

37. Malcolm L. Diamond, *Martin Buber,* p. 112. See also Gershom Scholem, *The Messianic Idea,* p. 321.

38. Malcolm, L. Diamond, *Ibid.,* p. 92.

39. Martin Buber, *On the Bible, ed. by* Nahum M. Glatzer, N.Y. 1968, p. 1.

40. *Ibid.,* p. 9.

July, 1978

Ethnicity and Survival

By YURI SUHL

ABOUT 50 years ago a sociology professor named Marcus Hansen studied the cultural patterns of the Scandinavian communities in the mid-West. He summarized his findings in one sentence which became known as Hansen's Law: "what the parents wanted to remember and the children wanted to forget, the grandchildren are now trying to recall."

I was one of the fortunate ones. I did not have to search for the connecting cultural link between my grandparents and myself. It was never broken. By the time I came here as a young immigrant of 15 that link had already been solidly forged to a long chain of customs and traditions, a history transmitted from generation to generation, a way of life consciously learned and subliminally absorbed.

What I left behind me was the poverty, the anti-Semitism, the precariousness of a physical existence in a hostile environment in Poland. What I was not conscious of then, but know now, was that among the few threadbare articles of clothing I carried in the straw basket as I stepped off the boat, there was also an invisible but richly embroidered possession called heritage.

My efforts at Amercanization did not estrange me from that heritage. In the delicate and sometimes painful process of striking new roots I was often sustained by the depth and firmness of the old ones. Indeed, so deep were those early roots that when I began writing poetry it was in the Yiddish language. When I felt sufficiently secure in the English language to use it as an instrument of literary expression, I started to write prose but continued to write poetry in Yiddish because Yiddish remained for me the mother tongue, the gut language.

Whether it was poetry or prose, fiction or non-fiction, central to all my work was an awareness of my Jewish identity in both the selection of the theme and in the treatment of it. "A writer's identity," says sociologist Michael Novak, "is the most precious resource he has." I fully subscribe to that statement.

In my frist novel, *One Foot in America,* and its sequel, *Cowboy on a Wooden Horse,* both autobiographical fiction, I dealt with the experience of the Jewish immigrant in the period of the 1920s. Next on my literary agenda was a third novel that would take the story into the 1930s, but I never got to it. I was side-tracked by a non-fiction project, the biography of

329

a Polish Jewish woman named Ernestine L. Rose, the daughter of a rabbi, who arrived in this country in 1836 and became a leading abolitionist and one of the founders of the woman's rights movement.

Soon after serving in the U.S. army in World War II, I returned to Poland for the first time since I had left it as a boy. Together with the remnant of Jewish survivors in Poland and delegations of Jews from all over the world, I attended the ceremony of the unveiling of the Warsaw Ghetto monument in April, 1948. Standing on the heap of charred rubble that had once been the site of the Warsaw Ghetto, I saw the source of my heritage in ashes, the ashes of Auschwitz, Maidanek, Treblinka.

Exile, suffering, pogroms, these had all been part of the Jewish people's history for over 2,000 years, yet the Jewish people had survived. But Hitler's "Final Solution" was genocide, the total annihilation of a people.

That moment on the site of the Warsaw Ghetto was a turning point in my life both as a Jew and a writer. I knew that my heritage would no longer suffice unless it incorporated this recent chapter in my people's history. For without a knowledge of the Holocaust and the lessons it entails for us, the survival of the Jewish people could no longer be taken for granted.

With all we now know about the Holocaust, who can say now that only the survival of the Jewish people is at stake? The Gypsies were not Jews and a million of them perished in the camps. Thousands of Catholics, including many priests, perished in the camps. On Hitler's scale of racial purity the Slavs were only one notch above the Jews and only for the time being. His blueprint for after the war called for the destruction of all Slavic peoples in Europe except for 50,000 select specimens to be distributed as servants among the elite of the "master race." Had his appetite for *Lebensraum* not been curbed in time, one could well imagine what would have happened to the minority peoples in this country.

To say that it could never happen again, or that it could not happen here is to repeat the mistake of an earlier generation that charcterized Hitler's storm troopers as "boy scouts having an outing, playing at war." This statement appeared in the *N.Y. Times* in 1923. As recently as May, 1977 Simon Wiesenthal revealed the shocking information that in this country there are 80 active Nazi-type organizations. Tons of anti-Semitic literature, printed in the United States, are flooding West Germany, Africa and South American counrties. The KKK, dormant for a while, is now active again from coast to coast. Only two weeks ago our ambassador to the United Nations, Andrew Young, sounded the warning that a race war in Africa is bound to trigger off a race war in the United States and he cited the American Nazi Party as the would-be instigator of that war.

Small wonder, then, that Elie Wiesel, a man who is not an alarmist, felt impelled to state in the *N.Y. Times* that "For the first time in many years I feel that I am in danger... that the nightmare may start all over again... the idea of another catastrophe is no longer unthinkable."

That is why I strongly believe that an awakened awareness of one's ethnicity must also include the lessons of the Holocaust, for without ethnic survival there can be no ethnic identity. That is also why in recent years the main focus of my work as a writer has been on the Holocaust theme.

In my latest novel for young adults, *Uncle Misha's Partisans* and *On the Other Side of the Gate,* the emphasis is not so much on the horrors and torments suffered by the Jews in the ghettos and camps as on their resistance, both spiritual and physical: how under the most unspeakable circumstances the victims managed to strike back at their tormentors.

Given the nature of the subject, I approached the task with a great deal of self-doubt and trepidation. Treating the Holocaust theme in fictional form can be a hazardous undertaking, especially for one who had himself not lived through the experience. How does one make the incredible credible, the unbelievable believable? I knew that to involve the reader personally in the world of the Holocaust is to engage his emotions and that is done best through the fictional narrative. So I took the plunge. When, after publication, I began to receive letters from my young readers both Jewish and non-Jewish, telling me how much they liked the books, and when the reviews characterized the stories as "realistic and believable," I allowed myself the feeling that I had not failed in my objectives.

Before concluding my remarks, I should like to tell you two stories about books in the ghettos. When the Germans surrounded the Vilna Ghetto in order to liquidate the last surviving Jews, the ghetto fighters hurried to their battle stations. They needed barricades to protect themselves and their meagre supply of weapons, but they had none because there was no sand in the ghetto for sandbags. Nearby stood a library called "Propagators of Enlightenment," so they filled the bags with books and they became their barricades.

The poet Abba Kovner, who was then the commander of the underground, recalls the event in these words: "I remember the books arriving volume after volume. During the intervals between the shootings my head was resting on the bags of books... Under my head there were generations of forefathers. Not flesh and blood — flesh and spirit." Books which historically have served as barricades against ignorance were here called upon to serve as barricades against barbarians.

My second story comes from the Warsaw Ghetto. With prophetic foresight the historian of the Warsaw Ghetto, Emmanuel [Menahem] Ringelblum (1900-1944), saw a time when, to hide the traces of their criminal deeds, the Nazis and their followers would rewrite and distort the history of that period. He therefore organized an underground organization of about 30 scholars, writers and teachers for the sole purpose of writing and collecting material that would present a true picture of fascist savagery, a warning to future generations. They labored at their task until Aug., 1942, when their ranks were decimated by mass deportations to Treblinka. They could no longer hold on to the material, so they sealed it in 10 metal boxes and in two iron milk cans and buried them in the ghetto grounds.

A 19-year-old youth named David Gorber was one of the people entrusted with hiding the material. This is how he expressed his feelings about his assignment: "I don't want any thanks. It will be enough for me if the coming generations will recall our times... I can say with assurance that this was the basis, the dynamic, of our existence then. What we could not cry out to the world we buried in the ground. May this treasure be deliverd into good hands. May it live to see better times so that it can alert the world to what happened in the 20th century." (From Lucy S. Dawidowicz, *A Holocaust Reader,* N.Y., 1976.)

It seems to me that the only way we can make his concern for us meaningful is to reverse the meaning of his very moving words. He said, "What we could not cry out to the world we buried in the ground." We must say, "What they buried in the ground, we must cry out to the world."

The most effective way for a writer to cry out is through his books and one of the most effective ways for this cry to be heard is through the intermediary between the writer and the people — the librarian.

I shall conclude my remarks with one final quotation written 2,000 years ago and as pertinent to us today as it was then. Rabbi Hillel, a great scholar and humanist, said: "If I am not for myself, who will be for me? And if I am only for myself, what am I? And if not now, when?"

April, 1978

The Legacy of Sholem Asch

By *ELI KATZ*

THE post-classical generation of Yiddish writers recedes; like that of its mentors, into the past; the year 1980 marks the centenary of the birth of Sholem Asch. Asch was a central figure in Yiddish literature from 1904 until his death in 1957. Moreover, while he was sometimes deprecated by critics both within and without the Yiddish literary milieu, he was without doubt the most widely translated and hence the most widely read Yiddish writer of his time. For those who did not read Yiddish, Asch virtually represented Yiddish literature. We are therefore indebted to Ben Siegel for a well-researched and informative introduction to the work of Asch and a valuable reminder of his significance to Yiddish and world literature.*

Sholem Asch moved quickly from Kutno, the Polish shtetl of his birth, first to Warsaw and then in dizzying sequence back and forth among such locations as St. Petersburg, Cologne, Zurich, Berlin, New York, Nice, Connecticut, Miami Beach, Tel Aviv and London. The cosmopolitanism evident in these migrations corresponds to Asch's view of himself as a writer of international significance and to his attempts to secure for himself a readership beyond (although by no means excluding) the Yiddish-reading Jews of East European origin or descent.

His personality was almost stereotypically that of the successful and lionized *litterateur:* impetuous, domineering, sometimes petty and often quick to take offense; but his working habits were impeccable and the volume of his writings prodigious. The speed and concentration with which Asch wrote may in part account for the superficial and scattered impression which his work often creates and for what the Yiddish critic S. Niger termed his "artistic distraction," which often led not only to inconsistencies of plot detail but also to disconcerting solecisms in language. If so, this tempo also reflects the driving energy and imaginative scope which characterize his best work.

Asch was one of that gifted group of young Yiddish writers who at the beginning of this century made the pilgrimage to Cieglana 1 in Warsaw

---

* *The Controversial Sholem Asch,* by Ben Siegel, Bowling Green Univeristy Press, Bowling Green, Ohio, 1976, 324 pages, indexed, $12.95, paperback, $4.95.

where I.L. Peretz (1851-1915), the acknowledged "rebbe" of modern Yiddish literature, held court. Together with such figures as Dovid Pinski, Avrom Reisin, H.D. Nomberg and Zalman Shneour, Asch benefited from Peretz's criticism, encouragement and occasional financial assistance. Asch continued to the end of his life to express his gratitude and devotion to Peretz but in fact was inclined neither to be a disciple nor to gather disciples about himself. He quickly embarked on his own path and even in his youth found little difficulty in disregarding Peretz's advice concerning his work.

Asch made his first great impression on the Yiddish-reading public with *Dos Shtetl,* a novella which appeared in 1904 in serial form and as a book the following year. This work affected an idyllic view of the Jewish shtetl and a subdued and understated style of narration; but neither the theme nor the treatment was to remain characteristic of Asch. In 1906 he wrote the play *Got fun Nekome* (God of Vengeance), which scandalized a substantial part of the Yiddish-reading community and, in effect, made Asch an international literary figure.

The play portrays Yanul Shapshovitsh, the Jewish proprietor of a brothel, who fails in his attempt to maintain the separation between his "business" and his family, which inhabits another floor in the house. He suffers God's vengeance when Rivkele, his daughter, is drawn into a lesbian affair with the prostitue Manka.

Objections to the play were directed against the generally lurid nature of the subject, the idea that a Jew could be portrayed as a brothel-keeper, and the explicit presentation on stage of a Torah scroll housed in a brothel. The *sefer torah,* Yankl vainly hopes, will act as a talisman to protect his daughter's virtue. Peretz's advice to Asch was that he burn the play. Instead the 27-year-old author saw it produced in Russian in St. Petersburg and five years later in German by Max Reinhardt in Berlin. During the early 1940s, however, reacting against Nazism, Asch did withdraw the play from performance. Only since his death has it again been staged.

If the themes of *Got fun Nekome* seem startlingly "modern" for a Yiddish play of 1906, this is partly because our own notions of Yiddish culture of the time are somewhat parochial. The play demonstrates, however, that Asch was thoroughly familiar with current trends in the European theater of his day and was prepared to make the right move at the right time. First Henrik Ibsen, and then Gerhardt Hauptmann, had, against Philistine resistance, succeeded in opening the stage to themes which had previously been taboo. Asch, while in no sense a stylistic innovator like Gerhart Hauptmann or Frank Wedekind (whose plays had provoked riots in Berlin shortly before), could nevertheless make use of the newly permissible but still daring themes to propel himself into the mainstream of European drama and literature.

Sholem Asch wrote countless stories, over 20 plays and a long list of full-length novels. Virtually all of the stories and most of the novels appeared first in the Yiddish periodical press of Europe and America and were published as Yiddish books. Of the novels, 19 were translated into English and many into German, Hebrew and other languages. He was probably the first Yiddish author to master the large-scale architecturally constructed novel, although not without several false starts. Critics of his earlier novels often complained of their lack of cohesion and of gratuitous episodes and characteriztions which appeared at times to have no integral relationship to one another.

The novel in which for the first time he largely overcame these defects was his monumental trilogy *Three Cities,* entitled in Yiddish *Farn Mabl,* "Before the Deluge." The three volumes contain close to a thousand pages and are set respectively in the cities of St. Petersburg, Warsaw and Moscow in the years preceding and during the Russian revolution. *Three Cities,* which appeared in English in 1933, was also the first of Asch's novels to gain wide prominence among the general American reading public.

The work exhibits in sharp relief both the virtues and the flaws of much of Asch's writing. Where he deals with a milieu in which he feels at home, as in the middle volume, *Warsaw,* he achieves a rich and convincing portrayal of Jewish life and of the complex interplay of varied social and political tendencies among diverse and interesting characters. Zionism, socialism, Polish nationalism; revolutionary militancy, enlightenment intellectualism and lingering Orthodoxy all have their exponents in what is clearly perceived and represented as an organic Jewish society. In contrast, his earlier portrayal of the St. Petersburg Jewish *haute bourgeoisie* and Russified intelligentsia (a minuscule proportion of the Jewish population in any case) tends toward one-dimensionality, extravagance and bathos. The final volume depicts the revolutionary events in Moscow in 1917-18 in a melodramatic manner that occasionally approaches caricature.

There is nothing surprising in the fact that novelists are apt to be more successful when dealing with familar material. But Asch's problems with *St. Petersburg* do not result mainly from lack of familiarity. He did in fact have contact with the circles he portrays as early as 1907, when *Got fun Nekome* was produced in the capitol, and his preferred associations from that time onward were with the cosmoplitan elite, both intellectual and social.

It seems, rather, that Asch, having early attained status among this elite, nevertheless remained bedazzled by it for most of his life. Prof. Siegel notes (p. 112) that even Asch's intimates were annoyed by "his near fawning over people of title and wealth." While his writing cannot be accused of fawning, he appears never to have achieved that degree of perspective on elite society or, alternatively, that degree of immersion in it which would allow him to produce a full-blooded and convincing portrayal.

Characteristically, Asch reveals once again in *Three Cities* his alertness to fashionable intellectual and cultural currents. In this case he fastens upon Freudian psychology, particularly the Oedipus complex, which in a naively obvious and superficial treatment provides the prime motivation for the protagonist, Zachary Mirkin. The Oedipal motif also allows for typical Aschian sensationalism, as in the quasi-incestuous seduction scene between Zachary and his attractive prospective mother-in-law.

Asch first visited the United States in 1909, settled here with his family in 1914 and became a citizen in 1920. America soon began to provide material for his fiction, and although he never was quite comfortable here (frequently commuting to Europe and spending the decade of the 1930s primarily in Nice) he was able to write a number of short stories and at least one novel which demonstrated successfully his absorption in the American Jewish milieu.

In *Uncle Moses* (Yiddish 1918, English 1920) he depicts the complex and often poignant transformation of Jewish life transplanted from the shtetl to New York. The novel is set in the garment industry, where Moses Melnik has become the boss of a shop employing almost exclusively his *landslayt* from the shtetl of Kuzmin. While the shop superficially replicates the patriarchial relations of the old world, distortion and irony are already evident in the fact that the roles are reversed; Uncle Moses, a personage of no stature in Kuzmin, here lords it over the former "cream" of the town. Not only employer, he is also the landlord of their tenements and the president of their congregation.

The demoralization of the transplanted shtetl is revealed as formerly dignified householders outdo one another in flattery of their benevolent tyrant. But even this inverted patriarchalism cannot survive in the conditions of modern urban capitalism. Gradually the powerful class-based antagonisms of capitalist society become the dominant forces while Uncle Moses, the apparently successful adaptor to American ways, loses his energy and drive and shows himself to be no lng "the Jewish idea, the Jewish spirit as it was incorporated in living Jewish life," at a time when the savagery of Nazi anti-Semitism had become apparent, Asch returned to the shtetl and the Hasidic milieu of his earliest work.

The action takes place in the 19th century and traces the reluctant development of a charismatic Hasidic rebbe. Yekhiel, the protagonist, acquires his following not by virtue of learning or spirituality, but because of an unmediated fear and love of God, which expresses itself in his compassion and his intuitive understanding of fellow human beings. In the work Asch takes occasion to depict the court of the gloomy and mysterious Kotsker Rebbe. Steeped in an East European ambience no longer contemporary but well within the historical memory of Yiddish readers, the novel reverts to thematic emphases familiar to them from earlier Yiddish literature: pre-eminence of moral concerns, definition of the individual in terms of the community and identification with the poor and downtrodden among the Jewish masses. It is perhaps not surprising that this work made little impression in translation, appearing in English at first only in an abridged version (*Salvatio*, 1934) and not until 1951 in its complete form.

The atmosphere of controversy which frequently surrounded Asch and which Ben Siegel makes a central focus of his study became most acute around his trilogy of "christological" novels, *The Nazarene* (1939), *The Apostle* (1943) and *Mary* (1950). These works were undoubtedly the result of complex motivations. In retrospect it seems fair to conclude that most prominent among them were Asch's exaggerated perception of himself as an interpreter and mediator between Jews and Christians and his obsessive desire for recognition by the literary arbiters of the non-Jewish world. He never troubled to conceal his frustration and bafflement at never having been awarded the Nobel Prize.

In devoting himself to the life of Jesus and the origins of Christianity he crossed the boundaries of parochial Jewishness, appropriated the central myth underlying the dominant culture of the West, and at the same time, he thought, struck a blow for Judeo-Christian reconciliation by reminding his readers of the common roots and shared values of the two religions.

Significantly, the *Forward*, which had serialized most of Asch's works before their publication as books, declined to print *The Nazarene*. The book, in fact, appeared in English four years before Asch could find a Yiddish publisher for it. Niger scoffed at the *Forward's* new-found concern for the sensibilities of observant Jews, the ostensible reason for rejecting the work, and defended the novel vigorously against intemperate accusations that it was Christian missionary literature. For Niger it was rather an elaboration of the theme of *Der Tilim Yid*, the celebration of faith, compassion and love of fellow human beings, as opposed to the dry pedantry and sterile legalism of institutional religion.

About *The Apostle*, based on the life of Paul, Niger would however later write, "this is a book which is truly more Christian than Jewish (in the religious sense of the word) — and the average Yiddish reader is not prepared psychologically or morally to accept such a work." By the time Asch had completed *Mary*, even his translator, Maurice Samuel, balked. Refusing to translate the work, he explained, "In the earlier books you were rooted in the developing Jewish traditions. But in *Mary* you make it appear that the Jewish law and ethics become petrified after Moses."

In other quotations Samuel suggested that his decision was based also on his assessment of the book as not very successful from an artistic point of view. Nevertheless Samuel streadfastly defended Asch against accusations of apostasy and against those who "stupidly accused [him] of seeking to convert Jews to Christianity... As it happened, Asch was Jewish through and through; apostasy was as remote from him, with his make-up and attachments, as from an orthodox Jew."

A curious consequence of the scandal surrounding the Christ trilogy was Asch's temporary association with the *Morning Freiheit* which, without endorsing his views, was happy to publish an author of Asch's stature and was for a time the only Yiddish newspaper to open its pages to him. This situation, illustrative of the complicated relationships between political ideology, for readers in the Yiddish literary and journalistic world of the 1930s and '40's, could probably have come about only in the context of the grand anti-fascist alliance of World War II. The denouement came in the 1950s when Asch was taxed with the association by Sen. Joseph McCarthy. Asch hastened to explain, "... somewhere I had to be printed. After all I'm a Yiddish writer. And when the *Morning Freiheit* opened its pages for me, I accepted. After all, America was at that time allied with the Communists against Nazism. but after the war, when the relations between East and West became sharper, I stopped writing for the *Freiheit.*"

On re-reading the trilogy it is clear that it adds little luster to Asch's reputation. He appears in these novels to succumb to his most characteristic literary vices: rambling prolixity, sentimentality verging on the maudlin and purple prose. The generally favorable reaction they elicited in the non-Jewish press was as much the result of a misconceived notion of Asch's purpose as was the consternation the books provoked among many Yiddish readers. There is, nevertheless, every reason to accept Samuel's assessment. Asch was neither apostate nor Christian missionary. But his elite cosmopolitanism, philosophical superficiality and inflated ego led him to overestimate his own insights and powers of "reconciliation" while ignoring the historically developed and deeply held sentiments of Yiddish readers. By no means averse to friendship among peoples, they could not avoid interpreting Asch's favorable depiction of the origins of Christianity as a form of aid and comfort to those who had historically denied the validity of their own beliefs and practices and who had made this denial a pretext for presecution.

The very fact that Asch's literary activity could provoke such vehement reaction is testimony to the extraordinarily active and vital relationship between the Yiddish reading public and its cultural personalities during the period when he wrote. While by no means enjoying the virtually universal admiration accorded such figures as Sholem Aleichem and Peretz, Asch as a writer was viewed as a public figure of enormous importance and the public assumed both the right and the responsibility to comment on and to judge both his writings and the positions he expressed on issues of the day.

As had been indicated, Asch's own situation was complicated by the fact that while he remained aware that his primary base was among the Jews of East European origin, he wished desperately to be recognized, as well, as an author of international stature. The 1930s in particular witnessed the translation into many languages and the considerable popularity of ambitious novels by such European authors as Thomas Mann, Romain Rolland, Arnold Zweig, Emil Ludwig, Stefan Zweig and Franz Werfel, the last two of whom were Asch's close friends. It was in this company that he wished to be and was, to a large extent, judged. It is clear today that of these Mann was the towering figure, but Asch could probably hold his own among the others.

Writing in Yiddish, however, Asch was not precisely in the same position as, say Mann or Werfel, who were, after all, representatives (in honorable exile from Nazism, to be sure) of German national literature, and acknowledgedly legitimate and respected tradition. Yiddish literature at that time was in many circles not accorded legitimacy. It could not be identified with the culture of a nation-state; the Yiddish language itself was still widely regarded as a sub-literary folk patois; and the Yiddish reading public, although probably a higher proportion of the language-population than was true for other languages, was not considered a respository of "high" culture.

For Asch, then, the tension between that which was appropriate to his primary audience and that which was admirable in the eyes of the literary establishment was bound to be greater than in the case of those who wrote in German, French or Russian. The situation was complicated by the fact that his readership, which was uninhibited in its propensity to criticise and proprietary in its assumption of the right to approve his choice of themes and treatments, nevertheless tended to be gratified by his non-Jewish successes, as if they too, to some extent, required confirmation of the validity of their own literature from external judges. The contradiction was never resolved on either side.

Milton Hindus' assessment that the work of Asch stands in the "No-man's land between the popular kitsch of the best-seller lists and a qualitative literature of serious intent" is perhaps a trifle harsh but seems not too far from the mark. For a figure like Asch, however, a purely literary assessment will not suffice; this one overlooks the enormous contributions Asch made to the modernization of Yiddish literature and to its recognition as a body of work to be taken seriously on the international literary scene. Hindus disregards, moreover, what Ben Siegel justly characterizes as Asch's moral seriousness and "his sense of *knowing* [which] shielded even his most hackneyed plots and characters from total distortion or travesty" (p. 227).

A new look at Sholem Asch is surely in order and Siegel's book can be a valuable guide. It may therefore seem churlish to draw attention, nevertheless, to some of its shortcomings. Addressed to readers of English, the book focuses largely on the English translations of Asch's work and on English language sources. While this approach is surely appropriate it is

339

also the occasion for some annoyance. Asch's works are always, for instance, introduced by English titles (even when they were never translated into English) and the original Yiddish titles and publication data must be looked for in the end-notes; there, it should be quickly added, they are always to be found. His disclaimer (p. ix) notwithstanding, the author would have done well to adopt a consistent system of transliteration from Yiddish (e.g. the simple and widely used YIVO system). Its absence results in some disconcerting renderings (*Gleben* [sic p. 239], English *Our Faith*), a situation which is compounded by outright errors in Yiddish *(Der* [sic] *Shtetl* [p. 238]; *Der Bund fun der* [sic] *Schwache* [p. 243]) and by occasional mistranslations.

More disturbing is the quasi "popular" perspective adopted by Siegel, presumably in order to capture the attention of an uninformed readership. Happily, the defects of this trivializing approach are confined primarily to the title of the book — was controversy the most significant aspect of Asch's activity? — and the heading of the first chapter, the rather tastelessly breezy " Sholem Who?" The text itself is for the most part interesting, well informed, balanced in judgment and well written. With its conscientious evaluations and the bonus of a rich bibliography and a chronology, the book makes an important contribution.

November, 1980

Not Without a Trace

By BER GREEN

Translated from the Yiddish
by Aaron Kramer

I SHALL not disappear without a trace;
within your hearts my flame shall find a place.
I'll carry this great truth across the earth;
that Man is holy, yes, beyond all worth.

From land to land I'll seek my radiant goal
till Man shall reach the heights of his own soul,
till every demon shall be overthrown
and freedom come at last into its own.

The path I choose leads on from heart to heart —
no, not without a trace shall I depart:
The treasures of my life are yours to keep —
the harvest of my days is yours to reap.

For it was your unfathomed life to me,
showed what a giant this poor dwarf might be.
Not every thing I reach for can be mine,
yet this I know: at least I'll leave a sign.

In every miracle of my refrain
I see your footprints: all your ageless pain
is mine now; all your laughter I've embraced.
I know: my life shall never be erased.

March, 1983

Contributors

CHARLES R. ALLEN, JR., author, journalist and pioneer investigator of the illegal presence of Nazi war criminals in the United States, has published the results of his inquiries in our magazine since 1962 and in other magazines. His latest volume is *Nazi War Criminals in America . . . The Basic Handbook* (1985).

ISAK ARBUS, a retired librarian, is a Holocaust survivor.

ROSA AND OSCAR BERGOFFEN came to the U.S. in 1940; both are now deceased. They were the parents of Hedy Shneyer, active in our Managment Committee.

GEORGE I. BERNSTEIN of Windsor, Canada, is an orthopedic surgeon who has published stories and poems in Canadian and U.S. periodicals.

JESSE BIER is Professor English at the University of Montana at Missoula. He is the author of two novels, a collection of short stories and a book about American humor.

MARTIN BIRNBAUM (1902-1986) was a poet in New York, author of many volumes of Yiddish poetry, a translator from the Yiddish and teacher in Yiddish *shules*.

THOMAS BLATT was a participant in the Sobibor concentration camp uprising; the account published here is excerpted from his yet unpublished diary of the time. He is now in Santa Barbara, Calif.

MARC BRESLOW took part in a Jewish Witness for Peace delegation to Nicaragua in Dec., 1984. He is a member of New Jewish Agenda National Steering Committee.

MILTON W. BROWN is the author of *Painting of the French Revolution, The Story of the Armory Show, American Painting from the Armory Show to the Depression* and *American Art to 1900*.

LAWRENCE BUSH is our Production Manager and a regular contributor. He has appeared in *Moment* and other magazines and is the author of a favorably reviewed first novel, *Bessie*. His latest book for ages 13 to 15 is *Rooftop Secrets and Other Stories of Anti-Semitism*.

ALISON B. CARB, a B.A. from Sarah Lawrence College, spent her junior year at Tel Aviv University. She received her M.A. from New York University in 1979.

MARC CHAGALL (1887-1985) is known around the world for his paintings, many of which center on Jewish themes.

SHIKE DRIZ (1908-1971) was a Soviet Yiddish poet, a victim of Stalinist repression. The poem here printed was written in 1953-1954.

MICHAEL ENGEL is a Los Angeles writer and filmmaker.

DR. FREDERIC EWEN is a retired Professor of Comparative Literature at Brooklyn College and author of *The Poetry and Prose of Heinrich Heine* (1948), *Bertolt Brecht, His Life and His Time* (1967), and *Heroic Imagination* (1984).

GORDON FELLMAN is Associate Professor and Chair of the department of sociology at Brandeis University and active in New Jewish Agenda.

LEO FRANK was lynched in 1915 in Georgia when he was falsely convicted of the murder of a Christian girl. This letter was written to a fellow alumnus of Cornell.

ITCHE GOLDBERG, recently Adjunct Professor of Yiddish Language and Literature at Queens College of CUNY, is editor of *Yiddishe Kultur*, organ of the Yiddisher Kultur Farband (YKUF) and director of the Service Bureau for Jewish Education. He was awarded the coveted Itzik Manger Prize in Israel in 1985.

HENRY GOODMAN, who was 85 when he published this story, often appeared in our magazine with stories, literary criticism, reviews and translations from the Yiddish. He is the author of *Our People Throughout the Middle Ages* in two volumes for young people. The story here is based on the real life Polish Rabbi Isaac Zavada.

MAX GORDON was formerly on the Editorial Board of the *Daily Worker* and in recent years his work has appeared in *The Nation, Science and Society, Socialist Revolution,* and *In These Times*. He is a member of our Editorial Advisory Council.

BER GREEN is a Yiddish poet, author of *Blumen Unter Shnay — Flowers Under Snow* (1939), former literary editor of the *Morgn Freiheit,* author of a book of literary essays.

MIRIAM GREENSPAN is a feminist therapist and a founding member of the Boston Committee to Challenge Anti-Semitism. Her "Feminism and Psychotherapy" appeared in the *Radical Philosophers News Journal* in April, 1977.

LOUIS HARAP was Managing Editor of *Jewish Life* (as *Jewish Currents* was named in its first decade) and has continued as a member of the Editorial Board ever since. He is the author of *Social Roots of the Arts* (1949), *The Image of the Jew in American Literature: from Early Republic to Mass Immigration* (1974) and *The Jewish Presence in Twentieth Century American Literature* (1987).

ANNETTE JAFFE, a member of New Jewish Agenda in Philadelphia, took part in a Jewish Witness for Peace delegation in Nicaragua.

CAROL JOCHNOWITZ, author of *Careers in Medicine for the New Woman,* is co-author of an unpublished biography of Waldemar M. Haffkine, Russian Jewish bacteriologist, and Secretary of our Editorial Board. She conducts our magazine's monthly column on women.

ELI KATZ is Professor of American Multi-Cultural Studies at Sonoma State University.

MELANIE KAYE/KANTROWITZ and IRENA KLEPFISZ have edited an anthology of women's writings, *The Tribe of Dina* (1986). IRENA KLEPFISZ is the author of *Keeper of Accounts,* a volume of poetry.

REGINA P. KRUMMEL is Professor of Education at Queens College (CUNY), author of *The Important Thing* (poems) and a novel *Looking Good* (1985) and a past member of our Editorial Board.

NORA LEVIN of Philadelphia is the author of *Holocaust* and *While Messiah Tarried.* The address included here was delivered at the Memorial Meeting for the Martyred Soviet Writers held by the progressive Jewish movement on August 9, 1984.

RUTH LEVIN of Shaftsbury, Vermont, was raised in the South. Her stories have appeared in *Bennington Review, Redbook, Ladies Home Journal* and *Mutiny.*

JUDAH LEVINSON is a semi-retired rabbi in London. His story is based on a true experience.

ELSIE LEVITAN of Philadelphia is a frequent contributor to our magazine.

A.B. MAGIL is the author of *Israel in Crisis* (1950) and numerous articles and reviews in our magazine and elsewhere. He was an editor of *The New Masses* and is a member of our Editorial Advisory Council.

MICHAEL MIRSKI is a noted activist and Jewish scholar who felt obliged to leave Poland during the 1968 anti-Semitic persecution. He fled to Sweden.

BOB NORMAN is a musician and writer who was editor of *Sing Out!* for many years. He is currently general administrator of the North American Congress on Latin America.

SAM PEVZNER is a member of the Editorial Board and a founding editor of the magazine. For many years he conducted the column "Inside the Jewish Community."

DAVID PLATT is an Emeritus Editorial Board member of our magazine and currently editor of the English section of the *Morgn Freiheit.* He was a movie critic for the *Daily Worker* for many years.

BILLIE PORTNOW of Seattle, WA, is a contributor to our pages and a member of our Editorial Advisory Council.

SID RESNICK of New Haven has been a frequent contributor to our magazine and to the English section of the *Morgn Freiheit.* He is also a member of our Editorial Advisory Council.

PAUL ROBESON JR. is a professional translator from the Russian and head of the Paul Robeson Archives. The address printed here was delivered on Aug. 12, 1981 in New York at a Memorial Meeting for the Martyred Soviet Yiddish Writers held by the progressive Jewish movement.

ISAAC ELHANAN RONCH (1899-1985) was a Yiddish poet, novelist and journalist for 55 years and author of 20 volumes. He wrote regularly for the *Morgn Freiheit.*

PHILIP ROSEN of Philadelphia teaches high school and lectures in colleges.

MAX ROSENFELD is a translator of many books and essays from the Yiddish. He is a member of our Editorial Board.

ANNETTE T. RUBINSTEIN is a literary critic and civil rights activist since the the 1930s. She is the author of *The Great Tradition in English Literature* (1953) and *American Literature, Root and Flowers: Significant Writers and Literary Movements, 1775-1955,* forthcoming in The People's Republic in China, where she taught English and American Literature to Chinese teachers and translators in Beijing. She is an Editorial Board Member of *Science and Society* and a member of our Editorial Advisory Council.

DR. KAREN SACKS is Assistant Professor of Sociology and Anthropology at Clark University in Worcester, Mass.

ANNE SAFRAN is a regular contributor to the Yiddish *Morgn Freiheit* and a Yiddish poet. Her books of poetry are *Nitzachon* (Victory, 1946), *Haint* (Today, 1950), *Lichtike Shtromen* (Radiant Streams, 1960). and *Dos Leben Ruft* (The Call of Life, 1968), and *The Fireborn* (1963) in English, and *Rikud Hahaim* (The Dance of Life, 1972), in Hebrew, both novels. She was 80 in 1982.

NEIL SALZMAN is Associate Professor of Political Science at Fairleigh Dickinson University and a member of our Editorial Board.

MORRIS U. SCHAPPES is Editor (1958-present) of our magazine, and a founding member of the Editorial Board in 1946. He was Adjunct Professor of History at Queens College of CUNY 1972-1976. He is the author of *Emma Lazarus: Selections from Her Poetry and Prose* (1943; 5th rev. and enl. ed. 1982), of *The Letters of Emma Lazarus, 1968-1885* (1949), of *A Documentary History of the Jews in the United States, 1654-1875,* (1950, 3rd rev. ed. 1971) and of *The Jews in the United States: A Pictorial History, 1654 to the Present* (1958, rev. and enl. ed., 1965).

THE REV. W. CHRISTOPH SCHMAUCH, an ordained minister of the United Church of Christ, is Executive Director of the World Fellowship at Conway, N.H.

MILTON A. SHAHAM is a psychotherapist in New York. He published a volume of poetry, *A Long Note,* in 1974.

CLARA LEMLICH SHAVELSON was a young girl when she electrified intensely exploited shirtwaistmakers in 1909 by calling for a strike. She continued to be an activist until she died in 1982.

JOHN SHERMAN, of Berkeley, Calif. was a founder of Local 1199 of what is now the National Union of Hospital and Health Care Employees and Editor of *1199 News* for several years in the 1940s and 1950s. He was also national organizer of the Medical Bureau and North American Committee to Aid Spanish Democracy in 1937-1940 and New York City Secretary of the Jewish People's Committee early in the 1940s.

WILLIAM SHNEYER, a retired engineer, has visited Israel a number of times. He is a regular contributor to our magazine and a member of its Managament Committee.

MORTON STAVIS, a long-time legal activist, heads the Center for Constitutional Rights and is a member of the Commission on Labor and Social Action of the American Jewish Congress. He is especially active in cases dealing with constitutional rights for Blacks.

GERALD STILLMAN, a translator from the Yiddish of Mendele Mokher Sforim's *The Parasite* (1956) and *Fishke the Lame* (1960), is a member of our magazine's Editorial Advisory Council.

YURI SUHL (1908-1986) was the author of four volumes of Yiddish poetry; his works in English include *Ernestine Rose, Cowboy on a Wooden Horse, One Foot in America* and *They Fought Back,* as well as a number of books for young people. The address here was delivered at a panel on Ethnic Pluralism at Queens College in 1974.

PHYLLIS TAYLOR took part in the Jewish Witness for Peace in Nacaragua in Dec., 1984. She is a member of the Philadelphia New Jewish Agenda and of the Agenda's National Steering Committee.

LOU WAX dedicates his story to his brother "Shlomo, who will never get a chance to read this."

RABBI BRIAN WALT is spiritual leader of the Reconstructionist Congregation Beth Israel in Media, Penna. He is active in New Jewish Agenda.

A.H. WHITE was a partisan in Radziwill Woods until 1944. He joined the Polish Army, and then the Soviet Army, as a Polish officer. He was among the first to reach Berlin. The story is excerpted from a larger work. He lives in Englewood, Calif.